Mothers & Others
for a Livable Planet

Guide to
Natural Baby
Care

Mothers & Others
for a Livable Planet

Guide to
Natural Baby
Care

Nontoxic and Environmentally Friendly Ways
to Take Care of Your New Child

M INDY P ENNYBACKER

&

A ISHA I KRAMUDDIN

John Wiley & Sons, Inc.

New York • Chichester • Weinheim • Brisbane • Singapore • Toronto

Copyright © 1999 by Mothers & Others for a Livable Planet. All rights reserved
Published by John Wiley & Sons, Inc.
Published simultaneously in Canada
Design and production by Navta Associates, Inc.

This publication is designed to provide accurate and authoritative information in regard to the subject matter covered. It is sold with the understanding that the publisher is not engaged in rendering professional services. If professional advice or other expert assistance is required, the services of a competent professional person should be sought.

Library of Congress Cataloging-in-Publication Data:
Pennybacker, Mindy.
     Mothers & Others for a Livable Planet guide to natural baby care :
Nontoxic and environmentally friendly ways to take care of your new
child / Mindy Pennybacker and Aisha Ikramuddin.
     p.   cm.
    Includes index.
    ISBN 0-471-29333-4 (pbk. : alk. paper)
    1. Infants—Care. 2. Infants' supplies. 3. Natural products.
I. Ikramuddin, Aisha. II. Mothers & Others for a Livable Planet,
Inc. III. Title. IV. Title: Mothers and Others for a Livable Planet
guide to natural baby care. V. Title: Guide to natural baby care.
HQ774.P45   1999
649'.122—dc21   98-31591

Printed in the United States of America

10 9 8 7 6 5 4 3 2

This book would not exist without the generous contributions of time and thought from the following team: Drs. Harvey Karp and Philip Landrigan, our medical advisors; Robert Bernstein and Don Wallace, our publication advisors; Judith McCarthy, Jennifer Campaniolo, and Diane Aronson at John Wiley & Sons; Brook Hersey, Lisa Lefferts, M.S. P.H., Chan McDermott, and Sandra Steingraber, Ph.D., our thoughtful reviewers; Carol Baxter and Joanne Camas, freelance writers and members of Mothers & Others; and Alexis Spakoski, the illustrator who makes us look good.

Within Mothers & Others, we'd like to especially thank Wendy Gordon, M.S., our executive director, who gave the writers guidance, time, and institutional resources for this book; Andrea Bernstein, Lynette Jaffe, and Meryl Streep, members of our Board of Directors, for their input and interest; Allison Sloan, who continually updated and checked the Appendices and other facts; and Kristin Ebbert, who provided in-house copyediting and art direction.

Finally, like all Mothers & Others' projects, this book was very much a cooperative venture employing the energy, ideas, and understanding of our wonderful staff—Frankie Colón, Mary Lou Dabulas, Sylvie Farrell, Lane Graves, Ruth Katz, Betsy Lydon, Dana Schwartz, Rebecca Spector, and Francine Stephens—as well as our families and friends.

Thank you, one and all.

Foreword xi

Introduction 1

PART 1   Preparing for the New Arrival

Chapter One   **The Importance of Your Child's**
                 First Environment   9
                 Why Babies and Children Need Extra Protection   13
                 Some Dangerous Chemicals Found in Most Homes   17
                 Nursery Ecology   19

Chapter Two   **Preparing Baby's Room**   23
                 Painting Baby's Room   24
                 Other Wall Coverings   30
                 Carpeting and Other Floor Covering   31
                 Choosing a Crib and Other Furniture   36
                 Crib Mattresses and Bedding   42
                 Window Treatments   50
                 Room Dividers   52
                 Lighting   54

Chapter Three **Other Baby Equipment**   57
                 Car Seats   58
                 Soft Carriers, Slings, and Backpacks   59
                 Infant Carrier Seats   59
                 Prams and Strollers   60
                 Playpens and Portable Cribs   60
                 Gates   62
                 High Chairs and Hook-on Chairs   62
                 A Word on Walkers   62

Chapter Four   **Environmental Babyproofing and**
                 Eco-Tips for Other Rooms   65
                 Parents' Room   66

Living Room/Playroom 69
The Kitchen 71
The Bathroom 74
Babyproofing for Child Safety 76
Energy Efficiency 78
Preventing Environmental Allergens
    and Asthma Triggers 80

Chapter Five   **Pollutants in Your House** **85**
Keeping Outdoor Pollutants Out 86
Chemicals That Go Up in Smoke: The Hazards
    of Gas Stoves, Fireplaces, Kerosene Heaters,
    and Cigarette Smoke 87
Cleaning Up 91
Pesticides 97
Radon 100
Asbestos 102
Moisture-Happy Molds and Microbes 103
Good Ventilation 107
Devices to Improve Air Quality: Air Filters, HEPA
    Vacuum Cleaners, and Air Conditioners 108
Electromagnetic Fields 111
Gardens and Lawns 113

Chapter Six   **Caring for Yourself During Pregnancy** **115**
How Environmental Toxins Affect
    the Developing Fetus 116
A Healthy Diet 122
Avoiding Alcohol 134
Checking Your Drinking Water 134
Personal Care Products 142
Checklist 143

PART II   *Caring for Baby the Natural Way*

Chapter Seven   **Dressing, Playing with, and Keeping Baby Clean . . . 147**
Bathing Baby 148
Soaps, Shampoos, and Other Baby Care Products 154
Diapering 159
Dressing Your Baby 166
Laundering Diapers and Baby Clothes 173
Choosing Nontoxic Toys and Playing with Baby 174
Exercise and Active Play 180

Chapter Eight **Feeding Your Baby** **183**
               The Benefits of Breast-Feeding 184
               Bottle-Feeding Dos and Don'ts 198
               Organic Baby Food 203

Chapter Nine   **Raising (and Protecting) Your Naturalist Child** . . . **219**
               Children's Books 221
               Outdoor and Indoor Activities 224
               Protecting Your Child Outside 229

Appendix A   **Resources for More Information** **241**

Appendix B   **Products Available by Mail** **259**

Appendix C   **Select Bibliography** **291**

               Index **309**

One of the first things that all new parents discover is that they must "childproof" their home to make it safe for their babies' exploring fingers and mouths. As with "childproofing," "environment proofing" also takes planning and foresight, and *Mothers & Others' Guide to Natural Baby Care* is the best "environment proofing" advisor I have ever seen!

This book is a commonsense, practical guide that tells us how to protect our children from needless exposure to chemicals and other easily avoided dangers in the household and out of doors. I have been a pediatrician for over twenty years and I know that this book comes at just the right time. Of course, all parents want to give their children the healthiest possible future, but today's parents are presented with many new choices on how to accomplish this goal. They need a handy source of clear and accurate information to help them do their best. Mothers & Others has provided this in an easy-to-use book that presents step-by-step, practical solutions to many of the everyday questions that new parents have.

New parents find no job more important than taking care of their child. Even well before the due date, many parents give up old, bad habits out of concern for their infant's health. They begin to eat better and drive more cautiously, start saving money and stop smoking, because they all want the same thing—to start their babies' lives in the right way by giving them health as well as happiness, security as well as love. Stopping smoking, and keeping cigarette smoke out of your home and car, are among the best things you can do to guard your child's future health. In much the same way, by avoiding the use of synthetic products that give off toxic and irritating fumes, you improve your indoor air quality and protect the extrasensitive lungs of your newborn. Finding better home and baby care products is easier to do than you may think. For a decade, Mothers & Others for a Livable Planet has been giving parents smart alternatives to dozens of polluting and unhealthy (and just plain dumb) products found in our homes. Now they've collected all that information for you in this exceptional book.

It's normal for expectant parents to feel more than a little awestruck by the new responsibilities they're facing. There are so many things to learn, from how to swaddle and diaper to how to protect vulnerable babies from germs, irritants, toxins, and allergens. But at the same time, please remember that you don't have to change the world—or your household—all at once. In fact, this book joins me in advising expectant parents not to embark on major renovations. The stress alone can be bad for a pregnant woman and the baby she's carrying, not to mention the exposure to fumes from fresh paint or pollutants that might be released when old materials are disturbed. This *is* a good time, however, to stop smoking, eat a healthier diet, and begin reading about the surprisingly simple steps you can take to get started with "environment proofing" your home.

If you're pregnant, *Mothers & Others' Guide to Natural Baby Care* contains a chapter on health tips to protect yourself and your unborn baby. It tells you how to check your walls and pipes (and even antique cribs) for lead, the most serious environmental threat to young children. It tells you how to eliminate dust, dust mites, and cockroach droppings, all of which are major causes of asthma, the number one chronic disease of children in the United States. From special mattress covers to the most efficient vacuum cleaners, this book will give you a full listing of the best asthma- and allergy-control products. Between these covers you'll find eco-smart, least-toxic choices of furnishings, from carpet to mattress and crib—not just for baby's room, but for the rest of the house, as well. And once baby arrives, you'll find the chapters on feeding, clothing, and caring for your baby fun to read.

One final thing I like about this book is its friendly, accessible voice. While it states the facts of what you want to avoid and why, it helps you put these risks into the proper perspective. Of course, worrying is built into the parental role, but this guide helps you replace worry with knowledge and action. So, relax—you're not alone. For natural home and baby care questions, you've got the answers in this book.

You can sit down and enjoy reading it, cover to cover, or use it as questions and concerns come up. So, enjoy! And, baby step by baby step, let *Mothers & Others' Guide to Natural Baby Care* help you get your baby off to the best start possible.

—Harvey Karp, M.D.
Fellow of the American Academy of Pediatrics
Assistant Clinical Professor of Pediatrics,
University of California at Los Angeles School of Medicine
Medical Advisor, UCLA Lactation Program
Practicing Pediatrician, Santa Monica, California

If you're the proud parents of a new baby, or have one on the way, Mothers & Others extends our warmest congratulations to you at this happy time, so full of promise. It's also a time in which this book can be very useful to you. *Mothers & Others' Guide to Natural Baby Care* is designed as a how-to manual to help you provide your baby or young child with the healthiest possible environment in which to grow and thrive. It is intended for expectant and fledgling parents, as well as the parents of older babies and anyone concerned about the effects of environmental toxins, such as lead and carcinogenic chemicals, upon our children's health. As all parents come to learn, we can't protect our children from everything; but there are simple and real things we can do to help them develop healthy, resilient bodies with which to tackle life's challenges.

Until now, very few books have addressed how to reduce babies' and children's exposure to environmental toxins such as lead in old paint and water pipes; fumes from paints, plywood and particleboard, carpets, cleansers, and insecticides; and pesticide residues, hormones, and antibiotics in food and milk. You will find all this information between these covers. In addition, this book discusses acute safety risks (poisonings, falls, choking, accidents) and allergenic hazards such as dust mites. And, while examining immediate risks to your own baby, we also consider collective risks posed to the whole ecosystem by our product choices.

Mothers & Others' Guide to Natural Baby Care came about through popular demand. For the past couple of years, our friends and members, most of whom are parents, have been asking us to write an environmental baby care book. Our membership nationwide—30,000 at last count, and growing—receives *The Green Guide,* a monthly consumer newsletter that combines cutting-edge reporting on environmental toxins with information about safer products and practices. Our readers said they wanted to have all that *Green Guide* information, and more, collected in a handbook on baby and child care. They needed one handy volume in which to find everything from nontoxic paints, cleaners, bedding, and carpets to untreated, natural-fiber clothes and diapers. For Mothers & Others, a consumer education organization dedicated to environmental protection for the sake of our children's health, this book was definitely the logical next step.

Mothers & Others has been advocating on behalf of children's health and the environment since our founding in 1989, with the goal of stopping the use of dangerous pesticides.

Partly in response to the consumer protest we spearheaded, Alar, a pesticide widely used on apples and classified as carcinogenic by the federal Environmental Protection Agency, was taken off the market by its maker, Uniroyal, in 1991. Until this time, risk exposures for toxic chemicals had been based on adult tolerance levels only. Mothers & Others was founded on the principle that children are more vulnerable to environmental toxins than are adults, and thus cannot tolerate as much exposure to risky substances. This principle was confirmed by the National Academy of Sciences in 1993 when it reported that federal pesticide standards, then based on adult risk tolerances, provided too little health protection for infants and children. In 1996, the Food Quality Protection Act reaffirmed that message, and, in 1997, the EPA formed a new Office of Children's Health with the goal of establishing new child-specific standards for exposure to contaminants in air, water, and food.

But until an adequate government policy is firmly in place, parents keep asking us what they can do to protect their children in their daily lives. The answer is, a lot. *Mothers & Others' Guide to Natural Baby Care* provides simple, practical steps you can take right now and every day to protect your children's health and reduce your worry load.

The best time to begin is when planning for a new baby, for whom your nesting instinct spurs you to make a safe, clean place. You're going to be acquiring a certain amount of stuff—baby equipment and so forth—no matter what, so why not make it the right stuff? This book will show you how to find environmentally sound, nontoxic products that are competitively priced with conventional ones. But it's also important to remember that, no matter what age your child is, it's never too late to make changes—when a room needs a fresh coat of paint or a floor refinishing, or you're buying a new chair or a bathroom or oven cleaner. Even as the mother of two "middle-aged" children, ages fourteen and eleven, I've learned a lot of useful information from this book. After all, my boys are still growing and developing, and I still worry.

As you leaf through it, you'll notice that this isn't just a nursery book. After all, no baby stays in just one room. We therefore have addressed potential environmental hazards throughout the home, in every room, nook, and cranny. This book contains everything from nontoxic building and decorating materials to water filters, detergents, clothing, personal care products, and toys, and an appendix listing where and how to get it all. In addition to product and company listings, we provide another appendix of resources, including telephone numbers of government organizations and other information services. We cover precautions to be taken in your yard and your neighborhood playground. There's even a chapter covering trips to the seashore and going on hikes, and a listing of environmentally themed books. This book is meant to be your companion for the long run.

It also contains the most current information you can find to date. Thanks to our patient editors at John Wiley & Sons, Inc., we've been able to update all the facts up to the moment this book went to press, incorporating the very latest scientific studies and environmental and health news. The past five years have seen rapid advances, both in our understanding of chemical threats, such as hormone disruptors, and the availability of alternative products. The names of companies that make or sell these nontoxic, more ecologically sound products are listed throughout each chapter in bold type; their phone numbers and other contact information can be found in Appendix B. Part of Mothers & Others' mission is to encourage consumers to buy from local retailers, supporting the economy in your area and reducing the environmental costs of long-distance shipping, which expends fossil fuels. Please contact us and tell us about any great resources you find; we can be reached at our toll-free number: 888-ECO-INFO.

And, if you're concerned about preserving what's left of the world's ecosystems, from mountain watersheds to the oceans, for our children and *their* children, this book is most definitely for you. In addition to protecting your baby's home environment, we draw the link between what we consume at home and the impact on our natural resources. Another major part of Mothers & Others' mission is to reduce our consumption of wasteful goods produced through polluting means, and to "vote" with our consumer dollars for organic food and other environmentally sound products. For instance, the lighting section of chapter 2 focuses on energy-efficient, compact fluorescent lightbulbs for baby's room. This part of our mission is implemented through a nationwide Shoppers' Campaign, which organizes individual consumers, manufacturers and growers, wholesalers, and retailers to make greener products more widely available. We hope that, after reading this book, you'll be moved to join Mothers & Others and work with us in our Shoppers' Campaign to effect social change, and protect the environment, through the power of our consumer demand. In the back of the book there's information on how you can send for a free *Green Guide* and also, if you wish, how to join Mothers & Others.

There's one more thing we'd like you, please, to keep in mind as you read: You don't have to do it all! In fact, you shouldn't try to. You should avoid the stress—psychological and physical—of major renovations while pregnant. You can go through this book and choose what seems manageable for you now, and what you might like to do later. Without further ado, then, here's a quick overview on how to use this book.

Part One, "Preparing for the New Arrival," explains how to prepare for your new baby.

Chapter 1, "The Importance of Your Child's First Environment," provides detailed reasons for avoiding environmental toxins, irritants, and allergens in the home.

Chapter 2, "Preparing Baby's Room," is a comprehensive treatment of the nursery, from paint and wallpaper and window treatments to carpeting and flooring and lighting, choosing a crib and other nursery furniture, mattresses, and sheets.

Chapter 3 gives a brief overview of other baby equipment, from car seats to playpens and portable cribs to gates and walkers—including the latest consumer information on these sometimes dangerous accessories, and safer alternatives.

Chapter 4 covers babyproofing, nontoxic furnishings and dishes, and an indoor air checkup for the whole household.

Chapter 5 presents an overall systems checklist: a broad and comprehensive sweep to uncover and clean up pollutants in and around your house.

Because a mother's environmental exposures to contaminants while pregnant can affect the developing fetus, chapter 6 is dedicated to caring for yourself during pregnancy. It provides a number of easy, but highly beneficial, things you can do while pregnant.

Once your baby has arrived, Part Two of *Mothers & Others' Guide to Natural Baby Care* comes into play.

Chapter 7 gives step-by-step instructions on nontoxic ways to bathe, diaper, dress, and play with your baby.

Chapter 8 focuses upon feeding your baby. Mothers & Others encourages breast-feeding, as do most pediatricians nowadays. How to breast-feed, how to pump and store milk, how to bottle-feed, and how to find and make organic baby food are also discussed.

As your baby grows, Chapter 9 will become increasingly relevant. It is aimed at helping you give your children an appreciation of nature.

Finally, Appendix A gives you contact numbers for getting further information from government agencies and other nonprofit organizations. Appendix B identifies companies that sell the products mentioned in this book by mail.

Among *our* resources, in putting together this book, Mothers & Others counted upon the talents and expertise of many staff members and friends. Our writers are Mindy Pennybacker, director of Mothers & Others' consumer research and education services (CRES), editor of *The Green Guide,* and mother of a twelve-year-old boy, and Aisha Ikramuddin, senior research associate and research editor, who heads the fact-checking department of *The Green Guide* and who thoroughly vetted this book for accuracy. Aisha and Allison Sloan, CRES assistant editor, are the voices who'll respond to you if you call our Mothers & Others' toll-free consumer research services information line. Members get free answers to their questions about environmental toxins and safer products. We listen carefully to our members' concerns: 25 percent ask about nontoxic home decorating and cleaning materials, providing ideas for *The Green Guide* and for this book.

Along the way, as Aisha and Mindy have asked me to acknowledge, they've had lots of help. We'd particularly like to thank our medical advisors, Dr. Harvey Karp and Dr. Philip Landrigan, both pediatricians. In addition to his private practice in Los Angeles, Dr. Karp is assistant professor of pediatrics at the University of California at Los Angeles School of Medicine. Dr. Landrigan, director of community and environmental medicine at Mount Sinai School of Medicine in New York, served on the first advisory panel for the EPA Office of Children's Health. He is also the coauthor, with Dr. Herbert Needleman, of *Raising Children Toxic-Free.* All three of these doctors contribute their medical expertise on the editorial advisory board of *The Green Guide.* Scientists Lisa Y. Lefferts, M.S. P.H., and Sandra Steingraber, Ph.D., also generously reviewed our manuscript.

We'd also like to thank Mothers & Others' members Carol Baxter, mother of two girls, and Joanne Camas, mother of three boys, who wrote first-person anecdotes for this book contained in boxes in chapters 1, 2, and 8.

Other first-person stories came from our program director, Betsy Lydon, mother of an eleven-year-old boy and a nine-year-old girl, who's been with us since 1989; and Lane Graves, regional director of Mothers & Others' West Coast office, whose son Angus was born during the writing of this book. As we went to press another staff member, membership coordinator Sylvie Farrell, became pregnant, and was able to update us on the challenges and joys discussed in chapter 6.

We owe our "look" to the talented Alexis Spakoski, our illustrator, whose daughter, Emma, was born soon after these wonderful drawings were completed. *Green Guide* managing editor Kristin Ebbert contributed in-house copyediting and much general support for this book.

Unfailingly supportive, full of useful ideas and good humor, Judith McCarthy, our editor at John Wiley & Sons, Inc., and the mother of a three-year-old boy, provided continual inspiration for this book from the proposal stage through final galleys. She made the writing and editing a fun and collegial process, and we will always be in her debt.

Mothers & Others is still a young organization. We started out as a project of the Natural Resources Defense Council (NRDC), from which we branched out in 1992, becoming our own, independent nonprofit organization. Since then, we've cultivated our growing membership and continued working with consumers, farmers, and retailers. We've helped spur the growth of the organic food industry. The new green mainstream is growing: According to market researchers the Hartman Group, 52 percent of U.S. consumers are open to and willing to buy greener products. Roper Starch's Worldwide 1993 Green Gauge Study classified 55 percent of the U.S. population as green consumers. Mothers & Others' goal is to increase those numbers. We hope that you'll join us!

My children were only five and two when I co-founded Mothers & Others with Meryl Streep, Roberta Willis, and other parents concerned about the effects of industrial pollutants on the environment and on our children's health. We believed, and continue to believe, that the health of our children and of the natural world are inseparable. And as Meryl, the mother of four, exclaimed the other day, while we sat in my office reviewing galleys, "I just wish there'd been a book like this when we were pregnant with our children!" But here, at last, it is: We're very proud to be presenting you with this useful guide on how to make your home environmentally safe for a new young life.

—Wendy Gordon, M.S.
Executive Director, Mothers & Others for a Livable Planet

PART 1

Preparing
for the
New Arrival

chapter one

The Importance *of* Your Child's First Environment

When preparing a baby's room in the not-so-olden days, we might have slapped on a fresh coat of paint, put down a new carpet, hung new wallpaper and drapes, bought new furniture, bedding, and clothes—and wondered why we felt so rotten afterwards. We'd probably chalk it up to exhaustion, a common side effect of the nesting urge. But nowadays we know better. We've learned that most new decorating and home furnishing products contain chemicals that give off fumes, which can literally be a headache, or worse.

Many of the synthetic chemicals used in common home products, such as solvents and pesticides, are known or suspected carcinogens. Others have been classified as hormone disruptors because they block or mimic the normal workings of reproductive, thyroid, and other hormones in our bodies. Inhaled or ingested by a pregnant woman, these chemicals in some cases can cross the placenta, affecting the child's pre- and postnatal development. Sometimes, chemicals released in the home can irritate the eyes, nose, and throat and trigger allergies and asthma. As a general rule, the more we're exposed to things we're allergic to, the worse our allergies get. One good way to give our children the best possible start in life is to limit their exposure to these substances.

Thus it's wise to know exactly what you are outfitting your nursery with, what the risks are, and whether healthier alternatives exist.

In most cases, they do. And when it comes to environmental factors in children's health, you are far better off preventing problems by maintaining surroundings as toxin-free as possible.

This chapter will acquaint you with some of the risks. The rest of the book will outline simple steps you can take throughout your home to protect your child. At the same time, we certainly don't want you to feel hopeless or unduly alarmed—you shouldn't feel pressured to do *everything* listed in this book.

Even Carol Baxter—a mother of two, and one of the most active, committed members of Mothers & Others—didn't try to do it all. "I did not create a pure non-toxic environment!" Carol says of her daughters' nursery. "We kept some of the plastic toys we got as gifts, and the crib and bed have conventional mattresses," she adds. Despite these minor lapses, Carol did, from the start, take some basic, simple steps to protect her children's environment. But before we look at what she did, let's examine the outfitting of a conventional nursery.

Here's a typical scenario:

An expectant couple—we'll call them Sally and Todd Maple—moves into a brand-new home in a housing development. They don't like the color of the small bedroom, which will become their baby's nursery, so they choose a nice sunny yellow paint. The proud salesman points out that the latex paint contains preservatives and fungicides that will keep it fresh for years to come. The Maples also choose an oil-based white paint for the baseboards, windowframes, sills, and doors. Because Todd is gone for most of the day, including a long commute to his job, and Sally left work at the beginning of her eighth month of pregnancy, she is happy to help out by painting the windows and doors, leaving the walls and ceiling for Todd to do on the weekend.

All the relatives, including both sets of grandparents-to-be, advise the Maples that synthetic carpeting, treated with stain-resistant finishes (to guard against all those baby spit-ups and spills) is the most practical and affordable, and that it should be well-padded to cushion a crawling baby or tumbling toddler. They choose a nice powder blue synthetic carpet and underlay. The carpet store installs the "system," gluing it all securely to the nursery floor.

At last comes the fun part, the furnishings. The Maples go to the baby emporium and choose a wooden crib. "What kind of wood is this exactly? Is it hardwood?" Sally asks the salesman. "No, it's a composite wood, pressed and laminated. Very strong. The bottom is good sturdy particleboard," he adds, lifting up the foam mattress to show her. "Everything's coated with a waterproof finish—crib, mattress—so you don't have to worry about accidents," the salesman concludes with a meaningful look. The upper bar has a sheath of soft plastic on it, to protect the crib from baby's gnawing during the teething stage. The Maples buy the crib, a matching pressed-wood changing table and chest of drawers, and a sturdy particleboard bookshelf and plastic toddler-size table and chairs. It's Todd's idea to buy the vinyl cartoon-character wallpaper to line the walls around the crib; he can't bear the idea of sticky little fingers ruining his new paint job.

When the furniture arrives, the Maples arrange it in the yellow-and-blue room. They place a fluffy polyester-stuffed quilt and matching overstuffed bumperguards in the crib, and make up the mattress with a fitted permanent-press sheet. On the changing table shelves they stack disposable diapers and many of the baby shower gifts, including hooded cotton towels and extra receiving blankets and comforters. Into the bureau they tuck the polyester terry knit, flameproofed pyjamas, the fleece creepers, and cotton and cotton-blend baby undershirts. They put the new books, including some cute vinyl bath books, on the shelves, along with plastic and stuffed toys.

After all the accessories have been neatly arranged, Todd has a surprise gift for Sally: an antique walnut rocking chair. With a cry of joy, she sits down immediately and puts her feet up on the child's table.

"I'm tired. And I have a headache. But I'm happy. We have made a beautiful nursery," she says.

"Not as beautiful as you," says Todd, his eyes watering—from emotion, he's almost sure, though it feels curiously like a hay fever attack. But this is winter, so there is no pollen for him to react to. He experiences two urges: to open a window and to smoke a cigarette. But he doesn't want to let in cold air, and he knows better than to smoke in the baby's room. He puts his hands on the back of the rocker and rocks Sally gently. In a little while, he'll smoke his cigarette in the living room, the one and only designated smoking room in the house.

What's wrong with this cozy scene?

First, a pregnant woman should avoid exposure to cigarette smoke, which enters the bloodstream from the lungs and crosses the placenta to affect the fetus. One clear example of prenatal harm is low birth weights of infants whose mothers either smoked during pregnancy or were passively exposed to secondary smoke. To protect a newborn's health, the family home and car should be made into completely smoke-free environments long before baby arrives—ideally, as soon as the couple decides to try for a pregnancy.

Next: Don't do any renovations while you're pregnant! You should never do any of the painting yourself; nor should you ever be present during the painting or the installation of carpets. This is because toxins ingested or inhaled by a pregnant woman readily cross the placenta, exposing the fetus to possible harm.

What could possibly be toxic about adorable baby accessories and such fixtures of daily life as a new carpet and a coat of fresh paint? Consider how too much of even a good thing can be smothering, and then think of the cumulative effect of a lot of not-so-good things. Sure, baby needs soft surroundings and warmth, but those overstuffed comforters and crib bumpers and the wall-to-wall carpet provide havens for dust mites, one of the most potent allergens known. And almost all of the synthetic decorating materials the Maples used, from paints to carpets to furniture, emit potentially dangerous fumes. So do many of the fabric finishes on the bedding and baby clothes, and the stain-resistant treatment on that carpet. Most powerful when new, the emissions from all these new products in the small, contained space of a nursery blend into a toxic atmosphere.

The principal culprits are volatile organic compounds, or VOCs, whose defining characteristic is that they contain carbon. They also evaporate faster than water—gasoline is a familiar example. VOCs readily evaporate as gaseous fumes into the air from paints, varnishes, cleaning products, glues, carpets, and many other products found in most homes today. This process is also referred to as "offgassing." VOCs occur most commonly in petrochemical-derived products, such as plastics and pesticides. Adverse health effects from exposure to many of the chemicals used in these products can range from allergic reactions, such as Todd Maple's itchy, watery eyes, to breathing difficulty, nerve damage and, in the long term and at high exposures, even cancer.

Cigarette smoke, for instance, contains a number of VOCs in its mixture of more than 4,000 chemicals. One of the worst is formaldehyde, a VOC ranked as a probable human carcinogen by the U.S. Environmental Protection Agency (EPA). Formaldehyde is also contained in, and offgasses from, such commonplace objects as pressed wood and glues, or bonding agents. The fiberboard used in the Maples' crib and changing table is a pressed wood; so is the particleboard used in the shelving they chose. Permanent-press finishes on fabrics, such as the no-iron crib sheets and the curtains, also can release formaldehyde. Formaldehyde also can be found in many paints. Health effects of exposure to formaldehyde vapors can include eye, nose, and throat irritation; coughing; skin rashes; headaches; dizziness; vomiting; fatigue; and nosebleeds, according to the American Lung Association (ALA).

As for the carpet, while most new systems do not contain formaldehyde, they do contain other toxic VOCs. And, as the ALA's Indoor Air Pollution Fact Sheet points out, ". . . carpets can trap formaldehyde emitted by other products in homes and then slowly release it thereafter." Some of the preservatives, fungicides, and solvents in the paint the Maples bought are toxic VOCs, too.

Finally, winter or summer, Todd should have opened that window—wide! Ventilation is crucial, because most modern homes are tightly sealed to hold heat in. This is good for conserving energy and dollars, but bad if you're also holding in dust mites and toxic fumes. Indoor air pollution is a particular problem in today's energy-efficient homes. Comparative risk studies performed by the U.S. Environmental Protection Agency (EPA) and its Science Advisory Board have consistently ranked indoor air pollution among the top four environmental risks to the public. The agency reports in its 1992 publication, "Targeting Indoor Air Pollution," that "indoor levels of pollutants may be 2–5 times, and occasionally more than 1,000 times, higher than outdoor levels." The EPA estimates that most people spend about 90 percent of their time indoors; in the case of a newborn, it's 95 percent.

Indoor air quality can be dangerously degraded by gasses emanating from all household furnishings, particularly in combination and when they're new—the typical nursery scenario. In decorating a nursery, just as we concentrate on making everything look harmonious, so should we make sure that it all comes together in terms of safety. Cumulative safety is the key. Measured on a product-by-product basis, the fumes from particleboard furniture, fresh paint, or synthetic carpeting and glues may not exceed health safety standards on their own. But in combination, these fumes might well cause adverse health effects. All these allergens and toxins, which are heavier than air, settle down into and collect in the carpet. "If truck-loads of dust with the same concentration of toxic chemicals as is found in most carpets were deposited outside, these locations would be considered hazardous-waste dumps," wrote Wayne R. Ott and John W. Roberts in the February 1998 issue of *Scientific American.*

But before you read further, please don't panic or feel overwhelmed! Through-out this book, there are a lot of problems and solutions—think of it as a menu you can apply to your own circumstances and needs. As when a child begins to walk, little steps can be transformative. When outfitting a new nursery, it's often just a matter of making different, "greener" choices in items you were already planning to acquire. This will lessen the overall, cumulative effect of chemicals in your home.

Is it really worth the trouble? We strongly believe that it is. The following overview of potential hazards and health problems will show you why.

Why Babies and Children Need Extra Protection

Our children live in a world vastly different from the one we grew up in even a generation ago. Since World War II, at least 75,000 new synthetic chemical com-pounds have been developed and released into the environment. Fewer than half of these have been tested for their potential toxicity to humans, and still fewer have been assessed for their particular toxicity to children.

While adults do suffer ill consequences from numerous home products, children are far more at risk than adults. In 1993, the National Academy of Sciences (NAS) and the EPA concluded that, beginning *in utero,* babies and children are different from adults; they are often much more vulnerable in terms of environmental toxins. The government has made it a matter of policy to protect our young ones from harmful substances in the environment. In 1996, in outlining the first "National Agenda to Protect Children's Health from Environmental Threats," the EPA announced that special assessments of chemical risk to our offspring must be undertaken as a matter of urgent national priority.

In 1998, in response to President Clinton's executive order on children's envi-ronmental health, the EPA and the Department of Health and Human Services allocated $10.6 million for new research centers at eight university hospitals nationwide.

Why Are Babies and Children More Vulnerable?

Pound-for-pound, children breathe more air, drink more water, and eat more food than adults. Thus, they are more exposed to air and water pollution and pesticides. For instance, a recent study at the University of North Carolina at Chapel Hill found that children inhaled proportionately more pollution than adults and teenagers did. Children's bodies grow and develop more rapidly, so chemicals that can harm development can do maximum damage at this critical time. They also play on the floor where allergens, such as dust and heavier-than-air chemicals, settle and collect. Then there's natural behavior: Putting everything in the mouth is a crucial part of normal development—the way a baby learns about the world. Rather than restrain development, it's better to provide a growing child with safe things to chew on.

Further complicating the matter, all these chemicals surround us in combination. And the cumulative effects of exposure to different chemicals, whether in the workplace or home, have simply not been addressed. To remedy this, the EPA has instituted a major change in its policy and approach: When it comes to children's health, in addition to examining and assessing each chemical's effects separately, the EPA will also measure their effects in combination, the way our children are most likely to encounter them. The goal is to examine "a child's total cumulative risk from all exposures to toxic chemicals," according to Carol Browner, EPA Administrator.

Dr. Philip Landrigan, former senior advisor to EPA Administrator Carol Browner on children's health and environment, chairman of Community and Preventative Medicine at the Mount Sinai Medical Center, Mothers & Others medical advisor, and coauthor, with Dr. Herbert Needleman, of the excellent medical guide *Raising Children Toxic Free,* has identified the following as the four most pressing health issues for children:

1. the rise of asthma
2. the rise in childhood cancers
3. endocrine disruptors
4. environmental neurotoxins (lead, mercury, solvents, pesticides)

The Rise of Asthma

An estimated 4.8 million Americans under age eighteen have asthma, which is also the number one reason for school absenteeism in America. Asthma deaths in children and young adults nearly doubled between 1980 and 1993, according to the Centers for Disease Control and Prevention (CDC).

Dust mites are principal culprits in asthma. Microscopic creatures, they thrive on moisture and the old skin cells we constantly shed. They infest bedding, upholstery, drapery, and rugs, and their excrement is a potent allergen that can trigger asthma attacks. "I ripped up my carpeting when my daughter first was diagnosed with asthma," says Patty Arlotta of the Bronx, New York. Patty says that thanks to bare floors and vigilant medical treatment, her daughter's symptoms have abated. Chapters 2 and 5 will show you how to keep mites out of your child's air without forgoing mattresses, pillows, comforters, and rugs.

Technically an irritant to airways rather than an allergen, cigarette smoke affects asthma sufferers severely. Also harmful are cockroaches, pet danders, mildews and molds, unvented gas appliances, fine airborne particulates, and smog. So are gasses released from vinyl interior materials, such as wall and floor coverings, researchers at the National Institute of Public Health of Norway found in 1997. These are all excellent examples of environmental factors that directly worsen and, in some cases, trigger, this debilitating disease. Throughout this book, we will tell how to reduce these environmental factors in your home.

The Rise in Childhood Cancers

The rate of cancer among American children younger than fifteen has been steadily rising at a rate of nearly 1 percent a year over the past twenty years, the National Cancer Institute reported in 1997. A child born today has about a 1-in-600 risk of developing cancer by the age of ten. While the death rate from cancer in children has steadily declined, thanks to improved detection and medical treatments, new cases are being diagnosed in ever-increasing numbers and cancer remains the most common form of fatal childhood disease.

"The strong probability exists that environmental factors are playing a role" in the rise of childhood cancer, Dr. Landrigan says. Environmental factors encompass everything from a child's food and water to the substances her skin comes in contact with and the air she breathes.

One study has found that the risk of childhood leukemia is three to six times greater for children in households using home and garden pesticides. Childhood brain tumors have been strongly associated with the use of household pesticides during pregnancy, particularly pyrethrin- and organophosphate-based flea and tick foggers. In Woburn, Massachusetts, where water was contaminated by industrial solvents and heavy metals, the childhood leukemia rate rose to four times the national average between 1966 and 1986.

Many of the ingredients used in home products such as pesticides, fungicides, and herbicides are known or suspected carcinogens. While, again, you shouldn't panic and throw out every plank of particleboard in the house, you can easily choose not to use the more dangerous pesticides in your home and garden, and certainly not to buy nursery wall paint laced with fungicides!

Endocrine Disruptors

Endocrine, or hormone, disruptors are synthetic chemicals that mimic or block the body's natural hormones, such as estrogen, thus altering the body's normal hormonal activity. They are suspected to be behind the increasing rates of endometriosis, breast cancer, low sperm counts, early puberty, undescended testicles, and hypospadias, a congenital deformation of the penis. These "hand-me-down" poisons readily cross the placenta. A classic example of a hormone disruptor, the fertility drug diethylstilbestrol (DES), an estrogen mimic, was banned after it was linked to increased infertility and cervical and testicular cancers in the children of women who had taken it. The worldwide dispersal of such known hormone-disrupting chemicals as the pesticides DDT, atrazine, chlordane, chlordecone, and lindane, and industrial byproducts such as dioxins, furans, and some of the polychlorinated biphenyls (PCBs), has effectively been drugging the environment for at least a generation. PCBs, oily compounds used for decades to insulate electrical equipment and now banned, remain in the bottom mud and banks of many waterways, from the Great Lakes to the Hudson River. PCBs, dioxin, and DDT rise in the food chain, accumulating in the fat of living creatures, such as fish and also humans. Most of us, certainly in the industrialized world, have these chemicals in our bodies. While few human studies have been conducted until now, the EPA's new agenda sets a high priority on evaluating hormone disruptors. The long-term effects on wildlife—from sterility in Florida's bald eagles to shrunken penises in alligators in contaminated waterways—have been collected in the groundbreaking book *Our Stolen Future* by Theo Colborn, J. P. Myers, and Dianne Dumanoski. What appears to be a worldwide decline in human sperm counts over the past fifty years has been tentatively linked to these chemicals, most of which did not exist until after World War II.

Babies can be exposed to hormone disruptors in four basic ways:

- through food;
- through prenatal exposures;
- through chemicals inhaled along with the air they breathe; and
- through other activities that put them in direct contact with toxins, such as putting objects in their mouths or crawling on or touching contaminated surfaces.

What's wrong with that soft vinyl teething shield on the Maples' crib? Phthalates, a class of chemicals used to soften vinyl so it can be made into teething rings, shower curtains, and other soft products, and another possible additive called nonylphenyl ethoxylate, may interfere with the human hormone system. Some phthalates are suspected to be carcinogenic. Phthalates are not permanently bonded to the plastic structure of PVC and can migrate to the surface of the plastic and offgas. In a Norwegian National Institute of Health study, exposure to phthalates in vinyl interior surfaces was shown to increase the risk of developing bronchial obstruction and asthma in the first two years of life. Phthalates were found to have offgassed from the plastic to become attached to house dusts and small air-borne particles, which are readily inhaled.

True, you'll say, but plastic surrounds us. And we agree that you shouldn't feel compelled to dispose of all the plastic in your life. As a guiding principle, simply be aware that these are chemicals found in plastics in the household, including pacifiers and toys—and so, when it comes to plastics, less is better than more. You can make the choice not to acquire more vinyl, particularly in home furnishing products where substitutes, such as wood and natural fibers, are readily available.

Environmental Neurotoxins
(lead, mercury, solvents, pesticides)

Neurotoxins, which include PCBs, affect the nervous system and brain development.

Lead, a heavy metal, is probably the most dangerous neurotoxin that children and pregnant women can encounter in everyday life. In 1978, lead was limited in interior house paints to 0.06 percent by weight, a level that eliminates lead poisoning dangers from paint. However, the primary exposure to lead comes from old lead-based paint remaining in layers on walls. Simple but frequent activities, such as opening a window or door, can create enough lead dust to harm a child. Though lead was phased out from gasoline beginning in 1979, it has settled from the air into the soil, where it remains a menace to young children.

And it isn't just a full-blown case of lead poisoning that can derail a child's growth. Lead's effects on intellect and development, even at low levels, can be tragically permanent. "It's now clear that lead in low levels can affect a child's ability to pay attention and avoid distractibility," says Dr. Herbert Needleman, a professor at the University of Pittsburgh Medical Center and leading researcher on the effects of lead exposure in children. Lead in higher levels correlates with antisocial behavior, aggression, learning disabilities, impaired hearing, and lowered I.Q. Though lead levels in children have dropped dramatically since its banning in gas and paint, still, according to the CDC, 4.4 percent of American children under the age of six have blood lead levels above the safety threshold of ten micrograms per deciliter (10 mcg/dl). More than 900,000 children in the United States have been exposed to lead levels that exceed the CDC's safety threshold.

Mercury, found in some batteries, thermometers, paints, and some fish, such as swordfish, is another heavy metal and neurotoxin. Elemental mercury causes numbness, memory problems, movement and speech problems, and tremors. Methylmercury, which accumulates in fish and crosses the placenta, can cause brain damage and birth defects as it did to the infants of Minamata, Japan, in the 1950s.

Organophosphate pesticides, another group of dangerous neurotoxins, are widely used in conventional agriculture, in homes, on gardens and lawns, and by municipalities battling mosquitoes. More than one million infants and children under five years old are exposed to potentially unsafe doses of these pesticides in their food, according to a January 1998 report called *Overexposed: Organophosphate Insecticides in Children's Food* by the Environmental Working Group (EWG). For more information on the problem of pesticides in food, see chapters 6 and 8.

Some Dangerous Chemicals Found in Most Homes

Most homes today contain hundreds of chemicals. Some, such as cleaners, pesticides, and building supplies, are deliberately brought inside. Others enter homes as a result of environmental pollution. These are the most serious environmental contaminants.

Dioxins

Dioxins are both potent carcinogens and hormone disruptors, and they provide a prime example of why less plastic is better than more. They cause cancer at levels far below those of any other known carcinogen. Possibly the most toxic man-made substances known, dioxins are primarily released into the air in the production and incineration of polyvinyl chloride (PVC), known to us as vinyl.

Dioxins are also released during the chlorine bleaching of paper, the incineration

17

of municipal and medical waste, and the manufacture of organochlorine herbicides and some household cleaners. From the air, dioxins settle into our water and soil, from which they enter the food chain and finally concentrate in the fatty tissues of animals and human beings. Human infants, at the top of the food chain, absorb dioxins across the placenta and through their mothers' milk. Sixty percent of the 10 billion pounds of PVC produced annually in the United States goes into home construction and decoration: in water, gas, and sewage pipes; window frames; doors; venetian blinds; shower curtains; imitation leather; furniture; and wallpaper. Sixty-six percent of American kitchens have vinyl flooring. It is also used in disposable medical supplies, from bedpans to IV tubing and syringes. Some water bottles and other plastic bottles are made with PVC (look for the triangular recycling symbol with the number 3). While we are not exposed to dioxin from PVC plastic in our homes, we should try not to buy it, as its manufacture and burning release dioxins into the environment. In addition, many PVC home products contain and release some toxins, such as phthalates and lead.

Volatile Organic Compounds (VOCs)

The pesticide chlorpyrifos is an example of a chemical that can vaporize and contaminate objects in a home. One obvious way such VOCs enter the air very readily is through spray applications, whether of paint, pesticides, foam insulation, or room fresheners. But VOCs don't have to be sprayed to enter the air. Fumes can rise from a stable-looking substance like a particleboard shelf or a synthetic carpet or any item held together by glues, for months on end.

As listed in *Raising Children Toxic Free,* by Drs. Landrigan and Needleman, some of the more toxic VOCs all too commonly found in conventional home furnishings (and in household air) include:

- *Benzene,* a solvent and known cause of leukemia and lymphoma, is present in some furniture and carpet glues, epoxies, and unleaded gasoline. It can be absorbed through the skin or by inhalation.

- *Formaldehyde,* an irritating gas and a probable carcinogen, has been implicated as a cause of cancers of the lungs and nasal sinuses. Formaldehyde gas may emanate from the glues in new plywood or particleboard furniture and cabinetry; some carpeting and other floor-covering systems (in glues, adhesives, and underlays as well as in the actual rug fibers or synthetic linoleum tiles); wallpaper; curtains; and certain fabric finishes, such as stain- and moth-proofing. As mentioned earlier, formaldehyde is also present in some paints, stains, and wood finishes, as well as in tobacco smoke.

Between 10 and 30 percent of the population may be sensitive to formaldehyde, but the actual health effects vary widely among individuals. At low levels, formaldehyde can cause headaches and irritation to skin and mucous membranes in the nose, eyes, and throat. Higher concentrations may result in dizziness, coughing, and constriction of the chest, and can trigger asthma attacks. The EPA also estimates that ". . . 10 to 20 percent of the U.S. population, including asthmatics, may have hyperreactive airways which may make them more susceptible to formaldehyde's effects." Formaldehyde is considered a probable human carcinogen by the EPA because it has been found to cause nasal cancer in rats and mice.

- *Styrenes* and *toluene* are solvents, present in airplane glue and some quick-drying paints, that are known neurotoxins. "Nearly all solvents can cause acute and chronic injury to the central nervous system," Drs. Landrigan and Needleman say.

- *Perchloroethylene,* the dry-cleaning solvent, has been found to be a neurotoxin as well as a cause of liver cancer. It has also been linked to bladder cancer in both occupational and epidemiological studies.

This book is dedicated to helping you take the best possible care of your baby by choosing less toxic products for your child's first environment. Have we convinced you that it's worth the trouble? Here's one more example: Babies and children touch everything in a room as they learn about the world. But what they touch can carry toxins that might be absorbed into their skin. Children may also ingest toxins by putting their hands into their mouths after touching a contaminated object or dust. A Rutgers University study showed how children can accumulate significant amounts of hazardous chemicals in their bodies simply by playing in a room after a pesticide fogger has been used there. The study found that children were significantly exposed, through their touching and handling of contaminated toys and other objects in a room, even as much as a week after spraying. The scientists found that vapors and residues from the pesticide chlorpyrifos, commonly used indoors against fleas and marketed under the names Dursban and Lorsban, were absorbed by both plush and plastic toys that were placed in rooms an hour after the areas had been sprayed.

In addition to choices that are healthier for your family, we also present you with choices that are sounder for the natural environment. Ultimately, a healthier natural environment is good for our health—individually and as a species.

Nursery Ecology

Beyond your concern for baby's immediate environment, there are global environmental considerations that all parents, as citizens of Earth, might want to consider in making product and decorating choices. By making a conscious choice not to buy petroleum-based products, consumers help preserve both the oil itself and the pristine areas, such as the Alaska wildlife refuges, imperiled by drilling and spills. By taking care not to select products made of tropical hardwoods, such as mahogany, we help protect the forests that are threatened worldwide. The burning and cutting of forests contributes 25 percent of all atmospheric carbon dioxide, a major greenhouse gas resulting from human activities, each year. In addition to its effects on your child's health, also consider the impact of how a product is made. The production of vinyl, or PVC plastic, for example, releases dioxins. And finally, what is the life cycle of a product? For instance, how does one ultimately dispose of a synthetic wall-to-wall carpet? Landfills are layered with such useless things.

Creating a nursery for my first baby was very exciting for my husband and me. Making it adorable, of course, was one of our goals, but making it as environmentally "clean" as possible was also of utmost importance to me. Since my infant had spent nine months *in utero,* the ultimate protected environment, I wanted to do all I could to create a natural environment and one that was environmentally responsible, free of chemicals, known allergens, and manmade synthetics.

Starting with the small, empty room, I was lucky to have a wood floor in beautiful condition. I tested the paint, especially on the window sills, for lead. The results, to my relief, came back negative.

Choosing wood furniture (crib, diaper table, rocking chair, and book shelf) was easy, but when it came to the mattress, I was at a loss. I was discouraged by the fact that every infant mattress I found was covered with vinyl. I was disappointed, but I finally went ahead and bought one because I didn't see any alternative. Most people like vinyl because it is practical since it cleans easily. But vinyl, a plastic, is made from petroleum, a nonrenewable resource, and its manufacture and disposal, when burned in incinerators, releases dangerous dioxins. New vinyl, like any plastic, offgasses VOCs into the air, so before I used the mattress, I made sure to leave it out in a well-ventilated area for a few weeks so that that process could take place long before my baby came to lie on it.

Painting was the next big issue. My original vision of the nursery was a rain forest theme, with a mural of monkeys, red-footed tree frogs, and toucans frolicking in a lush green overgrowth. But my baby, Lily, had received two beautiful, handmade cotton quilts, both pink. They belonged on the wall, and they wouldn't go with the rain forest scheme. I decided to use a solid pink color, but now I had to choose the paint.

I was aware that lead had been banned from paint for over twenty years; however, I also know that conventional paints still contain toxic VOCs, which offgas for a long time. I didn't want this. So, after weeks of research, I found Livos, a company in New Mexico, that makes paint free of VOCs. I chose a cheery pale pink, far from my first choice, but it ultimately turned the room into a lovely place to be. This nontoxic paint was exorbitantly expensive, $50 a gallon, but it was important to me. With each stroke I was reminded of its price, and I remember thinking that if I wanted to raise my daughter in an ecologically safe environment, it might be at a cost.

This was just the beginning of what I call "shift spending," going without one thing so that I can pay a little more for something that's important. Ultimately I remain within budget, while increasing the quality of life: my own, my family's, and the planet's.

Walls freshly painted and white cotton curtains with pink polka-dots hung, we now awaited the delivery of the furniture. I gave the floors a thorough cleaning with Murphy's Oil Soap before laying down a freshly cleaned, colorful antique wool throw rug.

Putting the nursery together, after the furniture arrived, was easy. I filled the bookcase with Lily's new books and wood and cotton toys. I opted to keep plastic toys out of her nursery because they, too, offgas. Her bed was made with 100 percent organic cotton mattress pads, bumper pads, sheets, and blankets. For the comforter, I made a pink-and-white-striped cotton cover. I put cotton diapers and clothing on the shelves, and toiletries made of natural ingredients on her dressing table. I stepped back and thought, "How adorable and crisp this room looks." I loved it.

It is years since I created that first nursery. Today costs have come down and selections have increased. For example, you can now purchase VOC-free paint, less expensively, at most paint stores. And you don't have to settle for a mass-produced vinyl mattress because cotton futons are now made for cribs.

The most important thing that impressed me when making the nursery was that my choices in making it eco-friendly were not bizarre. Natural fibers were the only thing available in our society two generations ago. My choices echo a simpler time. And I'm always pleased with the results.

Natural Fabrics

If you read the story in the box, you may have noticed that Carol Baxter, because she didn't know better at the time, broke a prime rule and painted her baby's room herself, while pregnant. At least she used nontoxic paint! Happily, both the baby she was carrying then, and her next child turned out perfectly fine. If you have also already painted or done other renovations while pregnant, don't worry! Just take sensible precautions from now on to reduce cumulative exposure to all these risks for yourself and your baby. This includes making sure that you have not disturbed and been exposed to old lead paint during your renovation, as discussed in chapter 2. Carol made many healthy environmental choices, and doing this made her happy and calm—a very healthy state to be in.

While Carol didn't stress herself out by creating a perfectly nontoxic nursery, she did take some basic commonsense steps to protect her children's environment *and* the environment at large. Rather than wall-to-wall synthetic carpeting, the Baxter nursery has all wood floors with just a couple of washable cotton and wool throw rugs. Rather than plastic, so ubiquitous in children's furnishings, all the furniture, including bed and crib, is made of real wood. Except for certain gifts, the bedding and toys are all cotton or wood. Already, Carol has reduced her family's consumption of petroleum-based products (plastics, synthetic fibers, and carpet glues); this helps preserve the environment at large, since petroleum is a nonrenewable natural resource. She has also reduced her family's exposure to irritating and toxic VOCs.

Plus, Carol's bare floors and throw rugs radically reduce the habitat of dust mites that teem and multiply in wall-to-wall carpet, which can't be taken up for a thorough wash. When it comes to floor washing, although Murphy's Oil Soap contains natural pine oil, it also has TEA (triethanolamine), which can form carcinogenic nitrosamines. Carol would be better off using a least-toxic, all-purpose cleaner such as Ecover.

If the wood Carol selected had been eco-certified, and the rugs bore the "no child labor" tag, so much the better. But products with these labels didn't hit the general marketplace until after her children were born, and to this day, savvy consumers still have to ask for them.

But also, as Carol Baxter's story amply demonstrates, there is room for joyful, creative nursery design: Less toxic, nonirritating alternatives are available in a wide variety of sizes, shapes, and colors. And, like Carol, you don't have to do it all. As you read on, please remember that our message is one of hope. You can take charge of your baby's environment and make a difference in his or her health while still creating a beautiful nursery. Your less-polluting choices will also help protect our common environment, the natural world.

chapter two

Preparing
Baby's Room

Most of your baby's time will likely be spent in the nursery, in the crib, since newborns sleep an average of sixteen to seventeen hours a day. Infants per kilo weight have a respirational volume twice as large as adults'. Therefore, it's important that the air your baby breathes be as fresh and pure as possible. Of all the spaces in the house, your baby's room deserves the most planning and care.

"From my point of view, in designing a nursery, infants fall into the same category as a hypersensitive person. The young are more open and vulnerable to environmental irritants, allergens, and toxins, so you want to take precautions, in assembling a nursery, against their developing asthma or other syndromes," says Mary Oetzel, a building consultant in Austin, Texas, who specializes in creating safe environments for people with allergies and environmental sickness, also known as multiple chemical sensitivities (MCS). And, as we showed in chapter 1, a safe, environmentally sound environment can be just as beautiful and full of personal details as a room filled with synthetic products. In other words, the two can look just the same. "If you've substituted the safer alternative product, nobody looking at it knows it's any different," Mary Oetzel says.

Children's bedrooms are often small. "A small room has a higher wall surface to room volume ratio than a large room; thus the emissions from building materials is highest in a small room," wrote Leif Øie and his coauthors in a Norwegian study on vinyl emissions. If toxic vapors emanate from the surfaces in a small room, the infant or child who sleeps there will be subject to a higher exposure risk.

In this chapter, we'll take a whole-room approach, while checking off the most environmentally sound and safe products for the nursery, in this order:

- Paints and Finishes
- Other Wall Coverings
- Carpeting and Flooring
- Choosing a Crib and Other Furniture
- Crib Mattresses and Bedding
- Window Treatments
- Room Dividers
- Lighting

Painting Baby's Room

Mothers & Others medical advisor Dr. Harvey Karp, an assistant professor of pediatrics at the University of California Los Angeles School of Medicine, says that no matter how strongly the nesting urge tells you to sand and paint the baby's room, you should *never* do it yourself when you're pregnant. Sanding can disturb old lead paint, resulting in toxic dust that is hard to avoid ingesting. Not only can this give lead poisoning to you, but since lead crosses the placenta, this can be very dangerous for your fetus, as well. And it takes a much smaller amount to harm a fetus.

This section will tell you how to test for the presence of lead paint, and how to find a lead-abatement professional to safely remove all traces of it. If lead paint is chipping or peeling, it is undoubtedly releasing fine, invisible lead dust into the air your family breathes. If lead paint is present and decomposing, the best course of action is for the family to move out while the paint is being removed by a professional, who will also take precautions to prevent the dispersal of lead dust throughout the rest of the home, and perform a thorough clean up afterward.

Whether there's a lead problem or not, any new paint, even a nontoxic one, gives off fumes. This is another reason why you shouldn't paint while pregnant. "When I was pregnant, my husband Alec painted the nursery," says Lane Graves, West Coast Regional Director of Mothers & Others. Lane, her husband, Alec Applegarthe, and their baby, Angus, born in January 1998, live in an authentic San Francisco Victorian house. Lane and Alec didn't know the age of the existing paint, but it was in good shape, not crumbling or flaking, so they left it alone. "Alec didn't do any chipping away of old paint; he just painted over it," Lane says. Lane and Alec generally followed a sensible course. A further precaution, one that they did not take, would have been to test the windowsills and doorjambs for lead. Lead paint, even when buried under many layers of safer paint, may become airborne as a result of friction from use that wears away the paint.

The Dangers of Lingering Old Lead-Based Paint

Children's lead exposure usually is greatest from thirteen months to three years because at that explorative age they ingest dust from lead paint that gets on their hands.

Despite the fact that leaded gasoline has been phased out in the United States, and lead-based paint has been banned in this country since 1978, lead poisoning remains a primary environmental health hazard for children, mostly from deteriorating old paint. Some lead exposure also occurs through drinking water (see chapter 6 for more on this). While the hazards of lead in poorly maintained inner-city rentals has been well publicized, and young children are routinely tested by city pediatricians, many Americans in suburban and rural areas have not been sufficiently informed that the problem also applies to them, Dr. Philip Landrigan, Mothers & Others' medical advisor and chairman of Community and Preventative Medicine at the Mount Sinai Medical Center, has observed. (See the box, "Country Dream Home Becomes a Nightmare.")

Detecting and Removing Lead-Based Paint

Some professionals, like Sheila Kennedy, an architect and professor at the Harvard School of Architecture, say that they can recognize lead paint immediately by its shiny, cracking surface. But this is not a reliable way to check for lead paint. You can't always tell if paint contains lead just by looking at it, and lead paint often hides under several coats of safer paints. If your home was built before 1978, when lead in paint was limited to a safe level of 0.06 percent by weight, it's best to have your home tested for lead. More than 80 percent of U.S. homes built before 1978— about 64 million private residences—contain lead paint, the EPA estimates. With a baby on the way, you should be cautious.

Whether you know your walls have some lead-based paint, or you simply aren't sure, always take care not to accidentally disturb lead-based paint during repainting or remodeling projects. "Lead dust can be invisible to the naked eye and is difficult to clean up," writes Lawrie Mott in *Our Children at Risk,* a 1997 report of the **Natural Resources Defense Council (NRDC).** If your remodeling plans include scraping paint or tearing down walls in a home built before 1978, have the paint tested and cleaned up by a lead-abatement specialist before embarking on the construction project.

The most reliable way to detect lead content near the EPA action threshold (0.5 percent) is to have a professional come into your home to test walls, windowsills, doorjambs, and house dust. Professional lead testers use sophisticated equipment that can detect lead underneath many layers of paint. The equipment is also sensitive enough to detect low levels of lead. **The National Lead Information Center and Clearinghouse (NLICC)** will give you a list of EPA-certified labs near you. You may send paint chips from cracks to one of these labs for testing. If lead is detected, NLICC can also provide a list of specialists who can remove the lead or, alternatively, seal (or "encapsulate") the surfaces covered with lead paint. Always take care that lead paint is removed *only* by a licensed professional; others, especially children and pregnant women, should stay out of the area until all dust is removed.

You can try **Lead Check** swabs, which can be found in many hardware stores for about $8. While do-it-yourself tests can't detect lead paint below the surface layer or the lower amounts that can still pose a hazard, they do provide a quick, inexpensive way to detect more obvious problems. Rub the tip of the swab on the painted surface, or on housedust or the soil outside. If the swab or the surface turns red, it indicates the presence of lead in amounts above the EPA safety threshold. Lead Inspector Kit from **Michigan Ceramic Supplies Inc.** is a similar test kit. In addition to using these kits on paint, you can also use them on ceramic dishes of unknown origin. (Some glazes used on pottery contain lead; see chapter 4.)

If you've found lead, ask your local health department or the EPA about safe removal or encapsulation procedures. Your EPA regional office, **U.S. Department of Housing and Urban Development (HUD)** offices, the **U.S. Centers for Disease Control and Prevention (CDC),** or the **American Industrial Hygiene Association** can help you locate certified lead removal contractors in your area.

In *American Journal of Public Health,* Dr. Landrigan and his coauthors write that "Lead dusts can invade all areas of a home, making the cleaning process very difficult and producing continued exposure."

As a temporary measure, you can clean up lead dust using a high phosphate detergent, such as a powder used for dishwashing machines. The phosphate bonds to the lead, making it easier to pick up with a mop or sponge. Rinse the mop or sponge in clean water between each swipe. Use this method to clean windowsills, doorjambs, floors, and baseboards, as well as children's toys—all things children may touch. Don't rely on this method long term; it is no substitute for professional lead abatement. And make sure all detergent is well rinsed off, so children won't accidentally ingest it.

Buyers' and Renters' Right to Know about Potential Lead Hazards

As of December 1996, all home buyers and tenants have the right to know about the presence of lead paint in a pre-1978 home they intend to buy or rent. The program, administered by the EPA and HUD, mandates disclosure in contracts or leases, and provides free public information pamphlets and sample right-to-know forms through the **National Lead Information Center and Clearinghouse.**

What This Means for You

What if you haven't, to your knowledge, got old lead paint lurking about and you just want to cover old paint? If your home was built *after* 1978, or the old paint is intact, you can do as Lane and Alec did, simply painting over it. If your home was built *before* 1978, you should also seriously consider having windowsills, door-jambs, and household dust tested, at the very least. But remember, if your house is pre-1978 and you haven't had a professional test all your layers of paint for lead, there may be some of the bad old stuff underneath, waiting to come out if disturbed. Test chipping, peeling paint in a pre-1978 home for lead before you cover it with fresh paint. If lead has been found in any area of the house, all work should be done by a licensed lead contractor.

Remember that when you're pregnant, you should not paint. You should stay out of the area where the painting, sanding, or scraping is taking place until the job is finished, cleaned up, and has been ventilated for at least a couple of weeks. The painter should wear a face mask designed to block out harmful vapors (not a dust mask, which will trap the vapor in the mask), gloves, long sleeves and pants, and leave the work clothes in the workroom, away from you, since dust gets on the clothes.

Country Dream Home Becomes a Nightmare

"We see far too many cases of young couples who get the nesting urge and decide to scrape down baby's room," Dr. Landrigan told us in a recent interview, pointing out that "lead poisoning affects all socioeconomic sectors, from decaying inner cities to rural retreats." In an article in *The American Journal of Public Health,* he and his coauthors recount one of the most tragic cases they've encountered, which occurred when a professional family renovated their Victorian farmhouse. The father was a doctor and the mother a magazine editor; they hired ordinary workmen to perform the renovations, which produced lead poisoning with astonishing rapidity and left permanent scars.

The family moved into the two-story wood-and-stone house in upstate New York in late June 1987. The walls, wooden floors, moldings, and doorframes had been covered with multiple coats of lead-based paint. From early August to mid-September, the family went away on vacation while workmen renovated the house; this entailed sanding, torching, or chemically stripping away all the paint and wallpaper and repairing two of the ceilings. All of these removal methods produce chips, fine dusts, and fumes that can be ingested or inhaled.

When the family returned, the work had not been completed, and a thick dust had formed and spread throughout the house. Work continued until late October. Aware that old paint could contain lead, though they hadn't had samples tested, the family did try to stay out of the work area. The husband worked in New York City, but the wife resumed work in her home office. The five-year-old was at school during the day, and the twenty-month-old was at home with a baby-sitter, who tried to keep him and her own two toddlers playing outdoors as much as possible. In mid-October, one of the dogs began suffering seizures and died. A veterinarian tested the dog's blood for lead, which was elevated.

A month later, when the wife complained of fatigue and weakness, and the five-year-old daughter of stomachaches, the families of both the owner and baby-sitter were tested for lead. All had elevated levels. The wife had blood lead levels close to 60 µg/dL, and her children had levels in the 50s—10 µg/dL is considered the accepted threshold, according to the CDC. "That level in a month or two would shave off a few I.Q. points," Dr. Landrigan says.

After the diagnoses of lead poisoning, the county health department measured the unrenovated painted surfaces of the house, using X-ray diffraction. Most had more than 10 milligrams of lead per square centimeter; the acceptable level for an area of the size tested is less than 0.7 milligrams of lead.

This family's story is fortunately rare. You can avoid a similar scenario by taking precautions:
- Have old paint tested professionally for lead before undertaking a renovation.
- Have any lead paint removed by a licensed professional.
- Keep yourself and your family out of the home until the work has been completed and cleaned up.

New Paint

Though lead-free, most new paint is not exactly safe. Most conventional paints and wood finishes contain volatile organic compounds (VOCs), which readily vaporize out of a liquid or solid form and into the air we breathe. Many VOCs commonly found in paint, such as benzene and formaldehyde, are suspected carcinogens. Other VOCs typically present in paints include ammonia, ethanol, glycols, kerosene, toluene, trichloroethylene, and xylene, which have been linked to headaches, nausea, and dizziness, nerve damage, and, in some cases, to liver and kidney disease. Paints may also contain fungicides and pesticides, which add to the mix of toxic fumes.

Oil-based paints tend to be the worst offenders, as they contain many dangerous petroleum compounds, such as benzene, toluene, and styrene, which readily offgas from the paint. Inhalation of these VOCs can result in irritation to the skin, eyes, nose, and upper respiratory tract; prolonged exposures can cause headaches and convulsions. Like car and truck fuel emissions and fumes from industrial combustion, these oil-paint VOCs contribute to ozone, or smog, out of doors. Oil-based paints contain about 50 percent petrochemicals by weight, as opposed to the 5 to 15 percent in water-based, or latex, paints.

However, latex paints can also be hazardous. According to Paul Novak of Environmental Construction Outfitters (ECO) in New York City, "A lot of water-based paints still have dangerous solvents, preservatives, and fungicides in them." Solvents, added to keep paint liquid, can offgas as do other ingredients.

Mercury, a potent neurotoxin, was once an ingredient in latex paints. One form, phenylmercury, was banned from indoor paints in 1990, and from outdoor paints in 1991. But if you have old paint in your garage or basement, and want to use it up, call the **National Pesticide Telecommunication Network** to find out whether that brand contains phenylmercury. If it does, don't use it. Dispose of it according to the hazardous waste regulations in your community. Mercury, even in small quantities, is dangerous and passes through the placenta to cause damage to babies.

Latex paint is most commonly used for interior walls and ceilings. Moisture-resistant oil- or water-based enamel paints are used for windows, doors, trim, bathrooms, and exterior surfaces. If you want to know what's in a given can of paint, ask the manufacturer for its material safety data sheets, which they are required by law to keep. "But again, is everything on them? Probably not," Novak says. The safest course, Novak says, is to choose low-biocide, low-VOC, or VOC-free paints.

"Low-VOC" on a paint label means that the manufacturer isn't exceeding a certain level of chemicals labeled as carcinogenic under California law, which has stricter than federal limits, but these paints can still offgas somewhat. "Low-VOC" paints are made by **AFM, Best Paint Co.,** and **Pace Chem Industries.** While **AFM**'s paints are technically low-VOC, they are formulated to emit no fumes so that they may be used in homes for people who are extremely sensitive to chemicals, Novak says. He also recommends Kurfees, made by **Progress Paint Company,** low-VOC paint, because it has a solvent made of baking soda, which evaporates in the first half hour.

"Low-biocide" paints are 90 to 95 percent free of biocides, which include preservatives and fungicides. Biocides are commonly added to conventional latex paints. Low-biocide paints, because they're more susceptible to mildew, should probably not be used in weather-exposed or humid areas, like the basement or bath, unless there's plenty of sunlight and ventilation. In such areas, you're better off using low-VOC oil- or water-based enamel paints, or, if a strong citrus smell doesn't bother you, one of the natural enamel paints discussed below.

"VOC-free" or "no-VOC" paints have even less-toxic chemicals than "low-VOC," but generally cost more. Manufacturers of VOC-free, low-biocide paints include **Chem-Safe Products,** which makes Enviro-Safe paint, **Miller Paint Company, Benjamin Moore, Glidden, Livos,** and **Kelly Moore.**

Lane Graves and her husband, Alec Applegarthe, used **Kelly Moore**'s Envirocoat, "a water-based paint that has no VOCs, according to the label," Lane says. "It was more expensive—the flat paint cost $24 per gallon and the enamel for the trim was about $39 per gallon, but it was worth it. The paint went on well, and there were definitely less fumes. A friend was painting her apartment with conventional paint at the same time, and the fumes were really noticeable—you could definitely tell the difference."

Natural milk or organic paints are also worth considering. Natural paints use primarily natural solvents, made from citrus and other plant oils, rather than petrochemical products; some still contain petrochemical solvents, but far less than do other paints. Made mostly in Germany, natural paints also contain plant resins, finely ground minerals, and earth pigments. They are free of preservatives and biocides; because of this, they have a shorter shelf life, and should therefore be used soon after purchase. Like other low-biocide paints, water-based natural paints are less resistant to mildews and molds; natural oil-based enamel paints can be used in humid areas instead. While better for the natural environment because they don't use petrochemical resources, natural paints are not necessarily healthier for everyone in the home. They can contain aromatic ingredients—such as the citrus-based solvent d,l-limonene, turpentine, and tung oil or pine resins—that, though natural, still emit fumes. These strong-smelling fumes can cause reactions, from watery eyes to respiratory problems, in sensitive people. Like any other paints, natural paints should be applied only with good ventilation—and you might want to test a sample first.

Manufacturers of both water- and oil-based natural paints include Auro (available at **Sinan**), **Bioshield,** and **Livos.** Bioshield's white organic wall paint (all the plant ingredients were certified grown organically) can be mixed with organic pigments. While these paints are more expensive than synthetics, and often require more care and effort to mix and apply, architect Paul Bierman-Lytle recommends them ". . . for those who want the highest-quality finish, both aesthetically and environmentally . . ." We agree that these paints can give your walls a truly individual, painterly look while freeing your indoor air from synthetic fumes. **Terra Verde** and **The Natural Choice** sell these pigments. If you've got plaster, cement, or stucco walls that you plan to paint simple white, a low-cost option is whitewash, which takes nicely to these surfaces. Natural whitewash consists of nothing more than lime paste, water, and salt. Auro (available at **Sinan**) and **Livos** make white-washes.

Natural milk paints are quite odorless, as they contain neither petrochemical nor plant-based solvents. Instead, they are made using the milk protein casein as a binder, along with earth pigments, lime, and clay. They come in powdered form, to be mixed with water. As with other natural water-based paints, milk paints, because they contain no preservatives or biocides should, once opened or mixed, be applied quickly. If left to stand for a few weeks, they can mold.

Finally, we can't stress enough that even the cleanest paints will give off some fumes, so steer clear of freshly painted rooms when you are pregnant, no matter what kind of paint is used. The room should be painted at least a month before the baby will occupy it. And it's best not to throw any leftover paint in the trash; it should be taken to a hazardous waste drop-off site. Check with your local sanitation department.

It's best to have only baby's room painted, unless it's currently occupied by parents or another child, or to move somewhere else or go on vacation while painting is done, allowing as much time as possible for drying and offgassing with windows open. But what if you're already pregnant, can't afford to go away, occupy a small apartment where fumes can't be avoided, and the paint on your walls is alarmingly old? Such was the situation for Mindy Pennybacker, Mothers' & Others' Director of Publications, whose son, Rory Wallace, was born in New York City in 1986. Their temporary solution: "As a shower gift, we'd received an antique cotton 'storybook' quilt. Hung on the wall, it completely covered the painted surface within the baby's reach." Before Rory reached crawling, dust-collecting stage, Mindy and her husband, Don Wallace, took him on vacation for a month and had the apartment painted, and ventilated, in their absence.

Dads and other nonpregnant painters should see page 27 for painting safety tips.

Biocide-free, VOC-free, and low-VOC paints can be obtained from **E.C.O., Eco-Wise, Environmental Home Center, Planetary Solutions, The Natural Choice, N.E.E.D.S.,** and **Nontoxic Environments,** or contact the manufacturers listed in Appendix B to find a retailer in your part of the country. Natural and milk paints are available from **The Natural Choice, Sinan,** and **Terra Verde. The Natural Choice** sells **Livos** whitewashes, as well.

Other Wall Coverings

In addition to a new paint job, you might be considering wall coverings and borders to decorate your baby nursery. Most wallpapers and adhesives are not a sound environmental alternative to paint. These days, many wallpapers are not paper, as the name would suggest, but are made of vinyl, which can offgas chemicals and may contain hormone-disrupting phthalates. Vinyl (PVC) is destructive to the environment because during its manufacture and incineration, the carcinogen and hormone disruptor dioxin is released. Fabric and paper wall coverings are usually dyed with chemical inks and treated with chemicals to prevent the growth of molds and insect damage, resist stains, and thwart fire; these may also offgas.

The adhesives for wall coverings may be worse than the treated paper, fabric, or vinyl. Once, people used wheat and water as a wallpaper paste. Today, this simple adhesive has been replaced by petroleum-based or urea-formaldehyde glues. These chemical-laden products may offgas for months, especially in hot or humid weather. (The fumes are usually strongest just after application, but they may continue to emanate from the walls for some time afterward in minute quantities.)

If you really want to hang wallpaper in your baby's room, there are environmentally friendly papers and glues to choose from. **Crown Corporation** makes wall coverings made of recycled cotton and wood. **Maya Romanoff Corporation, Pattern People, Inc.,** and **E.C.O. of New York** sell other low-pollutant papers. You can find natural and low-VOC wallpaper glues at **Sinan Company, The Natural Choice,** and **Roman Adhesives.**

Instead of hanging paper, you could also try painting murals or stencils on nursery walls using low-toxicity paints. Pre-cut stencils and kits are available at hardware, paint, and craft stores.

Carpeting and Other Floor Covering

As overwhelming evidence accumulates against the dust mites that trigger and worsen allergies and asthma, more and more pediatricians recommend no rugs at all in babies' rooms. Another reason is that synthetic carpeting contains so many chemicals, including VOCs, that it is frequently referred to as a "toxic soup." Keep in mind that, in the eyes of the $9.5 billion-a-year industry that makes and sells it, "carpeting" isn't just a rug, but a complex layered system. The typical wall-to-wall carpet includes adhesives to bind fiber to backing; underlay or rug pads; more glues or adhesive strips to attach carpet to floor; and chemical surface treatments to stainproof and mothproof.

Thus, although it may look innocent enough just lying there, synthetic carpeting is far from benign. All of the components of this complex layered system actively offgas VOCs into the air we breathe. The EPA has identified 900 of these pollutants in indoor air. Synthetic carpeting can contribute carcinogens such as benzene, formaldehyde, and styrene, and neurotoxins such as toluene and xylene, to that unhealthy mix. In 1988, the EPA itself had to remove 27,000 square feet of new carpeting from its headquarters when the staff reported that it made them ill.

What if you already have a wall-to-wall synthetic carpet installed in the room that will be your baby's? You can rip it up, as did Patty Arlotta, the mother of a child with asthma. Or you can leave it and use topical treatments, such as antidust-mite sprays and a vacuum cleaner with a fine-particle-trapping filter to control allergens (see chapter 5). If it's an old carpet, it may have done most of its offgassing by now. And if you're pregnant, it's safest not to rip up carpets, because doing so will release plenty of dust and VOCs from carpet glues and underlay into the air. Do it only if you won't be in that room until all has been cleaned and aired out.

Although offgassing drops off markedly several months after installation, carpets can issue these fumes for as long as five years in amounts that can irritate the chemically sensitive. If you don't have histories of allergies in either parent's family, you can probably keep your old rug. But remember, old or new, carpeting continues to absorb allergenic dust and toxic pesticides and cleaning agents. In humid environments, carpeting also may harbor allergenic mildews or molds. You'll need to use less-toxic cleaners, and really guard against excess humidity in your home.

"Allergens such as dust, or any chemical heavier than air, will settle down into the carpet. In addition, if insecticides and solvents are used in a room, residues will sink in the air and hover near the ground," Dr. Harvey Karp says, adding that, even if the windows are open, only the upper half of the room will be aerated. The toxic soup bubbles below. Babies and children, who play on the carpet and are naturally low to the ground anyway, receive the full onslaught of these fumes. "Imagine laying your face on the carpet and taking a deep breath—when your children are young, that's what they're doing," says Karp.

Finally, there are the environmental consequences of today's carpeting. According to **Green Seal**'s *Choose Green Report* on carpeting, in 1995 over 1.6 billion square yards of carpeting were sold for residential and commercial uses. "The manufacture of this 500 square miles of natural and synthetic fibers generated more than 1.7 million tons of solid waste," Green Seal reports. You can reduce waste by choosing carpets with long lifetimes, made of recycled, reusable, recyclable, or biodegradable material.

Except for a couple of small, natural-fiber throw rugs, Mothers & Others' member Carol Baxter went the bare floor route, and she's glad she did. However, like many prospective parents, Lane Graves and Alec Applegarth decided they'd go ahead and risk having a rug. "It just seems to make a room warmer, and we thought the added cushioning would help when the baby starts to crawl and walk," Lane says. "But when we went and looked at carpet, it seemed as if everything was synthetic." And wool, when they could find it, cost up to twice as much.

"We chose a white wool Berber from a big roll. We had it cut to 7 × 10 feet, exactly the size of the nursery. They bound the edges so that it looks nice. We didn't buy an underlay or rug pad, and we didn't tack or glue it to the floor. It has a sticky backing so it doesn't slide around, but it probably wouldn't, anyway, as it just fit the room," Lane says. She adds that she and her husband put the rug in their living room for a few weeks, so that it could offgas, before moving it to the baby's room. It's a good thing they did, because the "sticky backing" was a VOC-emitting latex adhesive. "Shopping for carpet was kind of a scary thing to do. The smells in the stores from all those giant rolls were overwhelming," Lane says. Remember, the mothproofing chemicals used on most wool carpets are pesticides, which will offgas dangerous VOCs. Choose an untreated carpet, or let your new one "breathe"—outdoors, if possible—before laying it down in a room.

Like Lane, American consumers are pretty much on their own when it comes to choosing less toxic carpets. In 1991, the attorneys general of twenty-six states petitioned the U.S. Consumer Product Safety Commission to require warning labels on carpets, but to no avail; despite the illness among its own workers, the EPA to this day maintains that there's no evidence that synthetic carpet causes health problems.

In this regulatory vacuum, the industry has sought to capitalize on consumer anxieties by issuing its own seal of environmental responsibility, the "Green Tag," administered by the Carpet and Rug Institute (CRI). However, the attorneys general of New York, Vermont, Connecticut, and Oregon have declared the testing behind this label to be inadequate, as the program tests only one sample from each carpet type and measures only the total amount of VOCs rather than specific ingredients or toxicity. It thus behooves consumers to do a little research of their own. Green Seal recommends that, as a *minimum*, carpets should satisfy the CRI "Green Tag" or have a label that says they meet the State of Washington's guidelines. These, however, should not be read as a guarantee that the carpet will not cause health problems.

Buying and Installing a Carpet

- Stick with natural fibers. Organically grown wool, cotton, hemp, jute, ramie, or goat hair cost more than nylon, but are environmentally the best choices. Also, particularly if not treated with pesticides and stainproofing, these fibers won't offgass VOCs. Note: hemp tends to be grown with less pesticides, as it's a naturally resistant plant; but if not certified organic, jute, like cotton, has probably been grown with heavy pesticide applications.

Real wool carpet

- Find out how the carpet fiber was colored; best choices are undyed or vegetable-dyed fibers.

- Inquire of store or manufacturer what sort of chemical treatments, if any, the carpet has undergone. Choose carpets with the fewest applied finishes.

- Check the backings. Tufted fibers are usually affixed to the carpet with an adhesive that contains 4-phenylcyclohexene (4-PC), which irritates the eyes and respiratory tract and can also affect the central nervous system. (That distinctive "new-carpet" aroma is the odor of 4-PC offgassing.) You can choose untreated natural latex rubber, but first make sure no one in your family reacts to this substance. Take a small sample and see whether touching it or sniffing it bothers them. Or avoid the hassle altogether by choosing a backing-free, flat-woven dhurrie or kilim.

- Scrutinize cushioning or underlays. Opt for an untreated wool or camel's hair felt pad rather than synthetic foams, foam rubber, synthetic, latex, or plastic. **Leggett and Platt**'s Permaloom Carpet Cushion, a less toxic pad, is made by **Southwest Fibers** in Mexia, Texas; or try Hartex Carpet Cushion (also made by Leggett and Platt). **Nontoxic Environments** and **Naturlich Natural Home** sell wool and camel hair sewn (not glued) to a jute backing.

- Before buying a carpet, you can have it tested for safety by sending two square feet to **Anderson Laboratories** for a $480 fee. But we don't recommend your spending your resources this way; why not simply choose a nonsynthetic, washable rug?

- Before buying a carpet, make sure the company will unwrap, unroll, and air it out in its warehouse for at least three days before delivering it to your home, Green Seal advises.

- Tack carpets down rather than gluing. Or try an adhesive that explicitly states it's low-VOC or water-based.

- Vacuum floors well before laying down new carpet.

- For at least seventy-two hours after installation, leave windows open to disperse VOCs.

Keeping Carpets Clean and Safe

- Try not to expose synthetic carpets, or natural-fiber carpets that contain synthetic backings or finishes to direct sunlight or temperatures above 80 degrees F. Synthetic carpets emit more fumes when heated up, as when spread on floors using radiant heat.

- Clean carpets with special care. Even a safe carpet, alas, will not keep itself clean. Yet many commercial carpet-cleaning solutions and powders are simply stronger than they need to be. **Nontoxic Environments** and **N.E.E.D.S.** sell safer carpet shampoos, such as **AFM** SafeChoice Carpet Shampoo. You can also steam clean carpets without a detergent, or use a mild all-purpose cleaner, such as Ecover or EarthRite All Purpose Cleaners, in most carpet cleaning machines. Use only a small amount of cleaner and aim for low suds, diluting $\frac{1}{8}$ to $\frac{1}{4}$ cup of cleaner in one gallon of water.

- Vacuum at least twice a week with a strong-suction machine, preferably one that uses a HEPA (High Energy Particulate) or ULPA filter, or one that traps dust particles down to at least 0.1-micron size or smaller. These small particles are the ones that irritate sensitive airways.

Some recommended carpets and manufacturers are:
- **Naturlich Natural Home** in Sebastopol, California, sells unpesticided wool carpet and Enviro-tech low-VOC carpet glue.

- **Sinan Company** in Davis, California, sells unpesticided wool carpet, as does **The Environmental Home Center** in Seattle, Washington.

- Nature's Carpet, available from **Collin Campbell & Sons,** is made from unbleached, undyed wool, giving the appeal of the sheep's natural color on a *natural* latex and jute backing. It is 100 percent biodegradable.

- All-hemp carpets are available from **Earthweave Carpet Mill** and **Ortex.**

- **Real Goods Trading Company** sells Dharmic rugs of vegetable-dyed hemp and cotton.

- **A Loomful of Hues** handweaves small area rugs in natural fibers, perfect for children's rooms.

Carpets Made without Child Labor

According to the Child Labor Coalition in Washington and the South Asian Coalition on Child Servitude, anywhere from 300,000 to 1 million children, mostly in India and Pakistan, are at work weaving rugs. Under the new Rugmark labeling initiative, you can obtain some assurance that the rugs you buy are not made with child labor.

Rugmark is an international nonprofit organization that monitors production by 145 manufacturers in India and Nepal; members' fees pay for three schools in those countries. It is the only label that tries to guarantee no child labor; however, in prac-

tice, since many rugs are made in private homes as well as in factories, this is hard to enforce, especially with only eighteen inspectors for 18,636 looms. The Kaleen program, run by the Indian government in cooperation with the carpet industry, requires that every loom be registered; fees also go to support schools; Kaleen also has only eighteen inspectors.

Swedish-headquartered Ikea and ABC Carpet and Home in Manhattan try to avoid selling products of child labor by commissioning random inspections of looms.

Other Floor Coverings: Hardwood, Linoleum, Cork, Ceramic Tile

If you choose not to cover floors with carpets, a variety of alternatives exist. But be careful. Even wood flooring, if treated with pesticides and petrochemical stains, waxes, and finishes, can offgas toxic or irritating VOCs. The safest types of flooring are *untreated* hardwood, true linoleum, ceramic tile, marble, and stone slate.

Untreated hardwood flooring can be bought from **Superior Flooring Company** and **Naturlich Natural Home.** You can treat these floors yourself with less-toxic finishes. **American Formulating and Manufacturing (AFM)** and **Pace Chem Industries** make paints, stains, and sealers that are water-based rather than solvent-based. You can find them in building supply stores that specialize in environmentally sound products or order them from **N.E.E.D.S., The Natural Choice,** and **Environmental Home Center.** Auro Products, from the **Sinan Company,** are natural, low-VOC waxes. Natural finishes such as tung oil can be mixed with cirus-based thinners and applied in two or more thin coats, then coated with beeswax, which needs to be reapplied once a year or so. For product information, call **E.C.O. Livos** makes a one-step clear natural finish "that acts just like polyurethane—it's the easiest natural system," according to Katherine Tiddens at Terra Verde. If you want to deepen the color, you can add **Bioshield** pigments sold by **Terra Verde** and **The Natural Choice** catalog. You can also use water-based polyurethane finishes, which can be found in hardware stores. Unlike oil-based polyurethane, the water-based type dries quickly and emits far fewer VOCs.

It's also worth enquiring after "reclaimed" or "recycled" lumber that can be used for floors. Companies include **Conklin's Authentic Barnwood, Crossroads Recycled Lumber,** and **EcoTimber International.** Other companies are listed in Appendix B. For a full list of lumber recyclers, contact **Rainforest Action Network.**

ALTERNATIVES TO VINYL TILES

For a nursery, resilient floor covering is an appealing alternative to carpeting to help protect energetically tumbling babies. While they won't literally bounce on resilient floors, much of the shock will be absorbed. Vinyl flooring, often incorrectly called "linoleum," is made of petrochemical plasticizers, pigments, and fillers formed under heat and pressure. An EPA study of emissions from these products found a number of neurotoxic solvents and aldehydes, including formaldehyde, acetone, ketones, toluene, xylene, and vinyl chloride. These chemicals affect the central nervous system, lungs, eyes, skin, liver, kidneys, gastrointestinal tract, and lymphatic system. In Norway, National Institute of Public Health researchers postulated that inhalation of phthalates emitted by vinyl floors was a likely cause for the rise in childhood asthma in that country.

As a healthier alternative, true linoleum, though difficult to find these days, is well worth the search. It contains the same natural ingredients used over a hundred years ago: linseed oil from flax, resins from pine trees, wood and cork with fillers composed of clay or chalk, and ground stone for colored pigments. It has a burlap or jute backing in place of the more toxic synthetic backings. It is durable and flexible. Note: because pine and linseed oil are aromatic, check a linoleum sample to make sure that you and your family aren't sensitive to these natural fumes.

True linoleum is available by mail order from **Naturlich Natural Home, E.C.O., Eco-Wise, Environmental Home Center, Forbo Industries,** and **Planetary Solutions.**

Cork flooring is produced from the outer bark of the cork oak, which grows mostly in Portugal and Spain. It's a renewable resource because the interval between stripping is regulated by law, so that the bark can regenerate. It can be bought in tiles or, more rarely, in carpeting sheets made with cork granules and linseed oil, backed with jute canvas. Rather than buy the usual commercial tiles coated with a layer of vinyl or urethane, look for unfinished tiles and have them sealed with a natural or low-VOC synthetic sealer. Cork tiles, according to Paul Bierman-Lytle and Janet Marinelli, authors of *Your Natural Home,* are moisture-, rot-, and mold-resistant, and, as Marcel Proust most famously demonstrated, absorb vibration and deaden sound. However, unlike true linoleum, cork does require periodic waxing or oiling. You can order cork tiles from **Classic Tile, Dodge Regupol, Inc., E.C.O., Eco-Wise, Environmental Home Center, Korqinc, Naturlich Natural Home,** and **Planetary Solutions.**

While not appropriate for the nursery, you may choose to use marble, slate, or ceramic floor tile in other rooms, such as the kitchen or bathroom. Marble, slate, and ceramic floor tile emit no VOCs. But conventional tile adhesives do. Less toxic alternatives are available from **E.C.O.** and **Sinan Company.**

Choosing a Crib and Other Furniture

Furniture you may want specifically for the nursery includes the crib, a comfortable rocking chair where you can sit to nurse or just hold your baby, a chest of drawers for clothes, shelves for easy access to diapers, and a changing table.

Easy Substitutions

Please remember: You don't have to *buy* everything. For instance, for a changing table, you could substitute a sturdy table, wide-topped shelves, or bureau. Just be sure it's of comfortable height, so that you don't have to bend over at the waist while wrestling with a rambunctious infant or toddler. As you will discover, there are enough surprise opportunities for backbreaking in parenthood; you should try to cosset your back when choosing equipment for the most common and repetitive tasks. A waterproof changing pad or simply a thick, folded terry cloth towel can be placed on top of this surface. While most changing tables come with belts, doctors advise that you always keep one hand on baby while changing him, anyway, and never leave your baby unattended on any surface, bed, or table, even for an instant, because of babies' propensity for sudden rolling. Or baby can simply be changed on a nice clean floor.

Rather than a chest of drawers, some parents use wicker laundry baskets: one for those necessary little snap-closure T-shirts, another for clean diapers. The unfinished material gives a fresh, clean look. Or you can get wicker stacking baskets from home furnishings stores and catalogs, such as **Crate & Barrel.** (Do dust the basket and check it periodically for mold, which can grow on damp basket fibers.) Wherever you change baby, make sure supplies—diapers, diaper covers, wipes, undershirts—are close at hand so you won't even be tempted to leave baby unattended for an instant. If you use a table without shelves built underneath, make sure it is next to shelves or a roomy bureau top, or place wicker or a short stack of wood shelves beneath the table—and not too far back—so you can grab items without taking your eyes off baby.

Toy or clothing chests are another common nursery feature. Most contemporary toy chests have slow-closing, spring-loaded lid supports; be sure to check this before buying one. Toy chests should also not have latches that could trap a child who climbs in; they should have ventilation holes or spaces in the front or sides, or under the lids. Beware of antique toy chests, which might lack these precautions. Your bedroom hope chest and other storage containers may be hazardous, as well. You can install a spring-loaded hinge on an older chest, or simply remove its lid.

The Crib

Despite its unfortunate resemblance to a small jail, the crib remains the heart of the nursery, the one new, specifically "baby" item most expectant parents feel they cannot do without. The bars, of course, are there to keep the baby safe; however, like any piece of furniture, a crib can, if inadequately built or painted, become a hazard in itself.

First rule: Look for a crib with a certification seal showing that it meets national safety standards.

Second rule: New or used, know your crib's age; while Mothers & Others generally recommends recycling and reuse, there are exceptions—and, when it comes to cribs, new—since 1990—is best.

There are three reasons to be wary of old, "heirloom," or even more recent hand-me-down cribs:

1. Cribs manufactured before 1990 may not meet the 1990 Consumer Product Safety Commission (CPSC) Standards (see box).

2. Structural weakness in used cribs. "Each year, about 50 babies suffocate or strangle when they become trapped between broken crib parts or in cribs with older, unsafe designs," the CPSC says. Even if a perfectly reputable friend or relative's used crib was made since 1990, it may have sustained damage due to vigorous use by one or more babies in the intervening years. Inspect used cribs carefully to make sure bars aren't missing or loose. "When choosing used or new nursery equipment, check for sturdy construction and stability. Avoid exposed screws, bolts, or fasteners with sharp edges or points; avoid scissor-like mechanisms which could crush fingers; and avoid cutout designs that could entrap a child's head," the CPSC advises.

3. Lead paint, which wasn't banned until 1978, may be present on older cribs, sometimes lurking beneath a more recent layer. "I thought, at first, we'll get a nice second-hand crib. But a lot of them were painted," Carol Baxter says. She opted for a new wood crib, whose label said it was painted with a nontoxic enamel paint. Lane Graves bought a new crib, but saved money because it was a floor sample. She chose an unpainted, solid wood crib treated with a clear low-VOC finish.

Crib Safety Standards

Here is a short list of CPSC safety standards for cribs and furniture.

A safe crib has:

- no more than $2\frac{3}{8}$ inches between crib slats, so that baby's head and body cannot fit through the slats
- no missing, loose, broken, or improperly installed screws, brackets, or other hardware on the crib or the mattress support
- a firm, snug-fitting mattress, so baby cannot get trapped between the mattress and the side of the crib
- a mattress support that does not easily pull apart from the corner posts (give it a hearty test tug)
- no corner posts over $\frac{1}{16}$ of an inch above the end panels, so baby's clothing cannot catch and strangle him

- no cutout areas on headboard or footboard that could trap baby's head
- no splinters or rough edges
- no cracked or peeling paint

To be certain the crib remains safe as long as your baby sleeps in it:

- Tighten all nuts, bolts and screws periodically.
- Check hooks regularly; open hooks may allow mattress to fall.
- Whenever crib has been moved, make sure all mattress support hangers remain secure.

In addition, to avoid choking and entanglement, pay attention to the placement of the crib within the room and take care not to use the crib to hang things from. Keep cribs and playpens a safe distance from windows, so that there's no chance your baby could fall out. Also, there will be less noise to disturb the baby if you place the crib against an interior wall. Always make sure there are no drapery or venetian blind cords or lamp cords hanging within your baby's reach. Move shelves and tabletops holding lamps, clocks, safety pins, or other dangerous objects well out of your baby's potential reach. Don't hang objects with strings or elastic (toys or laundry bags, for example) around cribs or playpens.

Keep all toys, including stuffed toys, out of baby's crib or wherever baby sleeps (see section on SIDS, page 46).

Crib gyms, exercisers, and kickers strung across crib or playpen should never be used once baby can push up on hands and knees or sit up, or reaches five months of age—whichever comes first. Remove them completely; don't just untie one end and allow the toy to dangle, because strangulation can still take place. "Our son enjoyed his crib gym, but even before he could push up we removed the toy from the top of the crib every night," Mindy says.

For a comprehensive list that encompasses baby-proofing and other baby equipment, ask **CPSC** for documents #4241 and #5020.

Buying New Furniture

You can choose more environmentally sound and healthier options when buying new furniture. Here are some tips:

- *Avoid furniture made of laminated wood, pressed wood, chipboard, plywood, particleboard, and synthetic veneers.*

"The major environmental drawback in the use of engineered wood products is the use of formaldehyde-based glues," writes Cassandra Adams, assistant professor of architecture at the University of California, Berkeley. In other words, all of the above wood products can release formaldehyde. "We went shopping for a crib and changing table at Albee's, the baby emporium on the Upper West Side in New York City," Mindy Pennybacker remembers. "The cribs had nontoxic stickers on them. What I didn't know then was that 'nontoxic' is an evolving concept—a lot of these substances haven't been fully tested. I didn't know that the bottom of the crib or changing table, or the back of a bureau might be made of pressed wood or particleboard," Mindy says. In general, particleboard looks like wood shavings glued together and doesn't have a grain. Plywood is usually fairly thin and has a grain. The cut edge shows that a number of layers have been stacked and glued together.

- *Avoid plastic, especially polyvinyl chloride (PVC) furniture and coatings.*
- *Allow time and space for offgassing.*

As both Carol Baxter and Lane Graves found, it's very hard to be completely ecologically "pure." It's also beyond most of our means. Therefore, if *some* synthetic fiber or particleboard does make its way into your nursery mix, you can minimize exposure by buying products made from them at least four to six weeks before baby's due date and letting them offgas in a well-ventilated area, as Lane did with her new carpet.

- *Your best bet: solid hardwood cribs with nontoxic finish.*

For about $500, **Ecobaby** sells a solid maple crib that converts to a toddler bed and can be bought either *unfinished* or finished with tung oil and beeswax. Though tung oil and other natural oils can be aromatic when applied, once these natural finishes have dried, they are quite safe. **Pacific Rim,** a wholesaler based in Eugene, Oregon, also manufactures cribs from certified, sustainably forested hardwood, available unfinished or with a plant-based stain, that can convert to a youth, or toddler, bed and a full-size twin bed. They

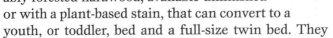

are sold at "green" stores such as **Terra Verde** in New York City, or you can call Pacific Rim to find out who carries their cribs in your area. If you're in a pinch, the **Eddie Bauer** catalog carries a Childcraft solid maple crib in white or natural wood colors although its "veneer finishes" make it a less than optimal choice. An attractive blond pine toddler bed, which fits a crib-size mattress, comes with a matching toy box/bench and nightstand from the **The Natural Baby Company.** Water-based finishes are used; however, the bed does have plywood crossboards.

- *Apply less-toxic, low-VOC sealants.*

You can also make your furniture and crib safer by sealing them with a water-based polyurethane sealant such as **Pace Chem Industries'** Crystal Air, available from **Environmental Home Center, N.E.E.D.S.,** and **Nontoxic Environments.** Other water-based polyurethane finishes are available at hardware stores. Make sure you don't pick up the oil-based kind, as it takes much longer to dry and off-gasses toxic fumes. Have the sealing done outdoors or in a well-ventilated area by someone who is not pregnant, and keep young children away until the furniture is completely dry. This kind of finish prevents VOC emissions by locking them under an impenetrable coating.

Choosing More Environmentally Sound Woods

No furniture material brings nature indoors better than wood. However, domestically and internationally, forests are in serious decline, being harvested at unsustainable rates—to put it mildly. Ninety-five percent of original, old-growth forests in the United States have been logged, and the remaining 5 percent have not been protected from the axe and saw. Between 1980 and 1995 alone, at least 2 million square kilometers of forests—an area larger than Mexico—were destroyed, the Worldwatch Institute reports. The destruction of forests releases tons of carbon dioxide, the main greenhouse gas, into Earth's atmosphere. Plus we lose more than just trees: Deforestation reduces the diversity of plant and animal species in these rich habitats.

The plight of forests internationally reached new emergency levels in the summer and autumn of 1997. Smoke from fires, set to clear land for crops on the densely forested islands of Borneo and Sumatra, spread from Indonesia to Malaysia, the Philippines, Singapore, Thailand, Brunei, and Papua New Guinea, and combined with pollution from industry and cars to cast a pall of smog and respiratory illness throughout the region. At the same time, reports from the Amazon revealed that Brazilian virgin rain forest was vanishing, through burning and clearcutting, at a far greater rate than previously thought.

Consumer demand for wood products, which helps fuel the destruction of forests, can also be harnessed to protect this resource if we make more ecologically sound choices. For instance, **Pacific Rim** in Eugene, Oregon, makes cribs with woods specifically *not* taken by clearcutting old-growth forests. **EcoTimber,** in San Francisco, specializes in sustainably harvested domestic hardwoods and tropical woods. In November 1997, EcoTimber told the *Wall Street Journal* that sales of environmentally certified wood (see below) had increased fourfold in the past year and, at $2 million, accounted for two-thirds of its business. Plus, it can be affordable. "Certified harvested redwood is competitively priced with non-certified redwood," according to the **Rainforest Action Network.** In general, certified wood products don't cost more than conventional—there's no "green premium," according to Stacy Brown of the Forest Stewardship Council. As with any product, "prices vary depending on the type of wood, fluctuating with supply and demand," Brown says. Availability, for instance, makes domestic U.S. species, such as maple and oak, more affordable than tropical hardwoods such as mahogany or teak. With regard to tropical species, a heated debate is currently raging over whether *any* logging in rain forests can be done sustainably, without damage to the delicate balance of biodiversity. We advise that, until this problem is solved, you think twice about choosing tropical hardwoods, and, if you do select them, make sure they bear FSC's label before you buy.

You can do your part to preserve forest resources—and combat global warming—by keeping a cool head and looking for the certified wood that has begun to penetrate the market. To be certified, timber companies must show that they use approved management practices for maintaining ecological balance, such as selective logging that allows the forest to grow back and preserves biodiversity and wildlife habitat. Here are some certified "green" wood labels you can look for:

- *The Forest Stewardship Council's "Certified Well-Managed Forest" label.* Founded in 1993, FSC is a nonprofit organization based in Waterbury, Vermont, and Oaxaca, Mexico, which gets support from the European Union, the World Wildlife Fund, and the U.S.-based Ford and MacArthur foundations, among others. Wood products with FSC's label can be found in the United States at Home Depot. Participants include Seven Islands, a Maine company that owns the largest certified forest (975,000 acres) in North America. In addition to their own label—a checkmark blending into a tree—FSC also accredits other forest management and product labeling programs; if wood bears any "green" certification label, make sure that it also carries FSC's.

- *The SmartWood program of the Rainforest Alliance.* The RA, based in New York City, has certified about 7.5 million acres of forest in the United States, Central America, and elsewhere. SmartWood's new "Rediscovered Wood" label certifies recycled lumber and wood taken from old orchards.

- *Scientific Certification Systems.*

If you're looking for a specific species, **SmartWood** or **SCS** can tell you whether it's available certified—and if not, why. **FSC**'s web catalog of certified-wood furniture and other finished products is listed in Appendix A.

Crib Mattresses and Bedding

From the earliest moments of their lives, babies spend a great deal of time sleeping. The average newborn sleeps sixteen to seventeen hours every day, waking every few hours to nurse. Over time, babies will gradually stay awake for longer segments of time. Even so, toddlers also sleep about twelve hours per day, or at least they should!

For this reason, making your baby's sleeping environment comfortable and healthy is important. Most of us don't think of bedding as a potential health hazard, yet fabric treatments and the materials used in mattresses can offgas for some time. In a nursery outfitted with new sheets, crib, and mattress, your baby may get a not-so-healthy dose of chemicals. You'll have to be especially careful to reduce biological contaminants, such as dust mites.

Choosing safe bedding is especially important because your baby will be in direct contact with the fabrics and other materials that make up bedding. A baby whose skin comes in contact with formaldehyde, toluene, benzene, and other VOCs, or inhales them, may experience acute reactions, such as headaches, dizziness, nausea, respiratory difficulties, and skin rashes. Early and prolonged exposure also may pave the way to serious chronic illnesses, such as allergies and asthma.

Biological contaminants, such as dust, dander, pollen, mold, and mildew, cling to fibers in bedding materials. Microscopic asthma-inducing dust mites thrive on skin cells, dander, and moisture in mattresses, sheets, pillows, stuffed animals, drapes, and carpeting. Other biological contaminants can also collect in and on these materials.

To restrict dust mite happy hunting grounds, steer away from overstuffed, overly fluffy comforters. You also won't want to oppress or overheat your baby under too-heavy bedding. When shopping for a crib blanket (or when you receive one as a gift), give it the heft test. Is it heavy? How would it feel on top of you if you weighed, say, seven pounds? Could a baby's tiny fingers and toes get caught in any loose stitching, crochet holes, or loops? Are you willing to wash and dry this thing every two weeks? If the quilt or blanket fails any of these tests, feel free to return it.

One thing you might invest in, in addition to a lightweight, washable comforter and some basic, washable plain cotton and wool blankets, are creepers. Many babies, once they're out of the swaddling stage, kick off all their bedding. This is fine in hot weather, if your home isn't drafty or overcooled, but in winter, one way to keep your baby from chills is to dress him in a little union suit, one that covers the feet, for sleeping. Some also cover the hands, so that baby can't scratch his face while he sleeps. This item should be in a light fabric rather than, say, fuzzy outdoor fleece, and is discussed in more detail in chapter 7. A lightweight blanket over a creeper-clad baby should provide plenty of warmth and comfort.

What You Should Know about Fabrics in General

There are many fabrics in a nursery—sheets, blankets, mattress pads, pillow encasements, and mattress ticking. The best choices for baby are natural and untreated fabrics, such as cotton and wool.

A WORD ON DYES

If you want more color variety while avoiding full-out chemical dyes, you can look for labels that say "natural" or "vegetable" dye, or "low-impact." Both these choices, while moving in the right direction, remain imperfect, however. Natural dyes, because of their poor colorfastness, are often accompanied by heavy metals in the mordant, or dye-fixing agent. If the label or tag says that no heavy metals were used in the dye process, be prepared for uneven fading—a lesser evil, in our opinion, than toxic but color-fast dyes! In theory, "low-impact" dyes should have used less chemicals and water, and produced less contamination of waterways; however, no guidelines exist, as yet, regulating these claims. Look for further specifications on the label: "fiber-reactive dyes" and "cold pad batch dyeing" are less chemically intensive, and result in less dyestuff going into water.

cotton plant

CONVENTIONAL, GREEN, AND ORGANIC COTTON

For babies, we often think of cotton as the best natural fabric choice. Cotton breathes, absorbs, and comforts. But how natural is conventionally grown and processed cotton?

About one-third of a pound of chemicals, including pesticides, fertilizers, and processing chemicals and dyes, is used to make just one cotton T-shirt, according to the Sustainable Cotton Project in California. Cotton is one of the most pesticide-intensive crops in the world. About 10 percent of the world's pesticides and 22.5 percent of all insecticides are used on conventionally grown cotton. In the United States, farmers applied more than 1.6 billion pounds of synthetic fertilizers and 53.4 billion pounds of pesticides on cotton crops in 1996. And, to process and bleach cotton a snowy white, chorine-based chemicals are used, creating hazardous dioxin. Finally, toxic heavy metals such as chromium and copper, which can leach into soils where fabrics are dyed, are commonly used to "fix" dark colors. Since cotton is naturally resistant to dyes, roughly half the chemicals used end up as waste in rivers and soil.

While the end product may contain only trace residues, if any, of these chemicals, putting the purest fabrics next to your baby's skin makes the most sense. These are two alternatives to chemical-laden cotton:

1. *Certified organic cotton* is cotton grown without the use of synthetic pesticides and fertilizers and certified as such by an independent certification organization. There are no uniform guidelines, at this time, for the use of bleaches, dyes, and other fabric treatments in organic cotton. So look for unbleached certified organic cotton, first and foremost. It is usually an off-white color instead of snowy white. Increasingly available is cotton that is naturally colored brown, pinkish orange (a sort of rosy umber shade), and green. These colors are often soft and muted—perfect for an infant.

2. *Green cotton* is cotton that has been conventionally grown, but is unbleached and has not been processed with chemicals.

You may also see *transitional cotton* on labels. This type of cotton has been grown organically on land that is being converted from conventional cultivation methods using chemicals. A three-year period, during which no synthetic chemicals are applied, is required before cotton grown on that land can be certified organic. We recommend buying transitional cotton; it will help the growers survive the transition!

You can purchase organic and green cotton crib sheets, blankets, and comforters from stores that sell environmentally friendly bath and bedroom products, like **Terre Verde** in New York City. You can also purchase them by mail from **The Natural Bedroom, Heart of Vermont, Ecobaby, The Natural Baby Company,** and **Nontoxic Environments.** Of particularly fine quality are the crib-size flannel blankets in natural-color organic cotton, with rose or blue hem-stitching, from **Forty Oaks Organic Textiles** in Petaluma, California. Forty Oaks also makes thinner rose or blue organic cotton receiving blankets for swaddling baby. Their wonderful brown-and-natural gingham quilted organic cotton throw would make an ideal floor quilt for baby, and could also warm your shoulders or lap while you nurse or just get some much-needed rest.

WOOL

Wool is warm, breathable, and naturally water-resistant and flame-retardant. For this reason, it makes an excellent choice in the nursery for blankets, mattress pads, and in the mattress itself. Wool may be processed with petrochemical detergents and oils, and it could be treated with moth repellents. A few companies sell untreated and even organic wool products. **Crown City Mattresses/The Natural Bedroom** offers bedding made of "Pure Grow Wool." Members of a certification program in California, Pure Grow ranchers pledge to follow environmentally sustainable management practices and limit medications given to sheep. They also do not dip sheep in pesticide baths. **Ecobaby** offers a "puddle pad" made of thin Pure Grow wool that can be used to keep baby's sheets and mattress dry in case of diaper leaks. **The Natural Baby Company** also sells wool crib mattress pads.

Avoid furry sheepskin mats as they may pose an increased risk of Sudden Infant Death Syndrome (SIDS).

Synthetic Fabrics and Fabric Treatments

Though synthetic fabrics—polyester, acrylics, nylon, and the like—offer the promise of easy care, you should avoid them as much as possible. Synthetic fabrics are spun from petrochemicals instead of natural fibers. They don't absorb moisture well, in general, nor are they good insulators for winter weather, because they do not "breathe." Synthetic fibers can also be difficult to clean. While some synthetic materials are inherently fire retardant, this doesn't mean they don't burn—only that they don't ignite into flames. (Burning polyester shrinks from flames and melts.) Other synthetics are treated during the manufacture of the fiber or after the cloth has been woven. Items sold as infants' and children's sleepwear must be treated with flame-retardants by federal law. If you choose to put your baby to bed in untreated clothing, first take precautions against fire hazards, install smoke detectors and fire extinguishers on each floor of your home, and plan and memorize a fire escape route. (We should all do this in any case.)

Some textiles made from polyester and nylon contain formaldehyde, either in finishes or embedded in the synthetic fiber. Formaldehyde is used as a finishing on many natural fabrics as well. Formaldehyde is used as a binder in dye pigments, a fire retardant, a fabric "stiffener," and a water repellent. Tetrakis, a fire retardant used on cotton, flannel, and rayon, contains formaldehyde.

Most sheets, comforters, and mattresses are treated with chemical dyes and finishes to improve the fabric's appearance, reduce the need for ironing, and retard flammability. Chemical treatments often stay embedded in fabrics even after washings. Airing linens outside on a warm day will allow some of the chemicals to volatilize and dissipate. But this is a tricky business because you can't control the heat and humidity that help release chemicals bound to fabrics and furniture. There is also no way to know if you've released all of the chemical. You may be able to wash some of the chemical treatments away using the method described in the box on page 46. This method is not guaranteed to work on all finishes, especially those designed to resist stains, which may contain some plastic resins, like those made of Teflon, or flame retardants embedded within synthetic fibers. Laundering will continue to break down the bonds between the fiber and chemical treatments.

So, in general, avoid textiles labeled permanent press, no-iron, crease-resistant, shrinkproof, stretchproof, water repellent, waterproofed, or those that have been treated with flame retardants—if you've taken other precautions for the latter.

Despite your best efforts, you might purchase sheets or clothing treated with finishes. While some finishes, such as flame retardants or stain guards, may be impossible to remove, try the following method to rid fabrics of that distinctive chemical "new" smell.

Fill a washing machine with water, add one cup of baking soda, and soak new clothing and bedding overnight, agitating the machine a few times (you could also use a large tub). Wash and dry at least three times, adding ¼ cup of baking soda to the detergent in the first two washes, and ½ cup white vinegar to the final wash. After three cycles, if water soaks into the dry fabric, most of the finish has been removed; if it beads up, wash and dry again.

While shopping for baby's sheets, blankets, and those sweetly decorated crib comforter and bumper guard sets should be fun, and really helps give your nursery a custom look, it's important to keep in mind the many safety issues related to babies left alone in their cribs. The most mysterious and wrenching of these is Sudden Infant Death Syndrome, and the following section will help you avoid products and practices that seem to put an infant at greater risk.

A Word about Sudden Infant Death Syndrome

Sudden Infant Death Syndrome (SIDS) is the leading cause of death in the United States among infants between one month and one year of age, claiming up to 7,000 lives per year. It is a sudden and silent killer, usually occurring during sleep; its cause remains unexplained. In June 1998, researchers in Italy announced the discovery of a correlation between SIDS and an irregular heartbeat. Peter John Schwartz, a coauthor of the study published in *New England Journal of Medicine,* estimates that one-third of SIDS cases are related to this unusual heartbeat. Other theories hypothesize that the causes for SIDS might include: stress in a normal baby caused by infections; a birth defect; failure to develop; and/or a critical period when all babies are especially vulnerable, such as time of rapid growth. But scientists still do not have a full answer to the riddle of what causes this mysterious syndrome. SIDS can strike seemingly healthy babies from all races, ethnic backgrounds, and socioeconomic origins.

Though it is not known how SIDS is caused, nor how it can be prevented, there are steps you can take to reduce the risk of SIDS. Following are the most recently available recommendations by the **Consumer Product Safety Commission,** the American Academy of Pediatrics, and the National Institute of Child Health and Development (NICHD).

1. *Place your healthy baby on its back or side to sleep, instead of on its stomach.* As of this writing, the American Academy of Pediatrics advises that infants sleeping on their backs carry the lowest risk of SIDS. When a baby is sleeping face down, her airway may become obstructed. In June 1996, the NICHD announced

that putting babies to sleep on their backs or sides reduced deaths from SIDS by 30 percent. Some pediatricians may recommend that babies with certain medical problems sleep on their stomachs. This is something to discuss with your doctor if he recommends a face-down sleeping position. Note that laying your baby down on his stomach is only a concern when he is sleeping. When an infant is awake and properly supervised, a stomach-down position is not considered hazardous.

2. *Use a firm, flat mattress.* Do not put your baby to sleep on a soft surface. Avoid pillows, water beds, lambskin or sheepskin rugs or pads, beanbag cushions, foam pads, foam sofa cushions, and thick, fluffy comforters, blankets, or mattress pads. The infant might sink in and suffocate.

3. *Eliminate tobacco smoke exposure.* SIDS has been associated with women who smoke during pregnancy. The National Center for Health Statistics found that babies exposed to smoke only after birth were twice as likely to die from SIDS as those whose mothers did not smoke at all. Constant smoke exposure during and after pregnancy triples a baby's risk.

4. *Avoid overheating your baby,* especially when he or she is ill. SIDS has been associated with the presence of colds and infections. Research indicates that overheating during illness may increase an infant's risk for SIDS by putting stress on the cardiovascular system and breathing control center in the brain. Signs that a baby is overheating include sweating, damp hair, heat rash, rapid breathing, restlessness, and sometimes fever. To regulate your baby's body temperature, maintain a constant indoor temperature between 68 and 70 degrees F., and dress your baby in as much or as little as you would wear.

5. *Breast-feed your baby,* if possible. The NICHD found that babies who died of SIDS were less likely to have been breast-fed. (For additional information on the benefits of breast-feeding, see chapter 8).

Other factors that may contribute to SIDS include:

- *Seasonality.* More babies die of SIDS during the winter months.
- *Maternal age.* The younger the mother, the greater the risk of SIDS.
- *Baby's gender.* Boys carry a higher risk than girls; 60 percent of babies who die of SIDS are boys.
- *Low birth weight.* Premature and low birth weight infants, as well as twins and triplets, have a higher incidence of SIDS.

For more information about SIDS, contact the **National Sudden Infant Death Syndrome Resource Center** or the **SIDS Network**.

Mattresses

A typical new crib mattress is stuffed with polyurethane foam and covered with material treated with fire retardants and water repellents. Chemicals, such as toluene, emitted from polyurethane foam can irritate airways, exacerbating respiratory problems and skin allergies. Federal law requires that all mattresses be treated with flame retardants. This law originated because of all the deaths from fire that occurred from people smoking in bed. Organic cotton and wool mattresses for cribs, untreated with water repellents or fire retardants, are available from manufacturers such as **Crown City Mattress Company/The Natural Bedroom,** but by law, to obtain a mattress that has not been treated with flame retardants, you must obtain a written statement from a doctor testifying that your child needs a chemical-free mattress because of allergies or asthma in the family.

This is a decision that only you can make. Obviously, we all want to guard our children as much as possible against accidents like fire; on the other hand, they won't be smoking in bed. Does anyone else in your household smoke? If you live in an apartment building, you have no control over other tenants' behavior. Equip your baby's room with a working smoke alarm that is checked periodically, and place fire extinguishers on each floor of your house. You may still want to opt for the extra security of a fire-retardant mattress.

On the other hand, wool, as mentioned above, is naturally fire resistant. Mattresses made of this fill will not require additional chemical treatments, and to purchase one, you will need a written statement from your doctor testifying that you have a medical reason for avoiding chemical treatments. Many doctors will comply with a parent's request. Natural, organic mattresses are expensive. An organic cotton and wool crib mattress may cost up to about $400. **Garnet Hill** sells a cotton crib mattress for about the same price. Although the materials are not organic and include 4 percent polyester, this mattress does not contain polyurethane foam. A crib-sized futon, stuffed with organic cotton and/or untreated wool, from **Crown City Mattress Company/The Natural Bedroom, Ecobaby,** or **Nontoxic Environments,** is more affordable, and the wool ones currently do *not* require a doctor's note. These fit standard cribs. Check the futon for firmness. Soft futons should be avoided as they may increase the risk of SIDS.

You can purchase a used mattress or get one from a relative or friend. Over time, the chemicals from the mattress will have dissipated. Inspect used mattresses carefully. A mattress should be clean, dry, and free from mold, dust, and animal dander (ask if the previous owner had pets). A used mattress should be encased in a dust-mite-impermeable cover, as the mites will have had an opportunity to grow in it over time.

If you decide to buy a new conventional mattress, contact the manufacturer about the materials. Try to avoid mattresses filled with polyurethane foam. Take the sniff test: if the odor is chemical-like or smells like plastic, reconsider your decision. Allow the chemicals in the mattress to offgas by leaving it in a well-ventilated area of your home, even outside if you can protect it from the elements. Don't allow it to get damp, as mold is difficult, if not impossible, to remove from mattresses. A display or floor sample, like Lane Graves's crib, is an excellent find, for it will have had time to offgas.

Make sure any mattress you buy, futon or standard, is firm.

Sheets and Blankets

Generally, choose natural fibers for your baby's bedding for the reasons we mentioned in the fabric section of this chapter. Organic and green cotton crib sheets can be ordered from **Earthlings, Ecosport, Eco-Wise Environmental Products, Heart of Vermont,** and **Terra Verde.** You can order cotton baby blankets from **Heart of Vermont, Terra Verde,** and other companies that carry bedding (see Appendix B). **EarthSpun Heritage Natural Fibers** and **Green Mountain Spinnery** make lovely handmade blankets from untreated, vegetable-dyed wool. Wool blankets are also available from **Heart of Vermont** and **Little Koala.**

Pillows, Comforters, and Bumper Pads

bedding

The temptation to cradle your baby in soft, fluffy pillows, comforters, and bumper pads may be great, but try to resist this urge. As mentioned above, soft and fluffy bedding is associated with an increased risk of SIDS. So are pillows, which should not be placed in a newborn or older infant's crib. Down and feathers in pillows and comforters can also contribute to allergies and may trigger asthma attacks, while foam rubber pillows are a haven for dust mites. Avoid these materials, or encase them! Look for 100 percent cotton or hypoallergenic pillows (for toddlers only) and comforters. You may want to install bumper pads on your baby's crib to prevent him from hurting himself on the bars or headboard. If you do, make sure the pads are made of cotton and that they are firm. Tie them down securely to railings.

You can order pillows, comforters, and bumper pads from **Heart of Vermont, Ecobaby,** and other companies specializing in environmentally sound bedding.

Mattress and Pillow Encasements

To reduce dust mites in your baby's nursery, be sure to wash mattress pads, sheets, and pillow covers and cases at least every two weeks in hot water (warm water will not kill the hardy mite). It's also a good idea, if allergies run in your family, to encase mattresses and pillows in impermeable covers that fit beneath the sheets. Unlike your standard mattress pad, the encasements must fully enclose the mattress, top and bottom. The zip-on covers suffocate the mites and prevent their food source (shed skin) from reaching them, and their extremely allergenic, microscopic droppings from being inhaled. Mites and their excrement easily pass through the most tightly woven cotton cloth, including very finely woven, 380-count sheets and comforter covers. Tightly woven "barrier cloth" covers are also available from **Allergy Control Products, Inc.,** and **InteliHealth Healthy Home.** Organic cotton covers, sold by **Allergy Resources,** are more costly. Barrier cloth, in general, is not as impermeable, alas, as their plastic counterparts. They must also be washed frequently in hot water with other bedding to remove dust mites. Vinyl covers, which offer a tight seal, cost between $15 and $50, but they may offgas. Softer, more fabriclike mattress covers made of polyester knit bonded to a polyurethane backing are about $70 from **Real Goods Trading Company** and **Priorities.** If you decide to go with vinyl- or polyurethane-backed encasements, remember to hang or spread out the encasement to let the chemicals dissipate for a few weeks before you put it on the mattress.

If allergies and/or asthma run in your family and you feel you can't afford a cloth dust mite barrier (which has to be washed frequently anyway), you should feel perfectly justified in buying a synthetic encasement. This is one of the few areas where affordable substitutes for synthetics are not readily available. We recommend any plastic but vinyl. Allow plastic covers to offgas by hanging them out in the sun or in a well-ventilated room for a few days before placing on the mattress and pillows.

Encasements are available from stores and companies specializing in products for allergy and asthma suffers. Some are listed in Appendix B. You can also purchase low-toxicity sprays and powders containing tannic acid that decrease dust mite populations on bedding from **Priorities, Harmony, Real Goods Trading Company,** and **InteliHealth Healthy Home.**

Laundering Bedding

Sheets, blankets, pillows, comforters, and bumper pads should be washed in *hot* water frequently, at least every two weeks. Of course, if they're soiled, as they often will be, you'll want to wash more frequently. Use a mild laundry soap, such as Ivory Snow Soap Granules, that is free from perfumes, as your baby may react to strong scents. Avoid using fabric softeners, which might irritate your baby's delicate skin. See chapter 5 for information on milder cleaning products.

Window Treatments

If the nursery will be located in a particularly sunny room, you are probably contemplating window treatments that will reduce the glare and heat that pour into the room. You may also want to install curtains or shades to create some privacy.

Curtains and Drapes

Fabric curtains and drapes, like bedding and carpets, will harbor dust mites. If you are concerned about allergies and asthma, you should avoid curtains and drapes unless you can wash them as frequently as bedding. Avoid synthetic materials for the reasons mentioned above. The heat and light coming through the window will cause synthetics to break down and offgas into the room. Natural fabric choices include cotton, linen, and hemp.

Blinds

Blinds are unobtrusive, durable, and easy to clean. They can block out the sun completely, even on a sunny afternoon, or lend privacy while permitting some daylight to permeate the room. Blinds now come in a variety of materials and colors that can enhance your infant's environment while permitting versatility.

You do need to be careful about the kind of blinds you purchase, if you choose to use them. The least expensive type of blind is the vinyl miniblind. As with other vinyl products, you should avoid these. Vinyl miniblinds could be especially dangerous to children. PVC may contain toxic heavy metals, such as lead and cadmium, used for both stabilizers and pigments. In June 1996, the **Consumer Product Safety Commission (CPSC)** found that vinyl miniblinds imported from China, Indonesia, Thailand, and Mexico not only contained lead, but also deteriorate from exposure to sunlight and heat, causing a lead dust to form on the blinds. CPSC tests revealed that the levels of lead in the dust on some blinds was so high that ingesting the dust from less than one square inch of blind a day for fifteen to thirty days could result in blood lead levels at or above the 10 µg/dL amount CPSC considers dangerous to children. And washing the blinds won't solve the problem; it won't necessarily pick up all the lead-laden dust, and between washings, the lead dust could migrate to other surfaces. The U.S. window covering industry voluntarily replaced lead as a stabilizer, but the safety of the alternatives to lead, such as tin, remains open to question. CPSC does not require premarket testing of the "reformulated" blinds, so there is no guarantee that vinyl miniblinds on the market are lead-free.

Instead you might consider hanging metal blinds made of aluminum or steel, which may be painted or covered with a baked-on enamel paint. This paint sometimes gives off an odor for a few days, but hanging them outside for a few days will diffuse the chemicals. Wood and bamboo blinds can be quite attractive and come in a variety of shades, but they may be finished with chemical-laden finishes. If you decide to purchase wood blinds, remember to allow them to offgas for a few days before installing them on windows.

Blinds may be dusted and cleaned with a damp cloth or vacuumed.

Shades

A window shade, simply a piece of material on a roller, can effectively reduce sun in a room. Shades are not quite as versatile as blinds, because you must draw them down completely for privacy. Look for shades made of fabric or paper in home decorating stores. Some shades may be made completely of vinyl or may be vinyl-backed to increase durability. Avoid these as you would other vinyl products.

You may also see shades made from reeds, plant fibers, or grasses. These may be treated with fungicides and insecticides. It's best to avoid these as there is no way to be sure. If you happen to find some used ones, they've probably offgassed to some extent and are likely to be safer.

Fabric shades will deteriorate faster from exposure to sunlight than metal or wood window coverings and they may be difficult to keep clean, especially those that are pleated. They generally can't be laundered because the fabric is attached to a roller. You can remove accumulating dust and dust mites by taking the shades down, opening them out, and vacuuming them every two or three weeks.

Room Dividers

In this day and age, many new families are short on space. We've added a section on room dividers because a nursery doesn't need to be—and sometimes can't be—a separate room. You might become pregnant while living in a one-bedroom apartment and not be able to move.

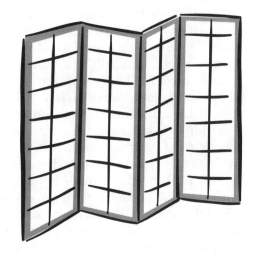

Or you might have a spare bedroom already occupied by another child or two who might disturb, or be disturbed by, the new baby. Space and economic considerations aside, you might feel more comfortable having the baby sleep in your room for better supervision and to ease frequent nursing. To provide some privacy for everyone in the family, a simple room divider can be the solution.

Simple is the key, as installing a whole new wall entails exactly the sort of major renovation doctors advise against during pregnancy or with a newborn in the house!

A room divider should:

- let light and air circulate through both sections of the room
- be firmly attached so baby cannot pull it over
- be made of unfinished materials, such as rice paper or solid wood, or painted or finished with VOC-free materials

As a temporary measure, a folding screen can make a handy room divider. If your baby's crib is in your bedroom, the screen can shield yourselves and the baby from each other's constant view, and your baby may sleep more comfortably as the screen muffles both your voices and your reading lights. Such screens typically measure 6 feet high by about 8 feet wide; even after baby can stand in his crib he won't be able to see over it. Inexpensive, Japanese-style screens are readily available at places like Pier 1 Imports. Made of light strips of wood and translucent plastic that looks like rice-paper, the screen should be wiped with a damp cloth and left in a well-ventilated area to offgas for a couple of weeks before you put it in place.

Another option: Buy a plain wood frame folding screen with three or four hinged sections. You can also scour flea markets for antique room dividers of the sort women used to change behind in boudoirs—and, who knows? It may remind you that even parents need a little romance now and then. Try to avoid those that are painted, as they may contain lead. You can test the paint with **Lead Check** swabs or look for a divider finished with varnishes, oils, or stains.

An added plus with portable screens: You don't need to have them up all the time. In fact, this type of screen should be put away as soon as baby can crawl, or he will pull it down upon himself.

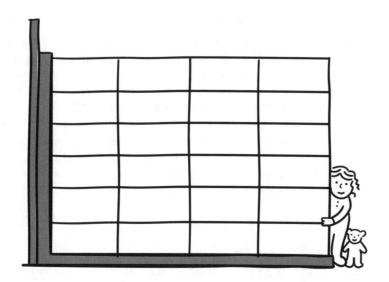

Or, you can go for the real thing, a permanent room divider. It should be securely fastened with brackets and screws to one wall and to the floor so that it cannot be pulled or pushed over. Because babies can pull over even very heavy objects, such as fully laden bookshelves, it is important that your room divider be secure, resting upon a stable base. Home entertainment wall systems, for instance, have fallen on and killed small children, even when standing against a wall. Such heavy, heavily laden pieces should not be used as room dividers.

When Mothers & Others member Sarah Hill's first child was born, she and her husband brought him home to a floor-through apartment in a New York City brownstone. "It was necessary to maximize daylight coming into the whole apartment from the small front bedroom, facing the street, which would be the baby's room," Sarah says. The room, which used to be a parlor, had no wall, so Sarah had a Japanese shoji screen custom made. "One of the things that I love about our screen is that it has four sliding doors—no fixed panel—so you can enter through the center or either side. There's one fixed panel on top, with grooves that the doors fit into, and grooves on the floor." Sarah bought her screen twelve years ago from **Miya Shoji,** a local store. "They installed it. They came in and measured, built it in the workshop, then took a day and put it in." The cost was about $1,100. "I have to get him in to replace all the screens that my children have punched out," she says with a laugh. Her panels are made of laminated rice paper. "They've actually stood up to a lot of wear and tear," she adds.

Japanese shoji screens make a good choice because they're traditionally made of nontoxic materials: solid wood, rice paper, nails, and rice-paper glues. We've installed one ourselves at Mothers & Others' New York office, to divide an office space from our library. It's a 4-foot-high, 8-foot-long screen that rests on top of a bookshelf of the same length. The shelf is fastened to one wall and the floor, and the screen is fastened on two sides, to the wall and to the top of the shelf.

We also bought our screen at **Miya Shoji,** a small Japanese custom furnishings shop on Seventeenth Street in Manhattan, just around the corner from our Twentieth Street office. Hisao Hanafusa, the owner, made it to measure from real rice paper and natural light pine; the wood is protected with a nontoxic finish. It attaches to the bookshelf and wall with a tongue-and-groove fastener he also provided. The cost, because we installed it ourselves, was $400. "Labor is the big cost in these things," Mr. Hanafusa says. He also makes full-size room dividers in all kinds of styles, and takes orders from all over the United States and the world. We hope you can find such a craftsman in your locale, to save on shipping, which has environmental as well as monetary costs (all that petroleum consumed). But if not, we recommend Miya Shoji.

Lighting

Lighting accounts for 20 to 25 percent of all U.S. energy consumption, the EPA reports. Buying an energy-efficient light fixture or lamp is an excellent opportunity to save on your energy bill, and to help the environment by reducing demand for oil and coal, whose burning in utility plants contributes to acid rain, particulates, gaseous air pollution, and global warming. The simplest way to do this is to purchase a compact fluorescent lamp (CFL), which is essentially a lightbulb, but not an incandescent one. To produce the same amount of light as incandescents, CFLs use only one-fourth the energy. They also last about ten to twelve times longer. After testing lightbulbs in 1996, *Consumer Reports* found that, while most incandescents lasted 1,000 hours, the CFLs were still glowing after 17,000 hours. As *E Mazagine* puts it, "One CFL bulb can keep a dozen used incandescents out of landfills." And these fluorescents are nothing like those horrible institutional tubes that hum and glow an eerie yellow-green. The light provided by CFLs is much softer and more natural.

CFLs can be purchased at hardware and other stores that sell light fixtures. They come in wattages from 25 to 150. Price ranges from $16 to $26. Some of the best brands, according to *Consumer Reports,* include **Osram Sylvania, Lights of America, General Electric,** and **Duro-Test.** If you can't find them at a local home improvement center or hardware store, call the company for a referral or buy them by mail from **Real Goods Trading Company, Harmony, Tomorrow's World,** or **Energy Federation, Inc.** Duro-Test will also sell their CFLs mail order.

Since CFLs are designed to fit into standard lamps and lighting fixtures, those that accept incandescent bulbs, you won't have to go out and buy new lamps to make this energy-saving leap. Still, some CFLs come in odd shapes, and won't necessarily be camouflaged by your lamp's hardware. On the market now you'll find many CFL-accepting lamp fixtures, including many table, overhead, and floor lamps. Makers include **Lightolier** and **Lights of America.**

In your nursery, you should avoid high-wattage halogen bulbs, as they burn at a very high heat and can cause serious burns to small, curious children or babies, who have a disproportionately long reach for their size, along with a built-in capacity for breathtakingly quick grabs. Halogen lamps are also a fire hazard because they get so hot.

Rather than floor lamps, which can be toppled and broken, select tabletop lamps and place the furniture upon which they rest in front of electrical outlets so that the cord, as well as the dangerous outlet, can be concealed from sight and reach. Another option is to install ceiling fixtures with the help of an electrician. All the wiring can be hidden in the walls, so everything will be out of your baby's reach.

You might also want to see about a dimmer attachment for your ceiling light fixture, if you aren't currently able to adjust light intensity. You may want to install a night-light in the nursery, but in general it's better to avoid unnecessary electric devices, which produce electromagnetic fields (EMFs), in sleeping areas. (See chapter 5 for information on the hazards of EMFs.) An alternative is to place night-lights in hallways, where no one will be sleeping. When summoned by a crying baby for 2 A.M. feedings, you will be guided safely to the nursery through a partially illuminated hallway. You can also purchase lamps with motion sensitive sensors, available from **Lutron,** so that as you move towards the nursery, the lamps will automatically switch on.

chapter three

Other Baby Equipment

When the arsenal of baby accessories and equipment rears its hydra head, you may wonder what on earth parents did when all they had to hold baby with was their arms. If you are suspicious of many of these items—such as bouncers, indoor swings, and walkers—as unnecessary gadgetry, you are quite correct; they can even be dangerous. And, since most of them are made of PVC, if you do not buy them you are helping to protect the environment.

Baby equipment, like basic childproofing, doesn't really fit within the environmental theme of this book, thus we will not go into great detail about these products, apart from listing what you'll probably need, what you don't need, and what you might want to avoid. We'll refer you to other resources for the details. An excellent and thorough resource is *Guide to Baby Products* from Consumer Reports Books. It also covers nursery furniture. And the **Consumer Product Safety Commission (CPSC)** has a Nursery Equipment Safety Checklist. You'll find their nursery equipment hotline number in Appendix A. Like the crib, baby equipment must be selected with baby's safety foremost in mind.

Here we'll cover these common items:

- Car Seats
- Soft Carriers, Slings, and Backpacks
- Infant Carrier Seats

- Prams and Strollers
- Playpens and Portable Cribs
- Gates
- High Chairs
- Walkers

Car Seats

Car seats for infants and small children are required by law in all states. The seats, fastened in by your car's seat belt, restrain baby in a safety harness. The seats must meet federal government safety standards. You will need a newborn-appropriate car seat in which to bring baby home from the hospital; some hospitals rent or loan them, but, at least for the well-baby checkups with the pediatrician, if you don't live within walking distance, you will have to buy or rent a car seat for your child. Some hospitals and state highway safety departments rent or loan seats. Up to one year of age, babies must sit in a rear-facing seat for protection of their necks and spines.

Typically, parents buy an infant seat for their newborn, since a child at that age can't sit up, and a bigger seat later on. Convertible seats that work from birth up to 40 pounds can be found, but *Consumer Reports* advises caution in selecting these, because overhead and T-shields can hurt a smaller baby. Their *Guide to Baby Products* recommends the convertible **Century** 1000 STE Classic as a Best Buy. While these seats are made of hard molded plastic, you have a choice of upholsteries. For your child's comfort, choose terry cloth or the most natural fabric available, instead of vinyl.

For children weighing between 30 and 60 pounds who've outgrown their car seats, *booster seats* are advised.

- WARNING: *Do not place an infant or child in a car seat, or any child age twelve or younger, in the front seat of a car with air bags,* as several fatalities have resulted from this. The center of the car's back seat is the safest position for your child, whether or not you have an air bag.

It's important to read the instruction manual and take the time to install your child's car seat correctly. Failure to do so poses a risk of serious injury. Yet nine out of every ten car seats examined were found to have been installed incorrectly, Drs. Wendy Moller and Anjana Barad found in a Detroit-area study which was presented at the 50th Scientific Assembly of the American Academy of Family Physicians in 1998. Car seat straps were clipped at the wrong position on the baby's body or were too loose, allowing excessive movement—mistakes which cost lives, the researchers said. Make sure that the straps are clipped at chest level on your infant, and that straps aren't too loose. Also check to make sure that the car seat is securely belted in by the car's seat belt. If you leave the seat installed in the car, make sure it's securely fastened each time you take baby for a ride. The researchers also found that one out of five seats had either been the subject of a recall, and thus shouldn't have been in use, or was found to be unsafe due to missing or broken pieces. **CPSC** has recall information.

If it's FAA-certified, your car seat can serve as an airplane seat to secure your child during takeoff and landing. "I recommend buying a ticket for your baby, so she'll be assured of a safe, belted-in seat," Mindy Pennybacker says. "Or, if you can't afford this, try to travel at nonpeak times when airplanes are less likely to be full, and carry your FAA-certified car seat on to strap into an empty seat."

Soft Carriers, Slings, and Backpacks

Varieties of soft devices have been used for thousands of years to carry babies while leaving parents' arms free (but you should never cook while holding baby in a carrier). The physical closeness can be comforting to both parent and child. Young infants who can't sit up on their own should be snuggled close to your body in soft carriers, which support their heads. There are several styles, from shoulder slings in which baby rests on your hip to more all-encompassing pouches suspended from both your shoulders. **Sara's Ride** has a hip carrier, available directly from the company and from **The Natural Baby Company.** Be vigilant with slings, to be sure that baby doesn't roll out. A 100 percent cotton Baby Bundler from **Baby Bunz & Company** ties on without any snaps or buckles, with an effect like Japanese couture. Another very popular soft carrier, by **Baby Bjorn,** can also be worn on the front of the parent's body. Kelty K.I.D.S. Kangaroo Child Carrier, a front carrier of sturdy nylon, has a hideaway hood to shield baby's head from sun or rain. It can be purchased at **REI** or **Earthlings.**

Babies six months and older can sit in metal-frame backpacks, which are great for hikes or long walks. These should have interior safety belts for baby, and the leg openings should be large enough to prevent chafing (padding helps) and small enough to prevent the passenger from slipping through. **Gerry**'s Explorer Backpack has a fold-up frame, a hip belt for balancing the load on the parent, and fits children up to 40 pounds. Kelty K.I.D.S. Explorer Child is a padded frame pack that can accommodate a child of up to about 40 pounds on backpacking trails and is available from **REI.**

Before purchasing, you should test a carrier for comfort and to make sure you know how to put it on!

Infant Carrier Seats

An infant carrier seat has a carrier handle, and the baby is carried as if in a basket. It looks like an infant car seat, but should *never* be used as such. A child should *never* be left unattended in such a seat. The CPSC advises that adults stay within arm's reach. Since 1986, the CPSC has had reports of over twenty deaths associated with infant carrier seats, either by the baby getting entangled in safety belts or straps, or by falling from the seat when the safety straps weren't used, or by the seats' falling over—sometimes from a tabletop. These seats should never be placed on a soft surface, such as a bed. *Consumer Reports' Guide to Baby Products* suggests using a convertible car seat instead. The same precautionary rules should apply to any object in which an infant is carried about.

Prams and Strollers

Prams, or carriages, are for newborns and younger babies who can't hold their heads up in a seated position; in a pram, a baby lies almost flat. Strollers tend to be more open, with the child sitting up. Most strollers these days recline nearly flat so they can serve as a pram, too; the padded fabric sides should be high enough to prevent baby from rolling out. Folding umbrella strollers with reclining backs, such as the MacLaren, seem comfortable for babies and are maneuverable for parents. "You should be able to steer the stroller in a straight line when pushing with one hand," according to the **American Medical Association (AMA)** "KidsHealth" website. Examine prams and strollers for seat belts with a necessary crotch strap to keep baby from slipping out. Look for a wide wheel base to prevent tipping, and for secure wheel brakes. For stability, the shopping basket should hang low on the back and directly over or in front of rear wheels.

Check that leg openings are small enough to prevent your baby's body from slipping through. Convertible models need some way of covering or closing leg openings. Some have a "boot" that fastens over baby's lower body for cooler weather. Some even convert to a car seat! In this combination, *Consumer Reports' Guide to Baby Products* says that the **Century** Deluxe Smart Fit 4-in-1 System meets all motor vehicle safety requirements for car seats as well as standard requirements for strollers. It ranges from $140 to $180. Running strollers for jogging parents start at about $200, and aren't suitable for a baby who can't sit up independently.

With a stroller, backpack, playpen, or any piece of baby equipment that folds or adjusts, make sure to keep your child's fingers away from pinching areas. The frame should have no sharp protruding parts that could cause injury. Once open, the stroller should lock into place that way; a child can be injured if the stroller accidentally collapses. The safety belt should be easy and quick to fasten. Try out different strollers in the store before you buy one. Never leave a child unattended in a stroller.

As for those clear plastic weathershields? "Never used one, whether in rain, sleet, or snow. I didn't want my baby looking at the world through a layer of PVC," says Mindy. "You can find a good rain cape with a hood that covers you, another to cover the baby and stroller (make sure the cape doesn't cover baby's face), and wheel into a bookstore or coffee shop for periodic dry-offs on rainy days."

Playpens and Portable Cribs

Once baby can creep or crawl, beginning at about six months of age, her playspace will expand beyond the living room area rug. At this stage, "you have to organize a child's environment a little bit so she doesn't get into trouble," says Dr. Harvey Karp, Mothers & Others medical advisor. Some parents find that playpens, also called play yards, are useful when their attention must temporarily focus on some other task. Others, not wanting to "cage" their children and possibly stunt development, take care to babyproof whole rooms while gating off others. If you do choose to have a playpen, just make sure not to leave baby in there too long. When she reaches up and signals she wants out, lift her out.

Playpens come in polyester or nylon mesh with steel or aluminum tubing supports, or in wood, which is harder to find. Drop-side mesh pens pose a hazard, as a baby can get smothered between the loose, sagging side and the playpen pad; the side should never be left in the down position, and the pen should bear a warning label. Mesh holes should be no more than ¼ inch in diameter; wooden playpens, like cribs, should have slats spaced no more than 2 inches apart.

Hinges should be well protected, and the floor support should be sturdy. A portable crib that has a certification sticker is certified to the voluntary industry standard for playpens. If built before 1997, a portable crib should never be used in place of a full-size crib. A specific portable crib standard that meets most of the requirements for full-size cribs applies to newer models.

Play yards built since 1997 have top rails that automatically lock into place when set up. Several faulty portable cribs and play yards sold between 1990 and 1997 have been recalled because their top rails can collapse, entrapping and suffocating children. For this reason it's advisable not to put your child in an older portable crib without first checking its safety status with **CPSC.** In 1998, a child died in a collapsed Playskool Travel-Lite play yard, manufactured by Kolcraft, that had been recalled five years earlier. Other play yards listed as faulty include Evenflo's Happy Camper, Happy Cabana, and Kiddie Camper; Century's Fold-N-Go models 10-710 and 10-810; Draco's All Our Kids; and Baby Trend's Home and Roam and Baby Express. Call **CPSC** at 800/638-2772, ext. 135 for information.

In November of 1998, CPSC announced a recall of almost 10 million foldable playpens, because protruding metal rivets posed a stragulation hazard by snagging children's clothing or pacifier strings. Brands include Bilt-Rite, Evenflo, Gerry, Graco, Kolcraft, PlaySkool, Pride-Trimble, and Strolee. Call 800/794-4115 for more details.

- WARNING: *The plastics used in playpens are not flameproof.*

Never add extra padding to the original playpen or portable crib mattress, and *never* leave baby or child unsupervised in one. "No matter which model you choose, keep the child in constant view," *Consumer Reports' Guide to Baby Products* cautions. Stop using the playpen once the child can climb out.

Gates

Gates, which fit in doorways or at the top or bottom of stairs, come in plastic or wood. Make certain that the openings are too small to entrap a child's head; for this reason, do not use accordion-style gates with large V-shaped openings along the top edge, or large diamond-shaped holes within. Good quality gates are available from **Perfectly Safe.**

High Chairs and Hook-on Chairs

The **CPSC** lists the following requirements for high chairs:

- Waist and crotch restraining straps should be attached to the body of the chair, not the tray; waist strap should have easy-to-use buckle.
- Tray locks on securely.
- Chair has a wide, stable base, and, if it's foldable, has a locking device to keep it from collapsing.
- Caps or plugs on tubing are firmly attached, and cannot be pulled off and choke a child.

Suitable for a toddler, a simple, trayless wooden high chair of the sort provided by many restaurants these days can bring your child right up to the table. They are available from **The Natural Baby Company.**

The obvious risk with hook-on chairs, which, instead of standing on legs, clamp onto the table so that baby's legs slide under it, is that they'll be kicked or worked loose and crash to the floor. Make sure that the clamp locks onto the table-top securely. These chairs, too, should have a waist and crotch safety strap, and, as with the high chair, tubing should not have any small detachable parts. The table should be sturdy enough to bear baby's weight. Make sure that you don't hook the chair on near a table leg or crossbeam, or another chair that the child can push at with her feet.

You don't need to buy a traditional high chair. Baby can be fed held in your lap, or in a car seat that converts into an indoor chair. A child who can feed herself can sit at the table supported by pillows on an armchair. Babies and children must be closely supervised when they're eating.

A Word on Walkers

Walkers are low seats surrounded by a tray, on a wheeled frame. They operate rather like bumper cars. We don't recommend these. You don't want to have your child careening about in a walker in the kitchen, as one good jolt of the table or stove might send hot food spilling down on her. "Nearly 29,000 injuries are treated in emergency rooms every year as a result of walkers," says the **AMA**'s "KidsHealth" website. Besides burns, injuries include concussions and broken limbs from falls. In addition, a recent study showed that babies who had used walkers were delayed in their motor and mental development compared with babies who had not. Researchers at Case Western Reserve University and the State University of New York at Buffalo point out that the walker tray blocks a child's lower body from view and prevents the child from picking up objects he drops, which happens if a baby is allowed to crawl around normally. So if you use a walker without wheels, like the Exersaucer, in which a baby can swivel, just be sure—as with a playpen—not to leave your baby in this restricted space for too long.

There are no safety standards, as yet, for indoor swings, which include mechanical windup and battery-powered varieties with different weight limits, to which strict attention must be paid. Stop using a swing once your child gets too heavy for it. Take care, also, not to put the swing on too high an automatic speed — baby's brains could quite literally get rattled. Use the safety belt, and stay within reach of a baby in the swing at all times. While babies enjoy swinging, they will enjoy it just as much—probably more—if you're pushing them in an outdoor baby swing and communicating, hands-on, or simply rocking them in your arms.

chapter four

Environmental Babyproofing *and* Eco-Tips *for* Other Rooms

"Young children are like Christopher Columbus. Their job is to explore everything, and do it with enthusiasm," says pediatrician Harvey Karp. Once you've supplied your nursery with the basics, you can consider making the rest of your home environmentally safe for your newborn, who will quickly grow into an explorer. This chapter is on how to environmentally babyproof your home. It focuses on avoiding exposure to, and ingestion of, environmental irritants and toxins. We'll show you how to avoid sudden accidents, such as the drinking of caustic drain cleaners, dishwasher soap, or bleach, as well as how to reduce cumulative long-term exposures to VOCs and dust mites. We'll also discuss allergens and demonstrate how one New York City Mothers & Others member, Laura Pope (not her real name), did an allergy-free renovation.

If you don't mop up those dust bunnies, your crawling infant will clean them up by licking them off the floor. Babies test the world with their mouths, which is why the number one rule in babyproofing your house is to keep toxins far from reach, removing as many as you can from the household altogether.

New parents will soon find that baby is not content to be confined to the nursery, but will quickly take over the whole house. Even before he can turn himself from stomach to back, he will have learned to give commands with voice, eyes, and gestures, ordering you to feed him and carry him and be your best attentive and amusing self. Your baby will want to be where the action is: your bedroom, living room, kitchen, bath—to him, all these will be playrooms and exploratoriums. Babies are the most companionable of creatures, and as they grow into preschoolers, they view the isolation of a "time out" as grave punishment. Not until the teen years will your child voluntarily go into his room and shut the door.

As you prepare your home to welcome this little conquistador, visualize a knee-high, downy-haired presence appearing at your elbow as you cook or clean, ready with one quick grab to upset a boiling pot or a bucketful of caustic suds; climbing into your lap as you sip your hot coffee, or sucking on an old printer ink cartridge as you sit hunched at your desk trying to make a deadline. Babies move, and grow, fast.

The point of babyproofing is also to enjoy your baby! These cuddly, clingy years pass all too quickly; you will want to savor this often-exhausting, yet delectable time when you are at the center of your child's life. This will be a lot easier to do if you've planned for environmental safety before baby arrives.

This does not mean renovations during pregnancy! Remember, once you're pregnant, it's too late for painting, refinishing, and structural changes to your home unless you haven't moved in yet, or can move out for the duration of the work.

Parents' Room

In the early going, given the frequency of newborn feeding schedules (every two hours), many babies will spend a lot of time in their drowsy parents' beds. "One of the most useful things the baby's nurse taught me in the hospital was how to nurse lying down," Mindy Pennybacker recalls.

The **Consumer Product Safety Commission (CPSC)** warns that infants' sleeping in their parents' bed has been associated with SIDS. But what if you fall asleep while nursing? Don't panic; it happens. The reality is, "parents have been sleeping with their babies for millions of years," Dr. Karp says.

Dangers can be avoided, he adds, by being careful to keep baby away from soft pillows or from getting tangled in the quilt, both of which are potential suffocation hazards. And as of this writing, pediatricians recommend that to avoid SIDS, wherever baby sleeps, he should be kept on his side or back.

An easy way to keep the baby from creeping under the covers during the first three months is to wrap babies up in swaddling. Dr. Karp often recommends this for helping babies sleep. "It lessens their involuntary startle movement, which often wakes them up during dreams," he explains. The baby nurse or midwife can show you how to swaddle your newborn in a cotton receiving blanket, and you can always get refresher instructions from your pediatrician. It is key to have the arms down straight at the sides, and to wrap snugly, but gently; otherwise, baby can wiggle free. However, a swaddled bundle can still roll off the bed, so be careful. To better guard against accidents, some parents, like M & O members John and

Deanna (Dee Dee) Kolivas, sleep on a mattress or futon on the floor. "We just got rid of our box spring. At least this way, if Kainalu rolls off our bed, he only falls a few inches," Dee Dee says.

Beds, Mattresses, and Bedding

We spend one-third of our lives in bed. (When you're pregnant, there will be a few times when you'll want to just stay there.) After your baby is born, late night feedings, nursings, and afternoon naps will bring your baby into that bed with you. Like her crib, your bed should be safe and comfortable. The same issues discussed in chapter 2 about baby bedding also apply to adult mattresses, sheets, blankets, comforters, and pillows.

You can obtain untreated, organic cotton and cotton/wool mattresses for twin, double, queen-, and king-size beds. Like high quality mattresses, they're not cheap. A queen-size organic cotton mattress and bedspring set costs about $1,400. One option is buying just an organic cotton mattress and placing it over a standard box spring. While the box spring may offgas somewhat, there's much more foam in a conventional mattress. Also, the mattress will be between you and the box spring. Adult mattresses are also treated with chemical flame retardants as required by federal law. You'll have to get a doctor's prescription for the untreated ones. Mattresses with wool fill (about $100 more than just cotton) are naturally fireproof, but you will still need a prescription from your doctor for them. Organic, untreated cotton and wool mattresses can be purchased from **Crown City Mattress Company, Nontoxic Environments, Nontoxic Hotline,** and **Heart of Vermont.**

If you can't afford to buy an organic cotton mattress set, you can opt for a cotton or cotton/wool futon made with organic, green, or conventional cotton. Futons—fiber-stuffed, 3- to 5-inch-thick mats—are firm and can be folded into sofas on convertible frames. Some futons have a polyurethane foam core, so be careful when you shop for conventional cotton futons. Organic cotton and cotton/wool futons can be ordered from the mattress vendors listed above. A 3-inch-thick, queen-size, wool wrapped organic cotton futon costs about $350, and currently can be bought without a doctor's note.

If you already have a conventional mattress, you can reduce offgassing by encasing it, and you'll block dust mites at the same time. A plastic encasement—available from **Priorities, Real Goods Trading Company,** and **Harmony**—is less permeable and less expensive, costing about $50 for a full-size encasement, than cotton barrier cloth encasements (available from **Allergy Resources**), and doesn't require frequent washings. But a plastic cover will offgas as well, so hang it out in the sun or in a well-ventilated room for a few days before putting it on the mattress.

Since your baby may be sleeping in your bed, try to stay away from soft and fluffy down pillows and comforters, which may contribute to SIDS. These are also problematic for allergy and asthma sufferers. A less allergenic, natural option is to use 100 percent cotton or wool pillows and comforters, available from **Crown City Mattress Company/The Natural Bedroom** and companies mentioned above. Hypoallergenic pillows, while often made of synthetic materials, are another alternative.

Sheets, pillowcases, duvet covers, and blankets should be natural—green or organic cotton and untreated wool. No-iron sheets are made with polyester and fabric treatments that contain formaldehyde. Natural is better anyway, because cotton and wool breathe. This will mean more comfortable sleep in all types of weather. You can find untreated and organic bedding at **Harmony, Tomorrow's World, Crown City Mattress Company/The Natural Bedroom, Coyuchi, Heart of Vermont, Eco-Wise Environmental Products, Earth Runnings,** and **Terra Verde.** You can also find 100 percent cotton sheets in department stores. Launder bedding frequently in hot water to kill dust mites.

Bedroom Furniture

If you don't opt for a metal bed frame (which you can usually buy with your mattress), you'll probably go for wood. You can order custom-made bed frames, dressers, nightstands, and bookcases from **The Loft Bed Store.** They'll ship them to you, if necessary. You can also have local craftsmen build furniture for you, avoiding the overharvested woods mentioned in chapter 2. Wood furniture is an elegant, long-lasting option, but it can be costly. A simple queen-size bed frame and headboard may be $1,000 or more. Cheaper wood frames, though, are often made of particleboard and plywood. Aside from offgassing VOCs for years, these may not stand the test of time, or a young child who views the big bed as a trampoline. In selecting and purchasing these pieces, you should follow the tips, including those for less expensive choices, offered for living room furniture, page 70. Many of the companies listed there also sell bedroom furniture. Buying unfinished wood furniture is best, because then you can have it finished with low-VOC stains and sealants. These can be ordered through **E.C.O., N.E.E.D.S., Environmental Home Center, Planetary Solutions,** and **Terra Verde.**

You can find unfinished futon frames at **Heart of Vermont** or the furniture manufacturers listed in the living room section. You may also be able to purchase an unfinished frame locally.

The Carpet Question

As with the nursery, you can minimize exposure to VOCs and dust mites by not having wall-to-wall carpeting in your bedroom. "We had a wall-to-wall carpet in our bedroom and on our stairs, and I had it ripped up when my daughter was diagnosed with asthma at two and a half," says Patty Arlotta, a mother of two in Bronx, New York. Patty took her daughter and her six-month-old infant and stayed at her mother-in-law's while the carpets were removed and the floors refinished. "Her symptoms have greatly improved," Patty says of her asthmatic child, attributing this to a combination of environmental controls and preventive asthma medication. She adds that her younger daughter, now two, had one asthmalike episode when she was four months old, and no symptoms since the wall-to-wall carpet was removed. Patty also keeps dust and other particulates under control with the help of an air purifying, or filtration, machine and a vacuum cleaner. For both of these appliances, she chose models that accommodate a high-energy-particulate, or HEPA, filter, which catches particles of less than 10 microns in size. These fine particles, which include dust mites and their droppings and other allergens such as animal danders, go uncollected by conventional vacuums and air cleaning machines. See chapter 5 for more information.

It's also a good idea not to use perfumes, colognes, or room deodorizers for two reasons: they can be an allergen/irritant, and "they smell sweet, so when the child begins to toddle around he will want to taste them," Dr. Karp warns. If you really can't bear to throw out your perfume, remember to always keep it on a high shelf. And try not to wear a lot of scent around your baby.

Living Room/Playroom

Where parents are, baby will want to be.

When they're not being carried, infants are safest playing on the floor, provided it's clean and not covered with an offgassing carpet full of dust mites. Young babies should, of course, be placed in a sheltered, designated area of the floor so that people do not accidentally step on them. You want to have some sort of shock-absorbent surface, so that when baby practices his pushups or rolls over, he doesn't get a hard bump on the head. A small cotton rug can serve just fine.

If you use a thin, easily washable area rug, padding or underlay can be used underneath to cushion impact and to keep the rug from rumpling or slipping underfoot. Try to get a rug pad that will not offgas VOCs, and that, ideally, can itself be washed periodically. A natural fabric, such as camel's hair felt, is best; a natural latex rubber pad (not sprayed-on synthetic latex) is preferable to urethane. Be wary of composite pads held together with vapor-venting glues. If the pad you choose cannot be washed in hot water, treat it with a tannic acid, anti-dust-mite spray, and, when vacuuming, be sure to lift off the rug and vacuum both sides of the pad, as well. Allersearch X-Mite Spray and Powder can be ordered from **Harmony** and **Priorities.**

Some thicker rugs, such as tufted Orientals, can lie without a pad, particularly if a piece of furniture, such as the legs of a heavy wooden coffee table, rests on at least one edge.

Some kind of rug is especially appealing for families like the Kolivases of Honolulu, who have a practical, natural, but very hard ceramic tile living room floor. When their son, Kainalu, began to push up on all fours and lurch back and forth, the way five-month-olds do before they crawl, Dee Dee and John bought an all-wool area rug for their living room. Although it cost about twice as much as a synthetic, and the Kolivases live on a tight budget (John is a freelance musician, and Dee Dee left her job to stay home with Kainalu), "We looked for wool because we wanted natural fibers as much as possible," Dee Dee says. "Though this Indich rug contains some acrylic, it didn't smell bad—I took a good whiff in the store—and it looks great in its undyed-wool color." To cover most of the floor, where Kainalu plays, they bought two 6-by-8-inch rugs and laid them side by side. The rugs are thick enough to stay flat, and pad Kainalu's tumbles, without an underlay.

On the other hand, why not a "rug" that can be mopped? As in the nursery, a wipe-cleanable option for your living room might be a resilient floor covering, such as natural linoleum or cork. If you don't want to re-cover your whole floor, you can make a cork area mat from Prontokorq Panels, an environmentally friendly cork "sandwich." The bottom layer is unfinished cork, which provides sound insulation and shock absorbency, and, because of its spongy surface, doesn't slide underfoot; the center is real wood, not plywood, for strength; and the cork top is protected with a low-VOC finish. The tiles fit together with tongue-and-groove sides, and can be glued with a nontoxic glue. The great thing is, they don't glue to the floor, so they can be picked up and moved. A box of six panels, enough to cover 18 square feet, can be ordered from **Korqinc,** which will ship anywhere.

Furniture

Furniture throughout your living room shares many construction and material characteristics with baby cribs, mattresses, and changing tables. Like these nursery pieces, furniture such as sofas, shelves, coffee tables, bookcases, dining tables, and upholstered chairs may contain toxic glues, particleboard, chipboard, pressed wood, plywood, and polyurethane foam. All of these can emit formaldehyde and other VOCs for months. Wood furniture finishes, particularly those that are oil-based, may also offgas chemicals.

You'll want your baby to be comfortable and safe no matter which room he's in, but that doesn't mean that you have to refurnish your entire home. If you've had your furniture for a few years, it's probably offgassed most of its VOCs. When you are considering new furniture, though, you should pay attention to the materials that it's constructed with.

Untreated, natural woods, especially sustainable woods, make beautiful, long-lasting, and safe furniture. You can have unfinished furniture finished with low-VOC stains and water-based polyurethane, available from **Planetary Solutions, Naturlich Natural Homes, N.E.E.D.S., Terra Verde,** and other eco-friendly building supply companies. **The Loft Bed Store** in Vermont makes and sells furniture made of sustainably harvested wood. **Green Design Furniture Company** offers solid wood furniture of interlocking joinery pieces that don't require glues or nails for assembly. You can also buy unfinished furniture kits from **Shaker Workshop** and **Heart of Vermont.** (See Appendix B for more companies.)

When you shop for wood furniture, try to be sure that the piece is solid wood. The most deceiving furniture looks like natural wood, but internal pieces, such as drawers, backs, and bottoms, may be made of particleboard or plywood. Natural veneers are sometimes used on cheaper, manufactured wood products. Inspect carefully. Unfinished edges are particularly telling.

Naturally, you'll want some upholstered chairs and couches for comfortable seating, especially in your more informal rooms. Like mattresses, upholstered furniture usually has some polyurethane foam. To avoid this VOC-emitting synthetic, you can have sofas, loveseats, and chairs custom-made with organic cotton and wool fill by **Furnature** and **The Natural Alternative.** Wool is flame retardant and substitutes well for foam. The cost can be high, but prices are usually in line with those of high quality and custom-made furniture in general. For example, a custom-made, all-organic chair may cost $500 to $1,000, while a sofa might be made for $2,000 to $3,000. Futons that convert to sofas and chairs are a less expensive option (see "Parents' Room," page 66). While you might not want your entire house to be furnished with futons, a piece here and there, especially in family rooms, will do double duty as safe seating and an extra bed for guests. And you can easily change futon covers for washing and new decorating looks. Make sure you buy futons made of 100 percent cotton. Avoid those with foam cores.

Seeking used furniture, which has already offgassed, provides a welcome excuse to go antique hunting. Even if you don't find mint-condition bargains, you may happen upon treasured heirloom pieces that will give your home a unique look. Sylvie Farrell, membership coordinator at Mothers & Others, scours flea markets and out-of-the-way antique shops for amazing bargains. For Sylvie, dents and scratches only add to their charm.

Old upholstered furniture presents another problem: accumulated dust, mold, and animal dander. Use a HEPA vacuum cleaner (see chapter 5), steam clean without the detergent, and apply tannic acid powders, such as Allersearch X-Mite Powder, that render dust mite particles innocuous to get rid of embedded allergens. Mold spores are almost impossible to get rid of in upholstery, so if a piece smells moldy, you shouldn't buy it, unless you plan to reupholster it.

You can pick up quality used upholstered furniture at thrift stores and garage sales, but give it a thump-and-sniff test. Here in New York City, as well as elsewhere in the country, a great time to find "almost new" used furniture is spring, when remodeling and redecorating season begins. You might even come upon designer furniture in good condition set out on the streets of wealthy neighborhoods, like New York City's Upper East Side, on garbage day. While you may cringe at the thought of snatching a couch from the clutches of garbage collectors, you'd be saving it and your community from unnecessary landfilling.

If the furniture is really dusty and hasn't been covered with a protective drape, you may want to forgo it. Removable, washable slipcovers for sofas and chairs will cover unsightly stains, but don't rely on them to block dust and mold. It may be worth having good quality furniture re-upholstered with organic cotton fabrics and fill.

The Kitchen

Because you will have less time to shop after baby arrives, it is good to lay in kitchen supplies now.

Baby Bottles and Nipples

Even if you are planning to breast-feed, it makes sense to have a few bottles and nipples on hand. Use silicone nipples and pacifiers, not plastic or latex rubber ones, Dr. Karp advises. "Silicone ones don't deteriorate and get sticky the way that yellow rubber does." If nipples do crack, throw them away, as bacteria can be hard to remove from them. Silicone nipples are available where baby feeding supplies are sold and through **Ecobaby.**

If you are breast-feeding your baby, it's probably still a good idea to select a few baby bottles made of non-PVC plastic and of tempered glass. Each has its benefits and risks. Hormone-disrupting phthalates are used to soften vinyl (PVC), used in toys, teethers, and some bottles. Many plastics leach their chemical additives, so it's best to avoid giving them to your baby. **Evenflo** makes glass bottles in 4- and 8-ounce sizes. See chapter 8, "Feeding Your Baby," for more information on bottles and other feeding equipment.

Kitchen Supplies

This is a good time to check your pots and pans for cracks or deeply scratched finishes that might harbor bacteria or flake enamel or Teflon into your food. We recommend stainless steel, cast iron, ceramic, and glass pans. These will not react with foods, nor do they have any chemicals that might leach into food. If you have aluminum or "nonstick" pans, you needn't throw them out. You can still use them for most cooking, as they won't leach much unless you cook acidic foods in them.

Some other equipment you will find useful includes:

- Stainless-steel, rubber-handled tongs make a good tool for taking hot bottles and nipples out of a sterilizing bath.
- Blenders and sieves can be handy when baby is older for pureeing cooked vegetables, fruits, or meat into baby food.
- Hand-held food grinders can conveniently chop up small amounts.
- Table-mounted food grinders are great for things you want to produce in bulk and freeze.
- Ice cube trays can hold baby food for freezing.
- Strainers will ensure a smooth puree for the first steps of baby's start at solid foods.

It's never too soon to invest in unbreakable babyware. Plastic bowls, plate sets, and cups are often given as gifts. You can trade these in, as chemicals may migrate from the plastic when it comes into contact with hot fatty or acidic foods, and order a wooden nonspill double bowl, which comes with an infant spoon, self-serve spoon, and pretend fork, from **The Natural Baby Company.**

Stainless steel bowls are a good option, but they conduct heat, so they must be allowed to cool down before serving warm food to a baby.

Lead-Free Dishes

The glazes on ceramic tableware—particularly that which is antique, homemade, or imported—remain a possible source of lead exposure. Lead can leach out of the glazes, particularly when the pottery holds acidic foods such as citrus fruits and tomato and apple sauces. **The Food and Drug Administration (FDA)** sets limits for lead that may leach from ceramic glazes, and requires that dishes containing lead above safe limits bear a sticker stating that they are not to be used to hold food. California's Proposition 65 is stricter than the FDA regulations, providing a much lower limit for the amount of acceptable lead. "In 1992, six hundred patterns of china dinnerware met the Proposition 65 standard; by 1994, more than eight thousand patterns were in compliance," Mott reports in *Our Children at Risk,* by the National Resources Defense Council. When buying imported china, or shopping in other countries, it is wise to ask whether the seller can certify that the ceramicware is made with a lead-free glaze. Completely lead-free pottery in stunning lapis blue, violet, linen, and celadon glazes can be bought from **Terra Verde** at reasonable prices. There's also a nice tea bowl size in which a child's hands could cup warm chocolate.

If you have pottery of unknown origin or antique ceramics, you can use **Lead Check** swabs to determine if they have lead. (See chapter 2 for information on testing for lead.) If they do, you can always use them as decorative knickknacks. **Environmental Defense Fund**'s pamphlet, "What You Should Know about Lead in China Dishes," provides information on testing dishes and lists 2,000 lead-free china patterns.

You should also avoid storing food in leaded crystal, and take care not to drink out of leaded crystal if you're pregnant. Do not serve drinks to children in leaded crystal glasses, as lead can leach from these in some cases (not all, but you might as well stay on the safe side here). If your baby is the recipient of one of those gimmicky leaded crystal baby bottles, don't feel guilty about returning it to the store! And while it's a good idea to stock your pantry for emergencies now, as you'll have much less time to shop after baby arrives, you should know that lead can also make its way into your food from some imported cans with soldered seams. (U.S. manufacturers have voluntarily discontinued the use of lead in food cans.) The solder may not contain lead, but it's not possible to tell just by looking. If you can feel a bumpy seam through a can label, it's soldered. Opt for seamless or welded (smooth seam) cans. Be especially careful to inspect cans of imported food.

Finally, the shopping bags in which you haul home those cans, and bags in which bread is sold, may also be contaminated with lead in the ink used to print them. Never turn plastic bags inside out and reuse them to store food. Magazines, comic books, newspapers, and other food wrappers may also be printed with lead-containing inks or dyes; red, yellow, and orange pigments are the most likely suspects. To be safe, keep the printed surfaces away from direct contact with food, and make sure that your baby doesn't put the papers in his mouth.

The Kitchen Physical Plan

It is one of life's ironies that the kitchen—the source of sustenance in the home— is often also the repository of toxins. Naturally leery of bacterial contamination, we all want the place where we prepare food to be clean and free of crawling creatures, which is why we keep cleaning substances at the ready there; however, it is time we reconsidered what "clean" means, and redefine it to include "nontoxic."

Basically, hot water and vegetable-based soaps will clean most dishes, sinks, and surfaces, including floors; and prevention methods, such as sealing cracks and fixing leaky faucets, will keep most pests away. And for those inevitable emergencies, a number of ready-made less toxic cleansers and pest deterrents exist. As discussed in chapter 5, some of these can also be made at home, in the kitchen.

Look under the sink and in mop, broom, and utility closets. Remove dangerous cleaners, paints, pesticides, and other chemicals from the lower shelves that a small child could get into. It is never too early to start engaging in safer habits that, it is to be hoped, will have become second nature by the time your baby is inclined to experiment in the kitchen.

STOVE PRECAUTIONS

As a rule, try to keep your baby or young child out of the kitchen while you cook, unless you are specifically doing a cooking project with a toddler, like making apple sauce or cookies. However, sometimes they get in when you least expect it, vaulting barriers or suddenly learning how to open a door or a gate. To that end, be prepared. Try to stay a jump ahead of baby's development by cultivating safe habits early on. Turn pot handles away from the edge of the stove; never let them extend out over the floor where a baby or toddler can grab them. Attach and use oven latches and stove guards. You can purchase them from baby stores or catalogs like **Perfectly Safe.**

CABINETS, CUPBOARDS, AND DRAWERS

From the age of eight months or so, when they can sit up and low cabinet handles are at eye level, babies become obsessed with opening and closing doors. It is time to get your child one of those busy boxes, as well as to let him open and close safe cabinets, like the toy cupboard, at will. We also cannot emphasize enough that cleaners mean danger, and should be removed from that tempting under-the-sink cabinet. "Dishwasher soap is dangerous," Dr. Karp says, "but cleaners have tasty-smelling fragrances added."

Do not use pesticide-impregnated drawer liners or table covers—or anything that promises to kill germs or ward off pests. These can offgas onto your cutlery and cooking tools, and residues can adhere to baby's exploring fingers, which inevitably go into his mouth.

Keep heavy and sharp objects out of reach in pantry and cupboards. "Toddlers can pull cans in a cupboard down and hurt themselves," says Dr. Karp.

Instead, put safe, fun objects where baby can reach them. "Have a Tupperware and wooden spoon space," Dr. Karp recommends. Rearrange low kitchen cupboards, drawers, and pantry shelves to put these safe objects within baby's reach. Like older people, he'll grow tired of his toy cupboard and go in search of more meaningful work. As the kitchen is the heart of the house, your baby should not be banned from it altogether.

The Bathroom

For various reasons, not the least of which is the pleasure they get from splashing in the bath, babies seem to be drawn to the toilet. This poses the risk of a drowning accident. A closed door should be sufficient to keep baby out of the bathroom until about the age of nine months. Then you can install toilet lid latches.

Babies love to turn knobs, which is why busy boxes have them. Tub and shower faucet handles invite turning, and an outrush of hot water can scald baby—a very common household accident. Make certain that your hot water heater is turned down to 120 degrees F, or lower. If you live in an apartment and cannot control the water temperature yourself, install an antiscald device, which slows water from tub spouts to a trickle if a dangerous temperature is reached. These devices can be found at home improvement centers.

Use handle restraints and faucet guards for bathroom sinks, showers, and tubs to help prevent scaldings, as well as the scrapes and bruises that sharp chrome fixtures can inflict upon tender heads. They are available in housewares stores.

When the time is right for toilet training, we recommend a solid wood potty chair, built low to the ground and with back and arm rests for comfort. One can be obtained from **The Natural Baby Company.** It even has its own book rack and toilet paper holder on either side. **Gerry** makes a less pricey wooden potty chair, though this one has a plastic seat, available from **Perfectly Safe.**

And when your toddler is ready to wash his own hands and make a stab at brushing his own teeth, it helps to have a stable wooden footstool on which he can stand at the sink while brushing. **The Natural Baby Company** has a nice one that also serves as a seat.

Unbleached, formaldehyde-free green cotton or organic cotton towels and bath rugs can be bought from stores like **Terra Verde** or catalogs such as **Garnet Hill** and **Harmony.**

One of the worst offenders, in terms of being made of PVC, is the lowly shower curtain. Make an eco-statement, and let something soft and natural touch your skin by trading in that vinyl shower curtain for one made of 100 percent green cotton canvas from **Harmony.** Hemp shower curtains, which are naturally mold-resistant, can be bought for a few more dollars from **Earth Runnings, Harmony,** and **Tomorrow's World.** And don't toss the old PVC curtain; use it as a tarp or dropcloth when painting.

A Word on Conserving Water

Conserving water makes good sense not just for your utility bill but for the environment, as well. Already, 20 percent of the world's population lacks potable water. The more wisely we use water, the less we detract from the natural water cycle of rain and snow feeding streams, which run into the sea, from which fresh water evaporates again. In areas such as reservoirs, where surface water is used as municipal supply, saving water at home leaves more water in streams and rivers. In areas where household water is pumped from the ground, conserving water means conserving energy used for pumping, and preserving the water table against times of drought.

In your kitchen, if you wash dishes by hand, use a pan of wash water or plug the sink instead of letting the faucet run. This can save more than 20 gallons. If you use a dishwasher, don't run it until it's full. The same rule should apply to your laundry washing machine. Maximize the amount of cleaning one water "load" does for you.

When buying new appliances, look for water-saving features. Many new dishwashers and washing machines, particularly front-loading clothes washers, use less water to do a job. (See "Energy Efficiency" later in this chapter.)

In the bathroom, install low-flow faucets and shower heads, and low-flush toilets that use less water. Why use potable water to water plants or wash the car? Water from hand-washed dishes or even family baths can be recycled for another use. Many innovative new "green" homes have "gray water" systems that funnel used wash water from sinks and appliances to plant and garden sprinkling systems. In any case, use a bucket and rag when washing the car—not the running hose, which can waste 80 gallons. Throw "gray water" over driveways and sidewalks, or just sweep them. Use mulch around plants to keep soil moist, and repair leaky hoses and pipes promptly.

Babyproofing for Child Safety

This book's focus is on environmental protection, essentially avoiding toxins and pollutants, rather than on giving medical advice. But everyday objects like drapery cords and electrical outlets suddenly become hazards when there's a baby around. As your infant reaches the different developmental stages, your pediatrician will review child safety issues with you. In addition, a very good comprehensive guide can be downloaded from the "Safety and Accident Prevention" section on the KidsHealth website of the **American Medical Association (AMA).** There's also a brief, useful, room-by-room "Baby Safety Checklist" from the **Consumer Product Safety Commission (CPSC).**

Most pediatricians take an age-based approach. But even before you bring the baby home, and if you have children of any age, we advise the following safety devices for your home:

1. smoke and carbon monoxide (CO) alarms (see chapter 5)

2. a fire extinguisher on every floor and one in the kitchen

3. an escape plan for an apartment or home with more than one story. A safety ladder that will reach from your window to the street is a good idea.

Take Age-Appropriate Safety Precautions from the Start

A basic rule of thumb: They're never too young to have an accident. "I start talking about accidents at the two-week visit; it's never too early for a baby to fall off the bed, or reach out and grab hot liquids," Dr. Karp says. "I had a case where a mother had her two-month-old in her lap and a cup of hot coffee in her hand; the baby whacked his mother's hand and got burned." From as early as three weeks old, Mindy Pennybacker's son, Rory, would reach out and pull his father's glasses off, Don remembers. "He had a lightning-quick grab, like a cat's."

At six months, it's time for intensive babyproofing. Remedies must be kept on hand against the baby's accidentally ingesting poisons. "At six months, I recommend ipecac, which causes vomiting, but it is only to be taken after calling your doctor for advice," Dr. Karp says. For environmental controls, one good way to start, he suggests, "is to get a lot of Post-its, then borrow someone's one-year-old to visit your house. They're like bloodhounds in their ability to find danger. Walk behind them putting Post-its on every dangerous thing they find." Then do something about them.

Some examples of dangerous things for babies:

- pennies, paper clips, fuzzballs, and other small objects, which can cause choking when put in the mouth
- electrical cords, telephone cords, and curtain pulls, which can strangle
- electrical outlets, which should be covered or plugged when empty
- plants, which can be toxic
- perfumes and other toiletries
- medicines, both prescription and over-the-counter
- cleaning products
- pesticides
- sharp corners on tables
- chests with heavy lids that can fall down on baby's head and neck
- top-heavy furniture that baby can pull down onto himself
- stairs, particularly stairs without risers, and with banisters more than 3 inches apart. Spaces between steps should be filled, preferably with hardwood rather than plywood or particleboard. If your stairway lacks banisters or rails on the side, it's a good idea to enclose it now.
- windows, from which baby can fall, and which can also come down suddenly, breaking a neck. Check to make sure that your windows work properly and safely.

Dangerous objects should be locked or covered up, battened down securely, and/or kept off the floor and well out of baby's reach, Dr. Karp advises. Stairs and windows can be blocked with gates, but these are not foolproof and cannot be relied on for complete protection; when awake and mobile, babies should be constantly supervised with a watchful eye. Before buying gates and other guards, check with your pediatrician and read a book that reports product-tested safety results, such as the *Consumer Reports' Guide to Baby Products.*

Perfectly Safe sells many types of gates, as well as electrical outlet and power strip covers, safety outlet plates that swivel to seal the holes, window blind cord shorteners, and drawer and cabinet latches and locks. However, when leafing through catalogs, note that the photographs can contain bad examples of parental behavior, or safety "don'ts," which should be avoided. In Perfectly Safe's catalog, for instance, a mother is shown opening a gate at the top of a stairway and letting a toddler go through it, down the stairs, ahead of her. Though holding the child's hand, the mother's body remains behind the gate, which would impede her reaction should the child pitch forward. Instead, when teaching toddlers how to negotiate stairs, the parent should be standing downstairs from the child in the event of a fall.

At six months, Dr. Karp advises, it's time to put latches on drawers and kitchen cabinets. Very hard floors, such as those made of brick, stone, or ceramic tile, should be covered with area rugs, laid over nonslip rug pads. (See chapter 2 for information on carpets and rugs.) Keep bathroom doors closed. "You don't need a toilet lid latch until nine months to a year old," he says.

At nine months: If you haven't already, put dishwasher soap, drain cleaners, other cleaning fluids and pesticides, perfumes, nail polish remover, pain relievers, vitamins, drugs, and toiletries in general up and well out of reach, or get rid of them. "Don't take vitamins or any kind of pills in front of kids; they will want to imitate you," Dr. Karp says. Safety latches on drawers usually work up until eighteen months, when children can figure out how to open them, but there's never a guarantee. There's no substitute for vigilance.

In addition, at all times, prevent burns and scalds from hot liquids and surfaces in the bathroom, kitchen, dining room, and elsewhere by turning down your hot water thermostat to 120 degrees F or lower. (This will help reduce your energy costs, too.) Always test hot water, both in the tub and from the tap, before putting baby in the bath.

Finally, make sure you're prepared for emergencies. Make up a first-aid kit with sterile gauze squares, flexible tape, and sterile bandages of various sizes, including a gauze bandage or clean cloth long enough to wrap a bleeding wound. Cotton swabs, a small pair of sharp scissors, and tweezers for splinters are also good to keep on hand. Ask your pediatrician for recommendations on what to have on hand to clean and dress cuts; 3 percent hydrogen peroxide is a common cleansing solution, and your doctor may recommend that your kit also contain an antibiotic cream. For any large or gaping cut, consult your doctor immediately.

To expedite emergency calls, make sure that phone numbers of pediatrician, poison control center, fire, police, and ambulance services are kept by the phone, or phones, or programmed into the autodial buttons, with clear labeling. Know where the nearest emergency room is, and how to get there. All baby-sitters, including your parents or other relations, should have all this information explained to them. Leave the phone number(s) where you can be reached, and a note authorizing the bearer to get emergency medical treatment for your child.

Energy Efficiency

In chapter 2, we discussed how the use of compact fluorescent lightbulbs (CFLs) can save energy and money. But lighting isn't the only way you can make your home more energy efficient at less expense to you, the environment, and our health. As Linda Latham, an energy consultant in Long Beach, California, and former energy specialist with the EPA, writes in *The Green Guide,* "While you may not think about it when you turn on your TV or your dishwasher, your electricity use causes a lot of environmental harm. In fact, the electricity used in an average U.S. household contributes more carbon dioxide (a cause of global warming) to the atmosphere than does the average car."

The sulfur dioxide from coal- and oil-burning electrical power plants is the major source of acid rain, which kills forests hundreds of miles from the source. Sulfur dioxide also is a major component of ozone, or smog; through its release, along with other pollutants, power plants directly contribute to human respiratory illness. "Power plants are a key contributor to our nation's air pollution problems. They also emit small particulates and heavy metals," Latham writes. A recent study estimated that approximately 64,000 people in the United States die prematurely each year from heart and lung disease due to particulate air pollution. That's more than the number who die each year in car accidents. So by reducing your energy use, you'll be reducing both air pollution and wasteful use of nonrenewable resources.

Finding Energy-Efficient Products

One simple way to identify energy-efficient products—including lightbulbs, air conditioners, dishwashers, washing machines, furnaces, hot water heaters, and refrigerators—is to look for the yellow Energy Guide stickers and Energy Star labels issued by the **U.S. Environmental Protection Agency (EPA).** For example, the agency estimates that the new Energy Star furnaces are 25 to 40 percent more efficient than old furnaces, thus reducing monthly heating bills, as well as air pollution.

Among home appliances, refrigerators are top energy guzzlers. If your refrigerator is a decade or more old and you've been wanting a new one, there are many good reasons to indulge yourself. Today's refrigerators, such as the Sunfrost, use less than half the energy of same-size models from the late 1970s. "Buying a new, specifically energy-efficient fridge can save you $50 to $100 per year in electricity bills, while keeping your food fresher and making less noise," writes Chris Calwell, an energy and transportation scientist, in *The Green Guide.* In addition, new fridges, like new air conditioners, do not contain chlorofluorocarbons (CFCs), a major atmospheric ozone layer depleter, in the coolant or insulation.

Because they tumble clothes through a pool of water, rather than filling the entire wash tub, front-loading clothes washers, used throughout Europe, use less energy, water, and detergent than top-loaders, and with less stress to the clothes. They also wring more water from clothes in the spin cycle, reducing drying time. **Frigidaire** makes an American model, soon to be joined by others. **American Council for an Energy-Efficient Economy** and **Rocky Mountain Institute** publish books and pamphlets on how to make your home more energy-efficient. ACEEE's book, *Consumer Guide to Home Energy Savings,* ranks appliances in terms of their energy efficiency.

Actions you can take to save energy without spending a lot of money:

- Where possible, replace existing incandescent lightbulbs with CFLs, available from hardware and lighting stores and from **Real Goods Trading Company, Harmony, Tomorrow's World,** and **Energy Federation, Inc. Philips, Osram/Sylvania, General Electric, Lights of America,** and **Panasonic** make 18- to 26-watt CFLs that substitute well for 60- and 75-watt incandescent bulbs. Circular or "2D" CFLs using between 28 and 38 watts can be installed in table and floor lamps requiring a 100-watt incandescent bulb. CFLs cost about $20, a lot more than standard light bulbs, but last fifteen to twenty times longer. The savings in energy also offset costs. Don't be tempted by cheap, high-wattage halogen lamps; they waste energy (you can feel the heat) and are a fire hazard. Halogen lamps with bulbs under 100 watts are energy efficient and less dangerous, but still get quite hot.

- If your fridge was made within the past fifteen years, it probably has an energy-saver switch inside. Make sure it's switched on. Also, take your fridge's temperature by leaving an outdoor thermometer in it for about twenty minutes. The freezer should be 0 to 5 degrees F, and the refrigerator 34 to 38 degrees F. Any more or less, and you're wasting energy. So adjust the temperatures accordingly.

- Make sure your water heater is set at no more than 120 degrees F. If its side feels warm to the touch, you're losing heat. Wrap it with an insulating blanket, made of fiberglass or reflective metal film, found for $20 at most hardware stores. Also wrap the hot water pipe leading out of the tank with pipe insulation, which costs $5 to $10 at hardware stores.

- Remember to clean your dryer lint trap before every load to increase efficiency. "Forcing a dryer to blow air through lint is like jogging with a snorkel," Chris Calwell says.

- Wash *full* loads of laundry rather than wasting water and energy on smaller ones.

- If your house is drafty, you can weatherstrip doors and windows for little expense. Caulk cracks; you can lose a lot of heat through them. Install foam rubber gaskets behind outlet and switch plates (turn off electrical power before you start) and rubber "sweeps" at the bottom of doors. Necessary materials are available at hardware stores.

- Set thermostats to 68 degrees F.

Preventing Environmental Allergens and Asthma Triggers

Where there is a family history of serious allergies, Dr. Philip Landrigan says, parents should try to eliminate such common (and unfortunately ubiquitous) allergens as dust mites. Laura Pope's childhood was made miserable by allergies, and when her son, Jeffrey, was three, blood tests showed he was allergic to dust mites, peanuts, and milk. Peanut allergies can be fatal, so the Popes have been vigilant about diet. Additionally, Laura took the dust mites seriously, because their doctor told them that allergies can often develop into chronic conditions such as asthma.

"If your child has specific environmental allergies, such as dust mites, you can remove them from the home environment. Thorough weekly cleanings, washing bed linens in hot water, and using HEPA air filters reduce allergens and reactions to them quite well," says Laura. "It's important to give all children a clean indoor environment as a healthy baseline. My son hasn't developed chronic asthma because we've kept the dust allergen level in his body down," she adds.

The Popes' is a model nonallergenic home environment. "We have no carpets. There's just one small wool Oriental rug in the living room, and one washable cotton rug in Jeffrey's room," Laura says. She replaced dust-catching drapes with wipe-clean, louvered wood shutters and roller shades. "The shutters are also useful when it's daylight savings time and the child has to go to bed when it's still light out," she says.

Laura uses filters that trap microparticles, less than 10 microns in size, in her HEPA vacuum cleaner, air cleaning machines, and air conditioners. She's a stickler for good ventilation and air circulation, as well. "Opening the window with the air cleaning machine nearby is wonderful for bringing oxygen into my son's room. I open the window about five inches and put the machine there." For the air conditioners, she uses 3M Filtrete filters, which cost about $6 each. "You can cut them to size." Filtrete filters are available from **3M, Priorities,** and most hardware stores. For specifics on filters and appliances, see chapter 5.

Laura's attack on dust mites intensifies in the realm of mattresses, pillows, and upholstered furniture. "Both foam and down are real dust mite feast foods," she says. "But if you're on a strict budget, don't spend everything on your mattress and box spring. They're not against your skin," Laura says.

She saves her resources for encasements, and saves on the cost of woven nylon barrier cloth encasements by purchasing the tightly woven barrier cloth from the **Allergy Control Products** catalog and making them herself. Whether you want to buy a ready-made encasement or just the material, ask and "They will send you samples, little tiny squares that you can sniff to see if there's any reaction," she advises, adding that you can call Allergy Control Products for advice. Laura also makes pillowcase covers that fit around her sofa pillows. She also takes covers when she travels with her son.

Laura is allergic to pesticides, and doesn't use them at all. She remembers Spectricide making her wheeze when her father sprayed it during her childhood.

Here is Dr. Karp's twelve-step checklist for keeping indoor air pollution and allergens down:

1. Make sure you have good ventilation and smoke and carbon monoxide alarms.

2. Spray carpets with tannic acid 3 percent spray (available at **Harmony** and **Priorities**) to kill dust mites.

3. Use air filters.

4. Use a vacuum with leakproof collecting bags and microparticle filters.

5. Clean out your heating system, and replace filters frequently.

6. Wash bedding in hot water every two weeks.

7. Wash curtains frequently.

8. Get rid of carpets and stuffed animals, unless you're going to regularly wash and dry them, or have enough room in your freezer to freeze them (this also kills mites).

9. Encase mattresses and pillows with impermeable material to keep dust mites down.

10. Keep home and car tobacco smoke-free zones.

11. Don't use smelly products. Use low-VOC, nontoxic household cleaners and pest controls; don't use air fresheners and perfumes.

12. Keep VOC-emitting products, such as surfaces and furniture made of plywood and particleboard, out of your house.

The Popes' Home: A Nonallergenic Renovation

Time and again, we've warned against home renovation while you're pregnant or have a young child at home. But what if you look around one day, with your vulnerable babe in your arms, and see that your old place is literally crumbling around you? Not to panic. These things happen. That's why the summer after her son Jeffrey turned three and tested positive for dust mite allergies, Laura Pope, before moving in, gave her new apartment a renovation aimed at reducing allergens in the home.

"I learned that our plaster was dying, that is, losing its gypsum and literally falling off the wall," Laura says. When plaster and paint crumble, they create lots of dust.

She specified no sheetrock. Molds and mildews can grow behind this surface. Her contractor replastered in an elaborate, old-fashioned way, canvassing the wall between two skim coats of plaster.

In her campaign against dust and mold, Laura put a strict cleanup clause in the contract, stipulating that the workers clean and wipe down the walls before they built cabinets. When they opened holes in the walls to insert air conditioners, she demanded that they clean up and seal the openings thoroughly. Under general notes, the architect stipulated that the contractor vacuum between radiators and walls when redoing the walls, and that ventilation ducts also be vacuumed before any sort of cabinetry was put over them. "Contractors are famous for trapping dust and paint chips and even their cigarette butts behind new cabinets, flooring, and wall," she says.

She used a natural, white base paint to which her painter added tints. You can choose from thirty natural organic pigments for custom-color paint or stain to mix for floor, walls, or trim. The pigments are available from **Eco Design** or **Terra Verde.**

She had the hardwood oak floors sanded and finished with Moisture Cure, a nonpolyurethane stain. "It takes three days to soak in, then you add a second coat and let it sit for two days. It doesn't wear like the synthetic ones, but it's a lot softer and more natural."

Finally, no matter what, don't move back in too early. Living in a virtual construction site happens so much these days you'd think it was hip. A man we know, after two years of dragged-out renovation was completed, looked around and said he missed his contractor. But it's bad for your health and your child's. Laura also kept the renovated rooms sealed with the air purifiers on for a couple of days after the construction was done. "It makes a huge difference in the smell and the quality of the air; it gets all those little particles out."

Laura Pope was as thorough as anyone could be, and she's happy with the results: a home that can easily be kept dust-free. Precautions can definitely work wonders.

chapter five

Pollutants
in Your House

Modern homes are composed of thousands of chemically based building products, from PVC plastic pipes and particleboard subflooring to urea-formaldehyde adhesives and fiberglass insulation. We decorate them with fume-emitting paints, synthetic carpets, vinyl flooring and wallpaper, and toxically finished furniture. Then we spritz, spray, and wipe every surface with chemicals to clean, degrease, deodorize, disinfect, dust, polish, waterproof, and debug. For every household problem, there's almost always a chemical product to solve it. "Industry has done an incredibly good job of narrowing a product's purpose, so that an average home may have 150 different products in cupboards and utility closets," says Wayne Tusa, president of Environmental Risk and Loss Control, a company that conducts residential environmental testing. No wonder indoor air pollution is one of the top environmental risks to the public!

As your baby begins to roam your home, you'll need to be even more vigilant about pollutants throughout the house, even if the source is only in one room. Particles of lead and asbestos, and chemicals from the smoke of a fireplace or from pesticides might drift from room to room on air currents or be tracked in on shoes. This chapter focuses on hazardous indoor pollutants that can be found throughout your home and how you can reduce your baby's exposure to them. You'll find sections on:

- Keeping Outdoor Pollutants Out
- Chemicals That Go Up in Smoke
- Cleaning Up
- Pesticides
- Radon
- Asbestos
- Moisture-Happy Molds and Microbes
- Good Ventilation
- Devices to Improve Air Quality
- Electromagnetic Fields
- Gardens and Lawns

Keeping Outdoor Pollutants Out

Even if you don't use toxic pesticides in your yard, drift from neighbors' yards or from nearby golf courses or public parks may settle on the ground outside your home. Or airborne droplets of freshly sprayed pesticides might waft in through your windows. And although lead began to be phased out from gasoline in 1979, in many areas it had settled over the years from the air into the soil, where it remains in high concentrations—especially near homes close to highways. Also, lead was banned more recently from exterior than from interior paints. Lead dust and chips from neighbors' or your own house's outdoor surfaces, especially during renovations, can easily be tracked to your door.

With regard to keeping out airborne pollutants, from pesticides to smog, your best recourse is to learn when the air is likely to be polluted by heeding smog and pollen count advisories. Check your newspapers and local TV and radio stations for the air quality index daily. Smog counts tend to be highest between 3 and 6 P.M. When it's very windy, airborne dust counts are higher. At such times, close your windows and use an air conditioner for ventilation and filtration.

For blocking tracked-in pollutants, the lowly doormat can play an effective role. "Wiping one's feet on a commercial-grade doormat appears to reduce the amount of lead in a typical carpet by a factor of six," Wayne R. Ott and John W. Roberts wrote in *Scientific American* in February 1998.

You can also do as the Japanese and Hawaiians do: leave your shoes at the door. You can assure visitors that, thanks to this practice, the floors in your home are very clean! "Removing one's shoes before entering is even more effective than just wiping one's feet in lowering indoor levels of the toxic pollutants that contaminate the environs of most homes (such as lead from peeling paint and pesticides from soils around the foundation)," Ott and Roberts say.

Chemicals That Go Up in Smoke:
The Hazards of Gas Stoves, Fireplaces,
Kerosene Heaters, and Cigarette Smoke

The burning, or combustion, of wood or fuels like natural gas or kerosene can be a formidable source of pollution, particularly if your home is poorly ventilated. Smoke, whether from a fireplace, cigarette, car emissions, or incense, contains thousands of chemicals, including cancer-causing substances and allergens. We now know that secondhand smoke can cause lung cancer, heart disease, asthma, and respiratory infections. Infants are even more vulnerable than adults. Exposure to tobacco smoke has doubled the incidence of pneumonia, bronchitis, and other respiratory ailments among infants and children up to age three. Similarly, exposure to pollutants from combustion appliances, heaters, and fireplaces also increases the risk of cancer, respiratory infections, heart disease, and retarded fetal development. Children living in homes heated with wood are more likely to develop respiratory illnesses. In the United States, 37 percent of all deaths in the first year of life are the result of lung disease and breathing problems, which are the leading cause of disease and death among newborns, according to the **American Lung Association.** Wood smoke has become a significant part of outdoor air pollution, too. In Washington state, for example, residential wood stoves and fireplaces release 10 percent of the state's total air pollution.

Because many of the particles and gasses found in smoke and fuel emissions are undetectable to us, we often don't realize the dangers that we may be exposing ourselves and our loved ones to. Some of the gas and particle byproducts of combustion include:

- *Carbon monoxide (CO).* A colorless and odorless gas, carbon monoxide is absorbed easily into the bloodstream and starves it of oxygen. Automobile exhaust is one of the main sources, but other combustibles (see page 88) also produce CO. At low levels, this gas causes fatigue in healthy people and chest pain in those with heart disease. Symptoms of exposure to moderate to high levels include impaired vision and coordination, headaches, dizziness, nausea, vomiting, memory loss, and flulike symptoms. At high doses, CO is fatal. Nearly 300 people die each year from CO poisoning in their homes, according to the **Consumer Product Safety Commission (CPSC).** Another 5,000 are treated in emergency rooms after exposure, but this is believed to be an underestimation, because many confuse the symptoms with those of the flu.

- *Nitrogen dioxide (NO$_2$).* A sharp-smelling, colorless gas, nitrogen dioxide irritates eyes, nose, throat, and lungs and can cause coughing, headaches, and nausea. In homes with gas stoves, kerosene heaters, and unvented gas space heaters, NO$_2$ levels often exceed outdoor levels, according to the EPA. Short-term exposures can increase the risk of respiratory infection, especially in young children, and trigger asthma attacks. Long-term exposure may result in permanent damage to lung tissue.

- *Sulfur dioxide (SO$_2$).* This gas is produced by sulfur-containing fuels such as kerosene space heaters and wood-burning stoves and can aggravate symptoms of asthma and bronchitis.

- *Small inhalable particles, or particulates.* Particles produced by combustion are often small enough to penetrate deep into the lungs. "Particulates can remain suspended for up to three weeks and can travel up to 700 miles," says Jamie Craighill, wood smoke coordinator for the Washington State Department of Ecology's Air Quality Program. These particles may also attach to other toxic substances and carry them into the lungs and mucous membranes. Long-term exposure may lead to lung cancer, asthma, and bronchitis. When walking or running, we kick up these particles, making it more likely that we'll breathe them in. Children risk even greater exposure to these particles. Crawling on the ground, they may ingest five times more dust than an adult, as much as 100 milligrams per day, report John Roberts and Wayne Ott in the February 1998 issue of *Scientific American.*

- *Polycyclic aromatic hydrocarbons (PAHs).* These can be found in either gas or particle form in the home. Tarlike PAHs are found in smoke, soot, ash, and creosote from wood, coal, and tobacco. Some PAH compounds have been linked to cancers of the lung, stomach, skin, and bladder in humans. They may also impact reproductive systems. Every day, the average urban infant will ingest 110 nanograms of benzo-a-pyrene, the most toxic polycyclic aromatic hydrocarbon, according to Ott and Roberts. A child would take in the same amount of this PAH by smoking three cigarettes.

Particles and PAHs produced from combustion cling to soil and dust, which may be tracked around the house on shoes and infiltrate rooms through open windows and ducts. These pollutants can be inhaled, absorbed through the skin, and ingested from hand-to-mouth contact.

Sources of Combustion Pollutants

There are three primary sources of combustion pollutants in the home. *Unvented appliances,* such as gas stoves and kerosene heaters, can be worrisome because they do not have an exhaust fan or flue that carries pollutants out of and away from the house. Even unvented pilot lights in gas appliances can increase indoor air pollution, according to the EPA. It's best to vent appliances to the outdoors whenever possible. And kitchen windows must be easily opened so that gases and particles can be dispersed.

Vented appliances, including most furnaces, wood stoves, fireplaces, gas water heaters, and gas clothes dryers, are supposed to exhaust pollutants outdoors through vents, flues, or ducts. But exhaust leakage, due to cracked heat exchangers or blocked vents, may cause the pollutants to seep into the home instead. Blocked flues or chimneys can cause backdrafts, or a reversal of airflow through a chimney or flue. Backdrafts push smoke into the house instead of outward. They are also caused by lowered air pressure, or depressurization, which occurs when other chimneys, exhaust fans, or forced air systems pull air from the house without adequate air replacement, producing a "suction" effect. "Even operating a clothes dryer, which expels air outdoors through a vent, can cause a backdraft, particularly when the fire is low," says Jamie Craighill.

Secondhand smoke, or the smoke from smoldering tobacco, emits more than 4,000 particles and gasses. At least forty of these, such as formaldehyde and benzene, are carcinogenic. Infants of smokers have a higher incidence of ear infections and may suffer reduced lung function and lung growth. Maternal smoking impacts fetal development as well and increases the risk of Sudden Infant Death Syndrome (SIDS).

Other activities related to combustion may also degrade indoor air quality. Pollutants from an idling car or fuel-burning heaters in the garage may seep into the house. Grilling or burning food, the oven-cleaning cycle on your kitchen stove, welding and soldering projects, and incense and candles release particles and gasses into the air as well.

Polluted outdoor air from passing traffic, outdoor barbecues, wood stoves and fireplaces in neighboring homes, and gas-powered lawnmowers can enter your home through open doors and windows.

Reducing Combustion Pollutants in Your Home

Once combustion pollutants contaminate your home, they are very difficult to remove. Particles cling to carpets, furniture, curtains, and household dust, and gasses spread throughout the house. You need not replace all your gas appliances and board up your fireplace. Instead, reduce contamination as much as possible by doing the following:

- *Install carbon monoxide alarms,* which cost between $50 and $80, in hallways outside bedrooms and the nursery. CO disperses fairly quickly and evenly throughout the house, so you won't need alarms next to every gas appliance, which might cause the alarm to react to short-lived, but high, amounts of CO. If you have a multilevel house, place one alarm near sleeping areas and others near, but not in, the kitchen and furnace room in the basement. Look for CO detectors that meet the Underwriters Laboratories standard 2034—this code is usually listed on the product and its packaging. *Consumer Reports* recommends plug-in detectors, such as those in the Nighthawk 900 series, American Sensors' CO920, and Lifesaver FYCO-6N, over battery-operated models. Don't rely on inexpensive plastic or cardboard detectors that indicate the presence of CO by changing color. Such devices will be useless when you are asleep.

- *Make your home as smoke-free as possible.* Keep as many smoking and burning activities as you can outdoors and away from open windows and doors.

- *Make sure gas cooking stoves have adequate ventilation.* Use a range hood with exhaust vents that direct smoke outside, or open windows for cross-ventilation each time you use the stove. Never use gas cooking stoves and ovens to heat your house.

- *Avoid kerosene or gas-fired space heaters.* If you need a space heater, use an electric or ceramic radiant heater. Both may outgas when first operated, but you can dissipate harmful fumes by operating the new heater on "high" in a ventilated garage or outdoors under close supervision. If you must resort to fuel-powered space heaters, use them only during emergencies for short periods of time in well-ventilated rooms (open a window slightly). Try to avoid using fuel-powered space heaters in small rooms. Follow manufacturer's directions faithfully, and never leave a space heater unattended.

- *Never use charcoal grills, hibachis, or portable camping stoves indoors,* in garages and sheds, on balconies, in tents, or near open windows. About twenty-five people die and several hundred become ill each year from use of charcoal indoors, according to CPSC.

- *Decrease the operation time of unvented combustion heaters by weatherizing your home.* Several books on energy efficiency listed in Appendix A explain how.

- *Avoid operating motor vehicles, lawnmowers, or other combustion engines in an enclosed garage attached to your home or near open windows.* Weatherstrip doors leading from the garage to the house to reduce the amount of car exhaust entering the house.

- *Limit the use of woodburning stoves and fireplaces,* particularly if your child has asthma or another chronic respiratory illness. Fireplaces are an inefficient and expensive way to heat your home, and they backdraft easily.

- *If you do choose to use a fireplace or wood stove, clean and inspect the flue and chimney annually.* A wood smoke or charred-wood smell at any time while a fire is burning usually means that something is obstructing the flue or chimney or there is a backdraft. Have it inspected before using it again! Wood stoves manufactured after 1992 are less polluting, using catalytic converters that burn fuel more completely, and require less wood to produce more heat. An EPA label on a wood stove certifies that it burns cleanly under laboratory conditions. Burn only dry, seasoned, and untreated wood for more efficient combustion and less pollution. Hardwoods, such as oak and maple, are better than soft pine and spruce. Never burn pressure-treated wood, particleboard, or plywood, which are filled with toxic chemicals. While it's okay to start a fire with newspaper, don't feed the fire with more newspaper, advises Jamie Craighill. "You don't know what kind of chemicals are in the ink," she says. Give the fire lots of air to make it burn as hot as possible. "The hotter the fire burns, the cleaner it burns," says Craighill.

- *Have a trained professional inspect, clean, and tune gas appliances annually.* She should examine heat exchangers, chimneys and flues, vents, ductwork, and filters for cracks and obstructions. Signs that you might have a leak or obstruction include:

  - a constantly running furnace or one that cannot adequately heat the house
  - sooting, especially on appliances

- decreasing hot water supply (if you have a gas water heater)
- a burning odor or other unusual smells
- visible rust or stains on vents and chimneys

- *Make sure your home is adequately ventilated.* See "Good Ventilation" later in this chapter.

Cleaning Up

When her baby began to fuss and cry while she was cleaning, Maria Santos of New York City became alarmed and puzzled. "My baby's eyes tear up every time I clean my house," says Maria. Maria doesn't experience any strange symptoms when she cleans, but her baby is very sensitive to the fumes and fragrances emitted from cleaning products. Rather than have her baby suffer, Maria now takes her baby to her sister's home, then returns home alone to clean. For most of us, this solution is inconvenient and may not be enough. Cleaners can cling to surfaces, fumes may linger for hours, and perfumes in laundry detergents can cause allergic reactions even weeks after washing. Even storing cleaners in your house can be hazardous to children. Babies find cleaning bottles an intriguing curiosity, which could spell disaster. In 1996, more than 21,000 children under the age of six were reported to poison control centers around the country as having ingested chlorine bleach. Another 10,000 young children reportedly swallowed glass cleaners. No deaths and very few life-threatening injuries resulted from these incidents, but all the worry could have been prevented simply by not using cleaners made with toxic chemicals.

Most people have become accustomed to using a large variety of chemicals to clean up. Hundreds of highly specialized chemical products have been designed to combat grease, dirt, mold, mildew, dust, and bacteria in every conceivable location of the house, from kitchen counters to shower tiles. More than 70,000 chemicals are registered with the EPA for use in cleaning products, including suspected hormone disruptors and carcinogens. Many of these chemicals contribute to indoor air pollution, are poisonous if ingested, and can be harmful if inhaled or if they come into contact with the skin. Despite this, manufacturers of cleaners are not obligated to list all the ingredients and their concentrations on labels, even if the ingredients are hazardous. While some companies print warnings on bottles, these often do not necessarily express the full range of the products' toxicity. In addition, so-called inactive or inert ingredients are not necessarily benign.

Irritating, Toxic, and Burning Chemicals

Infants and others may suffer acute reactions to some common cleaning chemicals, such as ammonia. The reactions may include irritation to skin, eyes, nose, and throat; dizziness; and headaches. Some fumes and fragrances may produce an allergic reaction, from rashes to sneezing and headaches. Ingestion of many chemicals can produce cramps, nausea, vomiting, and tissue damage and may even cause death. Caustic lye, an ingredient in some drain and oven cleaners, can cause burns. Chlorine bleach is a strong irritant to eyes, nose, throat, and lungs. Initial exposures may not cause any symptoms, but with prolonged use, sensitivities may suddenly appear. Chemicals from different cleaning products can also react with each other.

- WARNING: *Never mix ammonia-containing products with products that contain lye or chlorine bleach, or chlorine-based products with those containing acid.*

An ammonia-lye or ammonia-chlorine combination produces chloramine gasses that can damage the lungs. Chlorine bleach mixed with acid, which is used in some toilet bowl cleaners, forms toxic chlorine gas. Used during World War I for chemical warfare, chlorine gas can damage airways. Because so many household cleaners contain either chlorine bleach or ammonia, don't mix any cleaners, or use one cleaner on a surface that you have just cleaned with another. Better yet, avoid completely products containing either ammonia or chlorine bleach to prevent an accident from occurring.

Be very cautious with all extra-strength cleaners. Often they are simply not necessary. The most dangerous cleaning products are corrosive drain cleaners, oven cleaners, and acid-based bowl cleaners, says Philip Dickey, executive director of **Washington Toxics Coalition (WTC)** in Seattle. Corrosive products are dangerous because they burn human tissue easily. Ingestion can mean damage to mouth, throat, and esophagus. Inhalation may result in scarring of membranes in the nose and lungs, and contact with skin and eyes can produce severe burns. Corrosive cleaners may also react violently with other products. Safer, milder alternatives, such as Bon Ami Cleaner (a scouring powder), work just as well. Lisa Lefferts, Mothers & Others science advisor, says, "I find baking soda works fine on sinks and tubs." Preventive measures, such as lining your oven with aluminum foil to catch spills or installing screens on drains to catch hair, eliminate the need for cleaners that "eat away" stains and clogs.

Hormone Disruptors in Cleaners

A worrisome class of chemicals, alkylphenol ethoxylates (APEs), are used in many cleaning products, hair dyes, and pesticides as surfactants, an important cleaning agent in any cleaner, from soap to laundry detergent to shampoo. APEs don't biodegrade readily or completely, and, worse, they can break down into nonylphenol, which can disrupt hormone functions in animals and possibly in humans. Professor John Sumpter of Brunel University near London discovered a link between APE exposure of fish in rivers and a gender-bending characteristic—male fish producing female egg-yolk proteins. Drs. Ana Soto and Carlos Sonnenschein found in the late 1980s that p-nonylphenol can cause the growth of human breast cancer cells.

Philip Dickey of WTC has found APEs in 477 products, though there are probably more because many companies don't list them on labels. Dickey discovered that supermarket or drugstore brand laundry detergents are more likely to contain APEs than brand name products. In laboratory tests, three out of four nonchlorine disinfectants, as well as some "environmentally friendly" cleaners, contained APEs. But because manufacturers are not required to list ingredients, you wouldn't be able to tell by looking at the label. Dickey lists some APE-containing products in a WTC fact sheet called "Hormones in your Haircolor?"

Disinfectants

Disinfectants, for the most part, are also not necessary. Disinfectants are EPA-regulated pesticides that kill bacteria. But you don't have to resort to chemical warfare to maintain a clean and safe home. You can adequately clean household surfaces with hot, sudsy water and a little elbow grease. In the bathroom and kitchen, you may feel a little more power is needed. Some herbal oils and extracts, such as Australian tea tree oil, pine oil, and citrus seed extract, are thought to have antibacterial and antifungal properties. But they have not been tested adequately to know which microbes they kill. They can be found in natural foods stores and increasingly in supermarkets. If you switch to these alternatives, bear in mind that homemade cleaners and disinfectants don't necessarily kill all bacteria and viruses (which is also true of some chemical disinfectants). For example, borax makes a good laundry detergent, mold remover, and bathroom cleaner, but don't rely on it for cleaning kitchen counters or cutting boards because borax does not kill *Salmonella* or the dangerous strain of *E. coli,* two worrisome bacteria that cause food poisoning. Earth Power's Power Herbal Disinfectant is a hospital-grade disinfectant made of herbs that kills some bacteria and viruses like *Staphylococcus aureus* and *herpes simplex I.* It doesn't necessarily kill all food pathogens, though, so don't rely on it to keep your kitchen safe. (See chapter 6 for food safety tips.)

Environmental Considerations

Cleaners also have many environmental consequences that shouldn't be ignored. Synthetic cleaning ingredients are made from petroleum, a nonrenewable resource. Many of these do not biodegrade easily. These cleaning agents enter our waterways, the air, and the soil, and may remain there for some time, affecting wildlife and their habitats. Because we dump them in the trash, cleaning products often contaminate landfills, making them hazardous waste sites.

Phosphates, water-softening mineral additives, are still around. Despite all the criticisms, not all manufacturers have phased them out. Many states have banned phosphates from household laundry detergents and some other cleaning products, but automatic dishwasher detergents are usually exempt from such restrictions. This additive overnutrifies rivers and streams, causing excessive algae growth. Overabundance of algae deprives fish of oxygen and contributes to declining populations in many waterways.

Aerosol sprays made in the United States may no longer contain ozone-depleting chlorofluorocarbons (CFCs), but they often contain a higher VOC content than nonaerosol products. Petroleum-based propellants, such as butane and propane, contain VOCs and are flammable. Disinfectants and solvent-based spot removers (made of petrochemicals) packaged in aerosol cans also have high VOC levels. Aerosol sprays produce a fine spray of chemicals that can be more easily absorbed by the body. With contents under pressure, aerosol cans are explosive at high temperatures or pressure.

There are many other chemicals to avoid in your home. We have provided a listing of some toxic chemicals in cleaning products in the chart below. Several books with more information are listed in Appendix C. Keep in mind, though, that reading the label of a cleaning product may not be helpful when you are making purchasing decisions. Most ingredient listings are vague and incomplete. Instead, avoid cleaners that have these warning words: Caution, danger, corrosive, or caustic.

Some Hazardous Ingredients in Cleaners

INGREDIENT	FOUND IN	HAZARDS AND CHARACTERISTICS
ammonia	glass cleaners, furniture polishes, floor cleaners, drain cleaner, toilet bowl cleaner	Irritating to eyes, nose, lungs. Can cause rashes, redness, and burning.
butyl cellosolve	extra-strength all purpose cleaners, degreasers, window cleaners	Easily absorbed into the skin. Can damage blood, liver, and central nervous system. Can cause kidney failure.
chlorine	cleansers, disinfectants, bleach, toilet bowl cleaners, tub and tile cleaners	Irritates skin. When ingested, can irritate mouth, esophagus, and stomach. Inhaled chlorine gas may damage lungs and airways. Especially dangerous when combined with acids or ammonia.
ethoxylated alcohols	many products	May be contaminated with 1,4-dioxane, a carcinogen that is easily absorbed.
formaldehyde	disinfectants, furniture polishes, detergents, water softeners (also found in glues, furniture and fabric finishes)	Suspected human carcinogen. May cause damage to central nervous system. Inhaled, can cause nasal stuffiness, itchiness, nausea, headache, or fatigue. Ingested, can cause stomach pain, bleeding, coma, and death.
hydrochloric, phosphoric, and hydrofluoric acids	metal polishes, toilet bowl cleaners, lime removers, rust removers	Extremely caustic! Causes burns on contact.
kerosene	furniture polishes, car waxes	May cause damage to central nervous system. May contain benzene, a carcinogen.
lye (sodium hydroxide)	tub and tile cleaners, toilet bowl cleaners, oven cleaners, drain cleaners	Corrosive. Will cause burns on contact. When mixed with acids, releases harmful vapors. When mixed with ammonia, forms corrosive chloramine gas.

Ingredient	Found In	Hazards and Characteristics
naphthalene	mothballs, carpet cleaners, air fresheners, toilet bowl cleaners, car waxes	Eye and skin irritant. Can cause corneal damage and cataracts. May cause damage to reproductive and central nervous systems. Can cause headaches, vomiting, confusion, excessive sweating, and urinary irritation.
paradichlorobenzenes (PDCBs) or 1,4-dichlorobenzene	toilet fresheners, mothballs, room deodorizers, insecticides	Suspected carcinogen. Hormone disruptor. Can cause liver and kidney damage. Highly volatile.
perchloroethylene (PERC); tetrachloroethylene	spot removers, dry cleaning solvent	Suspected carcinogen. May cause damage to nervous system. Eye, skin, and respiratory irritant.
petroleum distillates	many products	May irritate eyes, skin, and airways. Can cause dermatitis. May cause damage to central nervous system. May contain benzene, a carcinogen.
phosphoric acid	bathroom cleaning products	Severe eye, skin, and respiratory irritant. Can damage lungs.
sodium bisulfate	toilet bowl cleaners	Corrosive; may damage eyes, skin, and internal tissues if ingested. May trigger asthma attacks.
toluene	spot removers	Eye and skin irritant. May damage central nervous system.
triethanolamine (TEA)	liquid all-purpose cleaners, metal polishes, spot removers	Eye and skin irritant. May react with nitrites (a preservative; sometimes not listed on labels) to form carcinogenic nitrosamines, which absorb readily into the skin.
trisodium nitrilotriacetate	bathroom cleaners	Suspected carcinogen.
trichloroethylene	spot removers, metal polishes	Probable carcinogen and a narcotic. May cause dizziness and headaches.

Safer Alternative Detergents

Now is a good time to reduce or eliminate your use of most conventional detergents. Milder, less toxic cleaners are available. **Seventh Generation, EarthRite, Aubrey Organics,** Auro, Biofa, **Dr. Bronner's,** Livos, **AFM,** and **Ecover** are sold in many natural foods stores, or you can order these and other brands through the mail (see Appendix B). You can also find mild alternatives in the supermarket, such as Bon Ami and Mr. Clean. WTC's booklet, *Buy Smart, Buy Safe: A Consumer's Guide to Less-Toxic Products,* rates the environmental and health safety of hundreds of cleaning products. Remember to avoid chlorine and ammonia, to prevent the possibility of mixing them; caustic, corrosive, and extra-strength cleaners; dishwasher detergents containing phosphates; and aerosol sprays. Also, try to use unscented laundry detergents—such as Arm & Hammer's scent-free detergent—and fabric softeners; scented products might cause allergic reactions. You may want to stop using fabric softeners completely; these temporary fabric treatments that coat clothing fibers to prevent static cling are usually unnecessary. Natural fibers, such as cotton, wool, linen, and hemp, don't get static-y in the dryer the way synthetics do. Reducing the amount of detergent you use, too, will help reduce the itchiness and discomfort of just-laundered clothing. Often, detergent residues remain on laundered items, making them stiff.

You can also do most of your household cleaning and laundry with safe and basic ingredients: lemon juice, baking soda, vinegar, borax, salt, olive oil, and vegetable soaps. *Clean & Green* by Annie Berthold-Bond and *Clean House, Clean Planet* by Karen Logan have recipes for homemade cleaners. Logan also sells empty plastic bottles with her recipes on the labels for home preparations. Whatever you choose, homemade or commercial, keep cleaners out of the reach of children in secure cupboards. Even safer cleaners can pose a health risk when ingested.

Lingering Dry Cleaning Fumes

Having clothes professionally cleaned doesn't necessarily mean perfectly clean clothes. Nearly all dry cleaners in the United States use perchloroethylene (PERC), a toxic organochlorine solvent, to remove stains, dirt, and odors from all types of clothing. In January 1996, just after Mori Mickelson, who was living above a dry cleaner in New York City, learned she was pregnant, the New York State Department of Health began a pilot study to determine PERC levels in residents living above dry cleaners. Researchers found PERC in Mori's blood, urine, and breast tissue. After she had given birth to her son, they found PERC in her breast milk.

There is reason to worry about even a minute amount of this chemical. The EPA has classified PERC as a hazardous air pollutant. The International Agency for Research on Cancer (IARC) lists PERC as a probable human carcinogen. PERC has been linked to nervous system, kidney, liver, and reproductive disorders in lab animals and a higher risk of cancer among dry cleaning workers. Acute exposures may cause headaches, dizziness, burning in the lungs, and loss of consciousness. Even after dry cleaned clothes have dried, residues of PERC may cling to clothing fibers and then dissipate into your home.

Dry cleaning workers and people living in buildings where a dry cleaning establishment is located are at the greatest risk for harm, but people who visit dry cleaners and wear clothes cleaned in PERC regularly also may be at risk. In the 1980s, EPA studies found that people who reported visiting a dry cleaning shop showed twice as much PERC in their breath, on average, as other people. EPA also found that levels of PERC remained elevated in a home for as long as one week after placing newly dry cleaned clothes in a closet. In a March 1996 report, Consumers Union found that people who wear freshly dry cleaned clothes, such as a jacket and shirt, every week over a forty-year period could inhale enough PERC "to measurably increase their risk of cancer"—by as much as 150 times what the EPA considers "negligible risk."

Avoid dry cleaning any of your and your baby's clothing and bedding. Any PERC-cleaned clothes that you bring into your home may increase your child's exposure to this dangerous chemical. You can best avoid it by purchasing only machine- or hand-washable garments.

If you do have clothes that require professional cleaning, there are alternatives to conventional dry cleaning. Many garments, in fact, do not need to be professionally cleaned, according to *Consumer Reports*. Many manufacturers, rather than risk consumer ire due to shrunken or otherwise damaged garments, recommend dry cleaning for clothing that could be hand-washed safely. The key is knowing how to wash the clothes in the first place. (See "Can I Hand Wash This Dry-Clean-Only Garment?" on page 98.)

For garments that cannot be handwashed, due to intricate tailoring or lack of color-fastness, there are professional cleaning processes that do not pose the health risks of PERC. Professional wet cleaning, which involves customized treatment for each garment using soap and water, has been around for fifty years. Depending on the type of fabric and construction, clothing is either machine-washed in water with special computerized machines, steam cleaned, or hand washed; then it is machine- or air-dried, pressed, and finished. Wet cleaning can be used on almost any garment, and on average, prices are the same as at a dry cleaner. There are more than 150 wet cleaning operations across the country. Another recently developed, though not yet available, alternative to PERC is carbon dioxide (CO_2). As a gas, CO_2, which is what we exhale and use to decaffeinate coffee, is a benign and inexhaustible resource. To clean clothes, gaseous CO_2 is liquefied in a high-pressure washing machine. After washing, the CO_2 is reconverted to gas.

Greenpeace has a listing of wet cleaners in the United States and Canada on their website. **Ecomat,** a wet cleaning franchise, is opening new facilities all over the country, and they also take clothes via United Parcel Service (UPS). You can also ask around. Some dry cleaners don't wet clean themselves, but will send the clothes to another facility if you ask.

Pesticides

Many people use synthetic pesticides to kill roaches, fleas, and rodents indoors almost as a matter of course. We now use pesticides in disinfectants to kill germs,

Can I Hand Wash This Dry-Clean-Only Garment?

In 1997, *Consumer Reports* found that many dry-clean-only clothes can be safely washed by hand or machine, depending on the type of garment. Here are some of *Consumer Reports'* tips:

- Handwash plain-weave rayon in cool water, squeeze rather than wring, and lay flat to dry.

- Cool-water wash solid-colored silks by hand. Multicolored silks may bleed when washed; professional cleaning is recommended.

- Wash sweaters in cold water by hand or machine. Cashmere and cotton do best in the washing machine, inside-out. Dry sweaters flat, except cotton, which can be machine dried. Send angora to a professional cleaner.

- Send structured or lined garments to a professional cleaner.

- Extend the time between cleaning by blotting up spills right away; airing out clothes after wearing; using a clothing or lint brush; and wearing undershirts or dress shields. Crumpled clean clothes can be professionally steamed and pressed.

---

on children's heads to combat head lice, in wallpaper and paints to prevent molding, and even in sponges merely to stop odors. Some people don't even think twice when they reach for a can of roach spray to blast just one bug. As a result of our need to instantaneously obliterate offending insects, rodents, and intrusive weeds, we have contaminated our groundwater and air. In 1995, the **Environmental Working Group** found that twenty-one out of twenty-nine midwestern cities had four or more different weed killers in their tap water. DDT, now banned by numerous countries including the United States for more than twenty years, has migrated into many ecosystems and can even be found in Arctic polar bears and Mediterranean dolphins.

Pesticides used in the home are just as harmful as those used in agriculture. In 1991 and 1992, the San Francisco poison control center reported almost a thousand adverse health outcomes as a result of pesticide exposures. One-fifth of these reported cases were among children aged five or younger. And these are only the reported cases. Many poisonings go unreported because some acute symptoms, such as headaches, dizziness, or flulike symptoms, confuse diagnosis or dissipate before the cause is determined. Long-term consequences of pesticide exposures, too, are underreported. It is difficult to determine how many cases of cancer, reproductive failure, and birth defects can be attributed to pesticide exposures.

Children are very sensitive to pesticide exposures. In addition to their physical vulnerabilities, children behave in ways that increase their risk of pesticide exposure. They may accidentally ingest poisons out of ignorance and curiosity. But children also crawl on floors, carpets, and grass where pesticides tend to accumulate and lodge. Infants may take in particles by breathing or ingesting them. Some pesticides, like flea sprays, layer out close to the ground in rooms so that even though an adult may not smell the chemicals, a child crawling on the ground would inhale them.

Studies show that children living in homes where pesticides are applied suffer the consequences. A 1995 study published in the *American Journal of Public Health* found a four-fold increase in the risk of soft-tissue sarcoma in children living in homes whose yards were treated with pesticides. This study also associates the use of pest strips containing the pesticide dichlorvos with incidences of leukemia. Another study, published in the *Journal of the National Cancer Institute* in 1987, found that children exposed to pesticides in the home or garden are three to six times more likely to develop leukemia than children who were not exposed. More recently, in November 1997, *Environmental Health Perspectives* published a study finding that prenatal exposure to flea/tick products increased the risk of pediatric brain tumor, especially among children less than five years of age.

There are no safe pesticides. They are poisons, intended for killing organisms, and should be treated as such. Many pesticides have not even been adequately tested by the EPA. Others were registered when standards were less stringent and we knew less about the health and environmental impacts of these chemicals. In 1988, Congress amended existing laws to require that all pesticides be reevaluated. In 1996, Congress passed the Food Quality Protection Act, which requires all pesticides to be reevaluated to consider children's vulnerabilities when setting acceptable tolerance levels.

Least-Toxic Pest Control

The best alternative to using synthetic pesticides is Integrated Pest Management (IPM), a strategy that draws from a variety of disciplines to keep pest levels at minimum by emphasizing prevention, monitoring, and use of biological controls, such as a pest's natural enemy, or by interrupting its natural life cycle. IPM is a long-term strategy, not a quick fix. For this reason, it can be more effective than simply spraying pesticides, which only kills pests but doesn't prevent a new infestation.

Some basic IPM tips for homeowners include:

- *Prevention.* Pests are attracted by food and water, so you must eliminate these tasty treats. Fix leaky plumbing and clogged gutters and downspouts. Eliminate all standing water in your home and yard, even under houseplants. Cover pet food and water bowls (at least at night). Store food in sealed, airtight containers. Wipe up crumbs and spills. Place garbage in tightly covered containers. Rinse recyclables before placing in bins.

- *Monitoring.* Place traps (sticky paper or roach "motels") in various places around the infested area. Check daily to determine the kind of pest you are dealing with and where the pest infestations are worst. Inspect areas with the highest concentrations for cracks and holes, then seal them with caulk or silica aerogel. You needn't fill every crack in your house—only those near traps with the greatest concentration of pests.

- *Safe Management.* If an infestation has gotten out of control, you may have to come up with a plan of attack, such as least toxic pesticides. A good book to consult for solutions is *Common Sense Pest Control* by Peter Olkowski, Sheila

Daar, and Helga Olkowski. The nonprofit organization **Bio-Integral Resource Center** offers booklets about various common pests, such as ants, termites, and mice, and the safest ways of eliminating them. A number of other organizations that can provide you with information are listed in Appendix A.

There are numerous strategies employed by IPM proponents. Boric acid is a mild stomach poison that can be used in cracks that you seal (so that your child or pet will not be exposed). Diatomaceous earth (DE), chalky powder made of fossilized algae (use only food-grade DE as another type, used for swimming pool filters, is toxic!), and silica aerogel are desiccants that strip insects of their protective oils and cause them to dry up. Insect growth regulators (IGRs) usually harm only insects by inhibiting molting, so the insect cannot grow, or by interfering with reproduction. IGRs are usually placed in bait stations instead of being dispersed throughout the house. Insects enter bait stations, come into contact with the IGR and take it back to the rest of the insect colony.

Other treatments are also available, such as heat treatments for termites and use of beneficial organisms that kill only certain species, such as a fungus that kills termites and a parasitic wasp that kills cockroaches.

You can find a pest control operator who practices IPM by contacting your state pest control association. You can get their number by calling the **National Pest Control Association.**

If you have pesticides in your home or garage, place them in locked cupboards or closets high above the reach of children. Dispose of pesticides in accordance with the hazardous waste regulations in your community. Discarding them with your household garbage risks poisoning pets, wildlife, and even humans accidentally, and you'll be contributing to the pollution of landfills that contaminate groundwater and soil. If you have not used stored chemicals for a time, get rid of them. Most pesticide containers are not airtight, and gasses can escape from them.

Radon

While most of the environmental toxins discussed in this chapter are made by humans, radon gas is naturally occurring, yet quite dangerous. Radon is radioactive and is believed to cause more cases of lung cancer than anything besides smoking. In February 1998, the National Research Council (NRC) announced estimates that radon is responsible for as many as 21,800 of the 157,400 lung cancer deaths per year. Radon is a hidden threat, in part because it is odorless and colorless, but also because its presence in your home has no connection to things you might have brought into it. In addition, exposure to radon does not cause any acute symptoms, making it unlikely that it will be discovered unless a conscious effort is made. Fortunately, radon can be easily detected and steps can be taken to reduce levels if necessary. If you haven't already tested for radon, before your baby is born is a good time to do so, especially if you plan on living in the house for a long time. Early exposure to cancer-causing agents increases the risk of developing cancer.

Radon is a byproduct of the decay of uranium and radium, which occur in some soils and rocks. From soil, the gas seeps into basements through cracks in the foundation, where it can easily accumulate, especially in unventilated areas. As the gas decays, or breaks down, it releases charged particles that cling to dust and other materials. Both gasses and particles may rise to the living areas of the house. These particles produce high-energy radiation, called alpha particles, which, if inhaled, can cause damage to lung tissue and may lead to cancer. Smokers are at an even higher risk of developing lung cancer if they live in a radon-contaminated home. Nonsmokers are less likely to develop lung cancer, but still are at risk. NRC estimates that radon causes 2,100 to 2,900 lung cancer deaths among nonsmokers per year. Reduction of radon in the home to below acceptable levels established by the EPA would decrease these deaths to about 1,000 a year.

High radon levels have been found in every state and every type of house, according to *Consumer Reports,* although some areas of the country are hot spots. The EPA estimates that about 6 million homes in the United States have radon concentrations above the recommended maximum of 4 picocuries per liter of air. Levels may vary considerably from house to house in a given neighborhood and even from day to day. For example, depressurization of your basement—due to wind, exhaust fans, or duct leakage—can cause radon to be sucked in and increase indoor radon levels. How your house is built can also have an impact on radon levels. Don't assume that because your neighbor's house is radon-free after testing that yours will be, too.

Testing for Radon

Testing for radon has become quite simple. You can hire a professional or use one of two types of do-it-yourself test kits. Short-term radon test kits are available at hardware stores and by mail order from **Nontoxic Environments** for $10 to $30. A short-term test kit is a charcoal-filled canister. You open up the canister, exposing the charcoal, and place in it the lowest level of your house, since that is where the greatest concentration would be. Over the course of two to seven days, the charcoal traps the radon. After the recommended period, reseal the canister and send it to the lab.

Since radon levels tend to fluctuate, long-term radon test kits give a more accurate picture of your radon exposure over time. The procedure used for these kits is roughly the same as for short-term tests, but instead of charcoal, long-term test kits use a specially formulated plastic that is imprinted with alpha particles emitted by radon as it decays. Usually, you must set these test kits out for three months or longer to get accurate results. A list of recommended test kits is located in Appendix B.

Radon Remediation

If test results indicate that the radon level in your home is above four picocuries per liter, it's best to have radon remediation done by professionals. There are three methods of reducing radon concentrations in a home. *Dilution* is simply ventilating the house either naturally by opening the windows (not necessarily energy-efficient depending on the time of year) or mechanically by using fans to increase the exchange of indoor and outdoor air. *Sealing* requires caulking cracks and filling gaps of any kind in basement walls, floors, and crawl spaces. It is usually difficult to seal most homes completely because most are not air tight. A better solution is *diversion,* using an exhaust fan that funnels radon-contaminated air from the basement and blows it into the atmosphere. Call your local board of health or state department of health for information and the **National Safety Council Radon Hotline** about radon testing and remediation. Hire only contractors who are certified by the EPA's Radon Contractor Proficiency Program and by your state. Remember to retest after the work has been completed.

Asbestos

Asbestos is most often in the news when it is discovered in a school, apartment building, or other public structure. But asbestos can also be found in houses, particularly older ones. Though asbestos has not been widely used in building materials since the early 1970s, its extensive use as an insulator and fire retardant for much of the twentieth century means that it will remain a concern for some time to come. A house built with materials made with asbestos is not necessarily dangerous. In most cases, as long as an asbestos-containing product is intact and not disintegrating, it poses no health risks. With age, asbestos may deteriorate and become air-borne.

Asbestos comes from a group of silicate minerals that naturally separate into long, thin, durable fibers. It becomes a hazard when it breaks up into air-borne particles. If inhaled, these particles may cause asbestosis, a condition of irreversible scarring of lung tissue; lung cancer; and malignant mesothelioma, a cancer of the inner lining of the chest or abdomen. Asbestos can also cause cancer of the throat, larynx, and gastrointestinal tract. These cancers have a long latency period, from ten to fifty years. As with dust and smoke particles, harmful compounds in the air may attach to asbestos particles and lodge themselves in the lungs along with the asbestos.

The degree of health risk associated with asbestos increases with the degree of exposure. The vulnerability of children to air-borne pollutants in general makes asbestos exposure more risky for them. For this reason, determine whether your house contains any asbestos *before* your child is born. Even if you find asbestos-containing items, you may not need to do anything but monitor them. If it's necessary, any clean-up can be done before your baby comes home from the hospital.

Where Can Asbestos Be Found in Your Home?

Asbestos fibers can be spun and woven into cloth or mixed into cement and other materials for use in insulation, pipe wrapping, ceiling tiles, vinyl flooring and adhesives, beam coverings, fire-protection panels, roofing and siding shingles, fuse-box liners, drywall joint compound, texturized ceiling paint and soundproofing materials, paper or millboard near woodburning stoves, furnaces, stoves, hair dryers, ironing board covers, hot pads, and fireproof gloves. U.S. manufacturers no longer use asbestos in most consumer and building products. But older homes and appliances may contain asbestos, as might some newer imported products.

Identification and removal of asbestos is best left to professionals. If you suspect that your home may have been constructed with asbestos-containing materials, have a professional asbestos manager or laboratory assess your home. If you disturb what turns out to be asbestos, you may release small particles into the air and expose everyone in the house. You can obtain the names of laboratories accredited for asbestos testing by the EPA by contacting your state or local health department or the **National Institute for Standards and Technology Laboratory Accreditation Program.** Both visual inspections and laboratory testing may be required to determine whether any asbestos is present and the extent to which it may be airborne. If asbestos is found and it's still intact, asbestos abatement (removal or encapsulation) may not be required. Removal is generally the most expensive way to deal with an asbestos problem and poses the most risk for fiber release. It is only necessary if damage to the asbestos-containing material is extensive or you are undertaking construction on your home that would disturb asbestos material.

Be suspicious of flooring made of vinyl, rubber, or asphalt, and very old appliances. Old flooring that is in good condition is safe. But if you decide to replace suspect flooring, have a professional do it. Subflooring may also contain asbestos. Do not remove, sand, or use abrasive brushes on flooring or subflooring that might contain asbestos. Cooking or wood-burning stoves, clothes dryers, electric blankets, or hair dryers made before 1979 may contain asbestos. Contact the manufacturer to find out for sure. (Have the model number and age of the product on hand when you call.) You can also call the **EPA Asbestos Ombudsman** to obtain more information about appliances containing asbestos. Unidentifiable old appliances with heating elements should be dealt with cautiously.

If you see a gray dust accumulating under insulated pipes, from ducts, or from other construction materials in your house, be careful. Have it tested by an EPA-approved laboratory. (Wearing gloves and dust mask, very carefully scoop up some of the dust and place it a tightly sealed container, then send to the lab.) Do not vacuum or sweep up the dust—both will disperse it; instead, moisten the dust first, then clean it up with a wet mop.

You can obtain more information about asbestos and asbestos abatement from the **EPA's Toxic Substances Control Act Hotline** or your regional EPA office and your local office of the **American Lung Association.**

Moisture-Happy Molds and Microbes

Fighting mold and mildew in the bathroom can become a constant battle, especially when inadequate ventilation prevents moisture from drying rapidly. Just imagine if you had to worry about mold in the rest of your house. Most of us don't really think about it until we see or smell it. But mold and other fungi can grow just about anywhere there is moisture, hidden away in ventilation systems, behind walls, and in basements.

Molds are certainly unsightly and can be a health hazard. That distinctively unpleasant musty odor of mold comes from the gasses emitted as a byproduct of the growing mold. In addition to breathing these gasses, you and your family can inhale mold particulates and spores. Both can cause health problems such as respiratory infections, allergic reactions, irritability, and headaches. One class of fungi, called mycotoxins, has toxic effects ranging from short-term irritation to immunosuppression and cancer. Various types of mold spores can settle into a damp spot in your home, some more harmful than others. In 1993, the U.S. Centers for Disease Control and Prevention linked bleeding lung syndrome, or pulmonary hemorrhage, in ten Cleveland, Ohio, infants to a toxic mold, *Stachybotrys atra,* found in flood water left standing in homes. Eight of the ten infants died from related illness. Since then, this mold has been discovered in schools and libraries around the country, including the Tottenville Library in Staten Island, New York. In the fall of 1997, the library was closed after a black mold within its walls and ventilation systems was linked to skin rashes, heart palpitations, respiratory problems, headaches, and chronic fatigue among employees. This type of mold occurs infrequently, but you may be harboring other molds in your house that might cause fatigue, headaches, or sneezing.

Moisture can also encourage the growth of other harmful microbes, such as dust mites and bacteria. Inadequate ventilation and high humidity may increase transmission of other viral and bacterial illnesses. And moisture attracts insects, from roaches to termites.

If your home is airtight, moisture from showers, cooking, dishwashing, and doing laundry can build up. Even humans add moisture to indoor air from respiration and perspiration. But if the overall humidity level in your home is not high, you may still have problems with mold when water dampens something in your home, from wicker baskets to garbage and diaper pails. Dirty laundry, stuffed animals, fabric furnishings, carpets, and houseplants can also host mold colonies. Plumbing may leak and moisten plaster and wood in walls, ceilings, and floors, leading to mold growth inside wall cavities. Water may also seep into basements from soil because of lack of gutters or water flow towards the house.

Molds and bacteria may grow in air conditioners and humidifiers, then disperse when the machines are used, if they are not properly cleaned and maintained. Contamination of humidifiers is associated with hypersensitivity pneumonitis, a flulike respiratory illness, and humidifier fever, which is also flulike but without respiratory symptoms.

Preventing Mold Growth

Preventing mold growth is as simple as eliminating as many sources of water and condensation as possible. The tricky part is finding all of those places. Here are a few suggestions:

- Inspect plumbing for leaks. If you notice dampened ceiling or walls, you may have a leaky roof or faulty plumbing. Repair all leaks right away.

- Curled roof shingles may be a result of attic moisture, often the result of inadequate ventilation, tight insulation, and blocked vents. Unblocking vents and adding more and using attic fans can alleviate the problem.

- If your basement is damp, moisture may be seeping in from outside. You may need gutters or landscaping to rebuild your yard so that the ground slopes away from the house. (This will cause water to move away rather than toward your basement or foundation.) Open basement windows, if you have them, as often as you can to release moisture.

- Clean up dying and rotting plants that are close to your house. Mold spores could come through windows and doors from moldy plant beds.

- Use exhaust fans in bathrooms and kitchens or open a window when showering or cooking to decrease moisture, especially if you see condensation on windows. Install fans if you don't have windows in these rooms. Make sure the vents lead outdoors and not to attics. And make sure that they are working properly. Depressurization can cause exhaust fans to "backdraft" (see section on combustibles earlier in this chapter).

- Dry damp carpets as soon as possible using a portable radiant heater. Don't steam-clean dampened carpeting as it will remain damp even longer than necessary. Avoid wall-to-wall carpeting in bathrooms and kitchens.

- Keep garbage and diaper pails clean.

- Promote good air circulation and ventilation (see page 107) in your home.

- Clean regularly all appliances that come into contact with water, such as heat pumps, air conditioners, and refrigerators. Don't allow water to sit in drain or drip pans or humidifier water tanks.

- Use air conditioners to reduce moisture in hot, humid climates after you've taken the above measures. Change filters often. If you've taken all of the above steps and moisture is still a problem in your home, you might consider buying a dehumidifier, available in appliance stores and from **Nontoxic Environments.** Empty and clean frequently. **Harmony** sells a room air dryer that reduces moisture in an area up to one thousand cubic feet.

- For more information, call **EPA's Indoor Air Quality Hotline,** the **CPSC,** and the **American Lung Association** for fact sheets and pamphlets on biological pollutants such as mold.

Cleaning Up Mold

Mold may be visible, but it often grows behind walls, in and under carpets, and inside upholstered furniture. Your only clue may be the odor or allergy symptoms, such as headache, runny nose, and fatigue. To be certain that your problem is mold, you can use a mold test plate, available from **Allergy Resources.** You can also have your home tested for mold by a local laboratory or environmental consultant listed in your telephone directory.

To kill mold, you must eliminate the moisture available to it. Once it no longer has water to live on, the mold will die on its own and won't produce more spores.

A portable radiant heater will speed up the drying of walls, carpeting, and furnishings. Resist the temptation to use a hair dryer or fan; they will blow mold spores around, increasing the chance that a new colony will sprout. After you've dried up the mold, clean it up with soapy water. Even dead mold spores can cause allergic reactions in sensitive people, so be as thorough as possible. Avoid vacuuming up the mold—the spores will pass through the filters and waft back into the room—unless you have a specially equipped HEPA vacuum cleaner (see page 108), which has a more effective filter. While you don't need a fungicide if you clean up well, borax, vinegar, or hydrogen peroxide (full-strength) kill mold spores effectively. Use one of these cleaners if the mold-infested wall or carpet will remain wet for an extended period of time. This will prevent continued mold growth. Once you've cleaned up, seek out the source of moisture that fed the mold colony and eliminate it to prevent a recurrence.

Some Notes on Humidifiers

During winter months when artificial heat contributes to an already arid environment, you and your baby might feel some discomfort. Dry conditions rob our bodies of moisture, causing skin, eye, and nasal irritation. Many people use humidifiers to increase humidity in their homes. Some also use them to help relieve nasal and chest congestion. But, as mentioned above, humidifiers can harbor mold and bacteria and spew them out all over the room. So we suggest you avoid them, if you can.

Try the following before resorting to a humidifier.

- Lower the room's air temperature by a few degrees. The cooler a room, the higher its relative humidity.
- Place water in clean pans on steam radiators.
- Drink more water to keep your mucous membranes moist.
- Boil water on the stove in an uncovered pan. The steam will hydrate the room.

If, after you've tried these, you still feel a humidifier is necessary, choose one carefully—frankly, none are ideal. *Steam* humidifiers do kill microorganisms when water is boiled in the unit, but they can release minerals from tap water into the air as fine particles that settle as a powdery white dust that can irritate your lungs and even cause scarring. And it's not wise to use appliances that produce high heat around your infant. Many steam humidifiers have safety features, such as automatic shut-off when water level is low or the unit is tipped over. *Cool-spray* humidifiers avoid the problem of heat, but won't kill mold and bacteria and also release minerals. Some cool-spray humidifiers are equipped with ultraviolet light, which kills mold spores and bacteria, but these also emit minerals. *Ultrasonic-dispersal* humidifiers use high-frequency sound to break up minerals and microbes in water droplets before they are emitted. These particles are extremely fine and can be inhaled into the lungs, so it's best to avoid this type of humidifier. Don't use *evaporative* humidifiers, which work by blowing air across or through water-saturated foam or other material to cause evaporation. The foam will become a microbe factory without very careful attention.

Whatever type of humidifier you decide on, make sure that it is the right size for the room. One that has a large capacity will potentially inundate the room with moisture. Purchasing a humidifier with a *humidistat,* a device that will detect relative humidity levels and turn the humidifier off when a preset level has been reached, will eliminate the possibility of increasing moisture to mold-sustaining levels. You can also monitor humidity levels with a hygrometer, available in hardware stores and Radio Shack. The **Consumer Product Safety Commission (CPSC)** suggests maintaining the relative humidity between 30 and 50 percent, as levels above 60 percent increase the likelihood of mold growth.

CPSC recommends using distilled or demineralized water in humidifiers to reduce scale buildup (which can harbor bacteria) and the release of minerals from the humidifier. Clean humidifiers, using a brush to scrub off mineral deposits, at least as often as the manufacturer suggests or more. Change water daily, and do not allow water to sit in the tank for more than a few hours.

Good Ventilation

There's only so much you can do to prevent pollutants from entering your home. Many of the measures we have mentioned thus far will go a long way to improve the indoor air quality of your home. But pollutants will still enter your home, from your mother-in-law's perfume to wisps of wood smoke from a neighbor's chimney. In spring, you'll have pollen tracked and blown into your house. In winter, dust will accumulate. And each person in your house will add his or her burden of moisture to the air.

A house that breathes alleviates this burden by circulating indoor and outdoor air. Good circulation, achieved through proper ventilation, prevents pollutant buildup by diluting the air. Imagine a glass filled halfway with water. Now, picture it with a few drops of red food coloring added. The water would be a pinkish red color. If you gradually add more water, though, the water becomes less red, more pink. Pouring water in so the water overflows will cause the pink water to gradually become clear. Pollen, dust, VOCs, and particulates in the air are like that red food coloring, except you can't see them. Adding air to the mix reduces the concentration.

As we've discussed, exhaust fans in the bathroom and kitchen push pollutants out and reduce moisture. You can also open windows to increase air flow. Won't that let bad air in? Yes and no. You will get seepage of outdoor air pollutants, and on days when air quality is low—when pollen and mold counts or ozone and smog levels are high—it's wise to keep windows and doors closed. But on clean, clear days, opening the windows, at least a crack, will be helpful. There's no hard and fast rule. Just use common sense. Too many days without adequate ventilation will mean pollutant build up. Watch weather reports on the morning or evening news for information on ozone, pollen, and mold levels to determine when to keep your house closed up.

Also keep in mind that cross-ventilation improves circulation. Opening more than one window allows air to exit through one with replacement from another.

When you use exhaust fans, opening a window a crack also helps circulate air. As dirty air is forced out, fresh air will be sucked in through the window to fill the gap.

Other means of ventilating homes include vents, strategically placed holes, heat-recovery ventilation systems, and whole house fans. To learn more about these, see *The Healthy House* and *Understanding Ventilation* by John Bower of **The Healthy House Institute.**

Devices to Improve Air Quality: Air Filters, HEPA Vacuum Cleaners, and Air Conditioners

After you've followed many of the recommendations we've already listed, you may still feel that your house could be more pollutant-free. In fact, there are a few more things you can do to reduce biological and chemical particles, including use of efficient air filters, vacuums, and electric air purifiers.

Vacuuming Up Pollutants

One of the most effective ways to get rid of accumulated dust and other particles is to thoroughly vacuum it up. Carpets, drapes, and upholstery—places where dust mites thrive and other particles cling—benefit from frequent cleanings. A vacuum cleaner is an effective way to pull these particles out from deep within the fabric. So try to vacuum well twice a week.

But you have to be careful. Standard vacuum cleaners backdraft—that is, they push particles right back out through their exhaust. In 1995, *Consumer Reports* found that canister-style cleaners spew out more dust than uprights. **Eureka,** Hoover, **Nilfisk, Euroclean,** and **Miele** now manufacture vacuum cleaners outfitted with HEPA and ULPA filters, which are very effective for capturing even minute particles (see below). This option may add $100 or more to the cost of the vacuum cleaner. HEPA and ULPA vacuum cleaners are sold by **N.E.E.D.S., Nontoxic Environments, For Your Health Products, Absolute Environmental's Allergy Products Store,** and retail stores specializing in supplies for allergy sufferers. Patty Arlotta, the mother of a child with allergies and asthma, bought a Hoover "Wind Tunnel" for $200. "I waited until it was on sale, plus I had a coupon. It's normally $300," she says.

While you can't use a HEPA or ULPA filter on vacuum cleaners that are not made for them, there are vacuum cleaner bags for standard machines that trap and retain small particles better than standard bags. You can obtain these at some vacuum cleaner outlets or through the mail from **Priorities, Nontoxic Hotline, Absolute Environmental's Allergy Products Store** and **Allergy Control Products.**

Air Filtration

Air filters work by capturing particles and gasses in some type of material before they can enter a room. Your home probably already has a few filters—in the furnace, air conditioners, ducts, and in your vacuum cleaner. Replace these frequently as they get dirty and clogged. You can also substitute more efficient filters for the old ones to improve filtration. And you can install them in places that usually don't have filters, like window screens and fans, and heating/cooling vents.

Filters can be used on ventilation systems to block pollutants in outdoor air before they enter the house. This only works in tightly constructed houses, though. Many homes, especially older ones, have air coming into the house from many places besides the ventilation system. An alternative is to filter indoor air through forced-air heating and cooling systems. Indoor air is pulled through the system and a filter, then forced back into living spaces. While outdoor air may enter the house, it will eventually get filtered as air moves through the forced-air system. Filtration is optimal if air-handling fans continuously operate.

Portable electric air purifiers, quite popular these days, have some advantages and some drawbacks. Prior to purchasing one of these devices, take as many steps as possible to reduce the entry of dust, pollen, mold, VOCs, and particulates into your house. Electric purifiers will not remove all pollutants and are much more effective contending with minor pollution. Preventing indoor air pollution in the first place will be more effective in the long run. If you've taken steps to keep your home pollutant-free, but feel that particles and gasses continue to find a way into your house, then a portable filter may help. It is important to select the right type of machine for your purposes (see below).

FILTERS FOR HOUSEHOLD APPLIANCES AND PORTABLE AIR PURIFIERS
Various types of filters are on the market. Some only block gasses, while others only eliminate particles. You can buy combination filters, for some purposes, that will do both. Filters that effectively block tiny particles, such as HEPA and ULPA filters, restrict airflow. This may mean having more powerful fans, in some cases, to push air through them. The following are some of the most frequently used filters.

Activated charcoal filters, for forced-air furnaces, air conditioners, and portable air purifiers, absorb gasses, such as some VOCs. They won't remove formaldehyde and other low-weight gasses, but there are specially treated charcoal filters that will. *Activated alumina filters* will also absorb low-weight gasses, including formaldehyde. You can obtain these filters from the **E.L. Foust Company.**

Medium efficiency particulate filters, used in ducts, furnaces, and air conditioners, capture 25 to 45 percent of the particles in the filtered air. This means that they will block pollen and mold spores, but tiny particles may escape them. The thicker the filter, the greater the probability that it will capture tiny particles. But thick filters may block airflow, which could damage machines. So make sure your furnace and air conditioner can handle them. They are available through **General Filters, Inc.** and **Research Products Corp.**

Electrostatic filters, usually made of vinyl, polyester, or polystyrene, rely on static electricity to attract particles to them. They filter only larger pollens, mold spores, and particles. Electrostatic filters also need to be changed often, about every month or so. They are useful in appliances that cannot be fitted with higher-efficiency filters, such as standard vacuum cleaners and window air conditioners.

3M's Filtrete filters can be cut to fit. You can order them directly from **3M** or **Priorities.**

High Efficiency Particulate Arresting (HEPA) filters are the most efficient filters available, for use in everything from specially equipped vacuum cleaners and filtration machines to central heating ducts. Made of fiberglass or polyester, a HEPA filter's tiny pores catch nearly everything—about 95 percent of what's in the air, including particles as small as 0.3 microns (a micron is one-millionth of a meter). Because of its ability to capture so much, a HEPA filter requires a powerful fan to push air through it. This means that some devices, such as vacuum cleaners, must be equipped to use them (see section on vacuum cleaners). Installed improperly, a HEPA filter used in appliances not designed for them may cause some damage. HEPA filters are also more expensive than other filters but last for a few years.

ULPA filters, used in Nilfisk vacuum cleaners, are similar to HEPA filters; they catch even smaller particles—as small as 0.12 micron.

You don't necessarily need a HEPA filter for every air conditioner, duct, and furnace in your home, especially if you've attempted to improve indoor air quality by eliminating sources of pollution. Instead, you may want to use a combination of filters. For example, medium efficiency particulate and activated charcoal/alumina filters could be installed in ducts, furnaces, and forced-air heating and cooling systems to catch gasses, pollen, mold spores, dust, and other larger particles. HEPA filters used in vacuum cleaners and portable air purifiers would clean up any remaining small particles.

You can purchase air filters for a variety of purposes from the companies listed above and from **Nontoxic Environments, N.E.E.D.S., Nontoxic Hotline, E.C.O., Absolute Environmental's Allergy Products Store, Allergy Control Products,** and **Priorities.**

SELECTING AND USING A PORTABLE ELECTRIC AIR PURIFIER

While portable air cleaners are not absolutely necessary, they can improve indoor air quality if they are used in conjunction with other measures. The best performing machines are the room-size type. Desktop or tabletop models don't work as well, according to *Consumer Reports*. Larger air purifiers pull more air through them at a faster rate than do smaller ones, thus cleaning more efficiently. Desktop or personal air purifiers are really too small to be of value.

Not all machines are equipped to eliminate gasses *and* particles. Look for a purifier that has a combination of filters that will handle both. Don't assume it will remove formaldehyde and other VOCs. Ask the salesperson.

We don't recommend ozone machines and negative-ion generators (which also produce ozone). At high concentrations, ozone attacks gas molecules, but does nothing to eliminate dust and other particles. Negative-ion generators spew out electrons that attach themselves to particles in the air and give them a negative charge. The negatively charged particles then cling to walls and furnishings. Salespeople will sometimes claim that you can simply clean the walls to remove pollutants, but this method of air purification is hardly efficient. And if the particles lose their negative charge before you've wiped them up, they'll just re-enter the air. The greater problem, though, is that ozone is a lung irritant. Asthmatics and children may feel discomfort and may possibly experience some respiratory problems while these machines are in operation.

Portable air purifiers work best when they are operated continuously. While using them, close the door to prevent contamination from other rooms. Also, if you have central heating or cooling, seal off the heating and cooling vents where the machine is operating to prevent entry of polluted air and escape of clean air. This may require installing a window air conditioner in the room for cooling in summer and a heater that is independent of the central system. If you want to purify several rooms, it may be more practical to install a central air filtration system. For more information about air purifiers, read the EPA booklet "Residential Air-Cleaning Devices: A Summary of Available Information" available by calling the **Indoor Air Quality Hotline.**

Air Conditioners

During the summer months, unbearable heat waves and high humidity prompt many of us to turn on air conditioners. Air conditioners have the added benefit of reducing relative humidity levels, which helps keep mold and dust mites in check. And since windows are kept closed, use of an air conditioner means less pollen entering your home. Use of fans, while more energy-efficient, can be problematic for asthma and allergy sufferers because they make pollutants airborne and pull unfiltered outdoor air inside (though you can buy fans with filters from **Priorities** and **Harmony**).

Central air conditioners can be fitted with HEPA filtration systems designed by **Allermed Corporation** and **Pure Air Systems.** Window air conditioners generally cannot be fitted with HEPA filters, but you can use electrostatic filters, such as **3M**'s Filtrete, for improved filtration.

To find the most energy-efficient air conditioners, consult *Consumer Reports'* annual buying guide and *Consumer Guide to Home Energy Savings* by Alex Wilson. Note that, in general, the higher the energy-efficiency or SEER (Seasonal Energy Efficiency Rating) of the air conditioner, the less effective it is at reducing relative humidity. To compensate, Rick Heede, a researcher at the Rocky Mountain Institute and author of *Homemade Money: How to Save Energy and Dollars in Your Home,* suggests lowering the air conditioner's fan speed on humid days to keep coils cool and, if your air conditioner has a recirculation setting, use it. Both of these books also offer tips on how to decrease your energy usage.

Electromagnetic Fields

There is no doubt that we all benefit from electricity. Without it, we wouldn't enjoy the many modern conveniences, such as refrigerators, answering machines, lamps, washers, and dryers, that make our lives easier, more efficient, and safer. Some people worry, though, that the amount of electricity surrounding us today may actually harm us, because of its creation of electromagnetic fields (EMFs).

All devices through which an electrical current runs, including household appliances, power lines, and electrical wiring, produce invisible lines of force called electric and magnetic fields. Whether or not they harm us is an issue of some controversy. Some studies suggest that a link exists between exposure to EMFs and some childhood cancers, such as leukemia and brain cancer. But other studies have found no connection. High incidences of cancers in some neighborhoods close to electric power facilities have raised some alarm. Some researchers say it is difficult to determine whether EMFs caused the cancers, though. It's possible that a combination of environmental factors are to blame. In June 1998, a thirty-member international panel convened by NIEHS voted in favor of categorizing low frequency EMFs as possible carcinogens based on epidemiological studies. They did not find the risks to be high, but believe that EMFs should be considered a public health concern. Researchers continue to study them in hopes of discovering how EMFs might cause cancer.

What is known about EMFs is that alternating current (AC) fields create weak electrical currents in the bodies of humans and animals. Strong EMFs, such as those under large transmission lines, can cause the hair on your head and arms to vibrate. The frequency, or intensity, of such a current is actually weaker than the electrical activity of our own hearts and brains and too frail, in general, to penetrate cell membranes. Some scientists believe that, even so, cell chemistry may be affected by these electrical signals.

While scientists continue to study the impact of EMFs on humans, the best course for parents to take is one of prudence. The following are some simple precautions, what the **National Institute of Environmental Health Science (NIEHS)** calls prudent avoidance, to take.

- Reduce exposure times by unplugging appliances that aren't in use, such as computers, lights, televisions, radios, and VCRs. Many electrical devices continue to conduct electricity even when switched off. You'll save energy as well.

- Maintain a safe distance from appliances in operation. The intensity of EMFs dissipates with distance, so the farther your baby is from an appliance or electrical line, the better. The NIEHS's booklet, "Questions and Answers About Electric and Magnetic Fields Associated with the Use of Electric Power," provides a listing of field measurements of various appliances at different distances.

- Minimize the number of electrical appliances in use in your baby's sleeping area.

- If you want to use a baby monitor in your baby's nursery, purchase one with a high sensitivity level so that you can place it as far away from the baby as possible.

- When deciding where to place your baby's crib (as well as your own bed), consider what might be on the other side of the wall. EMFs can penetrate walls. If there are electrical devices, such as computers or a refrigerator, on the other side, relocate the crib or bed.

- Avoid using electric blankets.

- Limit the time your toddler spends in front of computers. New "lapware," or computers and software designed for children from eighteen months to three years old, may be touted as developmental and educational tools, but they may cause more harm than good. Sitting an infant down in front of a computer screen exposes the baby to EMFs and may cause vision problems in developing eyes. Some experts worry that computer programs are overstimulating to infants. Dr. David Elkind, a noted child psychologist, told the *Wall Street Journal* in March 1998 that the bright, fast-moving images on computer and television screens are a likely culprit in the rise of attention disorders in children. Besides, according to Dr. Robert C. Calfee, a professor of education at Stanford University, there is no research showing benefits to infants and toddlers using computers.

Contact **NIEHS** and the **EMF Clearinghouse** for more information on EMFs.

Gardens and Lawns

Ideally, during warm weather, you and your baby will spend time outdoors. You'll want to introduce her to the delights of nature and its cycles, the smell of spring blossoms, and the chirps of crickets and songbirds. But as much as the great outdoors offers a curious infant, the way we treat our lawns and gardens make them treacherous places for children. If you're like most Americans, you'll have dumped chemical fertilizers, herbicides, and insecticides on your grass to maintain a manicured carpet of green. About 67 million pounds of pesticides are dumped on American lawns every year. One-fifth of the total volume of pesticides applied to lawns and gardens are considered potential human carcinogens by the EPA.

Pesticides used outdoors, on agricultural crops, golf courses, parks, and residential lawns, are having a tremendous impact on the environment. Populations of wild bees, which can pollinate just about anything, are on the decline. Some wildland habitats have lost up to 70 percent of their wild honey bees. The songs of birds on spring mornings are also disappearing. Pesticides like chlorpyrifos, the active ingredient in Dursban, have been implicated in large bird kills. Golf courses and sod farms were largely responsible. Now, the use of this insecticide is banned on these commercial grounds, but we are still allowed to use them at home. As much as half of the ground- and well-water in the United States is at risk of being contaminated by farm pesticides.

Even use of pesticides exclusively outdoors does not guarantee that the indoor environment will not be affected. A study in *Environmental Science and Technology* found that residues of popular lawn herbicides, such as 2,4-D and dicamba, may be tracked into homes and left on carpets or in household dust. Pesticides can persist longer indoors than outdoors because they are protected from degradation by sun, rain, and microbes. There isn't even a compelling reason to use chemicals to make your lawn a lush green carpet; regular use of synthetic fertilizers and pesticides makes your lawn chemically dependent and more susceptible to disease, drought, and insects. Chemical fertilizers kill soil organisms and promote shallow root development.

Integrated Pest Management, discussed earlier in this chapter, can also be used to manage pests in your lawn and garden. Promoting a healthy lawn is the best preventative measure; healthy grasses naturally crowd out weeds and resist disease. So, plant varieties of grass that are known to grow well in your region. Fertilize twice a year with organic fertilizer. Aerate your lawn. Don't mow low; instead mow frequently. Water deeply and in the morning to prevent growth of fungi. Consider alternatives to grass for landscaping that provide habitats for birds, butterflies, and beneficial insects (which will keep destructive insects at bay), such as wild meadows, native groundcovers, trees, and gardens. Two good books to consult are *Redesigning the American Lawn: A Search for Environmental Harmony,* by F. Herbert Bormann, Diana Balmori, and Gordon T. Geballe, and *The Chemical-Free Lawn* from Rodale Press.

Eliminate pesticides in the garden by practicing organic gardening. Ladybugs and lacewings can be released to control destructive caterpillars and beetles. Insecticidal soaps and oils are some least-toxic insecticides. Weed by hand and learn to accept a few weeds in your garden. **Rodale Press** publishes a number of excellent books and the magazine, *Organic Gardening,* that discuss alternatives to pesticide use in the garden. The **Brooklyn Botanic Garden** also publishes good gardening guides with least-toxic alternatives for pest control.

chapter six

Caring *for* Yourself During Pregnancy

Pregnancy brings on hormonal changes that can cause mood shifts and those legendary midnight cravings. You'll also experience other physical changes, meant to nourish and protect your baby during nine months of growth. But while in your womb, your baby will still be vulnerable to some substances that you unintentionally eat, drink, or inhale. "The placenta protects against lots of things, but by no means everything," says Dr. Landrigan. Some of the toxins that may pass through the placenta and affect your baby include PCBs and mercury, found in fish from polluted waters; pesticides in food, soil, air, and water; particles and chemicals found in smoke; some drugs; lead; and volatile organic compounds (VOCs) from plastics, paint, carpets, furnishings, and glues.

The levels of these contaminants in your body may be low enough to do *you* no harm, but even small amounts can pose significant risk to your growing baby. This is a crucial period of child development. While in the womb, a fetus goes through incredibly rapid cellular changes involving thousands of cells, particularly in the central nervous system. As a result, your baby is very susceptible to any interference. "If [exposure] happens during fetal development, certain critical steps may not take place," says Mothers & Others medical advisor Dr. Philip Landrigan. Chemical exposures can damage growing cells, increasing risks of cancer later in life, and may cause "miscommunication" between cells in different parts of your baby's body as he grows. This may result in birth defects, reproductive disorders, intellectual deficits, and behavioral problems.

This chapter will focus on how you can best protect your developing baby from exposure to toxic chemicals while you are pregnant. As we've already mentioned in earlier chapters, if you're pregnant you need to be especially careful to avoid exposure to lead, mercury, and other heavy metals; cigarette smoke; X rays; and VOCs, PCBs, and pesticides. Because so many conventional home decorating products, from paints and finishes to carpeting and furniture, emit VOCs, it's best to avoid painting, sanding and renovating during pregnancy. You should also watch out for food and water that may be contaminated by bacteria and other toxins. The sections in this chapter focus specifically on:

- How Environmental Toxins Affect the Developing Fetus
- A Healthy Diet
- Avoiding Alcohol
- Checking Your Drinking Water
- Checklist of Other Environmental Toxins

How Environmental Toxins Affect the Developing Fetus

Of the 3 million babies born in the United States every year, about 250,000 are born with birth defects, according to Drs. Philip Landrigan and Herbert Needleman, authors of *Raising Children Toxic Free.* They point out that, in as many as 60 percent of such cases, the cause of the birth defect is unknown. Genetic factors and inherited mutations account for only 5 percent of the known reasons for birth defects, while infections, such as rubella (German measles) and toxoplasmosis, trauma, radiation, and other physical factors, make up 35 percent.

Could the unknown causes be related to environmental pollution? Evidence increasingly indicates that this may be true. Reproductive and other mutations in wildlife may be the result of hormonelike chemicals, such as DDT and dioxin, in the environment. In their book *Our Stolen Future,* Theo Colborn, Diane Dumanoski, and John Peterson Myers provide examples of such damage, including sterility in Florida's bald eagles, abnormally small penises in alligators, and reproductive failure in minks fed PCB-contaminated fish from the Great Lakes. British researchers at Brunel University have linked estrogenic chemicals used as surfactants in detergents in English and Irish rivers to "feminization" of the male roach, a common British freshwater fish. Observers in many states have reported sightings of frogs with severe malformations of limbs, tails, eyes, and sex organs, and in many parts of the world frogs and amphibians are disappearing altogether.

Environmental toxins can harm human babies, as well. Even before the child is conceived, parental exposures to chemicals and radiation may damage eggs or sperm, leading to genetic damage that may result in hampered childhood development. For example, a 1989 study published in *Cancer Research* showed an increased risk of leukemia for children of people exposed to pesticides at their workplace prior to conception. Women's prenatal exposure to lead six months prior to conceiving may be associated with low birth weight of their babies, according to a 1996 study in the *American Journal of Industrial Medicine.* While a 1996 study in the *Journal of Epidemiology* found that children of Japanese exposed to radiation from atomic bomb blasts in Hiroshima and Nagasaki do not show an increased genetic predisposition for cancer, a 1997 study of male mice in *Radiation Research* revealed that small doses of radiation, such as those used for cancer therapy, caused the mice to pass on detrimental effects to their children, grandchildren, and great-grandchildren. Offspring of irradiated mice suffered from a growth disadvantage and reduction of sperm fertility due to DNA damage. For humans, even low levels of radiation, such as those from X rays, may affect birth weight and fetal growth. A study published in the *American Journal of Epidemiology* in March 1997 shows a downward trend in birth weight and fetal growth in babies of fathers who received diagnostic X rays prior to conception.

After conception, as the embryo develops, transplacental exposures to PCBs, lead, mercury, cigarette smoke, X rays, and drugs can impact reproductive, intellectual, and behavioral development and increase risks for cancers, respiratory illnesses, and birth defects. These will be discussed below.

How Toxins Cross the Placenta

The placenta is a porous barrier that filters out some substances while allowing others, such as nutrients, to reach the growing fetus. Chemicals and heavy metals may find their way into the blood stream after you eat, touch, or inhale them. From there, they are transported to the placenta. Not all of these substances can enter the womb through the placenta; it depends on their molecular size. Many drug molecules, for example, are too large to pass through placenta and have no effect on fetal development, while others, such as the synthetic hormone diethylstilbestrol (DES), thalidomide, Dilantin, tranquilizers, and amphetamines, do reach babies in the womb and may profoundly impact development of the fetus. Molecules of lead, mercury, and other heavy metals are also small enough to pass through the placenta to the fetus. Some chemicals, such as PCBs, accumulate in our body fat but may re-enter the blood stream to be carried to the womb during pregnancy. These substances may also enter breast milk (see chapter 8).

Radiation from X rays, radon, and nuclear accidents or leaks doesn't cross the placenta as a molecule in your blood or fat. But the charged particles or rays can reach the fetus; neither your body nor the placenta will block them. This is why experts recommend that you avoid X-rays and other exposures as much as possible during pregnancy.

PCBs AND DIOXIN

PCBs and dioxin are related organochlorine chemicals that are carcinogenic and hormone-disrupting. PCBs, once used as electrical insulators, are also neurotoxic. Both PCBs and dioxin are persistent in the environment and accumulate in animal fats. There is strong evidence that prenatal exposure to PCBs results in adverse health effects. The authors of *Our Stolen Future* recount how Taiwanese women who had consumed cooking oil contaminated with PCBs in 1979 later gave birth to children with birth defects, developmental delays, intelligence deficits, and increased behavioral problems. A study published in the *Archives of Environmental Health* found that these children also suffered from a higher incidence of middle-ear disease than unexposed children. American scientists discovered in the 1980s that women who consumed PCB-contaminated fish from the Great Lakes were more likely to give birth to babies of lower weight and smaller head circumference than normal. Long-term studies show that these children also suffer from neurological impairment resulting in lower I.Q. scores, memory problems, delayed speech development, and abnormal reflexes, according to the authors of *Our Stolen Future*. A team of scientists in Oswego, New York, on the shores of Lake Ontario, announced in May 1995 that their long-term studies revealed that babies of women who had consumed the equivalent of only 40 pounds of locally caught salmon during their lifetimes had more abnormal reflexes and other cognitive developmental abnormalities than babies of women who had not been exposed to PCBs through fish consumption.

Dioxin, formed through the manufacture and incineration of chlorine-based products like PVC plastic, is now ubiquitous in the environment. Animal studies show that dioxin inhibits testosterone, resulting in smaller penises, lowered sperm production, and altered sexual behavior in male rats, according to Lois Marie Gibbs, author of *Dying from Dioxin*. Dioxin also causes birth defects, such as reproductive and heart defects and learning deficits, in rat offspring. High levels of exposure to humans, such as occurred at Love Canal during the 1970s, is associated with high rates of birth defects, writes Gibbs. A study of 402 births in Times Beach, Missouri, where dioxin-contaminated oil was spread to control dust in 1972 and 1973, published in the *American Journal of Epidemiology,* found higher incidences of miscarriage among exposed women and low birth weight and birth defects in their children. Other studies suggest that prenatal exposure can cause behavioral, learning, and memory problems. Both PCBs and dioxin exposure during prenatal development may disrupt the normal action of thyroid hormone, which plays an essential role in brain growth and behavioral and intellectual development.

The Environmental Protection Agency (EPA) found that eating animal fats—in meat, fish, and dairy products—is the predominant human exposure route of dioxin.

LEAD AND MERCURY

Exposure to lead prior to and during pregnancy can have a significant impact on your baby's development. Lead flows directly through the placenta, so that contamination levels of mother and baby are usually nearly identical. But lead levels that would have no impact on an adult can severely hurt the fetus. And, even at low levels, prenatal lead exposure can cause premature birth, low birth weights, neurological damage, miscarriages, and stillbirths.

During pregnancy, if you don't get enough calcium from the foods you eat and from supplements, your body may release it into your blood, along with "stored" lead, from your bones. A study published in November 1997 in *Pediatrics* found that lead released from the mother's bones during pregnancy results in a baby of lower birth weight. To avoid this, it is important that you eat plenty of foods rich in calcium, including low-fat dairy products. If you decide to take calcium supplements, choose carefully. Some calcium supplements may have high levels of lead, especially those made from refined ground oyster shells, bone meal, or dolomite. Some manufacturers have pledged to manufacture calcium products with less than 0.5 microgram of lead per dose. These brands include CVS, Rite Aid, Walgreens, Wal-Mart, and Your Life. The **Natural Resources Defense Council (NRDC)** is a good source of information on this subject.

Mercury, like lead, is a heavy metal that affects the central nervous system. At low levels, mercury can cause neurological damage during prenatal development, which can result in impairment of speech, hearing, movement, and vision and deficits in learning, attention, and motor skills. Fetuses and children are four to five times more susceptible to mercury poisoning than adults. Metallic mercury, the kind found in thermometers, is also used in dental amalgam, or "silver" fillings. Mercury in this form is poorly absorbed through the skin, but it can be inhaled if it vaporizes. When you are pregnant, avoid having your teeth filled with dental amalgam and removing old fillings to prevent exposure. If you must have a cavity filled while you are pregnant, ask your dentist to use plastic composite, gold, or porcelain inlays instead of amalgam.

If you break a thermometer, do not vacuum it up as this will send mercury droplets and vapors throughout your home. And don't allow the mercury to sit exposed for any length of time, as it may evaporate and disperse. Instead, put on a pair of rubber gloves (if you're pregnant, ask someone else to do the clean up) and carefully wipe up the spilled mercury with a damp paper towel or adhesive tape, scoop it up with a piece of paper, or use an eye dropper to suck it up. (When you buy a thermometer, remember to also purchase an eyedropper from your pharmacist; keep them together in your first aid kit.) Place the entire paper or eye dropper in an airtight container, such as a jar with a screw top, a plastic container with a snap-tight lid, or a zippable plastic bag. Take the container to your hazardous waste dropoff site. To avoid this entire problem, you might consider buying a digital thermometer. Though it's a few more dollars, it doesn't have any mercury.

Some bacteria convert metallic mercury into a more readily absorbed form, called methylmercury, which is found in many lakes in the United States. In December 1997, the **Environmental Working Group (EWG)** released a report, *Catching the Limit,* stating that poor regulation of waste incineration and coal combustion, the primary sources of mercury pollution, has caused severe contamination of U.S. waterways and fish. The number of fish consumption advisories for mercury doubled between 1993 and 1996, and now the fish in some 1,600 bodies of water are too contaminated to eat. The EPA estimated that in 1996, 1.6 million pregnant women, children, and women of child-bearing age were exposed to unsafe levels of mercury from fish. *Neurotoxicology and Teratology* in 1997 published a study of 900 seven-year-old children in the Faroe Islands whose mothers consumed whale meat contaminated with methylmercury before and during pregnancy. The children had problems with attention span, memory, language, and other brain functions. But another long-term study of 700 children in the Seychelles found no connection between prenatal exposures due to their mothers' fish consumption and developmental problems. Until more research is conducted, pregnant women should avoid fish caught in contaminated waters by heeding fish advisories. **EWG** and the **EPA** have fish advisories on their websites for each of the thirty-seven states that issue fish advisories. If you don't have Internet access, call your state department of environmental protection for information. Even when eating fish deemed safe, it's best for you to keep fish consumption low while pregnant or breast-feeding (see "A Healthy Diet" later in this chapter).

RADIATION

Even the smallest dose of radiation can cause mutations in DNA, increasing the risk for cancer, according to Dr. Landrigan. And there is a direct correlation between the size of the dose and the likelihood of cancer. So it's particularly important to reduce exposure to all sources of radiation while you're pregnant by avoiding diagnostic X rays, including those done at the dentist's office. Studies show that even low doses of radiation through X-ray exposures, particularly during the last trimester of pregnancy, increase a child's risk for leukemia. Ultrasound is a safe alternative. Some conditions may require X rays for a complete diagnosis; discuss your concerns with your doctor. If you are seeing a specialist for a condition, be sure that person is in touch with your obstetrician or midwife.

Electromagnetic fields (EMFs) from electrical wires and appliances, and radon, a naturally occurring radioactive material, should also be avoided. While there is no conclusive information about the effects of EMF exposure, the **National Institute of Environmental Health Sciences** suggests prudent avoidance. See chapter 5 for more information.

PESTICIDES

A review article in the October 1997 issue of *Environmental Health Perspectives* documents that numerous studies have demonstrated that using pesticides in the home and garden during pregnancy or after delivery was associated with an increased risk of brain cancer and leukemia in children. Pesticides used at the parents' workplaces, too, may be a factor in the rise of these cancers, as these chemicals may be brought home on clothing and shoes. Pesticides can also affect a child's sexual and reproductive development. Some scientists hypothesize that hormone-disrupting pesticides and other chemicals are lowering sperm counts. A study published in the April 1998 *Journal of the American Medical Association* suggested that a decline in male births may be related to prenatal pesticide exposure.

Organochlorine pesticides, such as DDT (dichlorodiphenyltrichloroethane), persist in the environment and in animal fats. As a result, though it was banned in the United States, in 1972, researchers still find DDT and its byproduct, DDE, in human breast milk. DDT has been linked to birth defects in wildlife and animal studies. A 1997 study of 600 children whose mothers were exposed to DDT during pregnancy found that girls with the largest prenatal exposure entered puberty eleven months earlier than those with the least exposure. Organophosphate and carbamate pesticides, such as chlorpyrifos (Dursban), diazinon (Spectracide), malathion, and carbaryl (Sevin) are used widely on farms, lawns and gardens, golf courses, and schools, and by municipalities to combat mosquitoes. These pesticides can affect the cental nervous system. Your baby is undergoing a critical period of brain development while he's in the womb.

Avoid using pesticides in your home, and try to persuade your neighbors and employer to stop using them. You can get information about pesticides and less toxic alternatives from **National Coalition Against the Misuse of Pesticides, Northwest Coalition for Alternatives to Pesticides, Bio-Integral Resource Center,** and the **National Pesticide Telecommunications Network** (an EPA hotline). If you can't convince them, ask to be notified before a pesticide application is to take place so that you can stay away for a day or two.

CIGARETTE SMOKE

As we pointed out in chapter 5, cigarette smoke contains thousands of chemicals, many of them carcinogens, including polyclomatic aromatic hydrocarbons (PAHs), and solvents such as benzene, which are also found in emissions from combustion appliances. Children of mothers who smoke during pregnancy suffer from reduced lung function; respiratory illnesses such as bronchitis and pneumonia; and behavioral problems. And babies of smokers are at greater risk for Sudden Infant Death Syndrome (SIDS). In a 1996 study published in the *Journal of Toxicology and Environmental Health,* researchers at the University of Louisville School of Medicine in Kentucky found that the amount of tobacco-related 4-aminobiphenyl, a carcinogen, in the blood of a newborn of a mother who smokes is directly proportional to the number of cigarettes she smoked, although the concentration in the baby's blood is less than that of the mother's.

These medical researchers also found strong evidence that women who are exposed to second-hand smoke for six hours a day pass some carcinogens to the blood of the fetus. Studies of two-week-old babies born to women exposed to second-hand smoke show increased incidence of decreased lung function. Some scientists believe that the effects of second-hand smoke on fetal development may be similar to those for children of women who smoke while pregnant.

DRUGS AND SUPPLEMENTS

Drugs might also play a role in some unexplained birth defects. For example, diethylstilbestrol (DES) was once prescribed to prevent miscarriages, but has proven to cause reproductive defects and cancers in daughters and sons of women who took it. Researchers are now looking into the possibility that DES exposure may affect even third- and fourth-generation offspring. Other drugs, such as cocaine, damage the nervous systems of babies of addicted mothers, resulting in withdrawal symptoms, such as twitching and irritability, and long-term learning deficits and behavioral problems.

Even over-the-counter drugs can have harmful effects on developing babies. So before you take *any* medication, whether it's prescription or over-the-counter, ask your doctor if it is safe for both you and the baby. While you are pregnant, try to take medication only when absolutely necessary. Drugs are synthetic chemicals, after all, so it's best to keep your exposure levels down.

Be careful with herbal supplements, too. Since many herbal supplements have not been extensively researched, especially in terms of their effects on the fetus, it's best to avoid them during pregnancy. Some herbs, such as chaste berry, can produce hormonal effects, according to Dr. Adriane Fugh-Berman, chairperson of the National Women's Health Network.

While vitamin and mineral supplements are generally fine to take during pregnancy, talk with your doctor about the type and dosage of supplements before you start taking them. In some cases, high doses may be harmful to your baby. For example, more than 10,000 IU of Vitamin A can cause birth defects. As mentioned earlier in this chapter, some calcium supplements may contain lead.

While the number of environmental pollutants that can affect fetal development can seem daunting, taking steps to reduce your exposure will have a positive impact on your baby's healthy development. Since we've covered ways to reduce exposures in your home in earlier chapters, the rest of this chapter will discuss how to reduce consumption of contaminated water, food, and other products.

A Healthy Diet

Your doctor—and even your mother and friends—have probably discussed dietary changes that you should observe while you're pregnant. Don't drink anything with caffeine, such as coffee. Avoid alcoholic beverages to protect the baby. Eat foods high in calcium and folic acid and take vitamin supplements to give the baby and yourself plenty of nourishment. The list may seem endless, especially when you add yet another suggestion, avoiding foods that may be contaminated with chemicals. Fortunately, the healthiest foods—fresh, minimally processed, locally grown, and organic foods—are less likely to contain chemical residues. If you try to avoid junk food, and eat lots of fresh fruits and vegetables as well as grains and legumes, especially those that are organic, you shouldn't have too much trouble. But, if you're like many Americans, you probably eat out a lot and consume a diet that isn't exactly adhering to the USDA's food pyramid (a diet high in grains, vegetables, and fruits, and low in fats and animal proteins).

Now is a good time to change your eating patterns. With a child on the way, a change in how the entire household eats will improve everyone's health and vigor—something you'll need with a toddler crawling around! Books about nutrition during pregnancy, such as *Eating for Two: A Complete Guide to Nutrition During Pregnancy,* are excellent resources. You may want to consult a nutritionist to help you sort things out. And if you are making any dietary changes, you should always consult your doctor. These professionals can help you steer clear of unwise foods and vitamin supplement choices and suggest foods that are more beneficial to you and your baby.

The basic guidelines for healthy eating, from the perspectives of both nutrition and environmental health, can be found in the box, "Eight Simple Steps to the New Green Diet," later in this chapter. Think of yourself not only as eating for two, but as eating your way to a better world for you and your child.

How to Avoid Bacterial Contaminants

In general, you are not at an increased risk for food poisoning because you are pregnant, except for a bacteria called *Listeria*. Pregnant women are twenty times more likely to get listeriosis (an infection caused by *Listeria*), which sickens an estimated 2,000 people per year, according to the **U.S. Centers for Disease Control and Prevention (CDC).** The symptoms can be mild and flulike, but infection can lead to premature delivery and even stillbirth. Babies can be born with listeriosis if their mothers eat contaminated food during pregnancy. *Listeria* contaminates meat, dairy products, and processed foods—particularly deli foods, soft cheeses, such as feta, Brie, Camembert, and blue cheese, and cold cuts and processed meats, like hot dogs. It is very persistent, surviving refrigerator temperatures and sometimes even deep-freezes. The **U.S. Department of Agriculture (USDA)** and the **Food and Drug Administration (FDA)** maintain a policy of zero tolerance for *Listeria*. Even so, since the government only inspects a small percentage of food sold in the United States, it is not unwise to be cautious. Don't eat cold cuts, soft cheeses, hot dogs, and food on warming tables on buffets and salad bars if you can help it. In restaurants, go for something that is cooked, like a veggie burger, pasta, or soup. Follow "Keep Refrigerated" labels, and carefully observe "Sell By" and "Use By" dates on processed products. Also make sure to thoroughly reheat frozen or refrigerated processed meat and poultry products before eating them.

You will want to protect yourself from any kind of food poisoning to avoid having severe intestinal cramps and vomiting, which will have some impact on your baby. If you are in good health, it's unlikely that exposure to a food-borne pathogen will be life threatening. Serious illness as a result of food poisoning usually only affects people whose immune systems are compromised or undeveloped, such as those with autoimmune deficiencies, those undergoing cancer therapies, children, and the elderly.

Food poisoning is most problematic in meats and fish. Meats typically are tainted with bacteria at the farm or in the slaughterhouse as a result of fecal contamination. Some worrisome pathogens include:

- *Campylobacter jejuni,* which is present in 70 to 90 percent of all chickens, is the most common bacterial cause of diarrheal illness in the United States, according to the CDC. Up to 20 percent of those affected suffer relapse or suffer from prolonged illness. But worse than the bacterial infection are its side effects, which include reactive arthritis and Guillain-Barré syndrome, both linked to infections of *Campylobacter.*

- *Salmonella* primarily infects chickens and eggs, though it can be found in other foods, including grains and vegetables. Avoiding cracked eggs won't necessarily help, since *Salmonella* can pass from the hen straight into the egg, before it is laid. The CDC estimates that one in fifty consumers will be exposed to a *Salmonella*-contaminated egg each year.

- *E. coli* O157:H7 has been associated with hamburger meat, but also cross-contaminates fruits and vegetables. There are many types of this bacteria, including the generic *E. coli* that is in our own digestive systems, but this dangerous variant produces a toxin that ravages red blood cells and the kidneys. In children and others with compromised immune systems, an *E. coli* O157 infection can lead to hemolytic uremic syndrome (HUS). By the time HUS symptoms appear, the infection cannot be treated with antibiotics. Several children died as a result of eating *E. coli* O157-contaminated hamburgers at Jack-in-the-Box restaurants in 1993 and from drinking unpasteurized Odwalla apple juice in 1996.

- *Cryptosporidium parvum* and *Giardia lamblia:* These parasites have tainted imported strawberries and raspberries and caused outbreaks in 1996 and 1997. Both may be present in drinking water, rivers, lakes, and swimming pools. Symptoms include diarrhea and abdominal cramps, which may lead to weight loss and dehydration.

Nearly 50 percent of the antibiotics produced in the United States are given to farm animals to prevent infections and promote growth. This is an irresponsible use of antibiotics, since it can create strains of antibiotic-resistant bacteria (as can careless use of antibiotics by humans). For example, nearly all strains of *Salmonella* are resistant to the antibiotic tetracycline. If you are treated with an antibiotic to fight an infection of bacteria resistant to that antibiotic, it won't work. Some bacteria are resistant to more than one antibiotic—it could take some time for your doctor to find out which ones will effectively combat the infection. So, you're better off taking some precautions to prevent infection rather that relying on medications to cure you.

To avoid food poisoning:

- Wash all foods thoroughly before preparation, even those that will be cooked. Scrub produce with a vegetable brush and rinse several times (even if peeling). Soak leafy greens in cool water to remove accumulated soil and rinse at least three times. While peeling produce will eliminate surface germs, dirt, and pesticide residues on the skin or trapped under waxes, you will sacrifice some valuable nutrients and fiber.

- Cook meats and eggs thoroughly. Internal temperatures of meats should be:
    whole cuts of beef and lamb, 145 degrees F
    ground meat, whole cuts of pork and ham, 160 degrees F
    ground poultry, 165 degrees F
    poultry breasts, 170 degrees F
    whole poultry, 180 degrees F

- Eat only fresh fish. When you buy fish, look for clear eyes. Cloudiness means the fish is spoiling. There should be no fishy odor.

- Thaw frozen meats in the refrigerator or in cold water, changing water every 30 minutes.

- Avoid cooking meat in the microwave oven, which heats food unevenly.

- Wash hands before, during, and after food preparation. Wash everything that touches raw meat and eggs thoroughly in hot, soapy water. Don't allow utensils, such as knives or plates, that have touched raw meat to touch foods that will not be cooked.

- Use two cutting boards. One for raw meat and fish and another for vegetables.

- Refrigerate foods within two hours of cooking. Reheat foods until steaming hot throughout.

- Keep hot foods hot and cold foods cold.

Center for Science in the Public Interest, the **USDA Meat & Poultry Hotline,** the **FDA's Center for Food Safety and Applied Nutrition,** and the **CDC** can provide more information about avoiding food-borne illnesses.

8 Simple Steps to the New Green Diet

As consumers, we can make food choices that not only enhance our own health but also contribute to the protection of our natural resources and the long-term sustainability of the food system. The following guidelines, parts of which are adapted from Joan Dye Gussow and Katherine L. Clancy, "Dietary Guidelines for Sustainability," *Journal of Nutrition Education,* Vol. 18, No. 1, 1986, can help you plan your family's diet and make healthier, greener food choices.

1. *Eat a variety of food.* When you eat a wide variety of food, a broad range of nutritional requirements is likely to be met. You also draw on biological diversity. The proliferating "variety" in supermarkets does not reflect biological variety, since so many of the hundreds of available products are made from the same relatively few raw food materials—corn, wheat, rice, and potatoes. People today rely on just twenty varieties of plants for 90 percent of their food. Instead, you can eat a wider variety of whole foods instead of food novelties, whose claims to diversity are based on processing techniques and artificial colors and flavors. Choose different varieties of apples and potatoes, for example, instead of always buying the usual Red Delicious or Idaho russet.

2. *Buy locally produced food.* The average mouthful of food travels 1,200 miles from farm to factory to warehouse to supermarket to your plate. In comparison, food available from local farms is almost always fresher, tastier, and closer to ripeness. In addition, buying local products supports regional growers, thereby preserving farming near where you live and requiring less energy for transport. And, because it isn't being shipped long distances, local food is less likely to have been treated with post-harvest pesticides.

3. *Buy produce in season.* Out-of-season produce is extravagant not only because it costs you more to purchase, but also because it is so amazingly energy-intensive. It costs about 435 calories to fly one 5-calorie strawberry from California to New York. Out-of-season produce is also more likely to have been imported, possibly from a country with less stringent pesticide regulations than the United States. Eating frozen fruits and vegetables, especially from local producers, is your best option during the winter months. Frozen foods retain much of their nutritional content, in addition to cutting energy costs.

4. *Buy organically produced food.* Organically grown means that the food has been grown in a practical, ecological partnership with nature. Most organic food is minimally processed to maintain its integrity, without artificial ingredients, preservatives, or irradiation. Organic certification is the public's guarantee that the product has been grown and handled according to strict procedures without synthetic chemical inputs.

5. *Eat fresh, whole foods with adequate starch and fiber.* Whole foods—including fruits, vegetables, grains, legumes (beans), nuts, and seeds—are the healthiest foods we can eat. The National Cancer Institute recommends we each "strive for five" servings of fresh fruits and vegetables a day, since the complex carbohydrates and fiber they contain play a major beneficial role in protecting against cancer, heart disease, and common digestive ailments.

6. *Eat fewer and smaller portions of animal products.* Modern meat production involves intensive use of grain, water, energy, and grazing areas. It takes about 390 gallons of water to produce a pound of beef. Almost half of the energy used in Ameri-can agriculture goes into livestock production. Cattle and other livestock consume more than 70 percent of the grain produced in the United States and about a third of the world's total grain harvest. Animal agriculture also produces surprisingly large amounts of air and water pollution. Pork is the most resource intensive, followed by beef, then poultry. Eggs and dairy products are much less resource-intensive. Animal products, especially beef, are also a major source of fat in the U.S. diet. Reducing meat consumption and eating lower on the food chain protects us against heart disease, cancer, and diabetes.

7. *Choose minimally processed and packaged foods.* After it leaves the farm, food is subjected to a variety of processes (including packaging), most of which use fossil energy while removing naturally occurring nutrients. A typical highly processed (and highly advertised) "food product" may contain on average only 7 percent real food. Many processed foods are high in fat, salt, or sugar.

8. *Prepare your own meals at home.* Cooking from scratch can involve a little more labor and a little more time, but you can be sure you'll save money and resources. You're not paying someone else to prepare your food, to add nutrients removed in processing, to put it in a box or can, to ship it across the country, and to advertise it in slick TV commercials. You will also provide your family with healthier, more nutritious food since you are starting with fresh ingredients. And, cooking from scratch can be its own reward, providing a truly creative outlet that brings you pleasure and joy, rejuvenates the family meal, and nourishes our bodies and our souls.

A Green Diet Tour of Your Supermarket

Mothers & Others has created the following Green Diet Tour—an aisle-by-aisle guide—to help you identify the food choices in your regular supermarket that will be both healthful for you and your baby and supportive of a more ecologically balanced food system. The main theme of this tour is shopping for a green diet, so keep the "8 Simple Steps" in mind. Your food choices will make a difference in helping keep our water, soil, and air clean for your baby and future generations.

THE PRODUCE SECTION

Nutritionally, fresh fruits and vegetables are the healthiest foods you can eat—the more the better. The National Cancer Institute (NCI) recommends five servings a day of fruits and vegetables to help prevent cancer, heart disease, and common digestive ailments. Pregnant women should follow this recommendation faithfully. Except for avocados, fresh produce is low in fat. And most fruits and vegetables are packed with fiber, vitamins, and minerals, especially vitamins A and C, which pregnant women should get plenty of. Folic acid, a B vitamin that is necessary, especially during the first few weeks of pregnancy, to prevent neurological defects such as spina bifida, can be found in leafy greens, broccoli, avocados, strawberries, oranges, and many other fruits and vegetables.

There's much, much more to picking out fruits and vegetables than meets the eye. As you make your choices, ask yourself how the produce is grown (by conventional, organic, or Integrated Pest Management methods), where it comes from, and whether it's in season. Pesticides don't just remain on the peel; they can and do make their way into the "meat" of the fruit.

Always try to diversify your produce selections. Not only will you increase your intake of all essential vitamins and minerals, but buying different varieties of potatoes like fingerlings or Yukon Golds instead of the usual russet potatoes helps vary your diet and sustains demand for unique and diversified agricultural crops, so supermarkets will keep stocking them and farmers will keep growing them. Instead of plain lettuce or spinach, try mustard greens, bok choy, kale, beet greens, and other leafy vegetables. Biological diversity is as important in agricultural ecology as it is in the wild.

- *Organic or IPM Produce.* A sure way to reduce synthetic pesticide exposure and support those farmers who are not using them is to choose organically grown or IPM produce whenever possible. Certified organic produce is grown without the use of synthetic pesticides. Instead, organic farmers use only natural fertilizers and pest control methods, such as beneficial insects and biological pesticides like *Bacillus thuringiensis* (B.t.), a bacteria that kills pesky beetles in their larval stage. IPM growers also use biological means to control pests as much as possible, but they may use some pesticides if necessary, as a last resort. Both types of farming minimize pesticide residues, but there is no guarantee that any fruit or vegetable is completely pesticide-free; pesticides drift on air currents and through water.

  Look on the label or package for evidence that the product is IPM-grown or certified organic by a third party, either a government or a private certifier.

127

You'll see something like, "Processed in accordance with the California Clean Foods Act" or "Certified by C.C.O.F." A federal standard for certification of organic foods is being formulated at the time of the writing of this book. Even after the federal rules go into effect, third party certifiers will continue to carry out the certification process. However, all certifiers and producers will adhere to a single set of guidelines overseen by the USDA.

For the most part, organic produce is slightly more perishable than conventional. It's generally plucked closer to ripeness, which reduces its shelf life by a small factor. And produce begins to lose nutritional components after it's been harvested. So, lettuce, tomatoes, beans, and other perishable veggies should be eaten within a few days of buying them. Slightly wilted produce, however, can be perked up by soaking it in cold water. You should be able to keep storable foods—organic or conventional: potatoes, apples, beets, oranges, grapefruits, sweet potatoes—for a month or more in the refrigerator without any problem. Be careful to check for molds; they can form on fruits during long-term storage.

- *Waxes.* The glossy shine on that apple or pepper is due to waxes, which are not necessarily derived from natural ingredients and can contain animal products. Not all of them have been fully tested for safety. Numerous other fruits, vegetables, and nuts receive a wax coating: avocados, cucumbers, eggplants, grapefruit, grapes, lemons, limes, melons, oranges, parsnips, passion fruit, peaches, pineapples, potatoes, pumpkins, rutabagas, squash, strawberries, sweet potatoes, tomatoes, turnips.

  Many conventional fruits and vegetables are treated after harvest with chemicals and waxes to reduce deterioration and disease during storage and transport. Apples and potatoes, for instance, are dipped in a chlorine/fungicide wash to kill fungal spores. Imported produce, even organic, may be fumigated with fungicides, too, at international borders. When these chemicals are used with waxes, they cannot be washed off. Federal law now requires that retailers prominently display a sign for any fresh fruits and vegetables that are treated with post-harvest wax or resin coating, although the law isn't always enforced. Look for such signs in the produce department. If you suspect something is waxed, but don't see a sign, ask the produce manager.

- *Where Is the Produce From?* One of the most important questions we can ask our produce manager is where the produce comes from. Some countries don't have the same level of pesticide controls as the United States, so in some cases we may be importing produce that's been treated with chemicals that farmers here are not allowed to use. Food-borne pathogens may also lurk in foods imported from countries that do not enforce stringent hygiene standards.

  Choose locally grown produce, which can be found more easily in farmers' markets and some supermarkets. Being aware of what's fresh in your region according to season will help you discern what's local and what couldn't possibly be. In winter, for example, choose root crops, such as potatoes and turnips, and hardy greens, like mustard greens and kale, over summer vegetables like tomatoes. Fruits such as apples, pears, and citrus appear in fall and winter, but strawberries come into season in the summer in the United States. In general, even if the produce will remain unspoiled for a time, it's best to eat it as soon as possible after bringing it home from the store.

MEAT, POULTRY, DAIRY, AND EGGS

The best, and easiest, way to reduce intake of harmful chemical pollutants is by eating fewer animal products, such as red meat, butter, cheese and other dairy products, chicken, and pork. Contamination of rivers and lakes, soil and air exposes fish and farm animals to numerous chemicals. Farmed chickens, pigs, and cows may eat dioxin, mercury, and harmful bacteria through their feed. These toxins don't always pass through the animal. We can consume them right along with the meat or cheese. Eating foods with fewer animal fats also has numerous health benefits, from reducing cholesterol to decreasing the risk of heart disease, diabetes, and cancer.

Since you can pass toxic chemicals on to your baby through the placenta and breast milk, you should be careful about what you eat, even before and after pregnancy. While you can't change the past, making a change today will benefit you and your baby. Don't worry about risking a protein deficiency; the USDA food pyramid recommends eating only three servings of 2 to 3 ounces of protein (the size of half of a quarter-pound burger) per day. And if you eat a well-balanced diet, you'll get enough amino acids, the building blocks of protein, from other sources, such as beans, grains, vegetables, and tofu. You don't need to increase your intake of protein during pregnancy.

Avoid prepared meat products like hot dogs, luncheon meats, and sausage. They are more likely to be contaminated with *Listeria*. Processed meats are also high in fat, salt, chemical additives, and preservatives. If you buy cold-cuts from a deli, they should be thoroughly reheated before eating.

- *"Natural" and "Free-range."* Study these labels carefully. When used on meat and poultry, "natural" means minimally processed and free of artificial products, such as coloring and nitrites. "Natural" does not cover hormone use, organic feed, or other environmental practices. Some meat producers do make these "extended label" claims, which include "humanely raised," "raised without antibiotics," "milk fed," and "free range." To make an extended label claim on meat, a producer must submit a label and production protocol to the USDA.

   Organic meat, eggs, and milk come from animals that are fed organically grown grains instead of conventional animal feed, which may contain wastes such as chicken and pork byproducts, blood meal, euthanized cats and dogs, or chicken excrement. Organically raised livestock are not confined in chicken cages or pens. Organic farms keep flocks and herds small enough to be managed without resorting to antibiotics as a preventative measure. If they must use antibiotics to control infection, treated animals are sent to conventional markets. Until the federal regulations for organic cerification go into effect, you won't see "certified-organic" labels on meat (the USDA had prohibited their use), though you can find certified-organic eggs and dairy products. Until then, look for "raised on certified-organic grain," "free-range," and "not raised with antibiotics or hormones" on poultry and beef labels.

The **Humane Society of the United States** publishes *Humane Consumer and Producer Guide,* which can help you locate organic and "humane" producers of animal products. You can also find natural, free-range, and organic meats in natural food stores, some butcher shops, gourmet food shops, food co-ops, and some supermarkets.

- *Dairy Products.* While you should be reducing the amount of animal fats that you consume, you need not stop drinking milk and eating cheese and yogurt. You need more calcium when you're pregnant—about three to four servings of dairy products per day. If you don't get enough, your body may take it from your bones, along with stored lead. To avoid contaminants, choose low-fat or nonfat milk, yogurt, and cheese. Certified organic milk and dairy products (yogurt, cheese, butter, eggs) are available nationwide. To be certified organic, milk must be produced on farms where cows are fed 100 percent certified organic feed, forage, and hay. Unlike many of their conventional sisters, the cows are pastured rather than confined to feed lots. Organic milk does not contain recombinant bovine growth hormone (rBGH), a synthetic hormone given to cows to increase milk production. Avoid soft cheeses such as feta, Brie, Camembert, blue-veined, and Mexican-style cheese, because they are more easily contaminated with *Listeria,* a bacteria that can cause food poisoning in you and your baby. Cream cheese, cottage cheese, and hard cheeses are fine, though.

THE FISH COUNTER

Fish, from the standpoint of nutritional value, digestibility, and health benefits, is the most healthful flesh food in the world. It's an excellent source of protein, and contains a concentration of minerals, most notably iron, zinc, magnesium, and phosphorus. Fatty fish species, such as salmon, contain significant amounts of vitamin A and D, while dark, oily cold-water fishes, such as mackerel, sardines, and bluefish, are good sources of essential fatty acids (Omega-3), which are vital to our immune systems, but commonly missing from our diets. Sardines are also an excellent source of calcium.

Unfortunately, fish in polluted waters accumulate fat-soluble DDT, PCBs, and dioxins, and heavy metals like mercury. Clams and oysters absorb lead and cadmium. In general, larger fish carry higher levels of contaminants, and marine fish caught far off-shore pose less cancer risk from chemical contamination than freshwater fish or marine fish caught close to shore. But fish that migrate between clean, off-shore waters and polluted estuaries such as the Hudson River may accumulate dangerous levels of PCBs. And large ocean predators with long life-spans, such as sharks and swordfish, tend to carry higher concentrations of methylmercury. For this reason, the FDA advises no more than one meal per month of these fish for women who are pregnant or of childbearing age. Avoid raw oysters and clams—no other commercially available food poses a greater health risk. If you have AIDS, cancer, diabetes, or liver disease, or are a heavy drinker, you should never eat raw shellfish because of the risks of food poisoning. Likewise, women who are pregnant or are trying to conceive should be extra cautious.

A major environmental problem with fish is that we're depleting our supply. In

U.S. waters, 80 percent of marine fish for which we have data are classified as "fully fished" or "overexploited," reported the **NRDC** in "Hook, Line and Sinking: The Crisis in Marine Fisheries." Commonly eaten species, such as sole, snapper, bluefin and albacore tuna, cod, and swordfish have all made it onto the World Conservation Union's "red list" of the world's most threatened animals. Despite "dolphin-safe" labels, dolphins that travel with yellowfin tuna continue to be killed by fishing boats. Shrimp trawlers also kill millions of wild fish and the rare Kemp's Ridley sea turtles. Ask your fish merchant for Turtle-Safe Certified shrimp; the mark should be present on the packaging.

- *Farm-raised Fish.* While it would seem that farming fish, like cows and chicken, would be a solution to contamination and depletion of fish stocks, aquaculture faces the same problems plaguing agriculture. Farmed fish are kept in a confined area and are therefore more prone to disease. So farmers resort to a lot of chemicals—including formaldehyde, used as a disinfectant—and antibiotics to prevent outbreaks of disease. Shrimp-farm runoff—the wastes and drug residue—is ruining the coastal wetlands of India, Bangladesh, Southeast Asia, and Central America, decimating mangrove trees, an important habitat for marine life. And farmed fish, such as almost all Atlantic salmon, which spend part of their life cycle at sea, may escape from their pens and compete with wild fish for resources and taint the wild gene pool, says Michael Weber, author of an upcoming report on salmon aquaculture for the Consultative Group on Biological Diversity.

  The **FDA** advises that pregnant women reduce consumption of shark and swordfish to once a month. You should also limit consumption of tuna, salmon, and other fatty fish. The smaller and leaner the fish, the more unlikely that it will have a lot of toxins. Smart choices are flounder and sole.

  Ask your grocer to label where fish and shellfish come from. As a general rule, you should reach for local species that are not overfished and do not come from contaminated waters. Check with your state fish and wildlife department for health advisories regarding certain types of fish that may be contaminated with PCBs, mercury, or other toxins, especially if you sport fish. Pregnant women should always heed consumption recommendations of local fish advisories. You can also obtain information about contamination of waterways in your state by looking at the websites of **EWG** and the **EPA's Office of Science and Technology.** *The Audubon Guide to Seafood,* available from the **National Audubon Society,** is a great tool to help you avoid overfished species. But for a more comprehensive, region-by-region list of overfished species, from the Atlantic to the North Pacific, obtain the report, "Hook, Line and Sinking: The Crisis in Marine Fisheries," by contacting the publications department of the **NRDC** or surf to their website. While you're on the Internet, take a look at **Sea Web's** pages, too.

DRY GOODS

- *Grains and Baked Goods.* The USDA recommends eight to eleven servings of grains per day (one serving equals ½ cup of rice or other whole grain, a slice of bread, one tortilla, and so on). Grains, the seeds and fruits of cereal grasses, provide much needed fiber in our diets. Nutritionally, grains are the most valuable of all foods. Grains also contain proteins, fats, carbohydrates, vitamins, and minerals. These nutrients are found in the various layers of whole grains. Look for "whole grain" on labels. Vary your diet by choosing some of the many different grains that there are: amaranth, barley, bulgur, buckwheat, corn, couscous, quinoa, millet, oats, rice, wild rice, rye, triticale, and wheat berries. If you can't find some of these grains, ask for them. They are available and the store should try to provide them.

Baked goods, pasta, snacks, and cereals on the market today are made with refined flour and sugar, too much salt, hydrogenated oils, artificial colors and flavors, dough conditioners, and antioxidant preservatives. Added salt helps to accentuate taste in many processed foods because they have been stripped of flavor. And many products are so nutritionally deficient that they are often "fortified" with minerals and synthetic vitamins (though some whole-grain and bran cereals are also fortified). Nutritional fortification makes up for only a fraction of what has been taken away.

As a result, buying these products requires careful label reading. Look for those made with whole grains such as wheat, corn, oats, barley, rice, amaranth, and rye. Buy the organic variety whenever you can. But still read the labels. Increasingly, we are seeing processed organic foods that emulate conventional counterparts—down to their refined white flour, salt, and high sugar content.

- *Rice.* While rice is not one of the most nutritious of grains, its high fiber content helps flush out toxins in your body and prevent their reabsorption. Polished and milled white rice retains only the carbohydrates. But converted rice, sometimes called parboiled, is steamed and pressurized before milling, forcing 70 percent of the nutrients of the bran and germ into the grain, although some fiber is still lost in milling. Wild rice (which is actually the fruit seed of a tall aquatic grass) and brown rices are particularly nutritious. Try also arborio, jasmine, and white and brown basmati varieties, too.

- *Beans and Lentils.* These legumes contain more protein than any other foods in the vegetable kingdom, yet they have none of the cholesterol found in animal-source protein foods. Their high-quality protein rivals protein from meats and other animal foods, so you can substitute one or two servings of beans to meet part of your daily protein requirement. Beans have abundant complex carbohydrates, which we need for energy, and they are an excellent source of cholesterol-lowering soluble fibers. Unlike grains, beans do not go through processing methods by which they are stripped of nutrition. Thus you do not need to look for "whole" beans versus "refined" beans; all beans are whole beans. Beans contain a sugar that is difficult for us to digest; that's why some people suffer from gas after eating them. You can take Beano, an enzyme that helps digest the sugar, to avoid this problem.

Dried beans and lentils usually require soaking and simmering before they can be added to a recipe, but they taste fresher than their canned counterparts. There is also a much wider variety of beans available dried than in cans. But canned beans are a versatile substitute that you can use when time is precious. Some canned beans may have added sodium, so rinse them before using.

- *Nuts and Seeds.* Concentrated foods brimming with vitamins, minerals, protein, and polyunsaturated fats, nuts and seeds are among the most nutritious foods in the world and make wonderful snacks for you and your kids. (They are high in fat, though, so don't eat too many.)

   Whole nuts store well, but when they are sliced or broken, their oily flesh is exposed to air and can become rancid. Any rancid food is a toxic food and may cause illness, even liver damage. Aflatoxin, a carcinogenic mold, can grow on moldy nuts. Signs of rancidity: dark or discolored areas, rubbery texture, or mold.

- *Flours.* Most mills transform whole nutritious grains into nutritionally devoid white flour. The bran and germ layers are stripped away, leaving the white, pulpy interior kernel. When whole wheat is milled into white flour, 83 percent of the nutrients and its fiber are removed, leaving mostly starch. It must be fortified with synthetically manufactured thiamin, riboflavin, niacin, and iron.

   But whole-grain flour, when milled properly, does not lose its nutritional value. No synthetic nutrients or chemical additives are necessary. The various kinds of whole-grain flour are: whole-wheat bread flour, whole-wheat pastry flour, durum, gluten, cornmeal, blue corn, buckwheat, barley, brown rice, oat, oat bran, millet, amaranth, rye, soy, and carob.

- *Sugars.* Our bodies do in fact need sugar; it is essential to human life. But we get enough complex carbohydrates from whole grains, fruits, and vegetables to maintain a healthy blood sugar level. Still, as we all crave sweets from time to time, choose those made of natural sweeteners, which have some nutritional value. Take it easy, though—natural sweeteners still contain calories, can elevate blood sugar levels, and can cause cavities.

   Sucanat, the dehydrated juice of organically grown sugarcane in granular form, retains the vitamins, minerals, and trace elements found naturally in the sugarcane plant and can be used just like sugar. (Note: Sucanat is very expensive—as much as $3 per pound.) Other sweeteners include: barley malt syrup; brown rice syrup; date sugar; fruit-juice concentrate; granular fruit sweeteners; honey; maltose; maple syrup and sugar; molasses; sorghum syrup; and stevia, a very sweet-tasting but low-calorie product from a South American plant (slightly strange-tasting), sold in highly concentrated form.

PACKAGED FOODS

The rule here is to choose minimally processed and packaged foods.

- *Cereals.* Some commercial brands of breakfast cereals are a rogue's gallery of refined grains, high amounts of refined sugars, artificial colors, artificial flavors, and preservatives. It's not just the children's brands that are nutritionally compromised. Several so-called "natural" cereals are also loaded with refined sugar. Don't be fooled by the packaging, which may also display colorful banners proclaiming "with oat bran" or "high fiber." Forget all that and read the ingredients panel, which tells the real story.

- *Juices.* Other than fresh-squeezed juices, your best option is 100 percent pure, organic juice made from whole vegetables or fruit. There are many organic juices on the market today. Watch out for added sugar. Juice drinks, fruit punches, and fruit nectars can contain only 10 percent juice or less, along with added sweeteners and artificial flavors and colors. Look for pasteurized juices to avoid food poisoning. Several outbreaks of *E. coli* illnesses have been linked to unpasteurized apple juice.

Avoiding Alcohol

Consumption of alcohol during pregnancy can cause significant harm to the developing fetus. Like other chemicals, alcohol penetrates the womb through the placenta.

A wide variety of physical and neurological effects in babies born to women who drink significant amounts of alcohol during pregnancy has been documented. These children often have smaller-than-expected brain size and smaller heads. Researchers have also found that alcohol-exposed children may have microscopic changes in cell location, and missing or atrophied communication pathways in the brain, according to Paul D. Connor and Ann P. Streissguth at the Fetal Alcohol and Drug Unit at the University of Washington. As a result, these children suffer from deficits in attention, intelligence, memory, motor coordination, visual perception, complex problem-solving and abstract thinking—all of which usually persist into adulthood. Physical birth defects include heart malformations and facial anomalies.

Avoid alcohol throughout your pregnancy. While studies show facial distortions occur as a result of alcohol consumption during the first trimester, alcohol can impact the development of the central nervous system at any time during the pregnancy. A glass or two won't have a significant impact on your baby's development. More harmful is the regular consumption of large quantities of alcohol. Don't worry if you drank a glass of wine or two before you knew you were pregnant, as this amount is unlikely to cause serious injury, but otherwise don't drink while you're pregnant.

Checking Your Drinking Water

During pregnancy, you'll need to drink at least eight glasses (eight ounces each) of water to replenish essential minerals and body fluids that flush away toxins from our bodies. But is tap water safe to drink? While local water agencies test, filter, and clean drinking water, harmful substances are not always completely eliminated. Both natural and manufactured substances, from bacteria to radiation, can become water-borne. Human sewage, industrial waste, pesticide runoff (from both agricultural and residential use), backyard dumping, seepage from municipal landfills, and leaks from underground storage tanks threaten groundwater, rivers, and lakes. Even if your water is purified thoroughly by your water company, by the time it comes through your faucet, it may have accumulated bacteria and lead from some of the pipes through which it is carried.

For both mother and baby, a clean water supply is essential. You can easily find out what's in your water and whether you should take some decontamination measures after it reaches your tap. Not only will it be safer for you, but you will know that your child will be drinking only the purest water.

What's in Your Water

All large and most small water companies are required by the Safe Drinking Water Act to test their water for eighty regulated contaminants at regular intervals and report to the state and the U.S. Environmental Protection Agency (EPA). These contaminants include:

- generic *E. coli* and fecal coliform, which indicate the level of bacterial contamination

- nitrates and nitrites

- mercury, lead, zinc, and cadmium

- some pesticides, including atrazine, 2,4-D (Sevin), chlordane, glyphosate (Roundup) and others

- industrial chemicals, such as dioxin, PCBs, styrene, benzene, and tetra-chloroethylene

To get a free copy of the results of these tests, call your water company using the phone number on your water bill or in the phone book. You can also obtain test information and water quality reports from state water agencies. Ask for test results for the past two years. This is important because contaminant levels may fluctuate over time. Test results for a short time period may give you an incomplete picture. The results should contain what's in the water after it's been purified and before it leaves your local water company. The **Safe Drinking Water Hotline** has a list of all regulated substances in water and the maximum allowable levels. You can also obtain information on drinking water standards on **EPA's Office of Science and Technology** Website.

Don't forget, though, that water can become contaminated en route to your faucet. Some cities, like Boston, still have lead pipes in service lines. (See "Lead Flows into One Family's Home," later in this chapter.) Some PVC pipes made before 1977 may leach vinyl chloride, a carcinogen, into water as well, as was discovered in Troy, Kansas, in 1998. Within your own home, you may have lead pipes or pipes soldered with lead. Bacteria can grow in your hot water tank, the water tank on the roof of apartment buildings, or reservoirs between the water treatment plant and your home. You can test the water coming from your tap for lead and chemicals by sending samples to an EPA-certified laboratory, such as **Suburban Water Testing Labs** or **National Testing Labs.** The **Safe Drinking Water Hotline** can give you the names of other labs in your area. You can also obtain water test kits from **Allergy Resources** and **The Real Goods Trading Company** for about $100 to $150. To use these kits, simply collect water from your faucets and send it back to the laboratory as specified in the directions.

"Being an architect, I thought I had thought of everything," says Sheila Kennedy, a professor at Harvard University and mother of identical twin girls, Francesca and Ava. Sheila and her husband, Frano Violich, had even moved into a loft apartment in Boston's North End before their daughters were born, because their first, very old apartment, "...was covered in lead paint. We chose to move, rather than go through lead abatement. We never really considered that lead would be a problem in the water."

But after taking the twins to their doctor for a routine checkup that included a required blood test for lead, Sheila and Frano learned that both Francesca and Ava, twelve months old at the time, had lead levels of 13 and 14 micrograms per liter, respectively. Their doctor told them that 9 was thought to be normal. Ava had higher levels, perhaps as a result of the amount of formula she was drinking.

The twins nursed until they were about six or seven months old, after which Sheila put them on formula. "I immediately thought the problem might be the tap water we were using for the formula," Sheila says. "But my pediatrician was not concerned. She thought the levels would drift, and that we should just wait and see. I was not so unconcerned. We tested the paint in our apartment and found no lead there, but we live in an inner city neighborhood near a highway. We thought that the lead was coming from contaminated soil and dust.

"We found out from a community doctor specializing in lead that there really weren't that many cases related to contaminated soil from emissions in our area. He said that there usually was no smoking gun for lead poisoning, no single environmental factor. Instead, a lot of little contributing factors can increase a child's lead level. We actually did find a little lead on the window sills—probably coming from outside pollution. So we've had to keep a tidier home."

Sheila then called the City Department of Public Works in Boston, which has a computerized listing of the location of all the lead pipes in the city, and discovered that their apartment building had a lead pipe entering it. "They came within twenty-four hours to take the pipe out," she recalls. "They got rid of the pipe so quickly that we didn't even have time to test the water." Sheila also asked the building super if the building had any lead pipes within it, which it did not. "But we bought a water filter certified by National Sanitation Foundation anyway, because it gets rid of 98 percent of lead," Sheila says.

"We live in the oldest neighborhood in America, where Paul Revere once lived," says Sheila of the working class area near the Boston waterfront that is now being gentrified. "I thought I was living in a pretty safe neighborhood, but in retrospect I can see why it happened."

At fourteen months, Francesca and Ava were tested again, and the lead levels had decreased to 8 and 9 micrograms per liter, respectively. Sheila underwent lead testing, as well, and discovered that her blood lead level was only 4 micrograms per liter.

"I would definitely recommend testing for lead," Sheila says. "This can happen to anyone."

The following are substances that could be contaminating your water.

Pathogens. A number of harmful bacteria, viruses, and parasites can enter the drinking water supply from human sewage, animal feces (from both wild and farm animals) or rivers, lakes, and streams. Water-borne illnesses include hepatitis (A, B, or C), giardiasis, and Legionnaire's disease. Pathogens can cause higher miscarriage rates among pregnant women and also affect those with lowered immune systems, such as children, the elderly, AIDS patients, and people undergoing cancer therapy. Many water companies use fecal coliform levels as a general indicator for bacterial contamination.

Disinfectants such as chlorine, ultraviolet light, and ozone can kill many, but not all, pathogens. For example, chlorine, used in many areas of the country to purify water, does not kill all viruses or the cysts of *Giardia lamblia* or *Cryptosporidium parvum,* two parasites that cause painful intestinal illnesses. While a combination of disinfection and good filtration can eliminate most of these microbes, most water companies don't have the expensive equipment required to eliminate them completely. Find out if your local water company tests for parasites. They are required to test for viruses and *Giardia,* and some take the extra precaution of testing for *Cryptosporidium.* You may want to boil drinking water—for at least one minute—or use a water filter that removes particles of one micron or less (see water filter section later in this chapter) to ensure that your water is free from biological contaminants.

Heavy Metals. Heavy metals such as lead, mercury, cadmium, and arsenic exist in nature, but industrial pollution has increased levels in water. They can cross the placenta and cause neurological and reproductive damage to developing babies, as well as to children. Heavy metals concentrate in fat, so you may pass them on to your baby while you're pregnant and through your breast milk.

Of water-borne metal contaminants, lead is the most serious. According to the EPA, more than 800 U.S. cities have water that exceeds the EPA's "action level" for lead of 0.015 mg/l. Half of U.S. cities still send water through lead-lined or copper pipes with lead soldering. Lead pipes are the primary source of lead in drinking water. Sheila Kennedy discovered that her water was contaminated with lead after her twin daughters tested high for levels of lead in their blood (see the box "Lead Flows into One Family's Home").

Lead levels in water are usually highest in the morning after the water has been sitting overnight in pipes and faucets, where it has time to accumulate lead. If you're uncertain about the purity of your water, a good practice is to flush your pipes by running water from your faucet for at least one minute in the morning or if it hasn't been used for a few hours. You can capture the water in a bowl or jug and water your houseplants or garden with it. Hot water leaches lead, too, so use only cold water for drinking and cooking. Soft water leaches more lead from pipes than hard water. Testing your water for lead is a wise precaution, as is calling your local water agency, as Sheila Kennedy did, to find out if you have lead pipes leading into your house or apartment building. Some cities, like Boston, have computer listings of all the lead pipes in the city.

Nonmetallic inorganics. These include substances like asbestos, which may leach from cement water mains; cyanide used in insecticides; and emissions from metal refineries and plastic and pigment factories. Nitrogen fertilizers used in agricultural production and on lawns and gardens form nitrates, nitrites, and nitrosamines in water. Nitrites and nitrosamines are carcinogenic. Nitrates can cause "Blue Baby Syndrome," a condition in which blood is starved of oxygen. Since testing for nitrates and nitrites is now required, they are no longer a widespread threat. But they can be a problem in agricultural areas that are served by private wells. Private well owners should test their water regularly for them.

Synthetic Organic Compounds (SOCs). More than 50,000 SOCs, such as pesticides; solvents; industrial products; and ingredients for cosmetics, cleaners, and plastics, are produced today. This class of chemicals includes the VOCs discussed in earlier chapters. Many SOCs have not been adequately tested for toxicity. Of the EPA's 120 priority pollutants, 114 are SOCs. Some SOCs cause cancer, others reproductive and genetic damage. Some are neurotoxins, which damage the central nervous system.

- *Pesticides.* In 1995, Environmental Working Group, a Washington-based non-profit think tank, found that approximately 10.2 million people in the Midwest, 1.5 million in Louisiana, and 2.4 million in the Chesapeake Bay area are exposed to water contaminated with five heavily used herbicides: atrazine, cyanazine, simazine, alachlor, and metolachlor. Four of these are classified as probable or possible carcinogens by the EPA. In the Corn Belt, an estimated 65,000 infants drank formula mixed with pesticide-contaminated water.

- *Solvents.* Industrial chemicals used in paints, cleaners, and glues; benzene; trichloroethylene; p-dichlorobenzene; and styrene can cause neurological and reproductive effects and an increased risk for cancer. Solvents enter waterways as a result of industrial pollution.

- *Other SOCs.* These include dioxin, PAHs (discussed in chapter 5), phenols, and phthalates, a hormone-disrupting additive in PVC. Vinyl chloride (the building block of PVC) can cause neurological problems, reproductive effects, and increased risk for cancer.

Radioactive Substances. About 50 million people in the United States may be drinking water contaminated by naturally occurring or manufactured radionuclides such as uranium, radium, strontium, and radon. High levels of naturally occurring radionuclides, found in areas with granite substrata or those with known radioactive materials, may dissolve in the water. Manufactured radioactive substances enter the water supply from nuclear power plant leaks and accidents, weapons testing, medical waste disposal, and leaks at waste sites. As mentioned above, even small doses of radiation can cause genetic damage. Some pregnant women exposed to high levels of radiation after the nuclear accident at Chernobyl spontaneously aborted their babies, while some babies born to exposed women later developed thyroid cancer, which is rare among children. Under federal law, water companies are not required to test for radon and other radioactive substances, although some states may require it.

Chlorine and Trihalomethanes. Chlorine is used by most water treatment facilities to kill bacteria. But chlorine reacts with organic chemicals left in the water by soil and decaying vegetation, forming a group of chemicals called trihalomethanes (THMs), which includes chloroform. An analysis of studies on THM exposure in the *American Journal of Public Health* estimates that 10,000 or more rectal and bladder cancers each year in the United States are associated with these disinfection byproducts. Other studies show some possibility of reproductive effects, birth defects, and miscarriages due to THM exposure. A study in the March 1998 issue *Journal of Epidemiology* shows that 2 percent of 5,144 women who drank five or more glasses of chlorinated water containing at least 0.075 mg/l of THMs were at increased risk for miscarriages during their first trimester.

As of October 1996, the federal standard for THMs is 0.1 mg/l, but this standard may be lowered to 0.08 mg/l. You should check THM levels on the test results given to you by your water company, or have your water tested for them by an independent laboratory. THMs will dissipate from tap water if you leave it in an open container in the refrigerator for a few hours, or boil it for one minute.

Newer, nonchemical means of disinfection are being tested and introduced. Ozone has been shown to be an effective disinfectant, as has ultraviolet light.

Fluoride. This naturally occurring mineral is added to many water supplies to fight tooth decay, and it does a good job at this. But too much fluoride can cause mottling of teeth and can cause skeletal fluorosis (an accumulation of fluoride in the bones) in people with kidney disease. There is also some suggestion that fluoride is correlated with increased rates of cancer, but the evidence is not clear. Local drinking water programs are required to announce to the public when the fluoride level reaches more than 2 parts per million, at which level the possibility of moderate to severe dental mottling increases. There is much debate over whether the risks of fluoridation outweigh the benefits. For the time being, pay close attention to public alerts on fluoride, pathogens, and other contaminants, and use substitute drinking water until public safety officials say your water is safe again.

Should You Use a Water Filter?

Whether or not you should use a water filter depends on a few factors. After you obtain test results from your water company or state authorities, you may want to test the water coming from your faucet to determine what needs to be filtered out. Water testing can get expensive, though, since there are so many substances you could test for. Here are a few suggestions to help you narrow down the list:

- If your water company is not testing for some substances that you are concerned about, such as certain pesticides, radon, or arsenic, or some of the levels are high, you may want to have your water tested for those substances.

- If your water company is using chlorine for disinfection, but does not check THM levels, test for them yourself, since THMs may cause miscarriages.

- If you live in an agricultural area, test for pesticides. Some laboratories have pesticide package deals.

- If you live in a heavily industrialized area or near a waste dump, call the **Community Right to Know Hotline** to find out what chemicals are being released by industries in your area. Three websites—**EPA's Center for Environmental Information and Statistics, Chemical Scorecard,** and **EWG**—contain databases with information on reported toxic releases. EPA's website also contains information on water and air quality by county. If there has been a significant chemical release in your area, you may want to test for that specific chemical.

- Unless you live in a house built after 1978, you should test for lead.

If you find that the levels of contaminants are high (check with **Safe Drinking Water Hotline** for standards), or you want your water to be as free of them as possible, you'll probably want to invest in a water filter. Remember, though, that in order for the filter to be effective, you'll have to change filters and maintain the system; otherwise, it will be doing no good.

TYPES OF WATER FILTERS

The simplest—and often the cheapest—water purifiers are those that use a *carbon-activated filter*. These include the pitchers with filters built in as well as those that attach directly to faucets or to plumbing below the sink. Those using granulated charcoal may be slightly less effective than solid block charcoal filters. Carbon filters will generally remove chlorine, coarse sediment, lead, and some organic chemicals. The simplest types won't filter out pathogens, some pesticides, and some heavy metals, but those with a combination of filters are more likely to.

The most comprehensive—and most expensive—water purifiers are *reverse-osmosis systems*. These purifiers push water up against a membrane. The water that does not make it through contains the contaminants and is diverted as waste water. While reverse-osmosis systems remove a wide range of contaminants, including all heavy metals, many pesticides, and asbestos, they do not remove THMs, radon, VOCs, or pesticides such as lindane and atrazine unless they also have carbon filters attached. They also waste a lot of water; a few gallons for each gallon purified is flushed away as waste water.

Many people believe that *distillers* remove all substances from water. While distillers do remove heavy metals, nitrates, bacteria, viruses, and cysts, they do not get rid of asbestos, chlorine, THMs, most pesticides, or VOCs. In addition, distillation softens water, removes calcium and magnesium, which are beneficial to human health, and makes water more likely to leach chemicals from their storage containers.

Some water filters use ultraviolet light in combination with charcoal filters or reverse-osmosis systems to kill bacteria that contaminate water during purification as the result of bacterial build-up in the filter.

Water purifiers that are labeled "absolute one micron" will filter out cysts that have escaped disinfection by water companies. A word of caution: "Nominal one micron" *will not* remove pathogens!

The **National Sanitation Foundation (NSF),** a nonprofit organization, certifies water filters by the type of contaminants eliminated. NSF Standard 42 is used for filters that remove contaminants that reduce aesthetic quality (taste, smell, color), such as aluminum, chlorine, iron, and sediment. NSF Standard 53 is the most comprehensive, used for filters that remove most pesticides, VOCs, cysts, fluoride, most heavy metals, and THMs. You can obtain a booklet from NSF that lists the exact chemicals removed under each of their standards and the filters they certify.

Be careful when selecting under-sink filters with above-the-sink faucets. The **Center for Environmental Health (CEH)** in San Francisco announced in June 1998 that six popular under-sink water filters (Omni OT-2, Franke UF, Ametek CWF, Amway WTS, Aqua-Pure CRF, and Water Boss MPD) actually put lead into the water that they were supposed to be purifying. These water filtration systems had brass faucets containing lead, which leaches into the water left sitting in the faucet. The manufacturers of these water filters are either redesigning their products or taking them off the market. If you have one of these filters (purchased before November 1998) or plan to buy a similar one, contact the company or **CEH** for more information.

Consumer Reports has found that most under-sink models are not necessarily any better than countertop units. You can obtain a copy of their most recent ratings by calling **Consumers Union.**

Regardless of the type of filter you choose, remember to change the filters as often as the manufacturer suggests. Not only will clogged filters be inefficient, but they also may harbor bacteria. Many companies sell water filters, including **Real Goods Trading Company, Allergy Resources, N.E.E.D.S., Nontoxic Environments, Harmony,** and **Nontoxic Hotline.**

Bottled Water

In recent years, increasing awareness of water pollution, as well as a trend towards healthy living, have fueled the growth in bottled water sales. But if you drink a lot of water, buying it at a store can be costly. Bottled water is not necessarily more "pure" than tap water, nor is it more sterile, unless it's distilled.

Some companies bottle tap water that has been filtered to remove chlorine. The FDA requires labeling as follows:

- *Artesian water* is pumped from a confined underground aquifer.

- *Mineral water* contains no less than 250 parts per million of naturally occurring minerals, such as calcium, magnesium, and potassium. The minerals must come from the water's source, and cannot be added later.

- *Sparkling water* is naturally carbonated water, containing the same number of bubbles after treatment that it had when it emerged from the source.

- *Springwater* is water coming from a source that flows to surface through a natural hole.

None of these labels attests to the purity or safety of the water. Nonmineralized bottled water must comply to the standards in the Safe Drinking Water Act, but Lawrie Mott, a senior scientist at NRDC, says that monitoring bottled water is a lower priority than municipal water for the EPA.

If you drink bottled water instead of tap water in your home, you're better off investing in a water filter. Some bottled waters are merely filtered municipal water. Bottled water isn't necessarily harmful, but you shouldn't give it to your baby or to anyone with high blood pressure, as some bottled waters may contain high levels of sodium. A cheaper alternative to buying bottled water when you're outside of your home is to fill empty beverage bottles with filtered water at home. You can freeze them so the water will still be cold by the time you drink it later in the day.

NSF certifies bottled water. A list of those that adhere to their standards is available upon request. You can also obtain information about bottled waters from the **International Bottled Water Association.** And the **CDC** has some information on its website.

Personal Care Products

Although the chemicals in lotions, creams, makeup, and hair care products are small in comparison to other exposures, you should remember that they are absorbed into your skin. Avoid dyeing or perming your hair while you're pregnant. Some hair dyes contain lead acetate, and darker hair dyes may have ingredients that are cancer-causing. Hair dyes and some shampoos may also contain alkylphenol ethoxylates (APEs), which break down into hormone-disrupting chemicals. **Washington Toxics Coalition** has a fact sheet, called "Hormones in your Haircolor?", that lists products containing APEs. The corrosive chemicals in permanent solutions also may be absorbed into the skin.

The safest products to use are those that have a minimum of petrochemical and other synthetic ingredients. Just because the bottle says "natural" doesn't mean that every ingredient is. Some so-called natural products still contain synthetic ingredients—even petroleum comes from nature, and other natural substances, such as arsenic, are harmful. Watch out for the term "organic," too, since this doesn't necessarily refer to growing methods of ingredients; it can mean that the substance comes from a carbon-based material. Always read the ingredient list.

Fragrances and synthetic preservatives (such as those in the "paraben" group) can cause skin and eye irritations. Other chemicals that you might want to avoid are:

- formaldehyde, a possible carcinogen

- alkylphenol ethoxylates (APEs) (ingredients with "octoxynol" or "nonoxynol" on labels)

- amyl acetate, a neurotoxin

- triethanolamine (TEA) and diethanolamine (DEA), which interact with nitrites to form cancer-causing nitrosamines

The Safe Shopper's Bible lists brand names of personal care products that contain carcinogens. **Aubrey Organics,** a line of organic cosmetics and personal care products, only uses natural ingredients. **Tom's of Maine** and **Dr. Bronner's,** available in natural foods stores, sell mild personal care products. **N.E.E.D.S.**

offers products for the chemically sensitive. See chapter 7 for more information on personal care products.

Checklist

Take care to avoid the following when you are pregnant.

1. *VOCs emitted by home decoration products.*
   - *Paints.* Do not paint any room of your house while pregnant! Stay away from your home while it is being painted, even if you are using non-VOC paints. Ventilate well during and after painting. See chapter 2.
   - *New Furniture.* Avoid plywood and particleboard furniture. Do not apply finishes or stains yourself; have someone else do it, keep the area well-ventilated, and make sure the finishes have dried completely before bringing the furniture into the house. Offgas new upholstered furniture outside.
   - *Carpets.* Try not to install wall-to-wall carpeting. Choose natural over manufactured synthetics. See chapter 2.

2. *Cigarette smoke and polluted outdoor air.*
   - Make your home a smoke-free zone.
   - On high ozone days, keep your windows closed and minimize your outdoor activity.

3. *Pesticides and toxic cleaners.*
   - Do not use pesticides yourself or have an exterminator spray pesticides in your home while you are pregnant. For alternatives to synthetic pesticides, see chapter 5.
   - Stop using extra-strength cleaners now, before your baby is born. This is a good time to switch to milder cleaners. That way, you'll have reduced the chemical residues in your home and you'll be prepared for gentler cleaning for your baby.
   - Don't handle or dispose of toxic chemicals yourself. Ask your spouse, partner, or friend to take care of these in accordance with hazardous waste regulations.

4. *Dry cleaning clothes, bedding, and area rugs.*

5. *Unevenly cooked or raw foods* (such as sushi), as well as deli cold cuts, soft cheeses, and hot dogs.

6. *Hair dyes and perms.*

7. *Silver (amalgam) fillings.*

8. *X rays* unless absolutely necessary, and if there is no alternative.

You should do the following:

- Eat a well-balanced diet that is low in animal fat and high in vegetables, fruits, and grains.

- Use lead-free dishes. See chapter 4 for more information.

- Assess the quality of your water and determine whether you need a water filter.

- Test for radon as discussed in chapter 5.

- Install carbon monoxide and smoke detectors.

PART II

Caring for Baby the Natural Way

chapter seven

Dressing, Playing with, *and* Keeping Baby Clean

After all the preparations, and sometimes in the midst of them, baby finally arrives in a storm of tumult, pain, and joy. At some point following labor and delivery, after the essential bonding when you hold your baby for the first time and gaze into those deep, wise, newborn eyes, you will take a brief reflective moment to regain your bearings. Perhaps you'll look out the window of your hospital room, and whether it's night or day the world will never have looked so beautiful, because now your baby is in it. You'll also feel a fierce, primal, protective love. You'll want to make the world a better habitat for your baby, and you'll be glad of all the environmental preparations you've made.

Take a deep breath, because next a busy, hands-on learning time begins for both of you. Right away, you'll learn to breast-feed or prepare formula, and your baby will learn to feed. With the help of the nurse or midwife, you'll also learn how to change diapers and keep baby clean. You and baby will initiate a lifelong process of learning to communicate with each other. Baby will express needs through crying, and seek your company and engagement through looks and gestures even before she can smile. Ever attentive, as Nature made you, you'll be quick to learn and respond to your baby's nonverbal language. And, as parents have always known, babies smile earlier than scientists used to think they could. That come-hither grin you see on your baby's face at two weeks is definitely not just gas!

In addition to feeding, changing, and communicating, you'll learn to bathe, dress, and play with your young charge. You are your baby's first teacher, and babies learn through play. The great thing about babies is that almost every experience, from bathing to feeding to getting dressed, can be a playful one for them. Your attitude makes all the difference. Babies and children dislike being rushed, so taking time to experience the moment with them, playing peekaboo with an unfolded diaper or cat-and-mouse with a sock, can make changing and dressing a lot more fun for everyone. Baby will teach you, too, about her own inborn disposition and preferences: how she likes to be held and touched, how she doesn't, and when there's been enough play and she needs some space of her own. The world is a vast new place to baby, and she needs some time to reflect and get her bearings, too.

This chapter will cover bathing and dressing baby, and then move to quiet and active play—all with a natural, nontoxic theme—in this order:

- Bathing Baby
- Soaps, Shampoos, and Other Baby Care Products
- Diapering
- Dressing Your Baby
- Laundering Diapers and Baby Clothes
- Choosing Nontoxic Toys and Playing with Baby
- Exercise and Active Play

Bathing Baby

Babies need to be kept clean. Dribbles, drools, and spit-ups are regular occurrences, along with accumulations in the diaper. A baby's skin is highly sensitive, and even very tiny residues of milk, saliva, urine, or feces left on the skin can cause irritation and rashes. It's important to gently wash behind ears and knees, between fingers and toes, and within those creases formed by baby fat in a baby's neck, arms and legs, and groin and buttock areas. (This is excellent training, by the way, for searching for deer ticks, a must when older children play out of doors in areas where Lyme disease occurs.) It's also important to know that a bath doesn't have to mean full immersion. There are many instances when a sponge bath is perfectly appropriate.

You'd think that bathing a baby would come naturally, given our human affinity for water. After all, our earliest ancestors crawled out of the ocean, and fetuses sport gills for a brief time in the womb. Still, for many parents, baby's first bath is an anxiety-fraught experience. Drownings have occurred in less than an inch of water, so it's important to be careful. The first rule is to never let go of an infant in the bath, and never to leave a child of any age unattended in the water. "When my son Robbie was a newborn I always supported him on one arm, while bathing him with the other hand," says our editor, Judith McCarthy of Summit, New Jersey. "He didn't like his baths in that little baby tub—he seemed tense. Maybe he sensed my anxiety. Or maybe it was because he was such a big baby that the little tub made him feel constricted. Plus there was that foam mattress built into the tub, which might have made him feel uncomfortable. He started enjoying his bath when we put him in the big tub and he could move around."

Babies are individuals from the start, and they have their preferences. But as Robbie discovered in his own good time, baths can be fun. It's especially liberating for a baby, whose bottom is encased day and night in diapers, to get naked. The bath can be one of the most pleasurable play experiences for parent and child.

Whether you're giving a sponge bath or immersion bath, make sure the room is warm enough for a naked newborn. Keep the air warm, at about 85 degrees F. when bathing a young infant. When a newborn is dressed, 65 to 68 degrees F. should be a sufficient room temperature. Set your thermostat accordingly, and remember to turn the heat down to no more than 68 degrees F. once baby is dressed after the bath. If you live in an apartment without a thermostat, you can hang a thermometer on the wall in baby's room, and let in cooler outside air or turn radiators up or down as needed. Do avoid overheating. Once her weight reaches 8 pounds, baby can—and should—sleep in a cooler room, 60 degrees F., as there is now a layer of protective fat and her body can regulate heat well.

Sponge Baths

To avoid infection, doctors advise giving sponge baths until the stump of the umbilical cord drops off, which usually happens in a week to ten days. You can get a baby completely clean in this way. Some days, you might choose not to wash baby all over, but simply to focus upon areas that regularly get soiled, such as the bottom and genital areas and under the chin. In fact, a newborn doesn't need a complete bath every day. If you're tired (and you often will be) or run out of time, a bottom wash and a wipe under the chin are enough to freshen her up.

Here are the basic steps for giving a sponge bath, though you'll soon develop a procedure that feels right for your baby and you:

1. First, check that the bathing room is warm enough.

2. Gather all materials before you start. Here's what you need:
   - an unbreakable bowl of warm water (a large stainless steel mixing bowl works fine)
   - a smaller dish of sterilized water, boiled and then completely cooled, for washing baby's eyes during the first two weeks
   - clean baby-size washcloths or all-cotton, reusable wipes
   - sterile cotton pads or cotton balls
   - a thick, soft towel for baby to lie on
   - a towel with which to dab baby dry
   - baby fingernail clippers or manicure scissors

Soap and shampoo are not necessary for newborns; you can just wash them with water for the first couple of weeks or more, as you like.

3. Get the bath area ready: Baby can lie on a warm, soft towel on the changing table or on a clean counter beside the sink, or on a waterproof pad in the crib with the rail lowered, or on the floor. The latter is the most secure, should baby roll or slip in your grasp. If washing on a countertop, bed, sofa, changing table, or other raised surface, keep one hand on the baby at all times. This is a good habit to maintain even if you're washing or changing baby on the floor. Best bet: Put a thick, soft towel on top of a wool "puddle pad" from **Babyworks** ($24), which makes a natural waterproof surface. Do not place baby directly on the wool, as it could scratch.

4. Begin with baby's face. (With a sponge bath, you can focus on the areas that really need cleaning, such as baby's face and bottom, and leave the rest alone. Keeping the baby in her undershirt and diaper will help prevent chills.) Dip a sterile cotton pad in the bowl of warm sterilized water and dab eyes gently, washing one at a time, using a fresh pad for each eye to avoid spreading any infections, and wiping from inner to outer corner, to prevent water running from one eye to the other. Dip a soft washcloth in the larger basin of water and softly wipe baby's face. Use separate fresh cotton pads or clean washcloths for cleaning around mouth and under nose, the outer whorls of each ear, and for gently washing each hand. After the first couple of weeks, you can set aside the sterile pads and just use a clean washcloth for the top-down sponge bath, beginning with baby's eyes. If either eye has an inflammation, check with your pediatrician.

   - Do not put cotton swabs or balls into nostrils or the ear canal; they will only push dirt further in.
   - Do remember to wipe behind the ears and in back of the neck. Cleanse inside the creases of neck and those cute layered chins.

5. If you need to clean your baby's torso, you'll have to remove the baby's undershirt. A diaper or towel draped across his middle may comfort him as you work. Be extremely gentle.

6. To clean baby's lower body, remove the diaper. Wipe carefully around the stump of the umbilical cord. Wash baby's bottom, not neglecting any folds. As when you change the diaper, be sure to wipe a baby girl from front to back, to avoid getting fecal matter into the genital area. If your baby boy is uncircumcised, try not to pull back the foreskin of his penis to clean underneath. This should never be forced; the skin will eventually pull back naturally, and should not be disturbed, because tearing could result. Natural body mucus keeps the area under the foreskin clean; if there's any inflammation, call your pediatrician.

7. Gently pat damp areas dry. Wipe the leg folds and the backs of the knees, and clean between the toes. This may be a good opportunity for a game of Little Piggie.

8. Put a clean diaper and T-shirt on baby, along with a creeper or nightgown.

9. Readjust heat to normal room temperature.

10. It's a good idea to complete baby's bathing routine with a fingernail check. If the nails have grown long enough for baby to scratch herself, cut them carefully with a stainless steel, baby-size clipper or manicure scissors, sold at most pharmacies and baby stores. Ideally, you should do this while baby's asleep and less likely to fidget and fuss. Hold each finger gently and steadily and cut the nail straight across, and not too short (leave a rim of the white part showing).

Tub Baths

After the umbilical cord stump drops off, you can give baby a regular bath. But you don't *have* to. It's best to start when you and baby feel ready, perhaps when baby has filled out a bit more, looks less fragile, and is less likely to get chilled.

"I never bathed our baby, when he was very small, without my husband present," says Judith McCarthy. Her mother's intuition was right on point: It's a good idea, when you're new to giving baths, to have an adult helper at hand. Mindy Pennybacker had her mother with her to help during the first few weeks. "I was terrified of lowering our newborn into that small baby tub, because he was such a squirmy, slippery little thing that I could barely hold onto him while changing his diaper or during a sponge bath. "My mother, however, insisted that Rory was ready to enjoy his 'real' bath, and he was," Mindy remembers. She learned to support his head with one arm and hold his lower body with the other hand, and as she lowered him he got tense—it's a natural reflex newborns have against being dropped. But as soon as his body was enveloped by the warm water, Rory relaxed and stopped moving, and "his eyes got wide with his listening look. He was listening with his whole being to this new sensation," she says.

Here are the steps for a tub bath:

1. As with a sponge bath, make sure the air in the room is warm enough.

2. Gather all materials before you begin. You'll need:

   - a baby-size portable bathtub or a very clean dishpan or kitchen sink. Many doctors advise not putting baby in the big bathtub until she can sit up. If you do use the kitchen sink, though, make sure that baby doesn't bang into the hard taps or get scalded by hot dripping water.

   - a thick towel to pad the hard surface of sink or plastic baby tub. You can wring it out and let it dry between baths, or put it in the dryer (just make sure it doesn't mildew). Some baby tubs come with a thick foam pad, indented with a baby's shape, rather like a snow angel. We advise against buying these on principal, as they're petrochemical products. But if you want to use one, let it offgas first, and when you do bathe baby it might be a good idea to layer a diaper or towel over the foam, because its sticky surface can irritate baby's skin.

- sterile cotton squares for eyes—a good idea until about two weeks or so.
- washcloths.
- a warm hooded towel.
- a bath thermometer, if you like.

You still don't need shampoo or soap.

3. Get the location ready. The portable tub can be put on a steady tabletop or even inside the big bathtub. To guard against mishaps, Mindy and her mother felt safest bathing Rory, at first, in a portable baby tub on the floor.

4. Test the bath water on the more delicate skin of your wrist to make certain that it's comfortably warm, but not as hot as tough adult skin can take. It should be at about body temperature, 90 to 100 degrees F. If in the big tub or sink, get into the habit of turning the hot water off before the cold, so that if there are any drips, they won't scald the baby.

5. At first, you can leave baby wrapped out of the tub in her towel. Support baby's body along one forearm, with the back of her head resting in your hand and her bottom securely between your elbow and ribs, and hold her head over the edge of the tub while you rinse her face and hair. It's a good idea to wash eyes separately until age two weeks.

6. Next, take off the towel and gradually lower baby into the water with one forearm behind the shoulders so that her head rests on your wrist while that hand holds her around the shoulder and armpit. Be careful not to lower baby so far into the water that splashes might get into her mouth and nose.

7. Gently clean from neck to bottom as in the sponge bath, and gently splash warm water over her belly, chest, and legs. It helps to sing a little song about bathing or chant a little poem (it doesn't have to rhyme) to put baby more at ease. They love the sound of their parents' voices.

8. Before lifting baby out, make sure you have a secure grip on her, with one hand around her shoulders and the other under her bottom, holding her thigh.

Graduating to the Big Tub

Depending on the size of your baby, she may start feeling uncomfortably constrained by a small tub or sink around her sixth month of age, or earlier. To get her used to it, you can move a small tub into your porcelain bathroom tub for interim bathing sessions, until she gets used to being surrounded by those high tub walls. Or one adult can sit in the tub with the baby lying face up, head supported by the parent's lap and her body by the parent's outstretched leg. Then the other parent, kneeling or sitting on a footstool beside the tub, can serve as bath attendant, lowering and lifting baby in and out. An adult should never get in and out of the tub while holding the baby, as there's potential for slipping, even on a nonskid tub mat.

When you're ready to venture putting her into the big tub without a parent "chair," make sure there's a nonskid tub mat underneath her to prevent slipping. Test the water temperature both as you run it from the tap and when the bath is full. Keep water shallow. Make certain that you've turned your hot water heater thermostat down so that the hot water is always below 120 degrees F., to prevent scalding in the event your explorative infant or toddler grabs a tap. You can pad the metal faucet so that baby doesn't bruise her head on it. Instead of buying a PVC cartoon-animal cover, you can just cover the faucet with a thick sock and a rubber band, removing them between baby baths. Note: PVC tub mats, shower curtains, bath toys, faucet covers, and other accessories, while touted as waterproof, mildew as readily as natural cotton fabric or a natural rubber mat.

Kneel or sit on the floor beside the tub. If she cannot sit up on her own yet, let her lie back with her head and shoulders supported by your forearm, wrist, and hand and your fingers around her shoulder. If she can sit up on her own, be sure to keep one hand on her or hovering within reach at all times, as you wash her with the other hand. Once you've finished, drape the towel over your chest and lift her against you, then wrap her up.

Beware of gimmicks. It's amazing what makers of baby products will dream up and try and convince us we need, such as so-called tub safety rings, contraptions like small Hula Hoops on suction-cup feet, into which one sets an infant in sitting position. Judith remembers, "My sister gave me one of those bath rings, so of course I felt I had to use it. But I only used it a couple of times, because Robbie hated it. Again, he was a very large baby, so the ring didn't fit him too well. And it was so hard to get him in or out! You can't move the ring, because it's stuck with suction cups to the bottom of the tub. So I just bathed him with one arm supporting his back, and he could splash around and move his legs all he wanted."

Remember that no device can substitute for a parent's attentions.

Bath Accessories

- Untreated, affordable cotton washcloths can be had by the dozen from **Ecobaby**, which also carries washmitts and organic french terry washcloths. **The Natural Baby Company** and **Baby Bunz & Company** have all-cotton washcloths and economical terry wipes.

- Hooded Towels. "We received at least a dozen of these as shower gifts, which I found boring, but a friend who was already a mother warned me not to return them. She told me that hooded towels are one of the most useful things, and she was right," Mindy Pennybacker says. Newborns and babies, like the rest of us, lose body heat most rapidly through the scalp. The hood built into the towel immediately keeps baby's head warm, and its softness, if it's pure cotton, is very comforting; plus the rest of the towel wraps around for a gentle swaddling-dry—place the hood on baby's head, tuck up the bottom, then the sides, and you've got a warm bundle. **Babyworks** and **Ecobaby** have unbleached, all-cotton terry hooded baby bath towels. **Cloud Cottons** and **The Natural Choice** have them in organic cotton.

Hooded towels are one layette item the baby won't outgrow for a couple of years; many toddlers have been witnessed wearing hooded towels as costume capes as they run about after the bath, having an air-dry. You could even sew ears and a face on the towel; one of Rory Wallace's favorites was a green frog towel, worn proudly after swims at the beach. In this spirit, a generous-size Critter Cape, with ears on the hood, made of untreated, unbleached terry, fits up to three years old—from **Ecobaby.**

- Organic cotton shower curtains are available from **Real Goods Trading Company, Seventh Generation,** and **Harmony.** These really do keep water in without a liner, but we advise purchasing a nontoxic mildew treatment from **Harmony** to prolong the longevity of your curtain. Out of frugality, we tried it without purchasing the $12 spray, and mildew sprouted within a month. Washing your curtain regularly in hot water, once every week or two, and drying it thoroughly also helps stave off mildew. Hemp shower curtains from **Earth Runnings** and **Harmony** are naturally mildew resistant, but a bit on the pricey side.

- Organic or unbleached, untreated bath towels for adults are available from **Terra Verde, Ecobaby, Harmony, Heart of Vermont, Garnet Hill,** and other mail order retailers.

Soaps, Shampoos, and Other Baby Care Products

Babies have wonderful skin, and the general rule is to tamper with it as little as possible. Many doctors advise using nothing more than plain warm water and a wash cloth to get baby clean, at least until she's crawling about, indoors and out, and encountering real dirt, not just milk dribbles and drool. "Soap really just helps loosen things up," says one New York City pediatrician. At some point, you will probably decide that that grime on your baby's skin could use a little loosening. What is soap? It is a fat (vegetable or animal) converted by reaction with an alkali, usually lye, through a process called saponification, which is defined by *Webster's Collegiate Dictionary* as "the conversion of an ester, or organic compound, heated with an alkali into the corresponding alcohol and acid salt"; this process carried out with fats (glyceryl esters) produces soap.

Most pediatricians recommend using a mild soap, such as Dove or an olive-oil based castile soap. There are also many soaps marketed for babies that use natural ingredients. Be sure to rinse soaps off well, and to use them only sparingly; too much soap can dry the skin.

Antibacterial soaps are too harsh for babies and absolutely unnecessary, says Dr. Harvey Karp, Mothers & Others medical advisor. The active ingredient in many antibacterial soaps, triclosan, does not cause chronic health effects, but if these soaps are ingested, they may cause nausea, vomiting, and diarrhea. Antibacterial soaps are often liquid and brightly colored. Some come in "bubblegum" and "watermelon" scents that might confuse babies and young children into thinking they are edible. These fragrances may be irritating to your baby's skin or trigger an allergic reaction. Soap and water don't kill germs, it's true, but they lubricate and loosen them, so they can be rinsed away. This is a much safer alternative to using chemicals.

Baby shampoos are generally milder than adults', but you may want to try them on your own head before applying them to baby's, making certain that claims of "no tears" are true.

When buying foaming or bubble baths for your child, it is also wise to choose products for babies that use milder ingredients than those used for adults. Keep in mind, though, that many so-called baby baths use quite tough detergents. Also, it's best not to use bubble baths too frequently, as they have been linked to higher incidence of urinary tract irritation and infection. Dr. Karp recommends using a few drops of a mild baby shampoo in the water to produce some bubbles.

When buying soaps, shampoos, and other skin care products for your baby, bear in mind the permeability of the skin. As David Steinman and Dr. Samuel Epstein write in *The Safe Shopper's Bible,* "Cosmetic ingredients most certainly are absorbed through the skin." Synthetic chemicals abound in our daily lives anyway, so why compound your baby's exposure to them by putting them on her skin or hair?

The National Institute of Occupational Safety and Health has found that one-third of the substances—both natural and synthetic—used in the fragrance industry are toxic. However, the FDA does not test cosmetics for safety. In addition, perfumes and fragrances can be allergenic. If allergies run in your family, you might want to take care not to expose your baby to potential allergens, including fragrances. Once sensitized by contact with an allergic substance, some people more readily develop other allergies as well. If you notice any dermatological problems, such as a rash, or other symptoms, such as watery eyes or difficulty breathing, stop use of the product immediately and consult your pediatrician.

On the other hand, if products with fragrances and bubbles are used once in a while, say in a bath at Grandma's house, don't worry, unless there's a rare reaction like reddened skin, teary eyes, or difficulty in breathing. If your baby has a skin reaction, rinse the product off well. If respiratory problems continue for some time after you've removed your child from the bath, call the doctor immediately. Obviously, you won't want to use that product on your child again, and other caretakers should be informed of your child's reaction to that product. But in the absence of particular sensitivities, children relish the fun of bath products and cosmetics, and, like all of us, enjoy the occasional pampering.

To keep things in proportion, it's important to remember that the occasional exposure to chemicals that are rinsed off is *not* a toxic dose! It's simply that, as a matter of overall parental policy, you may want to limit cumulative exposures from all sorts of chemicals that your baby inhales, touches, and eats. In the case of bath products and shampoos, there are many safer and more natural alternatives, so it's a fairly non-labor-intensive way to reduce one type of exposure.

What's in a Label?

It can't be assumed that products labeled "hypoallergenic" are nonallergenic to everyone. They just don't use ingredients that are common allergens. While hypoallergenic products may not contain cornstarch, a common allergen, they may contain talc, an irritant whose fine particles can clog airways if inhaled.

"Natural" can be a meaningless label. Though "natural" products claim to be made primarily from plant, animal, and mineral ingredients, the FDA has set no clear legal definition for this word. Products labeled "natural" frequently contain petrochemicals. As Kristin Ebbert comments in *The Green Guide*, "basically all materials, including petroleum, have some basis in nature."

Some natural ingredients that can cause irritations and allergic reactions are: tocopherol (Vitamin E), glycolic "fruit" acids, fragrance (a natural citrus or flower scent can provoke reactions in allergic people just as synthetic mixtures can), lanolin (the oil from sheep's wool), cocoa butter, cornstarch, cottonseed oils. These common allergenic substances are absent from most hypoallergenic products, but again, that doesn't mean these products won't irritate your baby's skin.

"Cruelty-Free" doesn't mean that personal care products are free of animal testing. Often, manufacturers get around consumer concerns by using *ingredients* that have been animal-tested, although the finished product has not. For more information, contact **The Humane Society of the United States** or send for a free shopping guide from **People for the Ethical Treatment of Animals (PETA).**

Here are some ingredients to avoid, or use sparingly.

- *Strong fragrances.* Both synthetic and natural fragrances can cause headaches, dizziness, rashes, and coughing, and can make it difficult for asthma and allergy sufferers to breathe. Look for fragrance-free products, especially if there is a history of allergies or asthma in either parent's family.

- *Formaldehyde* is present in preservatives. Look on labels for quaternium-15, diazonlidinyl urea, and DMDM hydantoin, some of the pseudonyms of this potential human carcinogen that can also irritate skin, eyes, and airways.

- *Alkylphenol ethoxylates (APEs).* Found in many shampoos and conditioners, APEs are potential hormone disruptors. Look on the label for "octoxynol" or "nonoxynol," which signify APEs, or obtain a list of detergents that contain them from **Washington Toxics Coalition.**

- *Diethanolamine (DEA) and triethanolamine (TEA) compounds.* These surfactants, found in many shampoos and liquid soaps, are harmless on their own. But when combined with 2-bromo-2-nitroprone-1, 3-diol (BNPD), nitrites often used in these products as preservatives, they sometimes form carcinogenic nitrosamines. As these nistrosamines can be absorbed through the skin, it's probably a good idea not to regularly use DEA- or TEA-laced products on your child.

- *Methylene chloride,* a chemical commonly found in scented shampoos and various colognes, is also used as a paint stripper and can be found on EPA's Hazardous Waste list.

- *The persistent "parabens."* Some petrochemical derivatives, such as the methyl-, propyl-, ethyl- and butylparabens, are so ubiquitous as to be nearly impossible to elude without some intense sleuthing. Though the parabens have been shown to be safe in laboratory tests, they cause skin irritations in some people, not to mention the psychic irritation of finding them in so-called "natural" or "plant-based" products.

- *Talc.* Many baby powders contain talc, made up of fine crystals that actually scratch the skin—and the linings of the nose, throat, and lungs. "Cosmetic talc is carcinogenic," warn the authors of *The Safe Shopper's Bible,* adding that talc should never be used on babies.

While most powder manufacturers today say they do not use talc that contains asbestos, talc from whatever source is still made of sharp fine particles that can irritate baby's airways if inhaled. Any fine substance, such as cornstarch, can be an irritant as well, but cornstarch lacks talc's scratchy crystals. And, as the powder disperses readily into the air, it's difficult to prevent baby's inhaling stray particles when you pat talc on her bottom. For this reason, many pediatricians advise against using talc, or any baby powder, at all, unless the baby has a rash.

If you feel you *must* use something, some doctors recommend using cornstarch, unless there are family allergies. While diapering, you can dry baby's bottom more than adequately with a soft dry cotton wipe or washcloth.

In some cases, powders or cornstarch, which get damp and warm between baby's body and the diaper, may actually contribute to bacterial growth and diaper rash. If you do use powder, keep the container pointed away from baby's face when shaking it out of the container; shake it into your hand rather than directly onto baby's skin. "A terrible thing some people do is to give baby the talc container to play with," warns one New York pediatrician. Don't do this! The same goes for cornstarch, or any other personal care product.

Alternative Personal Care Products

Many conventional baby shampoos contain fragrances, colors, and surfactants like DEA. **Dr. Bronner's** and **Logona** make simpler, unscented baby washes based on potassium (potassium hydroxide, a natural mineral salt) and amino acids, respectively. **Aubrey Organics** makes baby soaps without methylparaben, claiming "no synthetic ingredients." Both **Logona** and Urtekram, a Danish company, make children's shampoos from organically grown ingredients; all are available at **Terra Verde.** You can also order **Logona** directly from the company. A gentle, vegetable-based baby bath from Neal's Yard Remedies can be used both as a skin cleanser and a shampoo. **California Baby** does not use DEA in its shampoo, body wash, or bubble baths; decylpolyglucose is used as a surfactant instead.

Massage Oils and Diaper Rash Creams

Babies, like all of us, derive great comfort from touch. In addition to basic cuddling, you might consider giving a gentle massage after the bath, or any time baby seems fussy and could use a little extra comforting. Lie baby on her belly and stroke the backs of her legs and arms towards her torso, which promotes circulation, and rub

A Twelve-Year-Old's Take on Kids' Bath Products
by Mindy Pennybacker

One of life's great joys for my son Rory is baths, bubble baths in particular. The latter we held to a once- or twice-weekly treat, because they have been linked to a risk of urinary tract infections. With Rory's permission, I recently had him test a few products. (He is twelve years old; obviously you should never test products on a young baby or toddler.) We tried **Logona**'s "Baby Cream Bath," which is supposedly fragrance free. It does, however, have a somewhat fruity smell, perhaps from the sweet almond oil it contains. It is free of synthetic preservatives. There's just one problem: it doesn't bubble. "It just feels like extra soapy water," said my disappointed son. Would that matter to a baby? "I guess a baby wouldn't really care," my son said. But then again, the more we thought about it, the more we couldn't see the benefit of exposing a young baby to extra soapy or creamy water.

We then tried **Terressentials** "Babykins Face & Body Soap," billed as a "fragrance-free, rich moisturizer for extra-tender skin," with saponified olive oil, cocoa butter, and aloe vera as ingredients. It is basically an unprepossessing brown square with a texture akin to smooth clay mixed with wheat germ oil. My son, who hates having his face washed, looked dubious; but I put a little of this soap on a washcloth and, as I stroked it over his face, his face relaxed. "It didn't feel like anything," he said. I asked him how it compared to the white Dove soap we usually use. "I hate that white soap. It burns my skin," he said. I told him that a soap doesn't have to do that, and expressed regret for all the years he'd spent bathing with what we considered to be a mild product. Fortunately, we never used soap on Rory's face when he was a baby; many pediatricians, including our own, advise against it before a baby is at least six months old.

Plus, everyone's different. When I tried the Terressentials soap, I had a burning sensation on my cheeks afterward. And it frustrated my husband, who uses Dove to keep his skin from drying out, because he said the baby soap was sticky and hard to wash off. What we learned from this is that people have their individual sensitivities, and that soap use should be kept to a trace on your baby's skin, as well. Also, watch baby closely for any reaction. If he really hates having his face washed, you might be scrubbing too hard, or, it might be that the soap doesn't agree with him. Try another one.

Next we tried a series of shampoos. **Logona**'s Kids Shampoo & Shower Gel, with a fresh orange fragrance that might be too strong for young infants, doesn't burn the eyes, and works up into a nice lather. It uses organically grown herbs (called biologics in Europe). We also tried **Terressentials** Baby-Baby Bar shampoo, a white square containing olive, corn, and other plant oils. In some ways, the readily softening soap is more convenient than pouring liquid shampoo over a child's head; but it's probably better to lather the bar between one's hands than directly on the baby's head, so as not to disturb the soft spot. Incidentally, you also have to take care about the cleaning products you use in your bathtub. Rory hates it when I use bath oils because the residue makes the tub slippery, and he used to be able to tell if I used Ajax or Comet scouring powder because, no matter how carefully I rinsed, the residue burned his skin. We don't have that problem since we switched to baking soda. See chapter 5 for more information on alternative cleaning products.

her back. Then lie baby on her back and gently knead her arms and legs and even hands, fingers, and toes. Stroke her chest and belly.

The native Hawaiians believe in gently massaging a baby's belly and back to promote digestion and relaxation; they traditionally used the oil of the kukui nut for massage, or *lomi lomi*. **Lakon Herbals** makes a lavender and calendula baby oil for skin care and massage. The bottle suggests that these ingredients might help soothe rash; it is probably most prudent, however, not to apply cosmetic oils to irritated skin. Check with your doctor first. If you use oil to massage your baby, you have to be careful that baby doesn't slip out of your grasp; make sure to wipe off any excess oil after the massage and before picking baby up. Furthermore, any fragranced oil, however natural, can smell rather strong, so it should be kept away from baby's face. Mustela, the French producer of hypoallergenic baby skin care products, makes a hydrating emulsion with natural oils, as well as baby soaps, shampoos, cleansing lotion with almond oil, and "barrier cream" for the prevention of diaper rash. Mustela is available through the **Biobottoms** catalog. **Weleda** makes a calendula baby oil that they recommend for massage, as well as baby cream, soap, and "diaper care" to relieve rash. The Swiss company says it doesn't use mineral oils or synthetic ingredients. Both the Weleda and Mustela diaper creams contain zinc oxide, as do Kiehl's diaper-rash ointment and creams, along with avocado oil and vitamins A and D. You can also buy oils, such as almond oil, apricot kernel oil, and avocado oil at natural food stores. They are somewhat costly, but a little goes a long way.

Using oils or creams may also help prevent diaper rash from developing. "They keep the skin protected by creating a barrier between the baby's skin and everything else. This barrier keeps poop and pee off the skin, which naturally is irritating to the skin and harbors bacteria," says Dr. Harvey Karp. Another preventative measure: Always keep your baby as dry as possible by exposing the affected area to air as often as possible. Covering the rash up will only trap the moisture in and perpetuate the rash. If the baby does develop a rash, Dr. Karp recommends the gel from an aloe plant, which you can also get in a tube at a natural foods store, and a baking soda wash (1 teaspoon of baking soda to 1 cup of water) to help prevent yeast from growing, especially when the child is taking antibiotics.

Diapering

Your newborn will, on the average, go through ten to fifteen diapers a day. Before you panic, consider this discovery that Eric Olsen, of Berkeley, California, confided to us when he was a brand-new dad. "Maybe it's the hormones, whatever, but parenthood makes you go through certain olfactory changes. Your own baby's poop doesn't smell bad to you. Nature does this so you won't mind cleaning them up," he said. Also, breast-fed babies' poop doesn't smell. It's once other food comes that they get really stinky! Actually, you should be happy to see soiled diapers. You want your baby to be wetting her diapers frequently and having regular bowel movements. Some newborns urinate as much as twenty times a day! (Don't worry, you don't have to change the diaper that often—every two or three hours will do.) These are signs of good health in your baby. But what about the health of the environment, not to mention the family budget? This is where parents with a conscience find themselves weighing the choice between disposable paper or washable, reusable cloth diapers. Before you read the pros and cons, know that the good news is, whichever you choose, environmentally sounder alternatives are available. There are disposables made with non-chlorine-bleached pulp, and cloth diapers made with both green and organic cotton. There are also low-VOC, more natural, and less irritating laundry soaps for both home and diaper service use.

The Debate

Your baby will go through an average 5,000 diaper changes before she's toilet trained. The biggest environmental plus for cloth is its reusability. Disposable diapers are made of paper, plastic, and absorptive acrylic gels. Though they may leave our sight and minds after we toss them, they do not vanish from the earth: they go straight to our landfills—at the rate of eighteen billion diapers per year, according to the EPA. Disposable diapers constitute the third-largest source of solid waste in landfills. While some manufacturers claim that their disposables are "biodegradable," they aren't. Cornstarch, added during the manufacture of diaper plastic coatings, merely helps the plastic to break apart rather than decompose. Plus, the cornstarch makes the plastic impossible to recycle.

In New York Harbor, where rare herons, ibis, and cormorants fish off marshy islands, birdwatchers in boats are regularly stunned by the putrid stench of Fresh Kills Landfill. Why contribute more dirty diapers to this or any habitat? Wildlife habitat—as New York's harbor herons and skyscraper peregrine falcons prove—is everywhere, intermixed with human habitat. We should follow our natural instincts against fouling our nest.

Then there's the use of natural resources: 1.3 million tons of wood pulp, or one-quarter million trees, are consumed in the production of disposable diapers each year. The production of disposable diapers also releases a toxic byproduct—dioxins—into the environment during the chlorine bleaching of the wood pulp.

Pro-disposable environmentalists, and there are some, argue that the production and cleaning of cloth diapers actually consumes more energy and water, and generates more water pollution, than the production of disposables. They also point out that diaper service delivery trucks consume gasoline, a nonrenewable resource, and release fumes into the air. Keep in mind, though, that they serve more than one household on their rounds. This might be more energy-efficient than all the extra shopping trips disposable-reliant households make for diaper runs. In addition, without disposable diapers, we might need fewer rounds by garbage trucks.

In the end, all we can do is present the different arguments. The decision is up to you. Of course, the environment won't be your only consideration. You'll be thinking about the wear and tear on your personal energy stores, and the impact on your household budget.

ARE DISPOSABLES REALLY EASIER?

Many parents feel drawn to disposables for their throwaway convenience. They are probably not thinking this through completely. The proper disposable user doesn't toss diapers full of bowel movements into the trash, where the smell and bacteria can create a public health hazard. As with cloth diapers, poop should be dumped into the toilet and flushed. "I read in *Mothering* magazine that diapers are not a toilet, but people treat them like that. And it's true," says Lane Graves, Mothers & Others West Coast Regional Director.

And for those who are afraid of diaper pins: things have changed since we were babies. You no longer need pins for cloth diapers. You fold them into a diaper cover, or wrap, which closes with Velcro or snaps, just like a disposable's sticky tapes.

ARE DISPOSABLES CHEAPER?

Not necessarily. After the initial outlays for cloth diaper covers, which cost about $20 each, disposables will cost you about the same as a diaper service, about $50 per month. Laundering your own, if you own your washer and dryer, should run about $35 a month. If you have to use coin-operated laundromat machines, your expenses for cloth could run somewhat higher. If you want to use cloth, and don't have laundry machines of your own, what better time to invest in them than with the advent of a new baby? Put one of the new, energy-efficient front-loading washers on your wish list for baby shower gifts, and friends and family can pool resources to buy you something you'll need and use from day one.

Is there a diaper service in everyone's locale? Here's the rub: There may not even be one in your state. About 90 percent of American households with babies use disposables, and this lack of demand for diaper services has resulted in scarcity of supply. As of this writing, the **National Association of Diaper Services (NADS)** has only thirty-seven members spread thinly through Arizona, Arkansas, California, Colorado, Florida, Iowa, Kansas, Maryland, Minnesota, North Carolina, Nebraska, New Hampshire, New Jersey, New Mexico, Nevada, New York, Ohio, Oregon, Pennsylvania, Texas, Utah, Washington State, and Wisconsin. You can call NADS for the address and phone number of diaper services in your state. If there's not a NADS service in your state, don't despair; not all diaper services are members of NADS. Check your local yellow pages. That's how Lane found Didy Wash and Tiny Tots, two services in San Francisco.

Your choice doesn't have to be set in stone, swearing absolute fealty to one or the other. You can have supplies of both types of diaper and choose to use them according to circumstances that particular day: Are you traveling or at home? Do you have access to a washing machine and dryer or clothesline? What's the weather like? A plain cloth diaper can feel a lot cooler than a thick disposable filled with absorbent gel and coated with waterproof plastic.

One type of diaper may make your baby happier than another, and, as you get to know your baby, you'll be able to tell. As Lane Graves observed about her baby Angus at five months of age, "He's much happier in cloth. Cotton is so much better on his bottom. And we wear cotton undies; why wouldn't we want the same for our babies? It's more healthful for us, but even more so for them." On the other hand, some parents and pediatricians believe that disposables wick moisture away from baby's skin and thus better prevent diaper rash.

How to Change a Diaper

On the average, babies need their diapers changed every two to three hours. You should check the diaper this frequently, and also when baby cries or seems uncomfortable. Not all babies do cry when their diapers are wet. You can check the diaper when baby wakes you to feed during the night; after they start sleeping for longer than two to three hours, you can let them sleep without changing the diaper.

Make sure you check for dampness well, particularly if you're using disposables. "A disposable might feel dry, but there is a lot of moisture trapped in there," says Lane.

Here are the basic changing moves, for both cloth and disposable diapers:

1. Have a fresh diaper ready at hand beside the changing surface. This can be the same set-up as you have for the sponge bath: a thick, undyed towel over a 100 percent wool waterproof pad. A disposable diaper is pulled from the sac and opened. A cloth diaper should be folded in thirds, lengthwise, ready to be placed on the opened diaper cover. You don't have to change the diaper cover every time; once a day is fine unless it's gotten soiled.

2. Place baby gently on her back. Remember to always keep one hand on her so that she won't roll off a changing table or bed.

3. Undo the tapes of the disposable diaper, or the Velcro of the cloth diaper cover, and lift baby's bottom with one of your hands around both her ankles. Slide the soiled diaper out from underneath. If the cloth diaper cover isn't soiled, leave it there. The expert, efficient diaper changer does steps 2, 3, and 4 with one baby bottom-lift; don't worry if you have to rest, and let baby have a rest, by lying her bottom back down in between steps.

4. Wipe baby's bottom clean with a wet cotton pad or paper towel, or a commercial wipe.

5. Slide a clean diaper underneath baby. The tapes of the disposable diaper should be at the back. Lower baby's bottom down. Aim for symmetry.

6. Pull the front of the diaper up between baby's legs (along with the diaper cover, if you're using cloth). Take care that the edge doesn't touch the umbilical cord stump; you can fold the diaper under to give it space.

7. Fold up the sides over the front panel, fastening with sticky tapes or Velcro tabs. Some cloth diaper covers come with all-Velcro front panels, which reduces fumbling.

8. Drop the wet diaper in the diaper pail, if it's cloth, and in a lined trash bin if it's disposable. If either diaper is soiled with a bowel movement, fold it up and put

it aside until you've put baby down in a secure place. Then shake the feces into the toilet, rinse the cloth diaper if necessary (holding it firmly while flushing the toilet once should suffice) or dispose of the paper diaper.

9. Wash your hands. You've done it!

When changing a diaper, try not to be rushed; chat with baby, making it a pleasant, social experience for both of you. Your baby will appreciate being allowed to lie there naked and kicking for a little while, so she can enjoy a brief "airing out." If it won't do any harm, let her lie, crawl, or run around naked for awhile. As Mindy's husband, Don Wallace, says, "Everybody needs a break from diapers." This extra air-drying will also help keep her skin less prone to diaper rash, which results from bacterial growth inside a warm, moist environment.

A Word on Wipes

Commercial baby wipes are fine in a pinch, but most of them contain alcohol or other ingredients that can irritate baby's skin, already irritated by urine. Teresa Farrisi, author of *Diaper Changes,* suggests buying cheap, thin, cotton washcloths in packs by the dozen at drug or department stores and washing these reusable wipes in hot water. Or indulge in "luxury wipes" from **Babyworks,** 100 percent cotton terry knit faced with flannel, or "economy wipes," 100 percent cotton terry washcloths, about $7 a dozen. **The Natural Baby Company** sells a dozen rainbow-edged terry wipes for about $12. When traveling or out and about town, you can carry homemade disposable wipes made of wet, unbleached paper towels in a plastic bag, along with a small squirt bottle—the kind you can buy empty in any pharmacy—filled with a gentle liquid baby soap or a mixture of 1 cup of water with 1 teaspoon of baking soda. Use this system to clean your hands, too, when there's no sink available. **Tushies** and Seventh Generation (available through **Harmony**) make disposable alcohol-free wipes. Seventh Generation's have aloe vera in them to help soothe irritated skin.

Storing Dirty Diapers Before Washing

Collect dirty diapers in a diaper pail (preferably one not made of PVC vinyl). You don't have to keep water in the pail and soak diapers; that just makes them heavier to lug to the machine. But if you do soak them, add borax to the pail to keep odors down. The dry pail can be deodorized with baking soda, vinegar, or borax. Never use a deodorizer cake, because they emit toxic fumes and pose a poisoning danger if a young child eats them (they have a cookie-like shape).

Cloth Diapering Equipment

Essentially, you will need diapers and at least a dozen waterproof diaper covers, to keep baby's outer clothing and parents' laps from getting wet.

DIAPERS

If you use a diaper service, it will provide you with absorbent, all-cotton diapers and even rent you covers. If you prefer to buy your own (and you can have your diaper service use diapers of your choice), you can find 100 percent cotton diapers in various thicknesses and prices in baby supply stores and in many catalogs. You can get diapers in infant, or newborn, and regular sizes. A basic set of six runs about $10 in newborn size, $15 in standard (for babies over 9 pounds) from **Baby Bunz & Company.** Prefolded diapers, thicker in the middle, cost about twice as much, from **Babyworks** and **Biobottoms.** You still have to fold them to fit them in the diaper cover. "Fitted" diapers contoured for boys or girls (thicker in front or back) are sold by **Biobottoms.** Unbleached cotton flannel prefolds are available from **Babyworks,** which also has unbleached flannel "no-folds," cut to fit perfectly inside a diaper cover.

A neat item for warm weather out of doors, when baby appreciates not being weighted down with covers or waterproof surfaces, is Popolino's untreated diaper that fastens with adjustable snaps from **Ecobaby,** which also offers a Sandy Diaper with snaps at the elasticized waist and leg openings—quite attractive. Snuggle-bottoms from **Baby Bunz & Company** are preshaped diapers that can be bought with Velcro wraps.

The most environmentally conscious diaper of all are organic diapers. **Ecobaby** has either rectangular or hourglass-shaped ones. At night, you can fortify a diaper's absorbency with diaper doublers, sold in a ten-pack of regular cotton flannel. **Baby Bunz & Company, HinderCovers, Glad Rags, Snugglebundle,** and **Biobottoms** also sell different types of organic cotton diapers.

PINS AND FASTENERS

You might as well have a few of these, along with non-prefolded diapers in an hourglass or traditional oversize rectangle that you can fold into a pinnable triangle yourself. You can also buy diaper clips, which remove the fear of sticking baby. Be very careful, however, to keep safety pins and clips, like all small objects, well out of baby's reach, as they are choking hazards.

COVERS

Diaper covers in wool or cotton that wrap around and close in front with Velcro or snaps range from about $16 to $20 each. Thick, all-wool diaper covers are naturally waterproof and also "wick" moisture out of cotton diapers. You can also get cotton covers with a polyester moisture shield to prevent leaking. **Biobottoms** sells both, with Velcro. Another popular brand, Nikkys, have cotton outside, a waterproof lining, and a full-Velcro front panel; they can also be found in breathable lambswool felt. Nikkys can be found in stores or through **Baby Bunz & Company** or **The Natural Baby Company.** The latter also sells an unlined, waterproofed cotton cover with Velcro fastening. But these, like other waterproofed fabrics, should be aired out to offgas before they're put on baby.

WOOL "SOAKERS" AND OTHER WATERPROOF PANTS

The key to soakers is breathability. These high-waisted wool diaper covers in creamy thick wool knit, with low-cut legs, have a certain old-fashioned charm. The makers of pull-ons recommend them for overnight wear. They are available from **Babyworks** or **Baby Bunz & Company.** Smoother, more sportif-looking soakers called "nappy pants," made of stretch, "non-itchy" merino wool tricot, with either short legs or long are imported from Finland by **Lill-ing.**

Wool items will last longer and stay softer if hand washed and line dried. Eucalan woolwash, made in Canada without phosphates, bleaches, or detergents, can also be ordered from **Babyworks.**

Softer than plastic and less toxic than vinyl, Bummi or Alexis nylon waterproof pants with soft Lycra stretchy bindings can be pulled on over Velcro, snap, or pinned diapers. From **Babyworks** and other mail order retailers. Babyworks also offers nylon, waterproof pants/diaper covers that close with Velcro.

You can also use "all-in-one" cotton flannel diapers with a waterproof layer sandwiched inside. They're expensive, but a dozen or so could make life a lot easier, and diaper changes swifter, when you need a break. **The Natural Baby Company** and **Ecobaby** have white or printed 100 percent cotton flannel all-in-one pants for about $70 to $80 for six. They fasten with adjustable snaps. Bumkins have six layers of all-cotton flannel with a sort of air-pocket layer in the middle, and a polyester waterproof outer layer, from **Babyworks** for about the same price.

CHANGING PADS

A washable cotton changing pad, with polyester padding and a waterproof plastic bottom can be purchased from **The Natural Baby Company.**

Theresa Farrisi, author of *Diaper Changes* and mother of five children, all of whom wore cloth diapers, suggests the following basic diapering layette:

- 3 to 5 dozen cloth diapers, or 5 dozen all-in-ones

- 5 diaper covers per size (This is a bare minimum. Those of us who do laundry less often differ with her here, recommending at least a dozen.)

- 2 to 3 dozen cotton washcloths

- a nonvinyl diaper bag (This should be capacious, as you'll line the pail with it, and again, we recommend having at least two, so that one can be in the wash while you're using the other.)

- 1 to 3 washable, waterproof ditty bags for traveling (Make sure at least one can drape over a stroller.)

- diaper rash cream or ointment

- pins or clips as needed

More Ecologically Correct Disposables

If you choose disposables (or, without a home laundry or diaper service, have no choice but), there are varieties that are less harmful to the environment and potentially safer for your baby. To keep chemical gels, perfumes, and plastics away from your baby's bottom as much as possible, use these alternative disposable diapers as much as possible. It's true that they are more expensive than the conventional ones. **Tushies** makes Tender Care Diapers, nonchlorine-bleached and free of gels, latex, dyes, and perfumes. They cost about $8 per pack from **Ecobaby,** ranging from thirty-four newborn-size diapers to eighteen toddler size. You could use these overnight, when your baby tends to spend more time in the same diaper, and line them for extra absorbency with Tushie Mates pads. These products can also be ordered directly from **Tushies.**

Lane Graves only uses Tushies when the family travels, for environmental reasons and because "they're just not as well made as cloth. They're more difficult to use in terms of size, and the tabs are difficult to use. And cloth diapers keep him drier."

Dressing Your Baby

While our consumer society tends to encourage the idea that the purpose of clothing is to make babies look cute, fussy, busily printed, elaborate clothing often has the reverse effect. If a baby is uncomfortable, he will look far from cute. The purpose of clothing is to protect us and keep our bodies within a comfortable and healthy temperature range.

Temperature

As with baby bear's porridge, a newborn should be kept neither too hot nor too cold. Newborns particularly need warmth because their bodies do not conserve heat efficiently. Their bodies are built to stay warm for the most part, but in most climates they'll need a little help. Just think of that bald little head—you'll need to put a hat on baby to conserve her body heat. If kept too scantily dressed in air that is chilly, the body heat will dissipate. The calories a cold baby takes in are used to generate heat rather than to grow and put on weight.

You also need to pay close attention to your climate both in and out of doors. For instance, if you live in a very warm climate or in an overheated apartment, you won't want to put baby to bed in a heavy creeper even in winter. Babies should not be left to play or allowed to sleep directly in front of operating air conditioners, heaters, heat vents, or radiators. Pay attention to your baby's signals. A fretting baby may be feeling either chilled or overheated. Physical signs of overheating include warm, red fingers and toes and sweaty palms, underarms, and necks. But be alert: if your central heating or building radiators are turned off at a certain hour of the night, baby may need an extra blanket at that time. When babies are chilled, they lose the color from their cheeks, their fingernails become bluish, and their legs, arms, and neck will be cool to the touch. Note: cool hands are normal in a comfortably dressed baby.

Fibers, Finishes, and Dyes

For environmental reasons as well as your baby's comfort, we recommend natural fibers, preferably organic or undyed, untreated cotton, or undyed, untreated wool, silk, or cashmere. Natural fibers breathe, unlike synthetics, which trap moisture and heat inside, promoting bacterial growth that can cause rashes. Undyed, untreated "green" materials are less chafing and irritating to a baby's sensitive skin.

Organic, untreated cotton clothing for infants and children can be ordered from **Patagonia, Earth Wear, Earthlings, Cloud Cottons, The Natural Baby Company, Ecosport, Baby Bunz & Company, Ecobaby,** and **Snugglebundle.** In addition, soft, high-quality, 100 percent cotton baby and children's clothes can be bought from **Hanna Andersson** and **Biobottoms. Globalwear,** a wholesaler, is one of the few companies that makes clothes in silk for children, starting at age two. **Lill-ing** has soft, undyed wool baby shirts, long johns, rompers, and bodysuits.

As mentioned in chapter 2, some fabrics are finished with formaldehyde to make them permanent press or to keep pleats in. Some finishes are applied to fabrics to make them stain or fire resistant. To remove fabric finishes, fill the washing machine, sink, or bathtub with water, add 1 cup of baking soda, and soak new clothing overnight, agitating occasionally. Wash and dry at least three times before baby wears the garment, adding ¼ cup of baking soda to the detergent in the first two washes, and ½ cup vinegar only in the final wash. After all three cycles, check to see if water beads up on the fabric or readily soaks in. If it beads up, wash and dry again.

Mothproofing and fire-retardant finishes also emit irritating VOCs. So do mothballs; do not dress infants in clothing that has been stored in mothballs until it's been washed and aired out well. A baby will be less likely to develop allergic skin reactions if exposure to VOCs and formaldehyde is reduced. Even after many washings, these chemicals can continue to be released from fabrics.

Fire-resistant and flame-retarding finishes must, by federal law, be applied to infants' and children's sleepwear. Before these standards were adopted in 1972, up to sixty children a year died because their garments caught fire, according to *The New York Times.* By 1991, the number of deaths had dropped to six per year. However, up to 300 children are still seriously burned each year when their cotton clothes, usually T-shirts, catch fire.

If you prefer to let your baby sleep in untreated cotton clothing, you owe it to yourself and your baby to be extra vigilant about fire hazards in your home. Some parents feel safer using standard treated pyjamas or nightgowns, but layering them over all-cotton undergarments, which are more comfortable against a baby's skin. As mentioned in the bedding section of chapter 2, pure wool is naturally fire retardant, and a wool-covered mattress does not have to be treated with finishes. If the room is cold, you can use a lightweight wool baby blanket or shawl in the crib, or put baby in a soft wool outfit, such as **Lill-ing**'s baby bunting, as extra security.

But the best security of all is a frequently checked smoke alarm in baby's room.

There is no organic certification for wool as yet, but some farmers do not use chemicals on their sheep's wool, and the labels on their products say so. If you're a knitter, look for these. Skin allergies or reactiveness to wool fiber, however, do run in some families; if this is the case in either parent's family, be careful about dressing your baby in wool. Some types of wool, like merino, and some knits, such as pointelle or stockinette, result in a finer feel that doesn't irritate many people as easily as coarse wools. Companies such as **Lill-ing** use very fine, untreated merino wools in their naturally off-white baby clothing. If you or someone in your family knits, **Green Mountain Spinnery** produces several undyed, untreated wools in natural gray, brown, and white, and several simple patterns for baby sweaters, soakers, hats, mittens, and booties. **Earthspun Heritage Natural Fibers** sells wool yarn that's been processed with vegetable-based soap, canola oil, and vegetable dyes.

For the chronically wool-allergic or just plain itchy, many items of baby outerwear come in polyester fleece from a plethora of companies. This stuff is virtually indestructible, so it's always welcome as a hand-me-down. We know little girls who avidly wait for their big brothers to outgrow the next item of fleece. Eco-spun, used by many of the baby clothes companies we've mentioned, and **Patagonia**'s PCR Synchilla fleeces are made from recycled plastic soda bottles, so buying baby and children clothing made of this material reduces, to some extent, our impact on the earth. WARNING: *Synthetic fleece is not flame-resistant.*

Then again, why buy? This is a question we should all be asking ourselves when we think we need something, including that cute, fuzzy, printed baby coat. The best way to keep our landfills from overloading is to recycle and reuse clothes. Take some time to visit school and church rummage sales, the Salvation Army, or your local thrift shop. You might find the perfect, puffy Japanese or French snowsuit in just your baby's size, and you can give it back when your baby outgrows it.

Just as babies naturally smell sweet and have fine, glowing skin, undyed, natural-color fabrics are most appropriate to clothe them with. It's also the most comfortable. "Dyes make sheets and clothing rough to the touch," says Katherine Tiddens, owner of **Terra Verde.** It's important to be watchful, because even organic cotton may have been dyed with caustic dyes. Give all baby clothing the "feel" test. Run it against your cheek. Does it scratch at all? Chances are it will even after it's washed. Chemical dyes are made to be color-fast, after all. Mindy Pennybacker has been given T-shirts that she's washed dozens of times, hoping they'll "soften up" enough for her sensitive skin (wool allergies run in her family), but they never do. Look for the words "low-impact dyes" on clothing labels. Some companies, such as **Patagonia** and **Ecobaby,** are starting to avoid harmful dyes and processes (such as "fixing" colors with chromium and copper) that release toxins into our rivers, streams, and groundwater. You can also try and dress baby in colors that don't require such high doses of heavy metals. That means not choosing black, turquoise, bright green, fuchsia, and bright red, according to fiber industry consultant Linda Grose. Vegetable dyes and "color-grown" cottons, the latter having subtle natural greenish, orange, or brown shades, are available in baby clothes from **Ecosport.**

Before you put any item of clothing on your baby, make sure you've washed it. Any new garment, even "green" cotton, does have a smell. Sometimes it's from the packaging. And, if it hasn't been wrapped in packaging, it may have accumulated fine dust in the warehouse or store.

Newborn's Layette

As newborns spit up and tend to produce frequent runny stools, they often need to have their clothes changed two or three times a day. The following layette should serve you adequately at first.

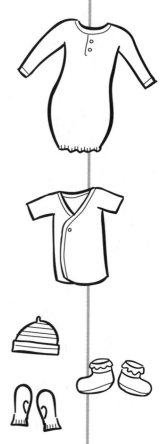

- 6 *swaddling, or receiving blankets,* de rigueur for calming baby at night and carrying during the day

- 1 *soft, breathable knit cotton cap* to keep newborn's head warm (Usually the hospital sends one home with you, but it's good to have an extra.)

- 10 *undershirts.* As with hooded towels, you simply cannot have enough of these. Plain, pure cotton T-shirts provide a soft layer between baby's skin and outer clothes. Because buttons can cause you to fumble or can fall off, make certain that undershirts fasten with snaps or ties, or have overlapping flaps at the neck (called "lap" or "envelope" neck tees) that enable them to spread wide when going on over baby's tender head. It's nice to have both long- and short-sleeved undershirts. Carter's, available at department and baby stores, are a great 100 percent cotton classic.

- 3 *onesies.* Lap- or snap-neck garments that cover the whole torso like a leotard and snap at the crotch (Because they don't ride up, they keep baby's belly warm.)

- 2 *play outfits,* such as overalls or a jumpsuit or romper, depending on the season (Snap crotches result in less wear-and-tear on baby and parent when changing diapers.)

- 3 *creepers or stretchies.* These unionsuits with feet look kind of homely; however, once put on your baby, they will look absolutely adorable. Some creepers are stretchy, some not. They should snap closed and have snaps up the insides of the legs for ease of changing. They do seem to feel comforting to newborns, and are nice— with nonskid soles—for babies who can stand, too.

- 3 *nightgowns or sleep sacks.* Also known as buntings, these nightgowns, which close beneath baby's feet with a drawstring or snaps, have a calming effect similar to swaddling. Try to find some with fold-over sleeves that turn into mitts, preventing baby from scratching herself with her fingernails.

- 1 *cardigan sweatshirt with hood,* in cotton (A snap-shoulder, pullover sweatshirt can also be a soft extra layer over a creeper or overalls.)

- 3 *pairs booties or infant socks*

- *soft cotton mitts for hands,* to prevent self-scratching

- *diapers and diaper covers.* Whether you're using cloth or disposable diapers, a soft terry cover gives baby a more put-together look and provides an extra layer of absorbency and cushioning.

Optional:

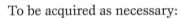

- *transport pouches or sacks.* We lose heat most rapidly from our extremities—head, hands, and feet—and that goes for babies, too. When preparing to drive baby home from the hospital, you have the conundrum of how to bundle a very tiny baby into a carseat. The safety harness comes up between the legs, so baby cannot be swaddled in the seat. A creeper will provide a layer of warmth, and you can and should cover baby with a blanket once she's strapped into her seat. (Double-check that the seat is properly strapped into the car's fastened seat belt, as well!) But an extra layer of comfort can provide the feeling of swaddling. Look for baby sacks—armless pouches with legs that can also be used in the stroller or in a Snugli. StaySnug is a 100 percent cotton flannel blanket with leg pouches from the **Crosby Company.** WARNING: *when using a sack, make sure it does not cover baby's face.* **Patagonia** has a Baby Bunting made of Synchilla fleece that converts from a "bag" to a suit with zippered legs; it can fit in car seats, Snuglis, or backpacks.

To be acquired as necessary:

- 1 *cardigan sweater,* in fine, nonitchy wool or cotton, depending on the season (Or maybe you can find a pullover sweater that snaps or laces closed at the shoulder. It helps to have a knitter in the extended family!)

- *a snowsuit in winter.* For a newborn, a one-piece probably makes most sense; for older babies, overalls with matching jackets help adjust body temperature readily.

- *a warm hat for winter.* If baby's skin seems irritated by wool, try cotton or polyester fleece, which insulates well and is generally less itchy. **Patagonia** sells fleece baby hats, and **Hanna Andersson** has a tremendous selection of soft

cotton and wool hats, pilot caps, and hoods. **Ecosport** has organic cotton baby skullcaps, in thermal and more breathable pointelle weaves, and **Baby Bunz & Company** has them in organic cotton interlock or thermal knits.

- *a coverall or overall and jacket for fall or spring,* to provide an extra outer layer

- *a sunhat or brimmed cap for spring and summer.* If you regularly plant a hat on your child's head from birth on, she'll become accustomed to wearing it, and be less likely to rip it off later on.

- *booties or footed creepers with nonskid soles* for when baby starts pulling up to a standing position (Remember, though, that bare feet are fine for baby at home. In the rare case of feet that turn in or out, needing correction, your pediatrician will consult with you on the type of shoe or brace to be worn.)

- *cold-weather foot covers.* There are many soft, warm pull-on boots with which to warm baby's feet in cold weather out of doors.

  It's an old wives' tale that babies need arch support. Babies have wide flat feet. Shoes aren't needed until and unless baby is walking out of doors. Shoes are necessary for protection from bees, sharp rocks, and hot sidewalks. Choose a nonslippery, flexible sole.

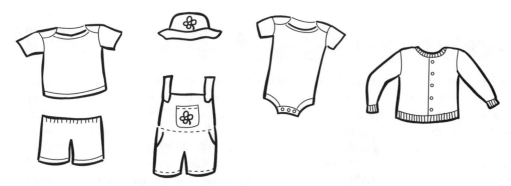

WHERE TO FIND NATURAL FABRIC, UNTREATED CLOTHES FOR BABY
All the baby clothes that **Terra Verde** carries are made from untreated cotton and wool. Brands include Bark & Seed, **Clean Clothes, Earthlings,** Family Clubhouse, and **Natureswear. Earthlings** makes wonderful organic cotton onesies, undershirts, hats, and ribbed cotton leggings, and Bark & Seed has a *really* soft drawstring-hem layette gown (we gave it the touch test).

Clothing Safety Tips

As closures, snaps, and zippers are preferable to buttons, which can be pulled off and choked on by infants and toddlers. It's difficult to find nonbutton clothes, so take the extra time to check clothing periodically to make sure that buttons are sewn on securely.

Avoid bulky zippers with pulltabs that can poke baby in the neck.

Hoods and hats that tie under the chin carry the risk of strangulation. Babies should never be put to sleep in hooded clothing or anything that ties around the neck. Hoods, with or without ties, should not be worn during active play, as they can catch on furniture or playground equipment, choking a child, particularly if she falls. But hoods are essential in some cases, such as the typical case of a child in a bitter winter who refuses to wear a hat or cap—a hood cannot be yanked off, and anyway, often feels less itchy. You can simply remove the cord from the hood; many hoods and jackets have string-free hoods that stay up reasonably well, many with a snap beneath the chin. Pacifiers should never be hung on strings.

AVOID OVERHEATING

In addition to taking chills easily, babies' bodies can rapidly and dangerously overheat in summer, resulting in dangerous dehydration. Take care not to overheat your baby in summer by overdressing her, and make certain that she gets plenty of liquids. Breast milk or formula should be adequate to keep a newborn hydrated, but in very hot weather, or if baby seems flushed, a supplementary bottle of water can be given. Just make sure that water is not used as a substitute for formula or breast milk, which are mostly water anyway but also contain necessary nutrients.

In cold weather, snowsuits and other outerwear, such as down jackets, will rapidly overheat baby indoors. Dress her and take her out without undue delay!

Children's Clothes Made without Child Labor

Now that brutal treatment of underpaid workers in Nike factories in Vietnam has made front-page news, most of us have become aware that much of the apparel sold in the United States has been made in inhumane sweatshop conditions—both abroad and sometimes domestically. As Jeffrey St. Clair, environmental editor of *Counterpunch,* writes in *The Green Guide,* "While these factories offer hope and jobs to the impoverished, the reality is that laborers work, without the most basic protections, for wages that fall short of what is required to survive." And many of these laborers are children. In June 1996, the Associated Press reported that more than 200 million children might be working in overseas sweatshops producing goods for American consumers. In 1997, for instance, it was revealed that Disney T-shirts were being made by Haitian children, and in 1996 the National Labor Committee unveiled the sorry fact that Wal-Mart's Kathie Lee Gifford clothing line was being made by child laborers in Honduras. In addition, some of Kathie Lee's blouses were being made in sweatshops in New York City.

When buying baby clothes, concerned parents should look beyond "Made in the U.S.A." labels for union labels, such as the International Ladies' Garment Worker's Union (I.L.G.W.U.) mark, which ensure that the product is made under fair labor standards. You can call the **Union Label and Service Department** of the **AFL-CIO** to verify if a specific product is union-made. Also, the **Council on Economic Priorities (CEP)** publishes a book called *Shopping for a Better World* that ranks companies by their policies and practices. The same information is available through an online database on **CEP**'s website. Once you've learned of a company's unfair labor practices, you can put pressure on them to change by boycotting their products and writing letters explaining why. Letters make a very effective tactic, according to Ellen Braune of the **National Labor Committee,** which has helped organize individual letter-writing campaigns to Disney and other companies.

As an alternative to buying clothing made by corporations abroad, you can look for products made by grassroots cooperatives of local peoples in Latin America, Asia, and India. Marketplace/Handwork of India is one example of a nonprofit alternative trade organization (ATO) that buys from grassroots cooperatives. These ATOs belong to the Fair Trade Federation, whose guidelines include paying a fair wage, using environmentally sustainable methods, and providing healthy, safe working conditions. While these producer-owned cooperatives cannot afford organic certification yet, or even find organically grown cotton for the most part, the human benefits they bring to local economies and low-income artisans merit our support.

Laundering Diapers and Baby Clothes

If your baby has a diaper or other skin rash, your laundry detergent should be on the list of possible culprits. As Dr. Harvey Karp says in the introduction to this book, he frequently sees children with rashes from clothes washed in allergenic laundry soaps. That can basically mean most laundry detergents, which contain dyes, fragrances, and harsh chemicals, residues of which can remain in clothes and irritate skin. Call your pediatrician about the rash. If it's not due to some other medical problem, your first step should be to try another laundry detergent for baby's clothes.

Seek laundry soaps labeled "fragrance-free" or "perfume-free." Avoid brighteners. Supermarket brands include Arm & Hammer Perfume and Dye Free, liquid or powder, and Tide Free. You can add borax to your laundry detergent as a cleaning booster. For diapers and baby clothes, Ivory Snow Soap Granules are mild yet effective. **Bi-O-Kleen** makes a laundry powder that's phosphate and chlorine free; it does contain oxygen bleach, which disinfects diapers. They also make a laundry liquid that uses grapefruit seed extract. **Logona**'s Sodasan concentrated laundry soap powder is biodegradable and made from organically grown vegetable oils.

If buying less-toxic laundry soaps from natural food stores or catalogs like **Harmony** or **Real Goods Trading Company,** be sure to ask whether they are scented, as even plant perfumes can irritate a baby's sensitive skin. Avoid chlorine bleaches, fabric softeners, and antistatic products, all of which can leave chemical residues on fabric after washing. Never mix chlorine bleach with products containing ammonia acids—including lemon juice and vinegar—since toxic gases can form.

You can add about ½ cup of white vinegar or lemon juice to the wash to brighten whites—just be sure there's no chlorine bleach in the detergent! Nonchlorine bleach alternatives include washing soda, sunlight, and Clorox 2 Liquid Bleach, **Ecover** Nonchlorine Bleach, Borax, and Borateam Dry Bleach. For fabric softening, add ½ cup of baking soda to the wash cycle. White vinegar also makes a perfectly good antistatic addition to the rinse cycle.

It's best not to wash more than a couple of dozen diapers at a time, or whatever your machine will hold without being packed. You want water to circulate freely around them. Wash with hot water and rinse twice. Chlorine-free bleaches can be used if you want your diapers to be white. But if you've bought "green" unbleached diapers, they won't show stains as much. And remember, the diaper will often be under a cover, so don't obsess about stains.

Dry at high heat, or, whenever you can, hang diapers outside in the sun, which will disinfect them naturally and also allow any residue odors from cleaning products to disperse. Sun-drying should be a top priority for all baby clothes, but especially for underthings. The sun seems to have a built-in softener, as well. When you use a clothes dryer, make sure that you put in a full load of laundry to save energy. There's no sense in operating a half-full dryer.

Before using a diaper service, ask them what sorts of detergents and disinfectants they use. If you (or your baby) are not happy with their choice of detergents, ask them if they can use alternative products.

Choosing Nontoxic Toys and Playing with Baby

It's wonderful to see how babies amuse themselves with the simplest articles at hand. They don't need or want a lot of toys in their first year, because they see almost everything as a toy. There will be a few favorites, of course, like a stuffed toy or flannel blanket, or even a diaper that baby cuddles for comfort. Through **Terra Verde,** you can also find wooden toys, including cars, a Jacob's ladder, clackers, and a cherrywood rattle by Mossy

wooden toys

Creek; the store also carries cuddly pigs and bears made of unbleached organic cotton with embroidered eyes by Foundlings.

But from the earliest age, it's wonderful to see how babies' play is also the way they challenge themselves to grow, step by developmental step.

In the first few months, a parent's reactive, engaging face is baby's favorite toy. You may think your baby is like a living doll, but actually the reverse is true. You are *her* life-size doll or teddy bear. You'd better get used to being a plaything, and enjoy it while you can, because someday, like Winnie the Pooh and the Velveteen Rabbit, you'll be outgrown—though you'll still be called upon for college tuition.

Other popular first toys are baby's fingers and toes. That's why "Little Piggies" is a timeless hit. But everyone welcomes a diversion now and then, and, happily for babies and parents, there are many nontoxic, developmentally appropriate toys available for each stage of growth. You will see your child work conscientiously to bring her hands together, to reach for and make contact with an object. Following her lead as she reaches out in the world, you can provide toys such as crib gyms for her to bat at, then grab at, as she lies on her back. Just be sensitive to giving her a break now and then; when she tires of an object, she will turn away from it. Then you can remove the crib gym and take her into your arms for a stroll to the window—even babies need to rest their tired eyes by looking into the distance. While babies want, and can take, a lot of stimulation, be considerate and don't overdo it. Read the signals. That includes knowing when to "get out of her face" when you're being your enchanting, singing, animated self and baby gets quiet and looks away. It's your signal to get quiet, too. She might also be ready for a nap, so you can try putting her down in her crib and lie down yourself. You need your rest, too, and the best time to take it is when baby does.

Newborns can be very alert and want to "play" right after a feeding, which can be a bit overwhelming at 4 A.M. In the first couple of weeks, play is more observational and intellectual on the baby's part than physical—just engaging the parent's attention and learning to focus her eyes a bit, and starting to reach for things, like a parent's eyeglasses. Don Wallace, Rory's father, tried to stay up for a while and hold him after Mindy fed him because Rory seemed to want to play. They'd sit by the window and watch the lights of the city, and Don would sing to him quietly. "I feel we really bonded in those early mornings," Don says.

As your baby develops month by month, she'll be ready for gradually more complex toys. However, if you give her a toy that's too advanced for her developmental stage, it can frustrate her and make her unhappy. Playing with your baby is a delicate balance between keeping her from getting too frustrated, and completing things she's trying to do, such as stack one block upon another, or discover the button that will open a door or ring a bell on the "busy box." Letting her do it by herself gives her an opportunity for growth. Be patient, and let her do things at her own speed.

Later in this chapter are some suggestions for types of toys and a few play ideas. You'll come up with quite a few yourself, as parenthood seems to get the creative juices flowing. Maybe it's hormones.

Keep in mind that our Appendices list some excellent guides for following and anticipating your baby's developmental changes and needs. There are books like Antonia van der Meer's *Great Beginnings* and Theresa Caplan's *The First Twelve Months of Life* that take you and your baby through the first twelve months of life, month by month and stage by stage, and books like Dr. T. Berry Brazelton's *Touchpoints* that cover emotional and behavioral development until age five. Remember to complete every interaction with your baby. Give her time to react. If you smile at your baby, wait for her to return the communication before you turn away. It is also very important to say good-bye to a baby or young child rather than just sneak away. We should be every bit as courteous with our children as we are with our coworkers or friends. After all, our babies first learn social skills and empathy from us.

Keep Vinyl (PVC) Toys Out of Your Child's Mouth

In the average toy store, "nontoxic" stickers can be found affixed to all manner of teethers, bath toys, and other flexible plastic toys aimed at the ages in which babies and children are most likely to put toys in their mouths. If these flexible plastic toys are made of vinyl, as they conventionally are, then they have not been proven to be nontoxic at all. Soft PVC toys contain chemicals called phthalate esters, which work as softening agents, or plasticizers. The problem: many studies on all kinds of vinyl products show that chemicals readily migrate from the plastic to other surfaces and vaporize into the air. Phthalates have been linked to cancer, kidney and liver damage, hormone disruption, and respiratory ailments such as asthma. A study by **Greenpeace** scientists and independent German labs showed that these hazardous chemicals can leach into children's mouths when they suck and chew on the toys. Greenpeace found that seventy-one soft plastic toys and teethers for children under age three made around the world contain from 10 to 40 percent phthalates by weight. Toy researcher David Santillo, a Greenpeace scientist from Exeter University in England, said that the smell from a new PVC toy comes from "the phthalates volatilizing from it." The German labs found that of twenty-three PVC toys tested, twelve were leaching chemical additives at levels five to six times the recommended limits set by German health authorities. Among the toys tested were several manufactured by U.S. companies.

A number of Swedish, Dutch, and Danish supermarkets, toy stores, and manufacturers, including IKEA, Lego, and the Dutch Toys 'R' Us, pledged to stop making or carrying PVC toys in 1997. In September 1998, Mattel announced that it was phasing out the use of phthalates in teething toys, and would begin shipping phthalate-free teethers in early 1999. Most of the teethers are made by Mattel's Fisher-Price division; the company will not, however, be recalling such phthalate-containing products as Activity Keys on a teething ring, and the Rock-a-Stack soft teething circles that stack on a plastic post. Gerber, Disney, Evenflo, Hasbro, and the First Years have announced a similar phaseout of phthalates in their toys. The Little Tykes division of Rubbermaid plans to phase out PVC entirely. In November, 1998, Toys 'R' Us, Target, Sears, Wal-Mart, and K-Mart announced their decision to remove phthalate-containing teethers, rattles, and pacifiers from their shelves.

A final safety rule of thumb for all toys from age newborn until three years: Make sure that toys—and anything else baby plays with—are too large to fit inside the mouth, and do not contain small parts that might get detached and pose a choking hazard.

Phthalates may not be the only potential toxins leaching from PVC toys. There may also be hazardous levels of cadmium and lead, as well. Attorneys General from several states are reviewing industry research about lead, cadmium, and phthalates in PVC products and seeking information about alternatives.

For these reasons, we are happy to list a wealth of alternatives for your child, that is, toys made of fabric and wood.

Age 0 to Six Months

Toys for a very young baby who can't hold things include small, soft stuffed toys that she can encompass in her still-dim field of vision as you hold it near her, perhaps stroking her cheek with it, and toys with rattles or bells that you can shake for her. You can introduce a crib mobile at two months or so, with swinging shapes that baby will gradually begin to swipe at. Some of them have detachable sections for different stages, converting to gyms with graspable objects when the baby becomes capable of this. (Make sure that any detachable pieces are not so small that your baby can put them in her mouth and choke on or swallow them.) A musical mobile, which should hang well above baby's reach, is entertaining to watch and comforting to listen to, but don't let it repeat for too long! It's a good idea to choose mobiles and gyms that swing away from the crib so that they're not always dangling above baby. Gyms and other toys that hang across the crib should always be removed when baby sleeps, and taken down permanently by age four to five months, to prevent possible entanglement as baby learns to sit up.

Studies show that newborns see bold contrasts and colors best, preferring mobiles and toys in black and white or in primary colors like red and blue. Also, babies do get bored with the same old toy. You can rotate toys, replacing a once-favored rattle or soft toy with something similar but in a different color, shape, or size. Baby will notice the difference. When interest in the new toy flags, you can rotate the old one back and it will be welcomed with open arms, as both familiar and new. Replace that mobile with another that plays a different tune. You can trade and rotate mobiles and toys with other parents you meet at the park. Just make sure to wash them or wipe them down with hot water and a nontoxic soap before they go on to the next child.

Until baby can sit up, at about five months, she will often be playing while lying on her back. When she's doing so, provide her with smallish, lightweight toys that won't hurt her if she drops them in her face. Terrycloth animals and soft rattles are nice. In velour of bright primary colors, Brio makes soft, stuffed rattles in the shape of a sausage dog or a clown, with bells inside. An important safety detail: Both toys have embroidered eyes rather than plastic eyes that can be pulled off and popped in the mouth. These toys are available from **Baby Bunz & Co.** Small organic cotton French terry boy and girl bears can be bought from **Ecosport.** You can hold your baby propped in your lap and hold things in front of her as she tries to swipe at, then touch and hold them, as she does with her crib mobile or gym.

In these early months, babies love to listen to their parents' voices. Perhaps they recognize our voices from hearing them in the womb; studies have shown that playing music or reading aloud to a pregnant belly, silly as it can make you feel, may contribute to intellectual development later on. It is really never too early to read to your baby—though again, don't let your fascinating voice drone on too long if she shows flagging interest. It's very important to read to your child, as everyone knows, and here's some recent proof: In a 1997 study, researchers from Johns Hopkins University and AT&T Laboratories read aloud from children's stories to eight-month-olds each day for ten days. They then read to the babies from a list of words from the stories, and a list of words that had not been used in the stories. The babies paid more attention to the words from the stories. The researchers concluded that the babies were already remembering the sounds and distinguishing between words.

That said, you must also take care that you're not raising a Type-A child. Don't whip out those French flash cards!

When baby is two months old and can lift her head when lying on her stomach, be very careful not to place toys under the neck or head—she could bring her head down suddenly and hurt herself or choke. We once saw someone wedge a fabric ball under a small baby's chin! This is very dangerous. In the third month, soft fabric cubes with different patterns on each side, and easily graspable toys can be introduced. Brio makes natural and painted wood rolling rattles, and a painted wood round cage with a bell visible inside, available from **Baby Bunz & Co.** An interesting wooden Woogle, a flexible wormy shape of segmented wood with a couple of sliding rings, or Rings and Rods provide readily graspable fun from **Ecobaby.**

Whatever you're doing with your baby, whether it's play, changing, bathing, or wheeling her in the stroller, talk to her about what you're doing and seeing. Tell baby what she's doing, whatever it is. She'll put it all together, from the words for facial features and body parts, household objects, toys and animals, trees, water, sky, houses and cars, to why people are doing what they do. Pause to let her verbalize, too. Ask her questions, and listen carefully to the response. There's a lot she has to tell you, even though she doesn't speak English yet.

Six Months to One Year

Now baby is trying to refine her grasp, working toward the pincer grasp in which an older baby can hold objects delicately between forefinger and thumb. Stacking rings in soft fabric or wood and big wood beads that she can move along on sculptural wire frames are good choices at this age. **The Natural Baby Company** has a simple bead-wire "roller coaster." **Ecobaby** has soft fabric rings that stack on a soft post, and big wooden beads. There are also activity boxes, or busy boards, that baby can play with while lying on her belly and, later, while sitting up. A good playboard will have lots of interesting bells to ring and squeaks to push at both eye levels. Baby is also probably becoming more interested in music, and as she begins to acquire language skills it's a good idea to play songs for babies and very young children to which you can sing along together. Simple folk songs are generally a hit.

Dramas involving dialogues between stuffed toys, who quickly take on distinct personalities, entertain babies and children and can also help with working through issues that come up, such as separation. For instance, Mother Rabbit can say goodbye, leaving Baby Rabbit with a babysitter Brontosaurus, and then come back. Father Bear can offer Baby Bear different items of clothing to choose from while getting dressed.

Seven-month-olds are very ready for books. **The Playstore** has little wooden picture books. Excellent books that can span the infant through beginning reading age include the **Little Bear** series by Arnold Lobel, which combines gentle humor and plenty of parental love with repetitions of key words. Bigger, more huggable stuffed animals become true companions to older babies. **Earth Friendly Goods** has a soft, but durable, organic cotton terry E.F. Bear, who comes dressed in a T-shirt and for whom other accessories can be ordered.

Babies love to look at other babies, or themselves in the mirror, and Helen Oxenbury's little board books engage them readily with simple, clear drawings of babies doing basic things. *I Can, I Touch, I Hear,* and *I See* can be ordered from **Baby Bunz & Co.**

At six months, you can also begin rolling a ball to baby as you sit across from each other on the floor. A seven-month-old will delight in playing patty-cake, peek-a-boo, and other classic baby games, or hand games of your own invention.

Keep in mind that everyday household objects will please babies every bit as much as toys. As soon as babies can crawl and sit, they will want to get into cupboards. It's a good idea to clear out lower cupboards in different rooms and put baby-safe stuff in them. For babies, there's nothing more satisfying than banging on a pot or pan with a nice rounded wooden spoon, except having you sit down on the floor to make music, too.

Eight Months and Beyond

At about seven or eight months, babies still delight in opening and closing flaps. They will be able to amuse themselves with a cardboard box with a four-flap top. They will also be fascinated with an empty box that they can fill with objects and then empty. They become able to distinguish shapes and textures. After your baby has reached the one-year mark, a shape sorter makes an interesting challenge. **Ecobaby** has them in stuffed fabric or wood. Later, when they're toddling at about twelve to eighteen months, they develop a fascination with garden gates and doors, swinging them open and closed, over and over. You'll have to watch for pinched fingers. They'll enjoy sturdy-paged books with window flaps you open to see characters beneath.

Brio, a Swedish toymaker, and **T.C. Timber,** a U.S. company, make wonderful wooden toys for babies and children up to about eight years of age. Both companies use nontoxic paints and varnishes that do not, in our firsthand experience, emit smelly vapors. They also make wooden train sets, complete with drawbridges and winches, if you like, and Noah's Arks with animals in pairs.

Large wooden beads on a string from **Ecobaby** and a natural wood hammer and cobbler bench from **The Natural Baby Company** will help develop hand-eye coordination for the older baby. The Natural Baby Company also has a small, baby-size wood-and-hide drum made by the Pueblo Indians in New Mexico. The nine-month-old will begin to enjoy stacking paper cups or wood boxes. The Natural Baby Company has six nesting wood boxes, with nursery scenes on each side.

Eleven-month-old babies will start examining objects in great detail. They will take toys from a bag, study each one carefully, and put it back in. They will begin to think about assembling toys, recognizing toys, like Lego sets, that have been built. They will enjoy taking them apart, but watch out, as Legos pose a choking hazard because of their small size. While we warn against too many plastic toys, there are worthy exceptions, and Duplo, the large-size Legos for ages eighteen months to four years, are one of these. They can be very satisfying for the youngest builders. Lego is also one of the few companies that has pledged to not use PVC plastic. Brio and T.C. Timber make wooden blocks in small sizes more easily grasped by the little hands of babies up to two years old. They come in lovely bright colors and exciting shapes, like arches, half-circles, triangles, and pyramids, too. **The Natural Baby Company** has thirty ABC wooden blocks in a basket.

For older toddlers and children, big, natural wood standard blocks in all shapes for some serious floor-covering building projects can be found in most toy stores and catalogues. A parent's involvement in such building will greatly enhance a young child's enjoyment. Ask baby what you're building. Remember to let her take the lead in the building plan, directing you to put what where.

Toddlers enjoy push and pull toys. **The Natural Baby Company** has a wooden lawnmower with clacking wood balls inside and an adorable wooden frog pull toy; **Ecobaby** has a wooden wiggle worm pull toy. WARNING: *Never leave baby alone with a toy that has a pull string, because of possible choking hazards.* Ecobaby and **The Playstore** also have wood wagons that can be pushed, like a walker. One-year-olds greatly enjoy ride-on toys—little horses or trains with wheels that they can scoot along on, pushing with their feet. Kid Classics makes a big, cheerful wooden turtle shape sorter, with star, circle, triangle, and square that fit into holes in the shell. It's available from **Learning Curve.** Plan Toys uses "replenishable rubber wood" for its Punch and Drop, which involves hammering wooden balls through holes in a slightly flexible box lid. Plan Toys also has a fun "sliceable" wooden vegetable set, with a blunt wooden "knife," lots of fun for two-year-olds who like to play at kitchen work; and fifty colorful blocks-in-a-bag, made from replenishable wood.

As your toddler develops, she'll be ready for puzzles and even very simple wooden board games designed for two-year-olds, where you roll a die and move a figure along. Good starters for this kind of play include wooden tiles with pictures to match in pairs, such as the memory game from **The Natural Baby Company,** with airplanes, zebras, roosters, frogs to turn up two by two, and match. They also have bright little wooden puzzles of very few pieces that are raised, so that chubby toddler fingers can more easily grasp them.

Most communities have baby stores and toy shops that carry toys made of natural materials. Seek them out. Shops like Dinosaur Hill in New York City, **The Play Store** in Palo Alto, California, and Child's Play in Honolulu, Hawaii, carry wooden blocks, vehicles, dolls, puzzles, and zoo animals, and toys made of other natural materials. **The Play Store** offers their products by mail.

Exercise and Active Play

For a baby, play, exercise, and intellectual and physical development are all intertwined. There's no such thing as a lazy baby; nor should parents worry about trying to make a baby exercise so she won't get fat. Babies naturally push and challenge themselves physically; they are driven to advance from stage to stage. The parents' job is to play with baby and provide a safe environment for baby's active, exploratory play as much as possible. A pattern of saying "no," for instance, each time a ten-month-old tries to crawl upstairs may both impede baby's developmental growth and facilitate the growth of excess fat. Instead, follow your child up the stairs, and begin training her to come down safely, backwards, by moving her legs and hands to lower stairs. You can also demonstrate, yourself. Always stand below your baby on stairs, so you can catch her if she slips.

Balls are great fun, starting at about age six months. While babies and toddlers can't really throw and catch balls much before the age of three—and then only quite big, light balls—they get a great deal of fun and exercise from chasing around and picking up balls that have been thrown or rolled to them. Frisbee, too, can be adapted to include the young child.

A fun form of exercise for baby and parent is dance. You can do this together, with baby in your arms, or apart. If she's at the lying-on-her-back stage, she can lie on the floor while you put the music on and dance, on your feet, in front of her. Choose something with a good beat, and she'll start waving her arms and kicking her feet. Her preferences in music will emerge. Or dance holding your baby in your arms. She'll start to bob with the beat. When she grows tall enough, she can stand on your feet and hold your hands while you dance. Older babies, toddlers, and children also enjoy games like Simon Says. Even before baby can talk, she can lead—for example, by putting a hand on her head and having you chant, "Simon says put your hand on your head," and following suit.

Ask your pediatrician, at monthly and bimonthly checkups, what sorts of physical activities baby is ready for. The doctor will give you cues in a normal visit, asking you whether baby is pushing up on all fours, or pulling to a stand. At six months or so, babies enjoy being pulled to a standing position in your lap. Hold her under the arms and let her bounce gently. She'll start to enjoy gentle roughhousing at times. She'll let you know when she's ready for more rambunctious play. Lie on the floor and let your baby attack you, and do a little mock-wrestling, groaning loudly with exertion as baby bests you. Babies also enjoy using a parent as a gym. You can play "horsie": lie on your back, and tuck your knees to your chest, and place baby so that she's lying on her belly along your shins. Then, making sure you have a good grip on baby's body, you can bounce her lightly. A toddler will be able to sit on your shins, really riding her horse. Warning: Some children never tire of this, no matter how big they grow.

Many YWCAs and health clubs have parent-and-baby exercise classes. In some of them, the goal is to exercise the mother while keeping baby entertained. This not only helps you get back in shape after birth, but allows you to meet other active moms with babies who can be friends with yours. Gymboree has exercise classes for babies. These can be a good place to learn games and songs, as well as a source for play dates. Even though babies mostly parallel play rather than interact until about age two, they very much enjoy seeing each other and making contact. They recognize each other.

It's also a good idea to make inquiries at your local Y about classes in cardiopulmonary resuscitation (CPR) specifically aimed at saving babies. Because babies are so much smaller than adults, various lifesaving techniques have been modified so as not to hurt them. Such classes also teach preventive measures, such as avoiding common choking foods like hotdogs and grapes.

If we can leave you with one message regarding your child and play, it's that you should take some time every day to get down to your baby or child's level, on the floor, make eye contact and play with her whatever game she likes. You'll start out lying face to face, maybe pushing a stuffed worm along. Then you'll be sitting, rolling a ball between you. You'll be building blocks and assembling wooden train tracks, populating zoos with little animals of all species. You'll get beaten at chess. At some point, even if or especially if you're a pacifist, you may find yourself setting up whole campaigns with miniature tanks and airplanes; if you're a feminist, you may find yourself dressing Barbie for a ride in her convertible. Children need to feel they have some choice and control over what goes on in their world. So in the realm of play, whatever your child wants, play along—within reason of course. So long as the play doesn't endanger children or others, and they understand these limits (a baby won't, but reason develops over time), it sets a healthy precedent. In eighteen years, after all, your baby will be an independent adult.

chapter eight

Feeding Your Baby

Soon after birth, your newborn will want to be fed. Having spent months in the womb, an environment that automatically provides nourishment to the developing fetus, he won't be used to feeling hunger. From then on, when his belly's empty, if he gets hungry enough, he'll cry. But, as a diligent parent, you won't wait that long. You'll learn to recognize the signs that a feeding is necessary, and you'll feel responsible for providing your baby with adequate nourishment, whether it comes from breast milk, formula, or eventually, solid food. It may seem like a tremendous burden, but in reality it's not so difficult. Giving your baby a nutritious, healthy, and safe diet is as easy as giving him—and yourself, if you're breast-feeding—the fruits (and veggies!) of nature. In this chapter, you'll find out how to do this easily.

We wholeheartedly recommend breast-feeding. It's the healthiest and most environmentally safe way to feed your baby. In this book, we'll explain why breast milk is the superior food for babies, how you can get over some difficulties, such as jaundice and allergies, and how to pump and store breast milk.

If you can't breast-feed, you needn't feel guilty. Formula offers nutrients that help a baby thrive. You do need to be a little discriminating as to your choice of bottles and the way you clean them, of course, as formula doesn't come in the sterile, natural package that breast milk does!

As your baby grows, he'll become more interested in solid foods. Start him out right by introducing a diverse and healthful organic diet. This chapter will provide tips on what to feed your baby and how to prepare baby foods without feeling overwhelmed, and how to be sure that baby's foods are safe from environmental and bacterial contaminants.

You'll find this chapter organized as follows:

- The Benefits of Breast-feeding
- Bottle-Feeding Dos and Don'ts
- Organic Baby Food

The Benefits of Breast-Feeding

While it may seem obvious, it bears repeating: Breast-feeding is the optimal way to feed your baby. And the American Academy of Pediatrics (AAP) agrees, promoting breast-feeding of infants as "the foundation of good feeding practices." Not only is breast milk the most appropriate, natural, and nourishing substance for infants, but the very act of breast-feeding nurtures a strong emotional bond between you and your baby. No substitute, be it cows' milk or synthetic formula, can include the nutritional components—the living cells, hormones, active enzymes, immunoglobulins, and unique compounds—that human breast milk does.

Moms gain some benefits from nursing, too. The low cost and convenience of breast-feeding makes it ideal for all women. Breast milk is free, whereas the cost of formula is about $1,000 per year. While you do need more calories to produce enough milk, that amount is not significant enough to cost you much. You only need to consume about 500 more calories per day—a bagel and a piece of fruit or two will do it—to produce enough milk for a newborn, according to Chan McDermott, a breast-feeding educator at the Texas Department of Health. "If you eat when you're hungry, you'll be fine," Chan says. If you work, you'll also need to invest in a breast pump and a few bottles, which should cost about $200 to $300. Otherwise, you won't need any extra equipment, nor will you have to sterilize bottles and heat formula. Breast milk is always ready to go, sterile, and the right temperature, no matter where you are; you won't need to carry around bottles of formula whenever you leave the house. And you won't need to feed your baby any kind of supplemental drink, food, or vitamins.

Breast-feeding also saves resources. The manufacture, packaging, advertising, and transportation of synthetic infant formulas and baby bottles use up energy, paper, and petroleum resources. Protein from animal sources is much more resource-intensive, requiring lots of grain and water. Packaging, bottles, and nipples are usually not recyclable nor are they made of recycled materials. Some are made of plastics that contain hormone disruptors, such as phthalates in PVC plastic, used for some nipples, and bisphenol-A in polycarbonate plastics, a common baby-bottle material.

Breast-fed babies become ill less often than formula-fed babies, meaning fewer trips to the doctor's office or hospital. This saves not only time and money, but also all that anxiety!

Nursing offers an experience that is emotionally satisfying. "Breast-feeding is psychologically good for both baby and mother. It provides an emotional bond between them," says Dr. Philip Landrigan, Mothers & Others medical advisor.

Health Benefits to Baby

"The number one reason I choose to breast-feed is the health benefits to my son, Angus," says Lane Graves, Mothers & Others West Coast regional director. Most breast-feeding women would agree with Lane. In terms of health benefits, human milk is unsurpassed by anything else. "Researchers haven't even identified all of the components in breast milk so there's no way it, or its health benefits, could be entirely duplicated in a formula," says breast-feeding specialist Chan McDermott, adding that, "Cows' milk, which is used for many formulas, is really designed for baby cows." While infant formulas serve as a good substitute if the mother cannot breast-feed or chooses not to, breast milk is a superior food for human babies.

Breast-feeding offers infants:

- *A perfectly balanced composition of fats, carbohydrates, and protein.* Breast milk adjusts to the needs of your baby. For example, just after your baby is born, you will produce colostrum, the first milk, which provides sugar, water, proteins, and minerals, plus antibodies. This first milk is quite laxative, so it helps move meconium out of a newborn's intestine. This sticky, tarlike substance promotes jaundice in about 50 percent of all babies if it is not pushed out of the intestine.

  If your baby is born prematurely, the breast milk that you produce will be suited for the nutritional needs of an early arrival whose immune system and organs are not as developed as the full-term baby. Note: A premature baby may still require some additional vitamin supplementation. If your baby is premature, follow your doctor's advice.

  The proportion of nutrients in your breast milk will change to match *your* baby's needs as he grows.

- *The most digestible form of food.* Breast milk contains an enzyme, not found in cows' and goats' milk, that aids digestion. Nutrients, such as protein, calcium, iron, amino acids, zinc, and vitamins in breast milk are more easily absorbed by the baby than those in cows' milk or formula. The curds in breast milk are smaller and more easily digested by babies than those in cows' milk and formula. And sick babies benefit greatly from breast milk. Unlike sick formula-fed babies, who may need to go on an artificial electrolyte solution because formula is too difficult to digest, breast-fed babies can usually continue to nurse. Substitutes don't have breast milk's antibodies, which speed healing.

  It is rare that a baby cannot tolerate breast milk. This is usually a result of allergy to something in the mother's diet or, very rarely, to conditions like phenylketonuria (PKU) and galactosemia, which prevent the affected baby from properly metabolizing substances in the breast milk. A baby cannot be allergic to breast milk.

- *Improved immune response.* Breast milk has antibodies and immunoglobulins that protect babies from disease. "It has been called 'white blood' because it has as many white blood cells as blood itself," according to Dr. Harvey Karp, Mothers & Others medical advisor. Breast milk also contains components that help develop the baby's immune system. In their policy statement on breast-feeding, the AAP states that breast-feeding decreases the incidence and severity of: diarrhea and other gastrointestinal disorders, lower respiratory infection, ear infections, bacteremia, bacterial meningitis, botulism, and urinary tract infection. A study published in the September 1998 issue of *Pediatrics* showed that premature babies in neonatal intensive care units who were fed breast milk had a 43 to 47 percent decreased risk of acquiring infections while hospitalized.

- *Decreased risk of Sudden Infant Death Syndrome (SIDS).*

- *Possible long-term protection against* allergies, asthma, some cancers, diabetes, Crohn's disease, and chronic digestive diseases.

- *Possible enhancement of cognitive development.*

- *Proper dental and jaw development and less likelihood of speech impediments.* Suckling and constant pulling encourages the growth of well-formed jaws and straight healthy teeth. Breast-fed babies get fewer cavities.

- *Reduced likelihood of becoming overweight.* Breast-fed babies drink until they are satisfied. But some parents encourage their bottle-fed babies to finish an entire bottle at each feeding, not realizing they are overfeeding. Children who begin their lives overweight are more likely to become overweight adults, according to a study published in the March 1998 issue of *Pediatrics*.

The AAP recommends that you breast-feed your baby for at least one year. The longer you breast-feed the greater the benefits to your child. Because Mindy Pennybacker is asthmatic, Rory's pediatrician advised her to breast-feed for at least one and a half years to provide him with antibodies against allergies that could trigger asthma. She did so, and Rory has been free of asthmatic symptoms. Even if you're not certain that breast-feeding is for you, it's beneficial to at least try it. Once you've started your newborn on formula, you can't go back because your breasts won't produce milk. But if you start out nursing, your baby will have a healthy start. Since there is no equivalent to colostrum, even a few days of breast-feeding will give your baby a nutritional and immunological boost during his adjustment to life outside the womb. You might also discover that you enjoy this time spent with your baby.

Remember that you aren't locked into your decision to breast-feed. You can always switch to formula at any time, knowing that you've at least given breast-feeding a chance.

Benefits for Mothers

Mothers also enjoy tremendous benefits by nursing. First, breast-feeding fosters a strong emotional bond between mother and baby. When Lane Graves returned to her job, she says that she gained a level of intimacy with five-month-old Angus before and after work that she would not have experienced if she were feeding him formula. Second, night feedings will be so much easier. You won't have to stumble around looking for bottles and mixing formula. You can lie down with your baby and let him do all the work! And, third, breast-feeding has positive health effects for mothers, including:

- *Reduced risk for premenopausal breast and ovarian cancers and osteoporosis.*

- *Faster return to prepregnancy size.* While breast-feeding won't necessarily make you lose weight quickly, as is commonly believed, milk production releases hormones that shrink the uterus, which expands to twenty times its usual size during pregnancy.

- *A natural cure for postpartum hemorrhaging.* Breast-feeding releases the hormone oxytocin, which discourages excess bleeding after delivery. Women who do not breast-feed must take synthetic oxytocin to achieve the same effect.

- *Less menstrual blood loss.* Nursing women may not ovulate for up to fourteen months after delivery, depending on how often they breast-feed and other circumstances. For some women, this can be a natural form of birth control for up to six months after delivery. The conditions are very specific, though, so don't rely on this. You should discuss nursing as a form of birth control with your doctor.

- *A calming, sedative effect.* Breast-feeding causes the release of prolactin, a hormone that dissolves anxiety. It may help you sleep better.

The How-Tos of Breast-feeding

Although breast-feeding is a natural activity, it can feel very awkward in the beginning. We rarely see women nursing, so it might seem complicated or mysterious. But once you start doing it, you'll learn that it is very natural and very easy. You won't even think about it after you and your baby get accustomed to each other.

Before you deliver your baby, you should talk with your doctor or midwife about breast-feeding and read a book or two on the subject. **La Leche League International** has an informative website and publishes an excellent resource book called *The Womanly Art of Breastfeeding*. They also have support groups all over the country and a hot line you can call if you need advice right away. You might find that these groups can not only offer information and advice, but can provide you with emotional strength and friendship as you battle your own misconceptions and those of your family and friends. (Because most of us have been kept in the dark about breast-feeding, don't be surprised by those well-meaning people who tell you that breast-feeding isn't all it's cracked-up to be.) *The Nursing*

Mother's Companion by Kathleen Huggins is another excellent guide on breast-feeding. General baby books, like Penelope Leach's *Your Baby and Child: From Birth to Age Five,* offer very good advice about breast-feeding. And you'll find at least a dozen or so books specifically on breast-feeding at your bookstore. Another good website to look at is that of **Promotion of Mother's Milk, Inc.**

Since excellent resources already exist, we won't delve into the subject of how to breast-feed in depth, but here is some basic information.

- The AAP recommends that you begin breast-feeding as soon as possible after birth, usually within the first hour. Long separations between you and your baby should be avoided, unless there is an exceptional medical reason.

- Though you may think that your baby should instinctively know that your breast will provide food, he doesn't necessarily make that connection right away. And sometimes your baby might be too sleepy to nurse, especially in the beginning, so he might not latch on immediately. You can help him along by using your free hand to cup your breast and softly stroke your nipple across your baby's lips to stimulate his sucking reflex. When he opens his mouth, gently place your nipple well inside his mouth. Sometimes, though a baby will appear to want to nurse, he doesn't have the sucking reflex down yet. Or you'll miss the magic moment. Relax and try again.

- Newborns should be nursed at any sign of hunger—increased alertness or activity, mouthing or "rooting" (actively turning his head towards the nipple and pursing his lips). Crying is a late sign of hunger. Newborns should be nursed eight to twelve times, or about every 90 minutes to 3 hours, during each 24-hour period. They usually nurse for about 10 to 15 minutes, but don't watch the clock. It's more important to watch your baby for signs that he's had his fill. Frequent nursing will help you boost your milk production. After a few weeks, your baby may begin to feed less often but for longer stretches.

- Don't try to breast-feed a baby who is very upset. Screaming babies will not latch on. First, try to calm your baby by rocking him or walking around with him in your arms. If you're having trouble getting your baby to latch on, you should also try having your partner take him from you for a few minutes. The smell of breast milk might only make a hungry, frustrated baby more upset. Having your partner calm your baby not only allows both of you to take a breather, but also gives your partner the chance to participate in the feeding experience and provide you with emotional support.

- Give breast-feeding a chance. The first few times you do it can be difficult. And it may take a few weeks to adjust to the rhythms of nursing. Relax. Ignore the naysayers. Seek support from other women who have nursed their babies and advice from your doctor and childbirth educators.

- You don't need to feed your baby any supplements while breast-feeding, unless your doctor recommends it. You also should avoid feeding your baby water, juice, and other foods before his sixth month, according to the AAP. Infants who drink too much water can suffer oral water intoxication. This occurs when sodium in the baby's blood becomes too diluted to allow the body to function properly, causing low body temperature, bloating, and altered mental state. Both breast milk and formula provide enough water to babies.

- Get enough rest and proper nourishment. While it is unlikely, you may not be able to produce enough milk if you and your body are under a lot of stress. And your baby's hunger and fussiness because he's not getting enough milk can increase your anxiety and lack of rest. "When I was nursing my daughter, Lucy, I was exhausted and couldn't produce an adequate supply of milk," Betsy Lydon, program director at Mothers & Others, recalls.

- If necessary, you can supplement breast milk with formula, if your doctor advises. Lucy's hunger, as it turned out, was making it difficult for her to sleep, causing an exasperating cycle to emerge. How could Betsy get enough rest with a baby who was irritable because she wasn't falling asleep? "It was a revelation when Lucy's pediatrician told me that the problem would be solved by supplementing my breast milk with formula," Betsy says. Both Lucy and Betsy began sleeping much better once Lucy was satiated. Dr. Karp advises that you don't give your baby breast milk and formula at the same feeding because formula interferes with the absorption of iron in breast milk. It's best to use a low-iron formula. Be aware, too, that introducing formula to a breast-fed baby can cause early weaning, and if you don't regularly nurse, your milk supply will diminish.

- Try, though, to avoid using a bottle until your baby is two or three weeks old, even if it's to feed your baby breast milk. The sucking technique for a plastic or rubber nipple is different than that needed for nursing. Your baby may become confused and refuse your breast or have trouble distinguishing which sucking technique he's supposed to use.

Dealing with Some Difficult Moments

Especially during the first few weeks, you may experience sore nipples. Not all women experience soreness. Betsy Lydon, for example, had no problems whatsoever, but Lane Graves experienced tenderness right from the start. "A friend told me that soreness subsides after six weeks, so I stuck with it. And it was true, I didn't have any more soreness after that," Lane says.

If you're beginning to experience some discomfort or pain, you might not have baby in the best nursing position, so try different ones. Your baby's tongue is rougher than you might realize. The friction on one spot may eventually become painful. But if you have him positioned correctly, your baby's tongue won't cause painful friction. Make sure not only your nipple but at least an inch of areola is in your baby's mouth. If you experience soreness for more than a few weeks, you should seek help from a lactation consultant; they can be found through hospitals, the **La Leche League,** or the phone book. A lactation consultant can help you determine which position will be the least painful or if there is some other reason that your baby is not latching on in a comfortable way.

Before you take your baby off your breast, wait for him to take his mouth off, or try to break his suction (and hold) by gently slipping your finger into his mouth. If your baby is particularly hungry, he might nurse with a vengeance. That strong suck can make your nipples hurt, so make sure you are feeding him often enough. It's extremely important to continue nursing regularly, even through the discomfort. Slowing down will make the problem worse. He'll be hungrier and suck harder.

When your nipples get sore, you can apply some USP lanolin, such as Lanisoh and Purelan, which has been purified to eliminate the pesticides used on sheep wool. You can get it from your pharmacist or from **Motherwear.** Some breast-feeding specialists recommend smoothing breast milk over sore nipples. Don't use harsh soaps on your nipples. These can make things worse. You might want to forgo soap entirely, because your nipples produce a natural lubricant that cleans and protects them as nature intended. In general, be careful about any cream that you might want to smooth over your entire breasts. Many substances can penetrate the skin.

Soreness can also occur if your nipples aren't allowed to dry completely between feedings. Let them air dry as often as possible. Leakage when you're not nursing can make it hard to stay dry. Fortunately, leakage usually stops within the first six weeks, though it may continue when you are engorged or when your baby cries. You might also find your breasts leaking when you are near other babies. It's a reflex you can't help. You can stop the leakage by applying direct pressure to the nipple. Also, using nursing pads will help you avoid any embarrassment from wet spots on clothing. Plastic-backed or waterproof pads will keep moisture in, so avoid these. Cotton pads will allow air to circulate and will prevent prolonged dampness. You should have enough maternity or nursing bras so that you can change them if your nursing pad doesn't do the job. A clean, dry, well-fitting bra will help reduce the chance of soreness and infections. You can obtain nursing pads, bras, and clothing that facilitates nursing (with discreet side or horizontal openings below your breasts) from maternity stores and mail order catalogs such as **Motherwear, The Natural Baby Company, Garnet Hill,** and **Ecobaby. Gladrags** sells organic cotton nursing pads.

Sometimes tenderness in the nipple or breast is caused by a plugged duct, which is a blockage in one of the tubes that carries milk from the glands to the nipple. This will cause redness, swelling, and tenderness. Wearing a tight bra, clothing, or baby sling may cause plugs. You should continue to breast-feed, trying different positions, and gently massage the plug before and after feeding. Use a warm compress, or try bathing the breast repeatedly in warm water. It should come out, but if it doesn't within a few days, visit your doctor or lactation consultant.

A plugged duct can lead to mastitis, or breast inflammation, caused when milk remains blocked and bursts into the breast's connective tissue and blood vessels or when the breast is invaded by bacteria. Mastitis can also result from an untreated cracked nipple or engorgement—when your breasts are too full. Symptoms of mastitis are similar to the flu, and your breasts may feel tender and warm to the touch.

See your doctor right away, get plenty of rest, drink lots of fluids, and continue to breast-feed. The milk is still safe and healthy for your baby. It is very important to take care of yourself when you have mastitis, as untreated mastitis could lead to an abscess.

Breasts that become swollen with milk can be very uncomfortable and even painful. This engorgement may occur just after birth and is alleviated within a day or two. You may also experience engorgement when the period between feedings is prolonged for some reason. Expressing some of the milk, either by hand or with a pump, will alleviate the pressure.

Your Nutritional Needs When Breast-Feeding

As when you are pregnant, you should take care to eat a well-balanced diet of wholesome, fresh foods. A healthy diet is not only important for milk production, but also to keep you feeling good. Follow the dietary recommendations in chapter 6. You will also need to consume more calories to compensate for those that go to breast milk production. In the first two months, about 500 calories will do. By four months, you may need about 500 to 700 more calories to feed your baby. Research has shown that women who consume less than 1,500 calories per day may suffer from decreased milk production, but Judy Hopkinson, assistant professor of pediatrics at USDA/ARS Children's Nutrition Research Center at Baylor College of Medicine, says that the actual amount of calories varies, depending on the woman's body type, metabolism, and other factors. If you feel tired and aren't producing enough milk, it may be worthwhile to consider your diet. If you eat a well-balanced diet and eat when you are hungry, you should have few problems. You may lose weight—$\frac{1}{2}$ to one pound per week is normal. In this way, you'll shed some of the pounds you gained while pregnant.

Keep your calcium and protein levels up and try to get them from plant sources rather than from animal products. You can obtain calcium from beans, tofu, and greens. Beans and tofu also provide lots of protein. Eating a variety of fruits and vegetables will provide vitamin C, which you'll need plenty of, as well as other essential vitamins. If you have dairy products or meats, try to keep fat content low by choosing low-fat or skim milk, low-fat cheeses and ice cream, and by trimming fat from all cuts of meat.

You don't have to give up spicy or strongly flavored foods. While these do impart a different taste to your breast milk that might not meet with approval from your baby, you shouldn't stop yourself from eating the foods you like. Just consume them in moderation. Try not to drink more than a cup or two of coffee per day, and avoid processed foods with a lot of additives. Caffeine can be passed through breast milk and might make your baby more irritable or anxious. Alcohol can also be consumed in moderation, but be careful, as alcohol enters breast milk (see page 193). There is little information about the effects of food additives on breast-fed infants, but it's still wise to keep intake minimal.

If your baby seems to be having an allergic reaction after a feeding, think about what you ate and read the section below on food allergies. The proteins in food that you've eaten enters your breast milk, and if your baby is allergic to those food proteins, he will suffer a reaction every time you eat them. While it's unlikely that your child is suffering from a food allergy, since less than 10 percent of infants under age three do, if you have a family history of food allergies, it's best to be cautious. Symptoms of allergy include skin rashes, swollen lips or gums, sneezing, wheezing, runny nose, diarrhea, or constipation.

Is Breast Milk Ever Unsafe?

Because breast milk is produced by your body, whatever you consume, inhale, and absorb through your skin—including some chemicals, drugs, and alcohol—may affect its quality. There also are a few diseases that you can pass on to your baby. Not everything that enters your body will move into your breast milk, though. And there are some steps you can take to protect your baby from potential harm.

ENVIRONMENTAL TOXINS

When you start lactating, your fat cells will release fat lipids, which are used in the production of breast milk. The release of these lipids causes the simultaneous release of fat-soluble chemicals—up to 20 percent of your lifetime accumulation—which then enter your breast milk. Human fat stores some chemicals found in the environment, such as DDT and other pesticides, dioxin, and PCBs. Studies have found all of these chemicals in samples of human breast milk. Lead and mercury can also enter breast milk in small concentrations. Lead stored in bones can be released and transferred to breast milk, according to a study published in the October 1998 issue of *Environmental Health Perspectives*. To prevent this from happening, both pregnant and lactating mothers should consume an adequate supply of calcium, either from dietary sources or supplements (see chapter 6).

"There aren't any women who don't have pesticides in their breast milk," says Dr. Walter Rogan, acting clinical director at the National Institute of Environmental Health Sciences. While it's true that your baby will ingest environmental toxins through breast milk, Dr. Rogan and other doctors, scientists, and breast-feeding advocates agree that the benefits of breast feeding outweigh the risks associated with exposure to toxins found in breast milk. In a long-term study of 700 school children, Dr. Rogan found that there was a slight advantage in the performance of breast-fed versus formula-fed children. "We did not see illnesses or developmental delays that we attributed to PCBs or DDE (a byproduct of DDT) transferred through breast milk," Dr. Rogan says. Only women who have experienced high levels of exposure to dioxin, PCBs, or other environmental toxins as the result of an industrial accident or through consumption of large amounts of fish caught in highly contaminated waters should be evaluated by their doctors before breast-feeding. Remember, even infant formulas will have some of the same pollutants as your milk, because cows' milk and soybeans also accumulate dioxins, heavy metals, and pesticides.

By reducing your exposure to pollutants prior to conception and during pregnancy, you can lower the chances that your breast milk will contain significant levels of dioxins, PCBs, and pesticides. Keeping your exposure low while you are breast-feeding will also keep the toxin levels down. If you've made some of the changes suggested in the first part of this book, you've made significant strides in reducing possible exposure to toxins. When you are pregnant and while breast-feeding remember to:

- Use least-toxic pest control measures. Don't use synthetic pesticides.
- Clean with mild cleaners.
- Refrain from painting, and leave your house while someone else paints it.
- Follow the fish consumption recommendations in chapter 6.
- Make sure your drinking water is lead-free. For information on water testing and filtering, see chapter 6.
- Avoid perming or coloring your hair. No studies have shown them to be harmful, but the chemicals can penetrate your skin.

While breast-feeding, it's best to lose weight slowly. While the release of fat stores caused by weight loss will free toxins that will enter your breast milk, the amount is usually not significant for women whose toxin levels are average, according to Judy Hopkinson. Rapid weight loss (more than one pound per week) could decrease the amount of breast milk you produce as well as the amount of the necessary fat in it.

DRUGS

Be careful about your intake of all medications, both over-the-counter and prescription. Some drugs—including antihistamines, psychotropic drugs (stimulants, tranquilizers, marijuana, and cocaine), and diet pills—enter breast milk. Doses that are fine for you are much too strong for your baby to handle. They can pose great harm and may even cause death. Other drugs, such as acetaminophen (Tylenol), penicillins, and milk of magnesia, are generally harmless. When you're sick, your doctor should almost always be able to prescribe a safe medication for you. Remember to always remind your doctor that you're breast-feeding. No matter what medication you take, it's very important that you talk to your doctor and pharmacist first to find out if it can enter your breast milk.

ALCOHOL

There's a popular myth circulating that beer increases breast milk production and that it's a good source of B vitamins. These rumors are unfounded. Good, healthy food is a much better source of nutrients. Alcohol will not increase breast milk production. Only a good diet, rest, and, most importantly, plenty of suckling will do that. But, a beer or a glass of wine now and then can help you relax. When you are feeling the stress that comes with your new role as a mother, and coping with an uncooperative infant, relaxation improves the chances that you'll succeed in your endeavor to breast-feed.

The important question is whether your alcohol consumption is harmful to your baby. Alcohol does enter breast milk, but the levels dissipate over the same time it takes to clear the bloodstream. Studies have not linked occasional alcohol consumption by breast-feeding mothers to physical or neurological defects in their babies. The AAP has placed alcohol in the category of those substances that are usually compatible with breast-feeding. But you should drink alcohol only in moderation. A 1989 study in the *New England Journal of Medicine* showed a slight difference in motor development at one year of age in babies of mothers who drank more than one drink per day. We advise not having more than one drink per day, and not more than two or three times per week, as other nutritional guidelines recommend, because numerous studies link alcohol consumption with an increased risk of breast cancer. In February 1998, the *Journal of the American Medical Association* published a study that shows that drinking one glass of alcohol per day increases a woman's risk of getting breast cancer by 10 percent.

It's best not to breast-feed immediately after you've consumed alcohol, even though a little alcohol won't hurt your baby. Wait at least two to three hours—this is how long it takes for one alcoholic drink, such as a glass of wine or one beer, to clear the system of a woman weighing between 100 and 160 pounds. Remember that absorption of alcohol is affected by your body weight, the rate at which you drink, and whether you're eating while drinking. Try to keep alcohol absorption down by sipping your wine or beer over time, and make sure you're not drinking on an empty stomach. Foods with high protein and fats, such as nuts, are good choices to have with alcohol. If you've had more than one drink in those two hours, it will take longer for the alcohol to dissipate. At those times, you might want to forgo breast-feeding. If you plan ahead by freezing some of your breast milk at an earlier time, you can feed the stored milk to your baby when you've consumed more than one drink. You may feel engorged if you don't breast-feed for a while, but you can alleviate the pressure by pumping the milk, with a manual or electric pump (see below). Discard this milk.

It's also important to consider how alcohol may impair your reflexes and judgment when caring for a baby.

ILLNESS

In most cases, you can nurse while you are sick. But there a few diseases that demand that you not breast-feed. Women with HIV or AIDS are advised against breast-feeding; there have been cases of women passing on the virus to their babies through their breast milk. Similarly, women with untreated active tuberculosis cannot breast-feed. And if you are undergoing cancer treatments, either chemical or radiation therapy, do not nurse your baby.

When You Can't Be with Your Baby: Pumping and Storing Breast Milk

At some point, you may want to return to your job or other responsibilities that take you away from your baby. But you may want to continue giving him the benefits of breast milk. This means some advance planning and expressing your milk with a breast pump so that your baby has a supply when you're not near him. The idea of doing this may make you feel uncomfortable. Some women worry that they'll feel like a cow, and the whole process will ruin the experience for them. But others, like Lane Graves, feel that the slight inconvenience is well worth the continuation of her breast-feeding experience.

You may be wondering why you should bother pumping. Couldn't your baby's caretaker give him formula while you're at work? While supplementing breast milk with formula is fine once in a while, if your breasts are not regularly stimulated by sucking or pumping, your milk supply will dwindle and you won't be able to nurse your baby. Plus, your baby could get used to the formula and may choose it over breast milk. Since the bottle itself might contribute to an early weaning, if you want to prolong nursing, try to feed your baby breast milk as much as possible.

There are several ways to express breast milk. You can do it by hand, but this will be inconvenient if you have to do it every day. "Though it's awkward at first, after doing it a few times, it can be as efficient as using an electric pump," says Dr. Harvey Karp. Books on breast-feeding explain how, and you might want to learn, just in case. Then, there are two types of pumps that you can use on a regular basis: hand-operated and electric.

Hand-operated or *manual pumps* create suction either with a pistonlike cylinder that works like a syringe or by a spring action. They can be very convenient when you are in a place with no electricity, like a public bathroom or an airplane. Many can be used with one hand and offer more control over pressure, and therefore sensitivity. In its *Guide to Baby Products, Consumer Reports* recommends that you avoid simple, "bicycle horn-style" pumps sold in drugstores because they may be ineffective and could hurt you. Look for a pump that is easy to clean, and make sure the gasket won't come into contact with the milk. If it does, you should be able to remove it easily for washing. Manual pumps cost about $40.

Electric pumps generally work with the same principles but are driven by electricity. The fancier pumps offer the capability of pumping both breasts simultaneously. **Medela**'s Pump-in-Style Professional Breast Pump can pump both breasts in about 10 or 15 minutes. Like pumps used in hospitals, it is designed to imitate the sucking action and pressure of actual nursing. It's a bit expensive, about $250, but it's light, weighing only 7 pounds, and has a built-in cooler to store the milk. You may feel it's worth it. If you have another child, you'll be all set, or you could pass it on to family members or friends who decide to breast-feed. Very efficient electric pumps can be rented from hospitals, baby stores, and medical supply houses for about $2 per day, too. You can try one out before you spend a lot of money. Medela and **Ameda/Egnell** also make smaller electric breast pumps that can pump one breast at a time. These cost between $60 and $80. Small battery-operated models are generally too slow and ineffective to be useful for a woman who needs to pump daily.

Even if you decide to purchase or rent an electric pump, buy a manual pump for emergencies, such as travel. The first time Lane Graves traveled to New York for a Mothers & Others board meeting, she didn't realize that delays in her travel schedule would prevent her from pumping. Her plane back to San Francisco was held on the runway for an hour. Then, after a six-hour flight, her bags were lost, so she spent some time at the airport at the claims' desk. Lane says she became very uncomfortable, because she was engorged, but was unable to pump because she had only an electric pump. "If I'd had a manual pump, I could have expressed some milk in the airplane bathroom," she says. Of course, if you learn how to express your milk by hand, then you'll always be prepared for an emergency.

You'll have to experiment with the breast pump, at first. Successful pumping requires that the nipple adapter fit your breast well so that pressure is exerted on both areola and nipple. You'll also need to have a quiet, private place to pump. Many employers now accommodate breast-feeding women by setting aside a room for this purpose. You may need to visualize your baby or look at a photograph of him to cue your body to "let down" your milk. Using a warm, wet compress or lightly massaging the breast might also help.

Most pumps direct the milk into a bottle, which should be sealed and refrigerated immediately. You can also keep breast milk cool in insulated coolers that use ice packs if a refrigerator is not available. Breast milk stays fresh for about 48 hours in the refrigerator. Place it in the back of the refrigerator, where it's coldest. If you want to store the milk for a longer period, you can freeze it for up to three months. Remember to label the container with the date, so you don't accidentally use old milk. Though it will keep longer, it's best to use frozen breast milk within a month, as some research indicates that freezing milk for longer may affect its folate, a vitamin necessary to a baby's growth.

STORING BREAST MILK

Try to use glass storage containers, whether the milk will be refrigerated or frozen. Plastic containers may scratch during cleaning. Bacteria may remain embedded in these scratches, even after washing, and contaminate the breast milk. Studies published in *Early Human Development* and *Nutrition Review* show that milk stored in some plastics, such as polyethylene and polypropylene containers, may lose some cellular components, fats, or antibodies because they cling to the plastic. Cellular components may also cling to glass containers, though.

Plastic containers made of polyvinyl chloride (PVC) or polycarbonate resin contain hormone-disrupting plasticizers that may leach into the milk. You cannot tell what kind of plastic you are dealing with if it has no recycling symbol on it, and this is often the case with baby bottles and other storage containers. Plastic containers marked with recycling symbol 3 are PVC. Polycarbonate plastic containers, which are generally clear and rigid, are in the "other" category and may be labeled with recycling symbol 7. Try to avoid using plastics marked with these numbers. See the next section on bottles for more information about which plastic bottles to use.

Polyethylene bags, such as those used in disposable bottle systems, have not been shown to leach toxic chemicals to date. While it's best to avoid using plastic, if you do use polyethylene bags to freeze milk, be careful when filling. Some of these bags are difficult to handle. And inspect them before you pour the breast milk in and when you defrost it—plastic bags may split at seams or tear, increasing the chances of bacterial contamination.

Glass can chip or crack, but if you inspect it frequently that should not be a problem. Whatever container you use, try to freeze breast milk in small portions, about 4 ounces, so you won't defrost more than you need. Lois Arnold, executive director of the Human Milk Banking Association of North America, suggests using wide-mouth glass canning jars, which are made of heavy glass that can withstand cold and heat. They come in a one-cup (8-ounce) size. Fill the jar only halfway to leave room for expansion so the glass won't crack. These jars won't screw onto breast pumps, but you can just pour the milk into them.

Thaw frozen breast milk by placing it in the refrigerator overnight or by putting the container under cool running water for about 15 minutes. *Never thaw breast milk in the microwave.* Microwaves heat unevenly. What you think is temperate might actually hide dangerous heat spots that can burn your baby's mouth. Microwaves may also destroy nutritional components in the milk. Once thawed, gently shake the breast milk to mix—it separates just like cows' milk. If your baby likes the milk warm, place the container under warm running water for a few minutes.

Thawed breast milk will keep for only 24 hours in the refrigerator, and it cannot remain at room temperature for more than a half hour without spoiling. Freezing destroys breast milk's antibacterial qualities. If you have any leftover breast milk after feeding your baby, it should be discarded. *Never refreeze thawed breast milk.*

You can and should continue to breast-feed for as long as you want to. Some women nurse their children until they are two or three. But if you decide to wean your baby earlier, you needn't feel any guilt. Infant formulas have been designed to be nutritious substitutes for breast milk.

Why I Breast-feed by Joanne Camas, copy editor and Mothers & Others member

You can't beat the feeling of putting a hungry, cranky, screaming baby to your breast, feeling the urgent sucking turn to contented feeding, and then getting a sleepy, adoring look and a quick milky smile.

The comfort of skin on skin seems as important to babies as the actual nourishment they receive. My three-month-old son is a hearty nurser, but grudgingly takes the same milk from a bottle.

Owen is my third child, and is following his brothers as a breast-fed baby. But unlike Aidan and Martin, he hasn't had any formula so far. I'm back at work, but this time I pump milk every day, and it's working out fine. My company has set up a spare office for me and another nursing mother so we can express milk on our breaks. We may work from home two days a week, making breast-feeding so much easier.

I enjoy the closeness of nursing and the ready supply of food—always fresh and at the right temperature. Your body produces milk at the sound of a baby's cry or even when you think about the child, tailoring production to the baby's current nutritional and growth needs. Amazing!

Even in these high-tech days, there are still some components of breast milk that scientists haven't been able to replicate in formula, which adds to my awe of the process of nature's way.

Why do so many women reject the idea of breast-feeding, even before their babies are born? Somehow formula has become the "natural" way to feed a child, even in Third World countries, where formula is expensive and the water supply may be unsafe.

When pregnant friends ask for advice, I admit that the first couple of weeks can be uncomfortable, and sometimes painful, but I stress the benefits that I've enjoyed.

I don't know if breast-feeding does produce more intelligent children, as suggested in a recent study, but I do know that there are many benefits for both mother and child. Breast-fed newborns, for example, enjoy strengthened immune systems and fewer ear infections. And breast-feeding can also make for a quicker return to the mother's prepregnancy condition. It may even help reduce the risk of some cancers!

Convenience is also a major plus for me. I'm an expert discreet nurser now. I've fed babies on planes, in cars, in the library, at the park, at breakfast in diners—you name it! During the night, you can bring the baby into bed for feedings, which is less disruptive for all concerned—no boiling bottles and heating formula while half-asleep!

I invested in an efficient double pump for my office and spend at most 20 minutes expressing enough milk for Owen's feeds the next day. In the afternoon, Paul, my husband, feeds him enough to keep hunger at bay, but not so much that he won't nurse when I get home. As I walk through the door, Owen stares me down, slips his eyes to my chest, and lets out a yell—time to feed him and earn myself another quick milky smile.

Bottle-Feeding Dos and Don'ts

Whether you choose to breast-feed or use infant formula, you'll eventually need to deal with bottles. Bottle-feeding can be both liberating and enslaving. If you choose to bottle-feed your baby, both parents can share feeding responsibilities. For a mother feeling stress and fatigue, a little help is always welcome. For dads, it's gratifying to be able to feed baby, too. Some nursing mothers feel tied down by breast-feeding at times. Bottle-feeding also means that you can leave your baby in the care of someone else without worrying about how the baby will be fed. But along with bottles come a few added duties. Bottles and nipples must be sterilized before their first use, and some pediatricians recommend sterilizing bottles and nipples for the first few months of the baby's life. If you're breast-feeding, you'll have to pump and carefully store your milk. If you choose formula, there's the preparation of the formula. It's not difficult, but certainly another thing to learn.

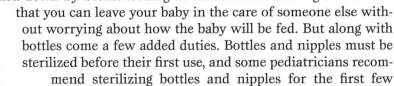

Infant Formula

"We are lucky that we live at a time when there is a good substitute for breast milk," Dr. Harvey Karp says. For women who can't breast-feed because of medications or illness, those who have difficulty with nursing, or those who have decided it's not for them, infant formula provides an alternative that gives babies roughly the same amount of calories and nutrients—fats, protein, vitamins, and minerals—they need to grow. Some formula companies are now adding nucleotides that are found in breast milk, such as DHA, that may have a role in infant cognitive development. (Note: It is not entirely clear that added nucleotides make infant formulas better or will improve a child's I.Q.)

It's true that infant formulas cannot duplicate breast milk in its entirety; breast milk has living cells that cannot be provided in a processed food. Nor will formula adapt to your baby's nutritional needs as he grows. But, infant formula is the closest equivalent to human milk available, and makers of formula continue to explore ways to improve their product. It will nourish your baby perfectly well.

Most infant formulas are based on cows' milk, which is modified to resemble human milk. For example, the fats in cows' milk are replaced by vegetable fats, which simulate the fatty acid balance of human breast milk. Mineral content (calcium and salt, for example) is reduced because a newborn's kidneys cannot handle the amounts found in cows' milk. Most formulas are fortified with vitamins, such as K and D, and iron.

Infants may have some difficulty with formula. Cows' milk contains proteins that are harder for human babies to digest than human milk, and about 2.5 percent of infants under three years of age may be allergic to cows' milk. Symptoms include vomiting, diarrhea (with or without blood), colic, skin rashes, frequent ear infections, nasal congestion, and unusual sluggishness. For these babies, a soy-based formula is advised. About 25 percent of babies who are allergic to cows' milk are also allergic to soy. Special formulas exist for these babies, but they are more costly. There is no reason for a baby who is not allergic to cows' milk to be fed soy-based formula.

Follow your doctor's recommendations for formula. The AAP recommends iron-fortified formula, but it may not be indicated for some babies. Otherwise, there isn't much difference between brands, but some may be better tolerated by your baby than others.

Formulas come in ready-to-feed bottles or cans, as liquid concentrate, or as dried powder. *Ready-to-feed formulas* are the easiest, but most expensive, choice. You merely open the can and pour into the bottle. Aside from cost, the biggest drawback is having to haul all those cans into your house and then out to the landfill. Once opened, ready-to-feed formula should be covered and has to be refrigerated. If kept refrigerated, it may be used for up to 48 hours after being opened.

Liquid concentrate and *dry powder* must be diluted with water before use. Follow directions carefully. You can use either tap water or filtered water to mix with the formula. Make certain that the water is free of lead, mercury, and other environmental toxins. See chapter 6 for information on how to test and filter your water. Bottled water is not necessarily better than tap water and may even contain contaminants. Cover leftover liquid concentrate and refrigerate for up to 48 hours. Dry powder formula can be kept for up to 4 weeks, covered, in the refrigerator.

Don't think you're doing your baby a favor by adding a little more formula concentrate or powder because he's especially hungry. You'll be giving him too much fat and salt. Adding extra water because it's a hot day, or to stretch the formula to give you more feedings, shortchanges your baby of the nutrients he needs and may cause malnutrition. Formulas are just right the way they are. They do not need to be improved. So don't add cereal or sugar or anything else.

All formula should be refrigerated once you've mixed it. Take it out of the refrigerator when your baby is awake and hungry, instead of preparing it for when he wakes up, as it spoils quickly. Be very careful with the milk. Unlike breast milk, formula has no antibacterial qualities. Babies who have not been breast-fed will not have their mothers' antibodies. A newborn's immune system is not fully developed, so until your baby builds up resistance, he will be vulnerable to bacterial attacks. Other safety tips you should follow are:

- Don't use formula that has passed its expiration date.
- Don't use dented or damaged cans of formula.
- Throw away formula that has an unusual texture, taste, or smell.
- Wash your hands thoroughly before mixing and pouring formula.
- Do not save formula left in the bottle. Your baby has contaminated it with bacteria from his mouth.
- Do not use formula that has been at room temperature for more than a half hour.

Equipment

BOTTLES

There are numerous baby bottles on the market, almost all of which are plastic. Most manufacturers have discontinued their glass bottle lines. It's not surprising, since the demand for glass bottles is on the wane. Many people are afraid that their babies will get hurt by a glass bottle. Plastic bottles seem so much safer. They certainly won't break or explode when sterilized or dropped. But many plastics contain plasticizers which could leach into breast milk or formula. In 1997, Food and Drug Administration chemists found that stove-top sterilization of polycarbonate plastic baby bottles releases bisphenol-A, a hormone-disrupting chemical, into infant formula. As of June 1998, Gerber and Avent plastic baby bottles were made of polycarbonate plastic. **Evenflo** markets 4- and 8-ounce tempered glass bottles at Toys "R" Us, Target, Sears, Wal-Mart, and **The Natural Baby Company.**

Medela baby bottles are made out of polypropylene, as are **Evenflo** clear and tinted plastic bottles. Evenflo makes their opaque pastel nursers from polyethylene. As mentioned above, breast milk stored in either of these plastics may lose nutrients, such as antibodies and/or essential fats. But, since neither polypropylene nor polyethylene contain hormone-disrupting chemicals, they are safer than polycarbonate plastic. If possible, don't store breast milk in these bottles. And don't heat breast milk and infant formula in plastic as chemicals are more likely to leach when you heat in plastic.

If you find bottles made by other manufacturers, call them and inquire about the plastic used. Avoid bottles made of PVC plastic, if you should find them. PVC may contain hormone-disrupting phthalates as well as lead.

Both plastic and glass bottles should be inspected often. Look for cracks and chips in glass bottles. Defective glass bottles will have to be discarded; pieces of glass might end up inside the bottle. Look for scratches in plastic bottles. These may harbor bacteria, which can contaminate formula or breast milk. Clear plastic bottles are generally easier to clean since you'll be able to see the inside much easier.

Avoid plastic bottles that have decorations printed on the inside. These have been found to come off into formula when the bottle's been heated.

Disposable nursers are not necessarily as convenient as they are made out to be. These systems use plastic bags that may leak or rupture. There have also been a few incidents of babies choking on the plastic tab inside. Disposable systems can also be more difficult to fill than standard bottles. They also use specialized nipples, which can't be exchanged for silicone nipples (see below). Furthermore, these systems waste resources and pollute the environment with a nonbiodegradable material.

NIPPLES

Nipples for bottles are usually made of rubber or silicone. The clear silicone nipples are generally better than the yellow rubber ones, which tend to deteriorate faster than silicone and get a permanent sticky feel to them. Rubber nipples may also release nitrosamines, which can be carcinogenic. Silicone nipples are less porous than rubber, so they harbor less bacteria than rubber, and they are heat-resistant, so they can be safely washed in a dishwasher. Do not try to enlarge the hole of a silicone nipple, as this may cause it to tear.

Both silicone and rubber nipples should be inspected for tears and cracks by holding them up to a light. If you find that a nipple has deteriorated, replace it, as it can hold bacteria. Avoid nipples made of PVC.

For thorough washing of nipples, **Prince Lionheart** offers an inexpensive sanitizing basket that fits over the water source of a dishwasher. These baskets are also available from **Perfectly Safe.**

Avoid using pacifiers. Pacifiers are associated with early weaning of breast-fed infants. One study also found that children who used pacifiers had significantly more middle ear infections than those who did not. Finally, some pacifiers are made with PVC plastic. Phthalates bonded to soft PVC may leach into your child's mouth. If you want to use a pacifier, Dr. Harvey Karp, Mothers & Others medical advisor, recommends silicone pacifiers only after breast-feeding is well established and only for the first few months of a baby's life. Dr. Karp says that it's best to wean your baby off the pacifier after three or four months to decrease ear infections.

OTHER USEFUL ITEMS

A funnel will be helpful when pouring breast milk or formula into bottles. You can buy stainless steel funnels in kitchen supply stores.

A ceramic or glass pitcher with cover can be used to store formula that will be used within a 24-hour period.

Sterilization

It used to be that if you were going to use formula, you had to sterilize the bottles, nipples, and formula for each feeding. You must sterilize bottles and nipples for about 5 minutes in boiling water before they're used for the first time. After that, in most cases, you can simply wash bottles and nipples thoroughly in warm, soapy water after each use, or put them through a dishwasher. If your baby is premature or vulnerable for any reason, your doctor may recommend sterilization. There may be other reasons you should sterilize, depending on your baby's health and your water supply. Your doctor will advise you on whether or not you should sterilize.

If you do need to sterilize, your doctor will recommend how long to boil bottles and nipples. Formula manufacturers also provide thorough instructions on sterilization procedures. When sterilizing bottles in boiling water, don't forget about them. Glass bottles can sometimes explode. If the water boils down, plastic bottles can ignite and send toxic fumes throughout your house. The safest way to sterilize is to use a unit with an automatic shut-off feature. **Evenflo** offers one for about $30.

Feeding with Bottles

When you are feeding your baby with a bottle, you may be tempted to make him drink the entire bottle. Ignore that temptation! There's no right amount a baby should be drinking. For a newborn, it could be as little as 1 ounce or up to 4 ounces per feeding. Each baby is different. But pushing your baby to drink more than he really wants teaches him to ignore the full feeling and overeat. Give your baby a bottle when he seems hungry and take it away when he loses interest. If he drinks all of it, you'll know that he was hungry. If he only drinks a little, it may be that he wanted the comfort of sucking and some attention from you. In the beginning, feedings will occur frequently and irregularly. After a few weeks, your baby will fall into a more regular pattern, or schedule of feedings, about 3 to 4 hours apart by six months of age.

Bottle-Feeding and Dental Care

When your baby begins to teethe, allowing him to have prolonged contact with the sugars in drinks in his bottle might cause baby-bottle tooth decay. A baby with this condition may develop cavities, and the protective enamel on his teeth, especially in the front of the mouth, may be stripped away. To prevent this from happening:

- *Don't put your baby to bed with a bottle containing breast milk, formula, or fruit juice.* Saliva's digestive action slows during sleep, and liquids from the bottle will pool around your baby's teeth. Bacteria will have ample time to wreak havoc. If your child is uncooperative, give him a bedtime bottle with water only.

- *Clean your baby's teeth after feedings, or at least once a day.* Use a soft child's toothbrush and water or baking soda until your child is two years old. Toothpaste containing fluoride is not advised before then, because a younger child may not rinse, swallowing the toothpaste instead. Most toothpastes have concentrations of fluoride that are too high for young children. If they swallow it frequently, their teeth may not develop properly. After age two, natural toothpastes are best. They have no saccharin (unlike most brands), preservatives, dyes, or artificial flavors. **Tom's of Maine** makes a toothpaste for children.

- *Don't allow your infant or toddler to hang onto a bottle for security.* A soft toy or blanket is harmless to teeth.

- *Don't put juice in bottles.* By the time your child is ready for juice, he'll be ready to learn how to use a cup. By fourteen months, he should be weaned from the bottle.

- *Begin regular dental checkups at about twelve to eighteen months.* Be wary of dentists who want to put dental sealants on baby teeth. Dental sealants are plastic. Some of them contain bisphenol-A, a hormone-disrupting chemical that one study found may leach from dental sealants into the mouth. With proper dental hygiene, including regular brushing and flossing, children should not get cavities. Dental sealants aren't foolproof anyway, as Mindy Pennybacker discovered after her dentist insisted that her son, Rory, get them at age two. Mindy gave in to the dental sealants after the dentist told her Rory was particularly prone to cavities. Rory got a cavity anyway.

Cavities in children under six are uncommon, but if your child gets one, try to avoid mercury amalgam, or "silver" fillings. Some mercury may leach, in minute quantities, into the mouth, but it has not been established conclusively that this type of mercury exposure poses a risk. Mercury at high levels can cause damage to the central nervous system, causing learning disabilities, tremors, memory loss, and dementia. But in studies of humans with amalgam fillings, no connection has been found between mercury exposure and cognitive function. A University of Calgary study found that sheep treated with fillings had impaired kidney function, but no human studies have indicated the same.

The National Institute of Dental Research maintains that no other restorative material offers the combined strength, durability, and affordability of amalgam. In the absence of conclusive proof of the safety of dental amalgam, it's best to seek alternatives when possible. Discuss the options with your dentist. The best, though more costly, alternatives to silver fillings are porcelain and gold fillings. An amalgam made of gallium instead of mercury has also been developed and is less costly than gold.

Organic Baby Food

Between his fourth and sixth month, your baby will become more interested in solid foods. He will begin to require more calories than is contained in the amount of milk or formula that fills his stomach. You'll want to give him the safest food, of course. You can easily avoid unnecessary additives, such as artificial colors and flavors, preservatives, and fillers, by reading labels. If you make your own baby food, you'll know that the ingredients are fresh and that there will be no additional salt, fillers, or refined sugar.

Dodging pesticides takes a little more effort. There is no way you can tell if the strawberries at the market bear traces of pesticides just by looking at them. And you can't just wash or peel them off. Many pesticides are systemic—they spread throughout the plant from the roots into the very heart of the fruit or vegetable. The federal government has set tolerable levels for pesticide residues on all produce. Until recently, standards for allowable pesticide residues on food were based on adults. The Food Quality Protection Act of 1996 required that EPA tolerances for pesticides be set to account for children's vulnerabilities and their exposures to pesticides from other sources, since environmental pollutants can have a cumulative effect, but the EPA has made little progress implementing the law. And data from the U.S. Department of Agriculture show that, in 1996, 72 percent of fruits and vegetables and 91 percent of wheat tested had detectable pesticide residues. In December 1997, **Environmental Working Group** discovered that as many as one million children were ingesting unsafe levels of organophosphate pesticides, a category of neurotoxic chemicals that are related to nerve gases developed during World War II. It may take some time before pesticide residues on food are limited to levels appropriate for children. And the federal government only samples a small percentage of foods on the market. Enforcement of standards is difficult.

Starting your baby out on organic foods or those grown by integrated pest management (IPM) methods ensures that he is eating only minimally treated and minimally processed foods. Certified organic foods are not sprayed with any synthetic pesticides. They are less likely to have pesticide residues. Produce grown by IPM methods are only sprayed when there is no other recourse to save the crop, which means reduced usage of pesticides.

The primary reason to buy organic or IPM foods, though, isn't to avoid pesticide residues. The reduction of pesticide use has ramifications that go beyond just personal health. Fewer pesticides in the environment from industrial agriculture means healthier ecosystems, cleaner water, and less air pollution. Use of organic matter instead of synthetic chemicals for fertilizers results in less nitrogen load in our atmosphere and waterways. Both organic and IPM methods promote the build-up of healthy soils, which means land that is stable and less likely to erode.

By supporting organic and other forms of sustainable agriculture, we also support small, local farmers who must compete against heavily subsidized agribusiness.

Buying produce that is locally grown and in season is also wise. Fruits and vegetables that don't travel far require fewer postharvest treatments to keep them from rotting, and they are picked closer to ripeness. The longer produce is off the plant, the greater the nutrient loss. Choosing fruits and vegetables seasonally means an increased likelihood that they came from your region instead of from across the country or a foreign land. Seasonal produce is usually fresher and riper.

Below you'll find tips on how to find locally grown foods in your region and how to prepare them for your baby. Chapter 6 contains a Green Diet Tour that will help you find wholesome and healthy foods in your supermarket.

First Introductions

Though not as nutritiously perfect for babies as breast milk or formula, solid foods offer a more concentrated source of calories. Introducing solid foods offers an opportunity for your baby to experiment with new tastes and textures and learn that there's quite a variety of treats that one can eat that don't come in a bottle or breast. At first, he might not take well to the idea of a spoon and more food may end up on his face than in his mouth. As a result, it might not be obvious that your baby is learning social norms that go along with eating. But it won't be long before most, if not all, of the food in the bowl will be directed smoothly into your child's mouth.

When you first begin giving your baby food, it'll be in the form of a smooth, creamy mush, since without teeth, that's all a baby can eat. You can mix in a little breast milk or formula to make it more familiar, but it must be bland, with no salt or pepper added. Baby cereal made of rice is a good starter, since it's somewhat similar in taste to your baby's usual formula or milk. You can mix up a "thinned" sample by adding a little extra formula or breast milk so it's not thick. Give baby a few teaspoons per feeding, gradually increasing the amount by a teaspoon per day, and you can gradually increase the thickness of the cereal as well.

You can also give your baby a few teaspoons of applesauce, mashed banana, or pureed pears, or mix it in with the cereal. Babies like the surprising and sweet taste of fruit, even if it's a bit unusual to them at first.

Don't force your baby to eat solids. Let him try some. If he likes it, give him a little more. But don't feel you have to give your baby a specific amount per feeding. These initial experiences with solid foods are more educational than nutritional. Solid foods will add some calories, but the nutrients will still come from breast milk or formula, which you shouldn't abandon yet.

Give your baby a variety of fruits, vegetables, and grains. Getting children to experience and enjoy the diverse tastes that nature has to offer will prevent finicky eating habits. Keep the "Eight Simple Steps to a New Green Diet" in chapter 6 in mind as your child increases his appetite for new foods and his diet expands.

Food Allergies

About 6 to 8 percent of infants develop food allergies by the age of three. The foods that most commonly cause allergic reactions include milk, eggs, peanuts and other nuts, fish, and shellfish. About 2.5 percent of babies develop an allergy to milk, but 85 percent of them outgrow the allergy by their third birthday. Some other food allergies may be outgrown, including those to soy, beef, and eggs. But nut, fish, and shellfish allergies, which can be fatal even if the allergic person is exposed to just a trace, often persist into adulthood. If there's a history of food allergies in either parent's family, or in a sibling, be sure to speak with your pediatrician about this.

It's best to delay introduction of solid food until at least six months. Food allergies occur less often among babies who are not fed solid foods until their digestive systems are better developed.

Since only minute amounts of a food protein can trigger a reaction, you should remain extremely cautious if there is a history of allergies in your family. Breast-feeding is highly recommended for infants whose parents have allergies. And delaying introduction of some foods to high-risk infants is recommended (see box on page 206).

There is some evidence that maternal diets that eliminate eggs, milk, peanuts, and fish reduce the development of eczema and possible food allergy in breast-fed infants. Eliminating these foods should only be considered if there is a family history of allergy, and only under the supervision of a doctor and dietitian to avoid nutritional deficiencies.

Regardless of your family history, always introduce one new food at a time to spot any allergies. Feed the new food to your baby for four or five days, along with foods that you've already introduced, before introducing anything else. During this time, if your baby experiences symptoms like vomiting, diarrhea, wheezing, skin rashes or hives, or runny nose and sneezing, consult your doctor.

Read labels carefully and remember that some potential allergens may be disguised by unusual names. For example, one milk derivative is casein. Dextrose is a derivative of corn. The **Food Allergy Network** can provide you with information on how to identify allergens hiding under other names.

Commercial Baby Food

Let's face it—commercial baby food is convenient. There's nothing to prepare. All you have to do is open a jar. Baby food makers have covered all the bases, from first foods to meals suitable for toddlers. Now, there are even organic baby foods on the market, including **Earth's Best, Gerber**'s Tender Harvest, and **The Well-Fed Baby.** Organic is generally more expensive than conventional, but both are more expensive than homemade.

Some conventional prepared baby foods contain additives, such as starches and sugars. Read labels to avoid these.

Homemade Baby Food

Homemade food can be better tasting and fresher than store-bought baby foods. When you make your baby's food at home, you'll know exactly what's in it and can

Foods to Avoid

- Up to six months: Spinach, celery, lettuce, radishes, carrots, beets, turnips, and collard greens may contain excessive nitrate, which can be converted to nitrite in the stomachs of young infants, according to *Consumer Reports*. Nitrite inhibits the blood's ability to carry oxygen.

- Up to nine months: Common allergens such as wheat, soybeans, citrus, corn, eggs, and cows' milk should be avoided if there is a family history of food allergies. Raw honey may cause botulism.

Use blackstrap molasses, which is high in iron, calcium, and fiber; brown rice syrup; or barley malt as sweeteners instead.

- Up to one year: Peanuts and other nuts, seafood.
- Up to two years: Avoid chocolate.
- Up to three years: If there is a family history of food allergies, avoid the most serious allergens—peanuts, nuts, and shellfish. Monitor infants carefully for signs of allergic reactions when these foods are introduced.

be assured that it's healthy. But you'll have to select and prepare the food, adding another thing to your busy life. Many people find a happy medium, serving both homemade and commercial baby food.

Making baby food from scratch is simple, though. It's really a matter of mashing or pureeing food. You can use a fork for many foods, or try pushing them through a strainer. If you want to use a more high-tech gadget, which will make the food very smooth, use a blender or food mill. **The Natural Baby Company** and **Perfectly Safe** sell baby food grinders for about $10; food is pushed through a cylinder with a blade and a strainer into a little cup. You can puree fruits, vegetables, eggs, grains, beans, lentils, and meat for baby food. Some fruits and vegetables must be cooked, by simmering or steaming in a little water or baking, to soften them before pureeing. Steaming is the most nutritious way to cook veggies. You can add a little water, formula, or breast milk if necessary to keep the puree thin enough. Before you feed your baby, check the temperature of the food. It should be cool enough to prevent scalding. Also make sure that the bowl and spoon are not hot to the touch before putting them on baby's tray.

Gradually, you can introduce texture by making purees a little thicker and lumpier. Pieces of food should remain small at first. But these can get bigger as your baby learns to chew up his food before swallowing. Be careful with foods like grapes, which children might swallow whole and choke on.

FROM FOUR TO SEVEN MONTHS, KEEP BABY FOOD SIMPLE.

Babies really cannot tolerate spicy foods, and even salt and pepper are not good for them. You can often take a small portion of foods that you are preparing for your meal and puree it for your baby just before seasoning. Make combinations of fruits, such as apples and pears, or vegetables, such as peas and carrots, with foods that you've already introduced to your baby.

The following simple suggestions come from *Feeding the Whole Family* by Cynthia Lair.

- Very ripe fruits make good Summer Fruit Puree. Bananas, melon, peaches, mangoes, and apricots don't require cooking. Just peel, remove seeds, and mash with a fork or puree in a food mill or blender.

- Make a Fruit Sauce with apples, blueberries, cherries, or pears (or a combination). Peel if the fruit is not organic. Cut up fruit. Put in a saucepan with 1 cup of water for every 1/4 cup of fruit. Bring to a boil; reduce to a simmer about 15 minutes or until the fruit is cooked. Puree the mixture in a blender or food mill, and strain if necessary. Don't add sugar or spices. If the fruit is really tart, sweeten with brown rice syrup.

You can freeze these in ice cube trays, as Carol Baxter suggests (see box on page 216). Make a large batch; freeze some for your baby and spice the rest with nutmeg and cinnamon for yourself to put on pancakes and mix with yogurt.

- Cooked squashes, sweet potatoes, parsnips, or rutabagas are just right for a Sweet Vegetable Puree. Cut vegetables in half, scoop out seeds from squash, and bake in a 400 degree oven for about an hour, or steam them for 20 to 25 minutes. You can cook these vegetables for your own dinner and puree a small portion in a blender or food mill for your baby.

- As your baby gets older, try mixing fruits or veggies for a little variety. You can also add pureed fruit to cereal.

FROM SEVEN TO NINE MONTHS, INTRODUCE TEXTURE AND LUMPS OF FOOD.
Make your baby's food a little thicker and lumpier. This will encourage chewing. Mashing with a fork will work with some foods, such as beans and cooked fruit. You can steam vegetables, puree half and roughly mash half, then combine the two. Cooked whole grains—such as millet, barley, oats, and rye—provide interesting and fun textures that are still soft and easy to swallow. Gradually increase the size of lumps in food.

You can introduce minced or pureed meat in small amounts (1 to 4 tablespoons) or substitute beans or lentils for protein. You can also feed your baby hard-boiled eggs (thoroughly cooked to avoid salmonella) about now. Start with about a teaspoon and gradually increase the amount.

Fruit juices may be given to your baby now. Don't let juice replace breast milk or formula, though, because it's not as nutritious. Baby juice or diluted "adult" juices (two parts juice to one part water) are best. The fructose and sorbitol in undiluted juices not made specifically for babies cause diarrhea. "It's just sugar water for kids," says Dr. Karp. Avoid citrus juices, which may trigger allergies, until your child is twelve months.

Teething infants can begin eating unsalted crackers, such as saltines and graham crackers, and dry toast. Supervise closely! Babies can easily choke on small pieces of food.

If there is no history of allergies to dairy products in your family, by the end of this period, you can feed your baby a few tablespoons of yogurt. Plain, organic yogurt is best. You can add a little pureed fruit for more taste. Monitor your baby for allergic reactions.

FROM NINE MONTHS TO ONE YEAR, GIVE CHUNKIER FOODS AND FINGER FOODS.
Continue giving your baby foods that are progressively lumpier. Finger foods, such as breadsticks, crackers, and cut-up steamed vegetables, can be given as well. Try pasta in small shapes, such as macaroni, alphabet noodles, and orzo. Mild cheeses and ground meat (beef or poultry) are also suitable.

Give baby raw fruits and vegetables when he has enough teeth, and the ability, to chew them.

You can increase the amount of juice you give your baby up to 8 ounces, but continue to dilute it.

After one year, most foods can be served in bite-size pieces. Continue to introduce new foods. Your baby should now be able to eat most foods. You can begin feeding him eggs and even a little fish. Be careful that there are no bones!

Ten Foods to Buy Organic, IPM, or Local

Whether you buy or make your baby's food, you'll want to be certain that these foods are as free from pesticide residues as possible. While it's not always possible to obtain local, organic, or IPM-grown foods at affordable prices, there will be some foods that your baby will eat more of, like rice or bananas. And certain foods have been found to contain more pesticide residues than others. For these, try to find organic, IPM, and local, in-season equivalents. The following ten foods are a good place to start:

1. *Baby Foods.* These include **Earth's Best, The Well-Fed Baby,** and **Gerber**'s Tender Harvest, and you can make your own by cooking and pureeing organic food. In 1995, the Environmental Working Group (EWG) tested eight nonorganic baby foods made by industry leaders Gerber, Heinz, and Beech-Nut. Some sixteen pesticides were found in more than half of the samples.

2. *Rice.* Look for baby cereal and foods made of organic rice from **Earth's Best** and **The Well-Fed Baby.** As your child grows, you can choose from brands like Eagle Agricultural Products, Lundberg Family Farms, and MacDougall's Wild Rice. Because rice allergies are practically nonexistent, this cereal grass is a primary ingredient in baby foods. But pesticide use on rice fields in California's Sacramento River Valley, one major growing region, has been so heavy that it has contaminated groundwater.

3. *Strawberries.* Organic brands include Golden River Farms, Cascadian Farms, and Boulder Fruit Express. Conventionally grown strawberries are the single most pesticide-contaminated fruit or vegetable in the United States, according to a 1995 EWG study. No surprise, in a crop that receives a dose of up to 500 pounds of pesticides per acre. Some 80 percent of the nation's domestic strawberry supply comes from intensively farmed lands in California. Strawberries and other produce bought out of season are the most likely to have been imported, possibly from a country with less-stringent pesticide regulations.

4. *Grains.* The USDA recommends six to eleven servings of grains a day (for adults). But in 1994, the FDA found illegal pesticide residues in a year's worth of General Mills' Cheerios oat-based cereal. And, in 1996, the FDA found residues from at least one pesticide in 91 percent of wheat samples tested. Try a healthy variety of organic offerings: oats, wheat, millet, quinoa, barley, couscous, amaranth, buckwheat, and spelt. Organic oatmeal is great for babies, and you can also make mushy cereals with other grains. Happily, there are too many brands of organic grain-based foods to list here, but look for flours, cereal, pasta, bread, and crackers.

5. *Milk.* There are no organic infant formulas at this time, but when your baby begins to drink milk (no earlier than 12 months), you'll find organic milk, such as that from Horizon Dairy, widely available. For local dairies, contact **Mothers & Others** for our Mothers' Milk List, which lists organic dairies around the country. Cows' milk comprises nearly a quarter of the nonnursing infant's diet, but many dairies inject their cows with recombinant bovine growth hormone (rBGH), a genetically engineered hormone used to boost milk production. Organic milk dairies don't use hormones or antibiotics.

6. *Corn.* Processed foods made with corn—cornbread, chips, and popcorn—were among the top fifteen foods likely to expose children to an unsafe dose of organophosphate (OP) pesticide residues, according to EWG's 1998 report. While you won't be feeding your infant these foods, check labels of processed foods. Many contain corn syrup and other corn-derived ingredients. Avoid these or buy organic versions, which can readily be found.

7. *Bananas.* Often the first fruit offered to babies, bananas are produced using benomyl (linked to birth defects) and chlorpyrifos (a neurotoxin). In Costa Rica, a major exporter, only 5 percent of farmland is used to grow bananas, but it accounts for 35 percent of the country's pesticide use. Ginger Ridge Farms, Made in Nature, and Eco-Fruit are organic brands available.

8. *Green beans.* In 1992 and 1993, contamination with pesticides illegal in the United States was found in 7.4 percent of green beans imported from Mexico. EWG's commercial baby food tests found three pesticides in green bean samples.

9. *Peaches.* A recent FDA study found that 5 percent of the peach crop was contaminated. Peaches lead the EWG's list of foods likely to contain unsafe OP exposures.

10. *Apples.* This fruit ranks second on the EWG list for OP residues, and baby apple juice also made the top fifteen. Since children consume a lot of apples, apple sauce, and apple juice, choose organic and IPM alternatives, which are increasingly available. Mothers & Others introduced its "CORE Values Northeast" label in 1996, certifying apples grown regionally by growers practicing IPM. These apples can be found in select supermarkets in the Northeast.

You may also want to seek organic nectarines, grapes and raisins, and kiwi fruit, all of which made EWG's "least wanted" list in their report on organophosphate residues on food. All of **EWG**'s reports are on their website.

RECIPES

Organix, a British organic food company, offers a line of baby foods. Founder Lizzie Vann recommends making these recipes with organic ingredients.

Pear, Apple, and Oats *(7 months +)*

1 tablespoon oats
3 tablespoons water
1 medium apple, peeled and chopped
1 medium pear, peeled and chopped

Simmer oats and water for 5 minutes. Add the pear and apple and simmer for 5 more minutes, or until soft. Puree roughly or mash; texture should be lumpy. Add extra water if necessary and allow to cool. Freeze leftovers in an ice cube tray.

Beans in Tomato Sauce

(7 months +)

¼ cup frozen or canned butter beans, chopped

2 tablespoons tomato puree

½ cup water

I medium carrot, peeled and chopped

I small onion, peeled and chopped

half a stick of celery, chopped

pinch of dried basil or parsley

Place beans, tomato puree, and water in a saucepan, bring to a boil, then simmer for 20 minutes. Add the vegetables and herb; simmer for 10 minutes longer. Puree roughly or mash; texture should be slightly lumpy. Add extra water if necessary and allow to cool. Freeze leftovers in an ice cube tray.

Making your own cereals is an excellent way to ensure that they contain only whole grains. Once ground, grains begin to lose nutrients rapidly. Grinding grains for cereals and flour as you need them provides you with the most nutritious foods. The following combination cereals come from Cynthia Lair, author of *Feeding the Whole Family*. The grains can be toasted in bulk, stored in airtight containers, then ground in a grinder or food processor in small batches as needed. You can feed these cereals to your baby after he's at least six months old. You can find the ingredients in many large supermarkets and natural food stores.

Sweet Rice-Sesame Cereal

(6 months +)

I cup brown rice

I cup sweet brown rice

½ cup whole oats

½ cup sesame seeds

Almond Millet Cereal

(I year +)

I cup millet

I cup brown rice

I cup almonds

Super Iron-Fortified Cereal

(I year +)

1½ cup millet

I cup amaranth or quinoa

½ cup sunflower seeds

3 tablespoons dulse flakes

Barley Oat-Pumpkin Seed Cereal

(I year +)

I cup hulled barley

I cup whole oats

½ cup sweet brown rice

½ cup pumpkin seeds

To toast grains: Place all grains, nuts, and seeds in a fine strainer; rinse and drain. Dulse does not need to be toasted, but can be added to grain mixture after toasting. For *oven toasting,* preheat oven to 350 degrees F. Spread grains on a cookie sheet and toast in oven until they give off a nutty aroma, about 12 to 15 minutes. For *skillet toasting,* place washed grains in a large skillet on burner and toast on medium heat, stirring constantly, until grains give off a nutty aroma, about 5 to 8 minutes.

To grind grains: Grind grains in an electric or hand grinder or food processor as you need them. Grinders can be purchased from **Back to Basics Products** or **The Bakers Catalog.** Hand grinders cost about $60, while electric flour mills range between $200 to $300. Use ground grains within 24 to 48 hours, as grains begin to lose nutrients just after grinding. As your baby grows and becomes accustomed to different textures, you can grind the grains more coarsely.

To cook ground grains into cereal: For baby-size portions, mix together 2 to 3 tablespoons of ground cereal and $^1/_2$ to $^3/_4$ cups water in a small pot; bring to a boil. Reduce heat to low and simmer, covered, for about 5 minutes.

For adults, use $^1/_3$ cup ground cereal and 1 cup water per person. Cook for 10 to 12 minutes.

These recipes make about 3 cups of dry cereal, which yields 9 adult servings or 12 to 15 baby-size portions.

Food Safety

Babies and children are more vulnerable to food poisoning than adults because their immune systems are not fully developed. For this reason, you should be very careful to maintain good hygiene practices in the kitchen. In chapter 6, a list of food safety tips is given. Follow these faithfully to avoid any illnesses. Children are very susceptible to botulism, salmonellosis, and *E. coli* poisoning. *E. coli O157:H7,* a dangerous strain of bacteria, can be fatal to children. Always wash your hands before preparing your baby's food and feeding him. When you start feeding your baby fruit juice, use only pasteurized juice. Remember to keep all cooking utensils, dishes, and storage containers as clean as possible. Do not let your baby's food or dishes come into contact with raw meat or eggs. Thoroughly cook all foods. Raw fruits and vegetables are fine as long as you wash them well and don't let them come into contact with raw meat or utensils that have touched raw meat.

Sources of Good Quality Food

In the past decade, the demand for organic and natural foods has increased tremendously. As a result, these foods can be found in more and more supermarkets around the country. But alternative marketplaces for these foods are also increasing. If you can't find good produce and a wide selection of whole foods in your supermarket, try these outlets:

- *Natural Food Stores.* More than 10,000 natural foods stores operate throughout the country. Natural food stores offer a wide variety of organic foods, including fresh produce, cereal, baby food, juice, coffee, peanut butter, dairy products, flour, grains, pastas and sauces, soups, and even frozen meals. A number of natural food store chains, such as Whole Foods Markets, Real Foods, Bread & Circus, Wild Oats, Alfalfa's, and Fresh Fields, may be in your area; also remember to look for smaller independent stores. These smaller stores are often locally owned, and many buy organic produce directly from local farms.

To find natural food stores near you, look in your local phone book under "Health and Diet Food Products—Retail," "Natural Foods," or "Grocers—Retail."

- *Farmers' Markets.* Most metropolitan areas and even small towns host one or more markets where farmers sell their products directly to the public. There are more than 2,400 farmers' markets across the country, according to the **U.S. Department of Agriculture (USDA).** The majority of these markets feature organic and conventional produce that is grown locally. Farmers' markets connect us directly with local farmers and how our food is grown.

  You can contact your local chamber of commerce or county courthouse to obtain a list of farmers' markets in the area. You can also obtain a directory from the **USDA.** While at the market, look for farm stands that have "certified organic" signs posted. If you do not see any organic signs, find the market coordinator (usually at an information table or booth) and ask that at least one organic farmer be represented there.

- *Food Cooperatives.* Food cooperatives, or buying clubs, allow consumers to purchase food in bulk directly from farmers and other suppliers. Some co-ops occupy a permanent site, such as a storefront or garage; others use a temporary site, such as a church basement, for a few hours a week while members divvy up a delivery of food. Purchasing food in this manner enables a collective of consumers to buy organic products directly from growers and distributors, usually at wholesale prices. To locate a co-op near you, look in your phone book under "natural food stores" or "buying clubs." Call the store to be sure it is what you are looking for. You can also contact the **Co-op Network** or the **Co-op Directory Service.** If there isn't an established co-op in your area, you can start one on your own! The **National Cooperative Business Association (NCBA)** has information on how to get started.

- *Community Supported Agriculture* (CSA). In a typical CSA, community members purchase a share in a local farm's operation at the start of each growing season, or a "subscription" to the farm for a set period of time. CSA members often provide their payment up front to assist growers with production costs and, in return, receive a box of freshly grown produce directly from their grower on a weekly basis during harvest, usually June through November. CSAs benefit farmers by guaranteeing them a direct market for their produce, and gives consumers a chance to know the farmers and the land where their food is grown. You can choose a CSA farmer who grows food organically or with minimal pesticide use. The cost is often significantly lower than organic foods at the supermarket.

The easiest way to find a CSA in your area is to contact the **Biodynamic Farming and Gardening Association** or the **Northeast Sustainable Agriculture Working Group,** two organizations that keep lists of CSAs nationally. The **Community Alliance with Family Farmers,** a nonprofit organization in California, specializes in lists of CSAs on the West Coast. If you can't find a CSA in your area, consider setting one up yourself. You can obtain information on how from **Community Supported Agriculture of North America.**

Genetically Modified Foods

Scientific advancements are such that some companies are putting foods on the market that have been genetically altered. A genetically modified plant is created by joining the genes of a plant with genes carrying special traits, such as disease resistance or pest control, from another plant, animal, bacteria, or virus. For example, Monsanto's Roundup Ready Soybean has been genetically modified to resist the popular herbicide Roundup. Bt-corn contains *Bacillus thuringiensis,* a biological pesticide that controls a number of insects and is used in organic agriculture.

Genetic modification of agricultural plants may significantly impact our agricultural lands and ecosystems. Roundup Ready Soybeans can withstand doses of Roundup that kill normal soybeans. Although Monsanto calls Roundup a safe herbicide, it is the third most commonly reported source of pesticide-related illness among California farmworkers. Roundup can also drift up to 800 yards from its application site, threatening neighboring farms. Genetically modified plants may also pass on their traits to other plants. Herbicide resistance that is transferred to weeds could wreak havoc on natural ecosystems, which could be invaded by superweeds. Some scientists are also worried that creating plants that are resistant to certain viruses or insects will result in more resistant strains of these pests. Studies are showing that crops of Bt-corn and cotton could potentially harm populations of beneficial insects that help farmers keep levels of harmful insects down. Loss of natural controls only means a greater dependence on synthetic chemicals.

The only known health problem associated with genetically modified foods is allergenicity. A 1996 study of soybeans implanted with genes from Brazil nuts in *The New England Journal of Medicine* showed that food allergens can be transferred this way. The FDA now requires that foods that are joined with genes from foods known to cause allergies, like Brazil nuts, be labeled. But all other genetically modified foods do not have to be labeled. Some scientists are concerned that genetically modified foods may contain unknown allergens, since genes from plants, animals, and bacteria not normally associated with food may become a significant part of our diet through genetically modified foods.

Since more than 60 percent of processed foods contain corn and soy derivatives, such as soy proteins and corn syrup, most of us have probably unwittingly eaten some genetically modified foods. In 1997, Genetic ID tested a number of popular foods and found genetically modified soy or corn in four baby formulas (Carnation's Alsoy, Similac Neocare, Isomil, and Enfamil Prosobee), Fritos corn chips, Tostitos Crispy Rounds, and Doritos Nacho Cheesier.

At this time, the only thing consumers can do is to purchase foods made with 100 percent certified organic ingredients and press our elected officials to require labeling of genetically modified foods. **Consumers International,** an international consumer advocacy organization, is campaigning for such labeling worldwide, and has information on their website. Other organizations that are working for labeling are **The Campaign for Food Safety, Mothers for Natural Law, Union of Concerned Scientists, Alliance for Bio-Integrity,** and **Greenpeace.**

Weaning

Even after you start introducing solid foods, your baby will continue drinking breast milk or formula. At meals of solid food, though, you can give him some water, formula, or breast milk in a cup with a flexible, spouted lid. This type of cup is a good intermediate drinking vessel, since the spout is somewhat like a nipple and allows sucking. These are made of plastic, but they are generally fine for drinking. Avoid heating drinks in them, though, as this may cause chemicals to leach into the liquid. Watered-down juice is fine, once in a while, after your baby's seventh month, but don't give him more than 3 or 4 ounces per day. Juice will not provide the nutrients your baby needs during the first year of life and the sugars are not good for his teeth. It's best to give your baby water as a thirst-quencher. When he gets used to water as an important drink, he'll be less likely to reject it in favor of sweeter juices. Tap or filtered water is better than bottled, for the most part, since some bottled waters have high sodium content.

By eight or nine months, infants can better handle a cup and don't need to suck as much to drink, so switch to a cup with a rigid spout. You'll find the lid to be a necessity for preventing spills. A baby of this age still does not have the coordination to manage holding and putting down the cup, at least not all the time.

Your baby may still want to breast-feed for months to come. But if you want to wean your baby, offer him formula or breast milk from a cup at meals. He'll gradually want to nurse less, taking only comfort feedings in the morning and before going to sleep. If you want to end nursing completely, but your baby is reluctant, give him a bottle instead.

You can start weaning your baby from bottles by not giving a bottle at lunchtime, when he can have a drink in a cup. When your baby begins sleeping through the night, which means his meals and snacks during the day are filling him up, stop giving a late-night or early-morning bottle. Try not to let your baby hold onto a bottle—it becomes a comfort piece. Don't use bottles for anything but formula or breast milk. If baby wants juice or water, give it in a cup to reduce dependence on bottles. In the first year, your baby will still require about a pint of formula or breast milk for adequate nourishment. So, even as you are weaning, remember that you should continue to provide formula in a cup, if necessary and if you are not breast-feeding.

Before I became pregnant with my first child, when it came to food, I considered myself health conscious and was a "sometime" organic food shopper. Although I understood the merits of organic food and was up-to-date on all the research on the health risks and environmental impacts of the use of pesticides, I only purchased organics when it was convenient.

It wasn't until the day I became pregnant that I became a full-fledged, committed, organic food consumer. I remember the overwhelming feeling of wanting to expose my baby to the best, the most natural, and the purest of things. And for me, that started with the most basic of needs: food.

My initial "problem" was to find organic sources, and they all seemed, at first, to be way out of my way. But once I shifted my routine and made these stores my priorities, all of my shopping and everything I needed conveniently fell into place. That was in 1991. Today, organic produce and food products can be found in most large grocery stores across the country.

After Lily was born, I breast-fed her, which made the connection between what I ate and what was passed on to her seem even more important. I grew to love the challenge of choosing high-quality foods: those that were organic, whole, unprocessed and that used no chemical additives, colorings, preservatives, or synthetic ingredients.

When she was old enough to go on solids, feeding her was easy. To my surprise, I conveniently made my own baby food, even though I, like most people, had been convinced that this is next to impossible! It was cheap, fresh, organic, and I knew exactly what was in it—just natural food. I would make batches of different kinds of cooked fruits and vegetables, grind it to mush, and freeze it in covered ice cube trays. When needed, I could pop out a baby-size portion and warm it up. For meals that we ate out of the house, I put the cubes in little plastic cups with lids (which lasted years, through many incarnations of

snacks!) and kept them cool in a thermal pouch. When it was time to eat, I added some hot water to the cup to warm up the food. As the variety of foods that Lily ate broadened, we fed her what we ate for dinner, blended with milk or water.

There were many times that I bought jars of organic baby food. From day one, I reached for Earth's Best, even though it cost a little more than Beechnut and Gerber. When Earth's Best went on sale, it was just pennies above the price of the conventional brands, so I stocked up.

When I couldn't find organic produce, I only bought produce grown in the United States and preferably that which was locally grown and in season. I avoided rBGH-treated milk and dairy products and opted for eggs from free-range, antibiotic-free chickens. Cookies and snacks were made of whole wheat, unrefined sugar, little salt and fat, and no chemicals or synthetic colors. This was all easy to do. It was simply a matter of making the choice. The selection was available.

I kept informed of the latest "food findings" in the news and still do. Helpful to me was a list compiled by the Environmental Working Group (EWG) in 1996 that listed the produce with the highest pesticide levels—strawberries, bell peppers, spinach, cherries, peaches, imported cantaloupe, celery, apples, apricots, green beans, grapes, and cucumbers. EWG suggested alternatives like oranges, grapefruit, blueberries, pears, U.S.-grown cantaloupe, carrots, bananas, broccoli, green peas, cauliflower, asparagus, Brussels sprouts, and potatoes.

Shopping "healthy" is a snap. My husband and I are always reminded how delicious "real," organic, and whole foods taste when we get a taste of food that has been processed or loaded with synthetic and chemical ingredients. My children are now three and six years old and the real challenge has just begun. I am well aware that I cannot control everything that they eat in the "outside world." It's hard to ignore the barrage of junk food that faces us on a day-to-day basis, but in my home, I choose to make the food as healthy as possible. We talk about what makes a food "good," and it's fun preparing a meal from scratch together. In the summer, we garden and shop at farmers' markets.

Food is not an incidental part of life, a quick fix or something to catch on the run. Food is a basic need. In trying to make quality food choices and focus on how food is grown and prepared, I feel that it not only nourishes my family's bodies and appetites, but it connects us to the world around us.

chapter nine

Raising (*and* Protecting) Your Naturalist Child

Children learn both good and bad habits from us. If you would rather not raise a child whose favorite activity is eating junk food in front of the television set, then the best thing you can do, no matter what the weather, is to get off the couch yourself. Get yourself and baby dressed and go outdoors. Baby will find plenty to be fascinated by. The world is new to her.

The low branches of a leafy tree can be as engaging as a crib mobile to a baby lying on a blanket on the grass. She'll wave her legs and arms and verbalize at the leaves, experiencing how the breeze, sunlight, and shadows play across her face (just make certain to keep checking that the moving sun is not shining directly in her eyes). If it's fine weather, take off the diaper and let baby air out on the blanket. You'll probably wash it anyway, so don't worry about accidents.

There are endless opportunities for engagement in the natural world. You can suggest looking under rocks for salamanders and bugs or make stops, as you perambulate down the street, at neighbor's front gardens to check whether yesterday's buds have opened up. You can collect yellow and red leaves and take them home to press between sheets of wax paper for a stained glass effect in your window. Or examine the different types of pine cones, acorns, or other types of seeds dropped by trees in the neighborhood. If there's a mulberry bush in your neighborhood you can check on the status of the caterpillars that will turn into chrysalises and then into Monarch butterflies.

Then there are the benefits of exercise for you. You have probably already noticed an increase in your activity as you find yourself running across a room, several times a day, to respond to baby's demands or to check whether she's safe. Soon you will be running after a crawler who can go amazingly fast while popping everything in her way into her mouth. Then you'll be trotting behind a racing, stumbling toddler. Balance these sudden sprints with some distance walking at the helm of a stroller, and you'll get in better shape. Try for 20 to 30 minutes at a stretch, to get some aerobic stimulation. As you push and walk, talk with your baby about what you're both seeing around you: pigeons, sparrows and crows, cats and dogs, butterflies, different trees and plants, whether it's a sunny or cloudy day or how the sky is changing. At the playground, hang from the chin-up bars to stretch your back and reverse "parent's hump." In fine weather you can explore parks and zoos. Many zoos have conservation-themed workshops for children of all ages and petting zoos with barnyard animals such as rabbits and goats. In the dead of winter you'll find the local natural history museum or children's library to be a great gathering place for the stroller set. And your zoo probably has some indoor environments, such as the reptile house, that are open in winter.

As for vacations, now that you have a baby, your fondest yearnings are probably for peace and quiet and rest, rather than scuba-diving in the Caribbean or the art and throngs of Venice—not to mention all those polluted canals. Baby will not appreciate being toted to fancy restaurants, and will make her displeasure all too audible. So think about weekends and vacations in a rented house or motel at the beach, a family hotel in the mountains, a cabin—or even a tent—in the forest. Nothing enthralls a young child more than a slow, meandering exploration up a burbling creek. It combines waterplay and the sweet slime of sand and mud between fingers and toes with the challenge of "bouldering" and the incipient thrill of a glimpse of chipmunks or deer. Most campgrounds in national and state parks have good restrooms and cooking facilities.

If you can't afford to go away and haven't got a back yard, don't worry. Think day trips. A young child doesn't need grand vistas. Grandma's back yard, or a meadow in a city park, is full of fascination for your baby. It's wonderful how even a day trip by bus or subway to a city beach can cool you off and smooth frayed nerves as soon as you're standing in water to your ankles and watching your child splash. And if you live where it snows, even in a city, nothing beats the joy of watching a snowsuited toddler bodysurfing snowy banks.

Nature is the best classroom. There's chemistry in that compost pile, aerodynamics in waves, behavioral psychology in the interaction between the blue jays and the squirrels. There's aesthetics in the sheer beauty of it all. The unstructured time spent observing and appreciating nature together will provide a lasting bond between you and your child. Young children are tenderhearted and adore animals and bugs, so this is a good age at which to get the message across that we can help other creatures. If your baby grows up to be an active environmentalist, joining with others to protect the earth, future generations—including your grandchildren and great-grandchildren, will be healthier for it.

All this can start with you and your baby, right now. Why wait? The great outdoors beckons. And it needs help. While this chapter also addresses avoiding hazards you might encounter in the great outdoors, its purpose is to help you maximize your child's enjoyment of nature, which needs not to be feared but understood. To that end, we've divided it into three environmentally themed sections:

- Children's Books

- Outdoor and Indoor Activities

- Protecting Your Child Outside

Children's Books

As new and nervous parents, Wendy Gordon, Betsy Lydon, Mindy Pennybacker, and others in the Mothers & Others family got a lot of ideas about how to experience and understand nature with our children from children's books. Here are a few of our favorites, along with activities that complement them. A common theme uniting this selection of babies' and young children's books is an appreciation and responsibility for the natural world. If you can't find any of the books below in your library or book store, they can be ordered by either one. Most libraries will obtain books at a cardholder's request. Or you can order these and other books from **Mothers & Others** online "bookshop" on our website, www.mothers.org. Of course, you'll also make your own discoveries; that's part of the joy.

The following books introduce babies and young children to the beauty of the natural world, helping them and you to better appreciate what's around you, and imagine, in close-up, what's not. Henry Cole's *I Took A Walk* (Greenwillow, 1998) lets toddlers (and book-friendly infants) open flaps of thickets, cattails, and ferns to see the creatures, plants, and flowers behind the screen. Robert McCloskey's classic *Make Way for Ducklings* (Viking Press, 1941) shows how an entire busy city can adapt to protect baby ducks, and *Blueberries For Sal* (Viking, 1976) reminds us that other species, like bears, gorge on wild fruit just as humans do. His tender *The Little Island* portrays a small rocky Maine island as an ecosystem, showing what happens to its denizens (including an adorable kitten) as the seasons change. *Where Does the Butterfly Go When It Rains?* by May Garelick (Mondo, 1997) answers this question for other creatures, too, including ducks, snakes, and bees. Children adore Eric Carle's soft-edged collages, which have influenced a whole generation of illustrators.

His *Brown Bear, Brown Bear, What Do You See?* (Henry Holt & Co., 1996), which portrays a number of other bright-eyed animals, including human children, has been a favorite of Kainalu Kolivas, Mindy's nephew, since he was eight months old. For a wintry change of pace, *Owl Moon,* by Jane Yolen (Putnam, 1987) conveys the mystery and wonder of the night forest as a girl and her father go owling.

Each blocky, colorful illustration and poem in Sally Rogers' and Melissa Baymathis' *Earthsong* (Dutton, 1998) is devoted to one of eleven endangered species, from blue whales blowing to Bengal tigers pouncing. In addition to detailing how habitat loss endangers these creatures, an afterword talks about the Endangered Species Act. Light and air and buoyant color abound in the seasonal watercolors of Jean and Mou-sien Tsengs' *Have You Seen Trees?* (Scholastic, 1995) in which a diverse palette of children, animals, and birds interact with these leafy splendors. And don't overlook *A Tree Is Nice*, Janice May Udry's Caldecott Medal winner, a simple celebration of the indispensable, now in its forty-second year (Demco Media, 1987).

Help foster children's natural empathy with books that bring you intimately close to wildlife. *Imagine You Are a Crocodile* by the writer/illustrator team of Karen Wallace and Mike Bostock (Henry Holt, 1997), depicts the swampy world of a mama croc and her babies.

Long before baby can snorkel, she can enter the sea in her imagination as you read to her from these gorgeously illustrated books, awash in light and aqueous colors. *Into the Sea* (Henry Holt, 1996) illustrated by Alix Berenzy, follows a sea turtle hatchling from her hole in the sand through various underwater habitats, populated by every imaginable kind of coral and fish, including sharks—but the gravest danger is posed by a fishing net. *One Less Fish,* by Kim Toft and Allan Sheather (Charlesbridge, 1998), counts backward in rhyme, listing the ways that fish on a coral reef—electrically colored angelfish, wrasses in all their varied glory—are destroyed by pollution and fishing. It finishes with the happier alternative of the protected Great Barrier Reef, and a glossary of some basic types of fish and pollutants. Nicola Davies's *Big Blue Whale,* with finely cross-hatched drawings by Nick Maland (Candlewick Press, 1997), chronicles the migration of a mother and a baby, how they feed and communicate and, despite their vast size, how vulnerable—and lonely—they are (only 10,000 remain). Diane Sweeney and Michelle Reddy's *Dolphin Babies* (Roberts Rhinehart, 1998), with fetching photographs of these aquatic geniuses, is sure to please human babies. *The Whales,* by Cynthia Rylant (Blue Sky, 1996), depicts these gentle giants with simple shapes and appropriately broad brush strokes that also convey a soothing sense of the whales moving through the sea. The funny *An Octopus Followed Me Home,* by Dan Yaccarino (Viking, 1997), builds on every baby's and child's wish to have all sorts of creatures living in the house—after all, we can put the penguins in the fridge. Another lift-the-flap book, *By the Seashore* by Maurice Pledger (Silver Dolphin, 1998), leads the children on a tactile beachcombing adventure.

Getting good and dirty means bliss for most babies and small children, who revel in the sensuality of mud. *Squishy, Misty, Damp & Muddy* (Sierra Club Books, 1996) looks at the value of wetlands—from potholes and ditches to marshes, bayous, and bogs—with inviting landscape and wildlife photos. Wendy Pfeffer and Robin Brickman's *A Log's Life* (Simon & Schuster, 1997), its leafy, loamy drawings virtually crackling off the page, gives the macroview of how one tree, even in death, provides a rich environment for lively salamanders, porcupines, fungi, and bugs. A companion piece is *What Rot! Nature's Mighty Recycler,* by Elizabeth Ring and Dwight Kuhn (The Millbrook Press, 1996), which celebrates decomposition and its agents, such as beetles, fungi, bacteria, and worms, in loving detail. A favorite with young children since its 1990 publication, Lynne Cherry's *The Great Kapok Tree* (Harcourt Brace, 1990) shows an Amazon woodcutter waking up among the inhabitants of the forest and ultimately deciding to lay down his axe for good. *Chameleons Are Cool,* by Martin Jenkins and Sue Shields (Candlewick Press, 1998), informs and entertains with zany, bulbous-eyed specimens, while warning against keeping exotic pets.

Birdsong, by Audrey Wood (Harcourt Brace, 1997), phonetically spells out the sounds different birds make, and pictures the environments where they're found. *Turtle at Long Pond,* by William and Lindsay Barnett George (Greenwillow, 1989), depicts the dramatic life of an ordinary American reptile. Jane Yolen's *Welcome to the Ice House* (Putnam, 1998) visits the mystical North with lovely paintings of polar bear, killer whales, seals, and hares.

Inside the Amazing Amazon by Don Lessem and Michael Rothman (Crown, 1995) displays foldout dioramas of ecosystems at different layers of the rain forest, from the floor to the treetops. Lizanne Flatt's and Allan Cormack's *My First Nature Treasury* (Sierra Club Books, 1994) contains clear, large-format illustrations of different ecosystems, including tundra, desert, lakes, prairies. In *Meeting Trees* by Scott Russell Sanders (National Geographic, 1997), a father takes his son out to look at and identify different trees.

Asking as many questions as it answers, the captivating *Keepers of the Earth* (Fulcrum, 1997) helps children place themselves in the world through a series of twenty-one Native American myths, illustrated in black-and-white line drawings. Each myth is followed by related activities designed to stimulate Earth stewardship. Activities include making water maps, "breathing" with a plant, studying soil, making bark rubbings and leaf prints, getting involved in local wildlife habitat management, and visualizing one's life as a sedimentary or metamorphic rock. In addition to fostering cooperative learning and a sense of oneness with the earth, this book stimulates creative thinking by asking questions, not all of which have one "right" answer. Gail Gibbons's *Recycle!* (Little, Brown, 1996) provides simple, cheerful illustrations of leaching garbage dumps; factories that recycle plastic, paper, and glass; and children at work picking up polystyrene litter and sorting trash. Endnotes contain quotable alarming statistics and a list of things we can do to improve the situation. We thought we'd had our fill of dinosaurs, an obsession with children from about the ages of two to six; however, in Laurie and Marc Browns' *Dinosaurs to the Rescue* (Little, Brown, 1994), the big green recyclers are full of fetching good cheer and display a far-from-fossilized fashion sense.

For diversion during free time spent at home, a luxury in these days of programmed activities and vacations, *Nature Watch* by Mick Manning and Brita Granshom (Kingfisher, 1997), tells children how to explore nature in their own back yard. Illustrated with lively cartoons of a diverse spectrum of children, this book concentrates on fun, simple things to do: making a worm farm or an underwater viewer (use a plastic bottle for the latter), observing how seeds spread, identifying tracks and droppings of animals, watching the creatures of the night (moths, bats, owls), and growing mold. Until you're a parent, you forget how much fun such elemental things can be. The lovely Arthur-Rackhamesque watercolors of *Linnea's Almanac,* by Christina Bjork (R&S Books, 1997), brings us once again the sprightly, straw-hatted young girl who visited Monet's garden at Giverney, this time with seasonal projects on bird feeding, flower pressing, fruit-compote cooking, and garland weaving. An earlier book still in print, *Linnea's Windowsill Garden* (Farrar Straus-Giroux, 1988), will please even very young children who love to see things grow but don't necessarily have an outdoor space. Mindy's one-year-old nephew Kainalu, for instance, loves to water potted plants, one by one, with great concentration.

Useful for outings in back yard or city park, or for trips slightly farther afield, the highly portable, small-format *Audubon First Field Guides* (Scholastic, 1997) include separate volumes on *Birds, Insects, Wildflowers,* and *Rocks and Minerals,* each lavishly illustrated with bright, engaging close-up photographs and charts of 175 North American creatures, blooms, and geological features. If you have attained parenthood without having hiked the Appalachian or John Muir trails, and never took an Outward Bound course, you will make good use of *Tom Brown's Field Guide to Nature and Survival for Children* by Tom and Judy Brown, Heather Bolyn, and Trip Becker (Berkley, 1989). After perusing this book, you will be much more knowledgeable about observing animals and plants, survival games, basic camping skills, building shelters, string walking at night, and swamp crawls.

Finally, while no childhood would be complete without Dr. Seuss's *Cat in the Hat* and *Horton,* don't forget to read your child *The Lorax* (Random House, 1971), the funny and sad tale of how pollution results from greed and a still-in-print classic of environmentalist storytelling. For many more titles, see Appendix A for how to order *The Amicus Journal*'s special issue on environmental children's books.

Outdoor and Indoor Activities

This section covers outdoor pursuits, such as hiking or sea-bathing with your child, and indoor board games for rainy or sick days, or snug family togetherness nights with the pressure turned off. At such times, you can also discuss the latest report on the status of a wild animal you've "adopted" through contributions to a conservation organization. It's one nice way for a child living in a city apartment, or one who's allergic to pet danders, to care for an animal without having a pet.

Backyard Habitats

No matter where you live, you've got potential habitat that can help support a healthy diversity of animal and plant life. In this section, we've separated out some books that can help you and your child identify the wildlife and habitat that surround you, whether you live in the city or the country. These books can provide a jumping-off point to such activities as making an organic wildlife habitat in your own yard, or bird-watching in your city.

You and your child can begin turning your yard into a conservation lot that creates wildlife habitat and preserves natural resources with the help of a new, free **U.S. Department of Agriculture** booklet "Backyard Habitats." The twenty-eight page booklet, aimed at families with children, gives ideas on how to attract and shelter butterflies, amphibians, and birds; and how to plant trees and bushes that attract birds that eat garden pests, along with other alternatives to using chemicals, such as using fruit and vegetable rinds to fertilize plants. One exciting goal for your child might be to have your backyard or school or community garden certified as a backyard wildlife habitat by the **National Wildlife Federation (NWF).** This national program encourages backyard cultivators to use native plants, while working with local environmental groups. The habitats must provide food, water, shelter, and a place for small mammals to raise their young. More than 20,000 schools, individuals, and businesses have certified their yards worldwide. Contact **NWF** and they'll put you in touch with a local affiliate.

If you have a garden or a yard of your own, or share one in your community, you can make good use of Constance Perenyi's *Growing Wild: Inviting Wildlife Into Your Yard* (Beyond Words, 1991), which could also serve as an updated companion to Virginia Lee Burton's *The Little House* (Houghton Mifflin, 1978), that classic tale of urban sprawl. *Growing Wild*'s lovely, clear collages depict an overgrown suburban yard gone to seed, and how it becomes a thriving wildlife habitat—as opposed to all those perfectly groomed, pesticide-doused lawns on which you wouldn't want your baby to spend too much time. Endnotes catalogue specific plants and animals, and instructions on how to make an organic garden that will shelter wildlife in your yard, with helpful instructions such as calling your local Cooperative Extension agency to learn about plants adapted to your area. It makes the important point that you don't need a large space; variety of plant species is the key. In a slightly different variation, *Where Once There Was a Wood* by Denise

Fleming (Henry Holt and Company, 1996), shows the species that once lived in North American back yards, while also instructing how to bring your back yard back to habitat.

Plants that attract pollinators to your garden are particularly desirable, because bees, butterflies, hummingbirds, and bats are dwindling in number as their habitats are lost to development. The **Brooklyn Botanic Gardens** in New York will provide a "pollinators list" of plants, by region and season, at your written request. If you have a vegetable garden, why not set aside a plot for your child? Make a little sign with her name on it. Let her choose what to put in the garden and where. You can also do this on a windowsill. Milk cartons can be handily recycled into seed planters; it's easy to punch holes in the bottom for drainage. **The Cook's Garden** has children's flower or vegetable seed collections, kids' garden gloves, and a book, *How a Seed Grows.* In big bright photographs of children harvesting and planting in the city and country, Robert Maas' *Garden* (Holt, 1998) is a wonderful introduction to this nourishing pastime.

A child-size tin watering can that meets all the specs for serious sprinkling is available from **The Natural Baby Company.**

There may not be many yards in the city, but there's plenty of habitat. While *Growing Wild* tells how to make bird feeders and bird baths, and what kinds of birds you're likely to spot in a North American garden, Barbara Bash's *Urban Roosts* (Sierra Club, 1992) shows how finches, sparrows, peregrine falcons, and owls make homes on skyscraper ledges, beneath bridges, inside traffic lights, and more. It's an inspiration to take your child bird-watching wherever you live—especially so in a city.

Encouraging Empathy for Animals

Children love to play at being animals. This makes for great outdoor games; instead of regular tag, one child can be a field mouse while another is a predator, such as a fox. The rules of the game can be dictated by true animal shelters and behaviors. You can also adopt specific animals with your child, or a whole preschool class can do this as a holiday gift to the environment. By adopting an endangered humpback or blue whale in your child's name, for $35, you can support the **Oceanic Society's** research and whale protection efforts on the coast of California. Or you can adopt a grizzly for $30 through **Brown Bear Resources** in Montana. Either program sends your child reports on the animals' progress. Other conservation organizations with similar programs include **International Wildlife Coalition, National Wildlife Federation, Bat Conservation International,** and the **Sea Turtle Survival League.**

At the Seashore

The combination of lots of relatively clean sand—that developmental treasure—and the entertaining, noisy, outreaching sea make the beach or lake a top pleasure destination for most babies. But because of overfishing and severe pollution, our oceans and waterways are far from as constantly regenerating as we thought. About one-third of fish species the world over are now threatened with extinction, and coral reefs are being poisoned and destroyed by nutrient overloads, warming seas, and the use of cyanide and dynamite by fishers to stun their prey. It's not so easy, of course, to identify with creatures who live out of sight, underwater. So until she reaches snorkeling age (about six or so), make it a point to take your baby to the aquarium as well as the zoo.

Participate in beach clean-up days sponsored by **National Audubon Society,** but also make every beach trip a litter pick-up day, explaining to your child that plastic objects often choke and entangle sea life. Separate recyclables from nonre-cyclables, and make a donation to an environmental organization with the pro-ceeds from returning bottles and cans. Most beach toys are made of plastic, alas, but a colorful tin set of pail, shovel, and sieve can be ordered from **The Natural Baby Company.**

Unfortunately, water pollution periodically makes many of our waterways unsafe for swimming and dunking, particularly for small children and babies, who tend to get water in their mouths. There were 3,685 beach closings and advisories in 1996, according to the *Testing the Waters,* an annual summer report by the **Natural Resources Defense Council (NRDC).** As a rule, don't take your child into the water after a heavy rainstorm, which may have washed sewage overflow into the lake or sea. Each summer, the **Environmental Protection Agency Office of Science and Technology** posts beach conditions on their website. You can also call **American Oceans Campaign** to find out if beaches in your area are under advisory.

Some Indoor Games and Activities

Before you know it, your child will be three years old and able to enjoy playing board games with you. It's a relaxing way to sit and chat and help children develop identification skills and learn about types of animals and how to protect their envi-ronments. For instance, one of Rory Wallace's special favorites is The Whale Game by Wildlife Games, whose goal is to reach home waters safely with one's mate and babies. "The Whale Game is a great environmental game because it simulates all that happens to whales, like oil spills and such, and makes you feel sad for them and think about how to change it," Rory says. Although he plays chess and com-puter games, at twelve years of age he still enjoys The Whale Game, which he's been playing since he was little. Animal Town has another Save the Whales Board Game, which looks at the different species of cetaceans. Look for these games at better toystores, environmentally themed stores, and zoo shops. For beginning gamesters, Ravensburger makes a number of lovely first games. Wildlife Bingo, for ages three and up, allows two to six players to play at matching photos of animals to the bingo game cards. There are nine animal cards, nine letter cards, fifty-nine cardboard tokens, and a drawstring bag to keep them in. They also make Baby Animal Lotto and Four First Games, including gentle Bird and Flower games, all for ages three to eight. Maisy's Color Game, featuring the cheerful mouse, and My First Matching Game are suitable for ages three to five. Ravensburger's WonderGame introduces a nature-protecting theme for children ages four and up, who must work cooperatively (noncompetitively) as a team to plant flowers before the sun goes down and thunderclouds form. **Frank Schaffer Co.** also makes an Animal Lotto with beautifully drawn wild animals, for ages four and up.

A terrific ecology board game called A Beautiful Place by Family Pastimes, for ages five and up, has as its aim to reduce pollution clouds with good ecology deeds.

For making your own nature images, put a stone, shell, leaf or your hand on the sun-sensitive paper in Solargraphics Kit by **Educational Insights** (for ages four and up). After a brief sun exposure, the image will develop in tap water as an elegant white silhouette against the blue. Your child can collect pages for her own nature album this way, or make greeting cards for grandparents and friends. Ages five and up may enjoy the traditional PommaWonga Indian Ring Toss Game, a wooden post and rings made by Francis Family Toys in New Mexico.

Safer Craft Supplies for Kids

Among the most satisfying activities you can do with your toddler, from about the age of two onwards, are painting and drawing. However, many art materials are hazardous. Here you can look for labels. The Labeling of Hazardous Art Materials Act of 1988 applies to many children's art products such as crayons, chalk, paint sets, modeling clay, and colored pencils. Labels must carry warnings if these materials contain the potential to pose a chronic hazard, or a conformance statement, "Conforms to ASTM D-4236," if a toxic hazard is not posed.

Organic watercolors, made in Germany of such natural substances as seaweed and beets, are available through **Terra Verde.** Wachsfarben makes wonderful beeswax crayons in chunky blocks, easy for toddlers to grasp; they're available from **The Natural Baby Company.**

Hitting the Trail

It can be great fun to take your baby, up to age two or so, on a hike in one of the carriers mentioned in chapter 3. If you're using a back carrier, it's best to go with another adult, who can keep an eye on baby—is she thirsty? has a bug gotten in her eye?—as well as share the carrying burden with you. Steer clear of branches and other protruding objects that might hurt the baby on your back. It takes time to adjust to this extension of your personal space, but you will. If you are alone with baby, you can stop and sit on a bench, log, or boulder every twenty minutes to half hour or so and take off the pack to rest your shoulders and back, check on baby, have a little face-to-face dialogue, and offer a drink. In hot or very dry weather, it's important not to let baby get dehydrated, which can be particularly dangerous for the very young. Remember to drink plenty of liquids yourself, especially if you're nursing.

If you have a carrier that distributes weight evenly, resting on your hips so as not to overly stress your shoulders and back, carrying baby on a hike can actually be easier than hiking with an ambulatory toddler or small child. They tire easily and get bored exerting themselves on what can seem to be an endless, monotonous trail—especially for someone too short to see a lot of the view. With a child who's too heavy to be carried, it's best to plan short nature walks instead of backpacking trips, and to focus on things close to her eye level.

To learn about nature hikes and species of plant and animal life in your area, contact your local **Audubon Society** or **Sierra Club** chapter. They also offer regular guided tours. Call your local botanical garden for a calendar of activities and seminars for children; many of them also have seasonal festivals.

Protecting Your Child Outside

Keep an Air Quality Watch

Because asthma is so dramatically on the rise, and air pollution has been found to exacerbate this disease, you need to be vigilant about air quality when you take your baby outside, or your older children go out to play.

As a general rule, take your children to play in parks, well away from highway fumes. Restrict outdoor activities when pollution is high. Check your local air quality index daily. Smog counts tend to be highest between 3 P.M. and 6 P.M. Ozone should not exceed 80 parts per billion (ppb) over an 8-hour period. That corresponds to 66 on the pollution standards index in local weather reports. Particulate matter should not exceed 50 micrograms per cubic meter daily. Particulates, or very fine particles of soot and dust, have been implicated in lung damage as well as smog. It's unsafe for asthmatic children, and unwise for everyone, to exert themselves outside in hot, smoggy weather, or when a dusty wind blows. If you live in the East or Midwest, you can check out **EPA**'s Air Now website to see ozone maps for these regions, updated several times a day. You can join Mothers & Others in urging EPA to expand their mapping regions by commenting by email while on the site.

Drive less, and fight pollution at the source. Paradoxically, asthma has soared while overall air quality has improved, at least in the United States, thanks to the Clean Air Act. But urban populations, surrounded by traffic and the clustering of factories, sewage treatment plants, and utility plants, remain especially at risk for asthma and other respiratory problems. To do your part bicycle, walk, or take public transportation rather than driving, whenever you can. (Make sure that when you take your baby or child bicycling, she wears a fitted helmet. Even a fall from a very low child's bike can cause lasting damage.)

Explain to your child why you choose public transportation. If you don't have a car, you should be commended, and your child should feel proud. You can always rent one for trips to places where you can't take a bus or train. If you feel you need a car, avoid gas-guzzling sports utility vehicles (SUVs), whose makers have gotten around Clean Air Act mileage standards by designating these vehicles as trucks, not cars. Pick the car with the highest mileage efficiency you can get. **The American Council for an Energy Efficient Economy (ACEEE)** publishes the book *Green Guide to Cars and Trucks,* which ranks vehicles according to their environmental impact and provides tips on how to keep your vehicle running cleanly and efficiently. *Consumer Reports* also considers gas mileage in making recommendations in their annual car buying guides.

If you live near industrial facilities, learn about possible emissions by calling the **EPA**'s **Community Right-to-Know Hotline.** Join with neighbors to seek monitoring and reduction of emissions from local power, incineration, and sewage plants; dumps; and large bus and truck lots. **The Center for Health, Environment, and Justice** will put you in touch with a nearby group, or advise you on how to start one.

The spraying of pesticides in your vicinity poses another air-pollution problem, as these toxic chemicals can drift from other properties onto yours. The droplets can be breathed in by children, come through open windows into your home, and coat toys left outdoors. Don't use toxic chemicals on your lawn, and ask neighbors to refrain from doing so. Give them the information about natural lawn care services listed in chapter 5.

Many municipalities or counties have Mosquito Abatement Districts (MADs) that are routinely sprayed. They should broadcast warnings, but many do not. Instead of toxic organophosphates and synthetic pyrethroids, you can ask them to use less toxic methods, such as Integrated Pest Management (IPM), which does everything from increasing circulation in wetlands to discourage the mosquito to using insect growth regulators, such as methoprene, considered safe for mammals. You can contact your MAD to ask what they spray and when they do it. You can request that the MAD not spray on or near your property. If you can't find their number in the local government pages of the phone book, try your local health, pest control, or agriculture department. For information on IPM, contact **National Coalition Against the Misuse of Pesticides (NCAMP), Bio-Integral Resource Center,** or **Northwest Coalition for Alternatives to Pesticides.**

Avoid biting insects without using chemical insecticides in the home or on your children's skin. Home foggers and sprayers are particularly dangerous, having been linked with higher incidence of childhood cancers. To fight mosquitoes, get them where they breed. Your child can help with this. Go outside and look for any containers that can hold rainwater—cans, buckets, saucers under plants, leaf-filled drains, old tires—and remove them. Make sure every window, door, and porch is fully screened, and check your screens often for tears. Use fans to discourage mosquitoes from coming near you and your child; mosquitoes don't like to be near circulating air. Wear protective clothing or try to stay inside at dusk, when mosquitoes are most active.

Local golf courses are also major sources of pesticide drift. If you live near a golf course, speak with the management about your concerns. Urge them to reduce or eliminate their use of synthetic pesticides and adopt IPM. Give them a copy of **Mothers & Others'** *Green Guide #37,* on the environmental and health hazards of golf course pesticides and golf courses that are successfully going "natural." Request advance notification of at least 48 hours before they spray the course, to enable you to close windows, leave home if necessary, or at least bring in or cover outside toys, tables, etc. NCAMP can advise you on getting a notification ordinance proposed by your local governing body.

Fending off Biting Insects

Many parents are justifiably concerned about Lyme disease, spread by biting deer ticks. The ticks are present throughout the Northeastern states. In the West,

Rocky Mountain Spotted fever is also spread by tick bites. In tick-infested areas, it's best to avoid going into long grass or underbrush. The best way to prevent tick bites is to wear protective clothing—including hats or caps, long-sleeved shirts, long pants tucked into socks—in light colors, so that ticks will be visible. Buy lightweight, gauzy clothing for summertime hikes. Preventive measures must be completed by a nightly inspection for ticks in every crack and crevice of your baby or child's body, and around the ears, back of the neck, and hairline. Immersing your child in a bath every night and washing her hair really helps. Ticks generally need 24 hours on the body to attach, so if you find them before this time you can brush or wash them off. Make sure they don't escape into your household!

If you find an attached tick, cover it with oil or petroleum jelly for 10 to 20 minutes to suffocate it and make it release its grip. Then, using a pair of tweezers or your fingers (protected by a latex glove or tissue), grasp the tick as close to the skin as possible, then pull slowly and directly up. Don't twist. Be careful not to squeeze or crush the tick, as it could regurgitate toxin into your child's bloodstream. Then wash your child's skin and your hands with soap and water, and disinfect the bite area and tweezers with rubbing alcohol. Save the tick in a bottle and take it to your doctor, who can have it tested for Lyme disease.

Insect repellents such as Cutter and Off! contain DEET, or N,N-diethyl-m-toluamide, which can be dangerous if overused—and in the case of children, less has more of an effect. In addition to the general special vulnerability of babies and children discussed throughout this book, children have more skin surface relative to their body size than do adults, and a child's skin is thinner, so there is more potential for absorption of, and thus toxic exposure to, repellents. DEET products should never be applied to the skin of anyone under two years old. And products used on children should not contain more than 10 percent DEET, the lowest effective dose. Repeated applications can be dangerous, producing a cumulative effect.

DEET is absorbed through the skin and can cause skin irritations, temporary eye damage, headaches, nausea, and neurotoxic problems. It can even be fatal in rare instances. "There have been five deaths we know about—all extreme cases of misuse," Robert Brennis, a researcher at the EPA, told *The Green Guide* in 1996. In the July 1998 issue of *Contemporary Pediatrics,* Drs. Adelaide A. Hebert, of the University of Texas Medical School in Houston, and Soni Carlton, an intern, reported that thirteen children under age eight have developed encephalopathy, with seizures and convulsions, after having been overexposed to DEET, most through repeated application of products containing 10 or 20 percent DEET. Three died.

We advise using safer alternatives to DEET, which should be applied, if at all, as a last resort—and then with the utmost caution and in the lowest concentration, 10 percent. For instance, **Lakon** has a completely herbal bug repellent called Bygone Bugz. Wouldn't it be great if the smell of herbs turned bugs off? You can try it and see—different products may also be less or more effective on different people. Soybean oil, another natural repellent, is quite effective in keeping mosquitoes off, Jane Brody reports in her health column in the July 7, 1998 *New York Times.* Bite Blocker, a product that contains 2 percent soybean oil, also has a sunscreen, though it can produce a stinging sensation on the skin. Brody concludes, "Although rubbing the skin with kitchen soybean oil has not yet been formally tested as a repellent, it would be safe for children and may be worth a try." We agree.

Oil of citronella, the active ingredient in **Avon**'s Skin So Soft, Natrapel, and other less-toxic alternative insecticides found in natural food stores, has been shown to be somewhat effective in keeping insects away, though far less so than DEET. Nor is oil of citronella proven safe, so use it only with caution and in the smallest amounts possible, making certain, as with any bug repellent, not to apply it near your child's eyes or mouth, or in her hands, which frequently travel to the mouth and eyes.

While home remedies such as herbs, blowing fans (a good idea while baby sleeps, but keep it low—you don't want to blast him with a great wind), and soybean oil may deflect mosquitoes, ticks can be more tenacious and difficult to detect. The insecticide permethrin, found in the tick repellents Permanone and Duranon, is more effective than DEET in the opinion of some doctors, but it hasn't yet been tested for safety as a product applied to skin. Therefore, Dr. Hebert advises in her *Contemporary Pediatrics* article that permethrin repellents not be put on a child's skin, but instead sprayed on clothing, shoes, tents, sleeping bags, and netting if you must use it. It could still be inhaled by your child, so use these products only when absolutely necessary.

If you feel you must use products containing DEET to repel mosquitoes and ticks during particularly dangerous or virulent infestations, choose a brand that has only a ten percent proportion or less. These include Skedaddle Insect Protection for Children and Johnson's Off! Skintastic Insect Repellent. The latter is fragrance-free. Remember, these should still not be used on babies younger than two years. The basic rule: Do not apply DEET near your child's eyes or mouth, on hands, or on any cuts or scrapes. Read labels thoroughly before use; wash skin and change clothes after returning indoors; if a reaction is suspected, wash skin immediately and call your local poison control center.

Safer Insect Repellents

The *Journal of the American Academy of Dermatology* lists the following products as safe for children (when used as directed, we must add).

Treo	0.05% citronella oil
Avon Skin So Soft	0.05% citronella oil
Bite Blocker (with sunscreen)	2% soybean oil
Permanone Tick Repellent	0.05% permethrin

Skedaddle (not for children under 2 years)	6.2% DEET
Off! Skintastic for Kids	7.125% DEET
Skintastic Lotion	8.125% DEET
Pleasant Protection	9.5% DEET
Skintastic Cream with Sunscreen	9.5% DEET
Sports Pack	9.5% DEET
Cutter Backyard	10% DEET

A good compromise is to put some repellent on a child's clothing, say on the outer brim of a hat or cap, or on socks—places where the child won't be rubbing his mouth or eyes. All clothing should be washed promptly after you've gone into an area that might have ticks.

While black flies can make life miserable, at least you won't get any disease from them. You should wear long-sleeved, long-pants protective clothing as you would against ticks, making sure it's loose and light enough to keep you as comfortable as possible in warm weather or while hiking. This will guard covered areas against sunburn, too. You can also apply, as minimally as possible, repellents such as OFF! and 6-12, which contain 1-ethyl-1,3-hexanediol, which is supposed to repel black flies.

To reduce the risks of insect bites, protective clothing and simple avoidance can be key. Know your insects, and teach your child about them, too. Never swat at or behave aggressively toward a bee, yellow jacket, or fire wasp. Running and waving your arms can make them chase you; it's best to walk calmly toward shelter. If they're known to exist in your area, check for fire ants before you sit down on a stump, rock, or mound of dirt. Keep out of black fly areas in their biting season— late spring in New England and the Upper Midwest. Deer flies strike in the autumn. Don't go into the underbrush or long grass in Lyme tick high season— April through October—though it's advisable to be vigilant year-round.

In addition, there is currently some debate as to whether products combining DEET insect repellents with sunblocks are advisable, as the need to reapply sunblock after swimming or exercise or heavy perspiration might result in overexposure to the insecticide. For instance, even so-called "waterproof" sunblocks, in our experience, need to be reapplied as frequently as every two hours, which would not be safe with DEET. There are some products that combine citronella with DEET, but in general we advise against using any repellent as frequently as you would a sunscreen. Therefore, it's best to keep them separate—then you'll be less likely to overuse the bug juice.

Sunblocks

For the next several years, it's especially important to take cover from the sun. The 1998 scientific assessment of the ozone layer, by the United Nations Environment Programme and the World Meteorological Organization, found that levels of ozone-depleting chemicals in the stratosphere are now reaching their highest point, and will peak around the year 2000. Risks of this thinning of ozone, which protects Earth from the sun's burning ultraviolet rays, include skin cancer, cataracts, and immune suppression.

Sunburns in childhood and adolescence correlate with a higher risk of developing skin cancers. But most sunblocks carry warnings that they are not to be used on children under six months of age. This is a prudent course of action, as sunblocks are chemically based. Until six months—and even when they're older— babies shouldn't be exposed to the sun between the ultraviolet-intensive hours of 10 A.M. to 3 P.M. If you keep your child in the shade of a tree, tent, or umbrella, and she's willing to wear a hat, remember that ultraviolet (UV) light can still bounce off other objects and reach her.

Use SPF 15 or higher blocks on children older than six months. Look for sunblock creams labeled "full-spectrum," which means that they protect against many UVA and UVB rays. UVA causes the familiar red sunburn; UVB damage is more insidious, occurring even before one gets symptoms of burn. Recent evidence reported in the May 1998 *Journal of Pathology* establishes a direct link between the sun's UVB rays and melanoma, the deadliest form of skin cancer. The most effective sunblockers for the skin contain either PABA, titanium dioxide, or zinc oxide, all of which block both UVA and UVB rays. The latter is the white stuff that lifeguards wear on their noses. Some children's and even adults' skin are irritated by PABA and other chemicals in sunblocks, so it's a good idea to do a test on a small patch of skin first. Currently, titanium dioxide and zinc oxide are believed to be less irritating because they don't absorb into skin, but instead create a physical barrier to rays. Aubrey **Organics** Green Tea Sunblock for children, SPF 25, has titanium dioxide and PABA. Mustela of Paris makes mineral-based, chemical- and fragrance-free sunblocks for babies and children, including a handy sunblock stick.

In addition, those little Lawrence of Arabia-style hats, with extra long bills and ear and neck flaps that protect vulnerable skin, should be standard issue on the summer dunes or at the park. Plus they appeal to young children's love of drama and dressing up. **Patagonia** makes these hats, which are also available at Patagonia stores and, by different makers, at most baby shops. Some makers are also producing UV-blocking cotton clothing and swimwear. They include **Koala Konnection** (swim and active wear), Solarweave SunFun Collection (fabric and hats) and **Sun Precautions** (clothing, hats, umbrellas).

The importance of this sort of protective clothing cannot be stressed enough, for both you and your baby. As the ozone hole grows, we need to be more and more careful not to let sunscreens lull us into a false sense of security. It's still best to avoid the sun's rays as much as possible.

If you have to or really want to be out, use sunglasses, hats, and visors, and protective clothing as much as possible. Children's sunglasses should have unbreakable plastic lenses that are labeled "Blocks ultraviolet rays," along with durable, flexible frames that won't break into sharp shards. While participating in water sports, for example, you and your child can wear the "wind shirts" popularized by surfers. They come in short- and long-sleeve styles and can be worn while swimming, snorkeling, boating, kayaking, and so on. Made of nylon, they dry rapidly and feel great against the skin. They're available from **Patagonia** and in most sport shops that sell surfing or diving gear. O'Neill, Local Motion, and Quicksilver are good brands, but Mindy was even given one made by Donna Karan as a gift, and she wears it surfing. "Out surfing in Honolulu, my home town, last summer, I wore a little brimmed cap that fastened under the chin—great for shading the eyes and face while surfing—and noticed other surfers out in the water with tennis and golf visors on. It's a sign of cool, like you're confident it won't get knocked off. But use a cheap visor in case it does," she advises. Mindy also wears knee-length surfer's "board shorts" in the water. These are available for children as well, and a good way to protect the tender skin at the back of the knees and thighs from nicks and scrapes against rocks and reefs, as well as from the sun.

Water Sports

Though we don't want to be a downer, especially as we love and recommend water play and outdoor activities so, we cannot emphasize enough the importance—particularly for babies and children—of minimizing exposure to the sun by simply keeping out of it as much as possible. One good reason: there is no evidence to date that proves that sunscreens protect us from melanoma, according to Dr. Philippe Autier of the European Institute of Oncology, writing with two colleagues in the April 1998 *Archives of Dermatology.* "Emphasis should be placed on physical rather than chemical sun-protection methods," the authors wrote. That means hats and clothing. Furthermore, a February 1998 report, based on ten epidemiologic studies, by Marianne Berwick of the Sloan Kettering Cancer Center, showed conflicting results: in five studies, sunscreen users seemed to have higher incidence of melanoma than nonusers; in two studies, sunscreen appeared to provide a significant protective effect against melanoma; three studies showed no association. However, the report asked only about sunscreen use in the prior ten years, while skin cancer takes many decades to develop; the subjects might have sustained damaging exposures as children, much more than ten years before. For this reason, the **American Academy of Dermatology (AAD)** says we should all wear sunscreen of at least SPF 15 whenever we go outdoors—in the city and the country, when it's cloudy or fair, and whether we are dark-skinned or fair-skinned or have brown eyes or blue.

Mothers & Others agrees with the AAD. Wear sunblock whenever you go outdoors, and make sure your child does, too. We advise the use of protective clothing over the sunblock. We also recommend that sun avoidance be the rule, to be broken only when conditions are irresistible. "If all else is the same, I'll choose to surf in the early morning or late afternoon, when it's less windy and crowded and the sun is plentiful, but weaker," Mindy says. She signs Rory up for sailing or tennis classes taught before 11 A.M. or after 2 P.M., never in the middle of the day. And when he was a baby, she and Don strictly observed the early-morning, late-afternoon rule when taking him for a swim. "Remember, you can also get badly burned during cloudy weather between those hours," she says.

Water, in addition to sun, is a potential hazard when you take your baby or child to the beach, lake, stream, or pool. Because of possible bacterial pollution, particularly in public children's pools where feces and urine may be accidentally released or leak out of diapers, you should not let your baby or child get wet without first checking out the water yourself. If the water is very warm and clean, it can be very relaxing for baby, even as young as two months, to be held by a parent in the ocean, pool, or lake. Just be very careful that water doesn't splash into the baby's mouth or eyes. The American Academy of Pediatrics discourages infant swimming classes because of the potential for accidental drowning. However, if you yourself are an aquatic person who understands the hazards of water and how to avoid them, getting into the pool with your baby can be wonderful exercise and bonding for both of you. Just make sure that you pick a class with a certified instructor. And you can also take a lifeguard water-safety course, yourself. For older babies who can hold their heads up and make crawling motions, starting at seven to eight months, swim classes are often offered at YMCAs or YWCAs. **Ecobaby, The Natural Baby Company,** and others offer cute swim suits, or modified swim diapers, for babies that won't weigh them down like diapers, and also fit snugly enough and are tightly woven or have a waterproof layer so as to contain poop and, possibly, some of the pee, though one never really knows.

It's a very good idea to start swim lessons by the age of two or three, of the kind where you are required to be in the water with your baby. You will learn a lot about water safety and also correct swimming strokes and fun water games to play with your child. Remember, even if your child knows how to swim, he or she must never be left unsupervised near water. Pools should be securely gated with child-proof latches—but do not trust the latches, only trust your very open eyes.

Never take your baby or child on a boat or canoe without a life vest specifically made for your child's size. You can buy life vests at a sporting goods store. It is advisable to buy a vest for your child because many boats provide only Type IIIs, the most popular life vests. Type IIIs aren't designed to keep the head and face out of the water in rough conditions. In addition, Type IIIs won't automatically turn you face up if you've been knocked unconscious or, in the case of a child, have landed face down in the water and can't maneuver. Though bulkier, Type I vests offer the most protection, according to water safety expert Wayne Williams, who started the Air Force Sea Survival School. When shopping for a life vest, or personal flotation device (PFD), read the "Think Safe" pamphlet that the Coast Guard requires to be attached to every vest sold. It will tell you how the vest will work in various conditions. No matter which vest you buy, remember to test it on your child before your first water outing.

Dr. Harvey Barnett, director of Infant Swimming Research, Inc., advises that parents look for the following in a child's life vest:

- asymmetrical front flotation
- no collar
- double girth straps
- adjustable crotch straps
- tethered D-ring on the back (for sailboat use)

Make sure your child can sit comfortably wearing the vest, without chafing from buckles and snaps. In addition, know the size of the seat your child will occupy; it should be able to fit her wearing the jacket. New inflatable life vests, like the ones used on airplanes, are an effective and less bulky option; however, the manually inflatable one, which is Coast Guard approved, wouldn't be operable by an infant or young child. The automatic inflatable is still awaiting Coast Guard approval.

Playground Hazards

Look carefully at the paint on the jungle gym, swings, and other equipment at the playground. Some public playground equipment has chipping and peeling lead paint, a potential lead poisoning hazard for children six years and younger, the **U.S. Consumer Product Safety Commission (CPSC)** reported in 1996. If the playground in your neighborhood has deteriorating paint, ask your city health department to test it for lead. Find another playground with intact paint or natural wood equipment. If there's no other playground and you want your child to be able to play in one with deteriorating paint, make sure she does not suck on the equipment or put her hands in her mouth while playing there, and wash her hands thoroughly afterward. For questions about lead on playground equipment that are not about the status of individual playgrounds, call CPSC's toll-free hotline or visit their website.

Playground sand should be periodically changed, because it collects dirt and pollutants from the air. Also, it's a good thing to learn about the composition of the sand itself. Beach sand is fine, but some sands made from crushed rock contain asbestiform tremolite, which has been known to cause asbestosis and lung cancer in exposed workers. Another type of fiber found in some manufactured sands, nonasbestiform tremolite, may present similar health hazards, some scientists warn, although this has yet to be proven. Until then, we recommend, as always, taking a precautionary approach and avoiding both types of sand. Nonasbestiform tremolite is more commonly found in playsand.

A problem: the CPSC doesn't require labeling of sand. When you or your child's preschool or your local playground buy sand, ask the merchant whether it can be certified that the sand comes from a beach and is tremolite-free. Crushed rock sands also tend to be much finer, whiter, and dustier than beach sands. Ask about the type of sand used at any indoor play arenas you visit, too.

Avoiding Poisonous Plants

WARNING: *Don't let your baby or child nibble on any plants, fungi, or twigs!* Talk with your youngster regularly about the difference between food plants that we pull from the garden and wild plants, which we should never eat unless they are brought home and looked up in a plant encyclopedia, or, if mushrooms, vetted by a mycologist. The toadstools that spring up after a heavy rain provide great examples for such a talk. Point out that many less-ugly mushrooms resemble edible ones but are extremely fatal. Educate yourself about poisonous plants of your area, and teach your child about the leaf shapes of such common irritants as poison ivy and poison oak. They should also be able to recognize oleander (notorious for fatalities when its branches are used for roasting marshmallows). If they get milk or nectar from a tree branch or flower on their hands, they must be instructed to never lick it off, but instead wash hands well. And don't touch their eyes.

Environmental Education at Preschool

When selecting a day care program or preschool for your child, ask what sort of nature studies and science projects they do, and whether the school recycles, involving children in some way—by sorting bottles, cans, and paper into the appropriate bins, or by taking lunch bags, drink containers, and sandwich wrappers home to be reused. When it's your turn to bring snacks, bring organically or IPM grown fruit, and organic crackers and juices. Explain how organic and IPM farming, by not using toxic pesticides, help protect habitat—ours as well as wild creatures'—and keep our water clean. Books such as **Mothers & Others**' *The Green Food Shopper* and *The Green Kitchen Handbook* will give you all the background you need to make the connection between how our food is grown and the health of the environment.

Most schools today include ecology in their curricula, helping children discover how humans share Earth with other life forms, and our responsibility to coexist rather than destroy.

Many preschools take a field trip to a nearby farm. What can be better hands-on learning than picking their own food while learning how and by whom it's grown? A popular excursion is to pick apples in the autumn, but you can adjust that to the season in which a crop is locally harvested. Or children can help plant. In Hawaii, children often visit taro farms, where Hawaiian farmers grow the plant whose roots they pound into poi, the staple of their traditional diet. While taro has to be cooked, so they can't pick and eat it, the children can get good and muddy helping to dig irrigation ditches linking the paddies to natural streams. In other parts of the country, children can see how cows are milked, pick strawberries, watch farmers till soil, and play with barnyard animals.

If your child's school doesn't do farm visits, speak with the teachers and administration about organizing one. You can ask farmers at your local greenmarket whether they're open to receiving visits from school groups. Or your state department of agriculture or local county extension should have lists of organic growers in your state. You can also contact an organic certifier in your state. Most universities also have agricultural extensions that list farms. Once you've found a willing farmer, ask the school to help you book school buses or vans for transportation. Make sure that the trip will be covered by the school's insurance policy. Or parents can organize into car pools.

Of course, you don't need an organized tour to visit a farm with your child. On a drive out into the countryside during harvest season you'll see signs for picking your own berries, pumpkins, and apples, and you and your child can go out into the fields and get busy.

Ecology 101 at Home

Before long, your child will be teaching you about the environment. But what you can and must provide is the active example. Children follow our examples, good and bad. So, as the parents who work at Mothers & Others are constantly being reminded, we need to practice what we preach. When you shop with your child, explain why you look on the undersides of containers to avoid those made of PVC (number 3 on the bottom of containers). Use nonchlorine-bleached, postconsumer recycled paper for your home stationery.

Separate and recycle your trash diligently at home. Rinsing bottles and sorting trash is an excellent job for a child, after they are able to be careful not to break bottles or cut themselves. Thinking of ways to reuse things is a wonderful stimulus to creativity. Any small, clear plastic container can have a glorious second life as a hummingbird feeder, after all.

In conclusion, though we've listed many activities for you to do with your baby or child, it's also important to remember how to do nothing but just be alive and aware, enjoying life, the way most of us can remember feeling on a midsummer's day when our time was all our own. In *Keepers of the Earth,* there's a lovely black-and-white photo of a young child sitting among reeds. It shows how children can develop a sense of place and oneness with the earth by picking their own special spot.

Resources *for* More Information

Chapter Two
Preparing Baby's Room

GENERAL INFORMATION

Children's Environmental Health Network
1515 Clay Street, 17th Floor
Oakland, CA 94612
Phone: 510/622-4440
Website: www.cehn.org

—National organization promotes sound public health and child-focused policies; educates health professionals, policy makers, and the community; and stimulates pre-vention-oriented research on environmental hazards to children. Publishes *Resource Guide on Children's Environmental Health.*

Children's Health Environmental Coalition
P. O. Box 846
Malibu, CA 90265
Phone: 310/573-9608
Website: www.checnet.org

—Coalition working to protect children's right to good health through a safe and clean environment by educating legislators and the public. Publishes *The CHEC Report* (newsletter) and *The Household Detective* handbook and video.

PAINT

American Industrial Hygiene Association
2700 Prosperity Avenue, Suite 250
Fairfax, VA 22031
Phone: 703/849-8888
Website: www.aiha.org

—Pamphlets on lead removal.

Environmental Defense Fund
257 Park Avenue South
New York, NY 10010
Phone: 212/505-2100
Website: www.edf.org

—Develops market-based approaches, working with large corporations, to protect the environment. Provides question hotline for members. Pamphlet available: *What You Should Know About Lead in China Dishes*

National Lead Information Center and Clearinghouse
National Safety Council
Phone: 800/LEAD-FYI (800/532-3394)

—Provides general information on lead and home renters' and buyers' rights to lead disclosure. List of contractors accredited through the National Lead Lab Accreditation Program (NLLAP) is available.

National Pesticide Telecommunication Network
Phone: 800/858-7378
Website: ace.orst.edu/info/nptn

—Has list of brands of latex paint made before 1992 that contain phenylmercury and answers questions about the toxicity of specific pesticides.

Natural Resources Defense Council
40 West 20th Street, 11th Floor
New York, NY 10011-4211
Phone: 212/727-2700
Website: www.nrdc.org/nrdc

—Monitors government agencies, brings legal action to preserve natural resources, conducts policy research, and disseminates information concerning damage to the environment.

U.S. Centers for Disease Control and Prevention
Phone: 800/311-3435
Website: www.cdc.gov

—Provides information and fact sheets on lead and food-borne bacterial pathogens. For pamphlet: *Screening Young Children for Lead Poisoning,* call 888-232-6789. Food safety fact sheets are available on Website: www.cdc.gov/ncidod

U.S. Consumer Product Safety Commission (CPSC)
Phone: 800/638-2772, 301/504-0580
Website: www.cpsc.gov

—Government agency overseeing product safety. Issues alerts on recalls and publishes factsheets on baby equipment, babyproofing, lead, and electrical and toxic hazards to children. "Baby Safety Checklist" available.

U.S. Department of Housing and Urban Development
The Lead Listing
Office of Lead Hazard and Control
Website: www.leadlisting.org

—This website lists qualified lead service providers (lead inspectors, risk assessors, and abatement contractors) and lead analysis laboratories. Also has a downloadable consumer reference guide and other documents.

CARPETS, BEDDING, FURNITURE, FLOORING, AND WINDOW TREATMENTS

Anderson Laboratories
P.O. Box 323
West Hartford, VT 05084
Phone: 802/295-7344

—Tests synthetic carpet samples for safety.

Certified Forest Products Council (formerly The Good Wood Alliance)
14780 SW Osprey Drive, Suite 285
Beaverton, OR 97007-8424
Phone: 503/590-6600
Website: www.certifiedwood.org

—Website has a database of certified wood suppliers. Publishes *Understory* newsletter.

Environmental Building News
28 Birge Street
Brattleboro, VT 05301
Phone: 802/257-7300
Website: www.ebuild.com

—Green building newsletter and other publications including "Carpeting, Indoor Air Quality, and the Environment," available online or for $12 by mail. Website has database of safe building materials.

Forest Stewardship Council U.S.
P.O. Box 10
Waterbury, VT 05676
Phone: 802/244-6257
Website: www.fscus.org;
www.certifiedproducts.org (for products)

—Provides information on wood certification and where to obtain sustainably harvested wood products. Website features database of certified wood furniture, flooring, musical instruments and other products.

Scientific Certification Systems
Park Plaza Building
1939 Harrison Street, Suite 400
Oakland, CA 94612
Phone: 510/832-1415
Website: www.scs1.com

—Certifies wood that is sustainably harvested. Certifies cleaners based on their biodegradability, toxicity, VOC content, and other criteria.

Green Seal
1400 16th Street, NW, Suite 300
Washington, DC 20036-2215
Phone: 202/588-8400
Website: www.greenseal.org

—Tests products under strict environmental standards and awards the "Green Seal" to those that comply. *Choose Green Reports* on carpets, paints, adhesives, and other building materials, as well as other household products, such as paper and household cleaners; provides information on their environmental hazards and recommendations for safer alternatives.

Greenpeace
1436 U Street, NW
Washington, DC 20009
Phone: 202/462-1177
Website: www.greenpeaceusa.org

—Grassroots activism to promote sound conservation policies and reducing environmental toxins. Some campaigns focus on PVC, genetically engineered foods, and dry cleaning. Website lists suppliers of PVC-free wiring, pipes, flooring, and windows. (Also see listing under chapter 5, "Cleaning Products.")

Institute for Sustainable Forestry
46 Humboldt Street
Willits, CA 95490
Phone: 707/459-5499
Website: www.isf-sw.org

—Provides information about sustainable forestry certification.

Rainforest Action Network
450 Sansome, Suite 700
San Francisco, CA 94111
Phone: 415/398-4404
Website: www.ran.org

—Dedicated to preserving the world's rain forests and protecting the human rights of those who live in them. Provides information about products made with rain forest resources.

Rainforest Alliance
65 Bleecker Street
New York, NY 10012
Phone: 212/677-1900;
802/434-5491 (for SmartWood)
Websites: www.rainforest-alliance.org
www.smartwood.org

—Develops and promotes sustainable alternatives to tropical deforestation that are both economically and socially viable. The SmartWood Certification and the ECO-OK agricultural programs certify that products have been harvested from well-managed sources.

Sustainable Sources

Website: www.greenbuilder.com

—Includes information on green building, a directory of green building professionals, an online bookstore, links to other good sites, and *The Sustainable Building Sourcebook,* which lists sources of environmentally sound building materials.

U.S. Consumer Product Safety Commission (See listing under "Paint" above.)

U.S. Environmental Protection Agency Indoor Air Quality Information Hotline

Phone: 800/438-4318
Website: www.epa.gov/iaq

—Information on indoor air pollutants and improving indoor air quality. Has booklets, such as *Residential Air-Cleaning Devices: A Summary of Available Information* and *The Inside Story: A Guide to Indoor Air Quality.*

Other Publications

Green Building Resource Guide. John Hermannsson. Taunton Press, 1997.

SUDDEN INFANT DEATH SYNDROME

National Sudden Infant Death Syndrome Resource Center

2070 Chain Bridge Road, Suite 450
Vienna, VA 22182
Phone: 703/821-8955
Website: www.circsol.com/sids

—Publishes information and answers questions about SIDS.

SIDS Network

P.O. Box 520
Ledyard, CT 06339
Website: www.sids-network.org

—Provides information on SIDS and a support network for its victims.

Chapter Three
Other Baby Equipment

American Medical Association KidsHealth

website: www.ama-assn.org/kidshealth

—Includes useful "Safety and Accident Prevention" pages.

U.S. Consumer Product Safety Commission

(See listing under chapter 2, "Paints.")
Pamphlets available: "Nursery Equipment Safety Checklist." CPSC doc. 4200.

Publications

Guide to Baby Products, 5th Ed. Sandy Jones, Werner Freitag, and the editors of *Consumer Reports.* Consumer Reports Books, 1996.

Chapter Four
Environmental Babyproofing and Eco-Tips for Other Rooms

American Council for an Energy-Efficient Economy

1001 Connecticut NW, Suite 801
Washington, DC 20036
Phone: 202/429-8873; for publications 202/429-0063
Website: www.aceee.org

—Conducts technical and policy assessments on energy efficiency and publishes several consumer guides, including *Consumer's Guide to Home Energy Savings.*

**American Medical Association KidsHealth
website** (See listing under chapter 3.)

Environmental Defense Fund
(See listing under chapter 2, "Paints.")

U.S. Consumer Product Safety Commission (See listing under chapter 2, "Paints.")
Pamphlets available: "Baby Safety
Checklist." CPSC doc. 206

**U.S. Food and Drug Administration
Center for Food Safety & Applied
Nutrition**
Phone: 800/332-4010
Website: www.fda.gov

—Provides pamphlets and information
on lead in dishes, food safety,
dietary supplements, and nutrition.
Information specialists respond to
questions from the public.

Home Energy Magazine
2124 Kittredge Street, 95
Berkeley, CA 94704
Phone: 510/524-5405

—Offers energy savings brochures on
kitchens, bathrooms, remodeling,
and air conditioners.

Rocky Mountain Institute
1739 Snowmass Creek Road
Snowmass, CO 81654
Phone: 303/927-3128 (Call only if no
internet access)
Website: www.rmi.org

—Publishes *Homemade Money: How
to Save Energy and Dollars in Your
Home* and other pamphlets on
energy consumption and efficiency
issues.

**U.S. Environmental Protection Agency
Green Lights/Energy Star Hotline**
Phone: 202/775-6650
Website: www.epa.gov/energystar

—Energy Star labeling system indicates the energy efficiency of participating household products and
appliances.

Other Publications

Consumer Reports Guide to Baby Products
(See listing under chapter 3.)

*Chapter Five
Pollutants in Your House*

GENERAL INFORMATION

American Lung Association
432 Park Avenue South, 8th Floor
New York, NY 10016
Phone: 800/586-4872
Website: www.lungusa.org

—Provides brochures and fact sheets
on asthma, air quality, and mold.

The Healthy House Institute
430 North Sewell Road
Bloomington, IN 47408
Phone: 812/332-5073

—Publishes books on residential construction for people with chemical
sensitivities.

**U.S. Consumer Product Safety
Commission** (See listing under chapter 2,
"Paints.")

—Pamphlets available: "Asbestos
in the Home," CPSC doc. 453;
"The Senseless Killer (Carbon
Monoxide)," CPSC doc. 4464; and
fact sheets on radon, pesticides,
kerosene heaters.

U.S. Environmental Protection Agency Information Resource Center

3404
401 M Street, SW
Washington, DC 20460
Website: www.epa.gov

—Library headquarters for the EPA is open to the public; responds to general questions over the phone.

Center for Environmental Information and Statistics Database

Website: www.epa.gov/ceis

—Environmental profiles for every county in the United States summarizing existing information on air quality, drinking water, surface water quality, hazardous waste, and reported toxic releases.

Community Right to Know Hotline:

800/535-0202

—Provides information on polluting industrial facilities in your area.

Indoor Air Quality Hotline

(See listing under chapter 2, "Carpets . . .")

Toxic Substances Control Act Hotline

202/554-1404
Website: www.epa.gov/opptintr

—Answers questions about regulations for specific chemicals.

Other Publications

"Health Effects Of Wood Smoke."
Washington State Department of Ecology, Air Quality Program, P.O. Box 47600, Olympia, WA 98504-7600.
Phone: 360/407-6832
Website:
www.wa.gov/ecology/air/airhome.html

Home Safe Home. Debra Lynn Dodd. Putnam, 1997.

The Safe Shopper's Bible: A Consumer's Guide to Nontoxic Household Products, Cosmetics and Food. David Steinman and Samuel S. Epstein, M.D. Macmillan, 1995.

Toxics A to Z: A Guide to Everyday Pollution Hazards. John Harte, Cheryl Holdren, Richard Schneider, Christine Shirley. University of California Press, 1991.

ASBESTOS

National Institute for Standards and Technology

National Voluntary Laboratory Accreditation Program
Building 820, Room 282
Gaithersburg, MD 20899
Phone: 301/975-4016
Website: http://ts.nist.gov/nvlap

—Provides lists of government-accredited asbestos professionals.

U.S. Environmental Protection Agency Asbestos Ombudsman

Phone: 800/368-5888
Website: www.epa.gov/sbo/

—Provides information on asbestos detection and abatement, as well as federal regulations.

ASTHMA

Allergy & Asthma Network/ Mothers of Asthmatics

2751 Prosperity Avenue, Suite 150
Fairfax, VA 22031
Phone: 800/878-4403
Website: www.aanma.org

—Offers publications and videos on allergies and asthma.

Asthma & Allergy Foundation of America
1125 Fifteenth St., NW, Suite 502
Washington, DC 20005
Phone: 800/7-ASTHMA (800/727-8462)
Website: www.aafa.org

—Support group for asthma and allergy sufferers provides patient education and advocacy and supports research.

CLEANING PRODUCTS

Center for Neighborhood Technology
2125 West North Avenue
Chicago, IL 60647
Phone: 773/278-4800, x 299
Website: www.cnt.org/wetcleaning

—Provides information on The Greener Cleaning Project and videos for both consumers and dry cleaners.

Greenpeace (Chicago Office)
417 South Dearborn
Chicago, IL 60605
Phone: 312/554-1028
Website: www.greenpeaceusa.org

—Greenpeace is an independent international organization that uses peaceful activism to protect the global environment. The Chicago office provides information about the hazards of perchloroethylene and locations of wet cleaners.

Scientific Certification Systems
(See listing under chapter 2, "Carpets...")

Washington Toxics Coalition
4649 Sunnyside Avenue North
Suite 540 East
Seattle, WA 98103
Phone: 800/844-SAFE (800/844-7233)
Website: www.accessone.com/~watoxics

—Offers fact sheets and booklets on cleaning products and other toxic chemicals found around the home. "Safer Cleaning Products" lists safe cleaners and "Hormones in Your Haircolor?" provides information on hormone disruptors in cleaners and personal care products. *BuySmart, BuySafe* rates cleaning products.

ELECTROMAGNETIC FIELDS

EMF Clearinghouse
Information Ventures
1500 Locust Street, Suite 1513
Philadelphia, PA 19102
Website: infoventures.com/emf

—Website has database with thousands of documents on EMFs. Publishes *EMF Health Report,* bimonthly newsletter.

National Institute of Environmental Health Sciences
EMF Infoline
Phone: 800/363-2383
Website:
www.niehs.nih.gov/emfrapid/home.htm

—Answers questions about exposures to electromagnetic fields from power lines and appliances and the potential health effects that have been studied. For booklet: *Questions and Answers about Electric and Magnetic Fields Associated with the Use of Electric Power* and *Electric and Magnetic Fields and the Potential Hazard to Humans,* call 919/541-5085.

Other Publications

EMF in Your Environment: Magnetic Field Measurements of Everyday Electrical Devices, U.S. EPA, 1992. Available from the U.S. EPA Information Resource Center. (See listing under chapter 5.)

GARDENS AND LAWN CARE

American Community Gardening Association
100 North 20th Street, 5th Floor
Philadelphia, PA 19103
Phone: 215/988-8785
Website: www.communitygarden.org

—Offers free publications on how to start a community garden. Membership in ACGA includes a subscription to *Community Greening Review*.

American PIE (Public Information on the Environment)
P.O. Box 340
124 High Street
South Glastonbury, CT 06073-0340
Phone: 800/320-APIE (800/320-2743)
Website: www.AmericanPIE.org

—Environmental clearinghouse. Will answer questions on all environmental issues. "Safe to Play On" program explains how to maintain a healthy lawn naturally.

Bio-Dynamic Farming and Gardening Association
P.O. Box 550
Kimberton, PA 19442
Phone: 610/935-7797

—Publishes journals and books that provide information on biodynamic agricultural practices.

Brooklyn Botanic Gardens
1000 Washington Avenue
Brooklyn, NY 11225
Phone: 718/622-4433
Website: www.bbg.org

—Excellent gardening publications. Send a self-addressed, stamped envelope to Publication Department for "Pollinators List."

Rodale Institute Experimental Farm
611 Siegfriedale Road
Kutztown, PA 19530

Phone: 610/683-1400 (for mail-order publications: 610/683-6009)

—Rodale is one of the largest education and research facilities for organic horticulture and sustainable agriculture in the United States. Conducts workshops, seminars, tours. Research librarian will answer questions from the public.

Washington Toxics Coalition
(See listing above under "Cleaning Products.")

—Offers fact sheets on least-toxic lawn care; the booklet, *Grow Smart, Grow Safe,* rates lawn and garden pesticides and fertilizers.

Other Publications

The Chemical-Free Lawn: The Newest Varieties and Techniques to Grow Lush, Hardy Grass. Warren Schultz. Rodale Press, 1996.

"Healthy Lawn, Healthy Environment." Free EPA booklet available through the National Center for Environmental Publications and Information, P.O. Box 42419, Cincinnati OH 45242-2419. Phone: 513/489-8190.

Organic Gardening. Monthly magazine published by Rodale Press, Inc., 33 East Minor Street, Emmaus, PA 18098. Phone: 610/967-5171.

PESTICIDES

Bio-Integral Resource Center (BIRC)
P.O. Box 7414
Berkeley, CA 94707
Phone: 510/524-2567
Website: www.igc.apc.org/birc

—Publications on controlling most pests without resorting to toxic chemicals. Sells a directory of suppliers of least-toxic pest control remedies.

Environmental Working Group (EWG)
1718 Connecticut Avenue, Suite 600
Washington, DC 20009
Phone: 202/667-6982 (Please call only
if you have no computer or Internet
access.)
Website: www.ewg.org

—Issues reports on national environmental policy issues, including
pesticides in food, contamination
of waterways in each state, and
agricultural subsidies.

**National Coalition Against the
Misuse of Pesticides**
701 E Street, SE, Suite 200
Washington, DC 20003
Phone: 202/543-5450
Website: www.ncamp.org

—Offers fact sheets and booklets on
least toxic pest control.

National Pediculosis Association
P.O. Box 610189
Newton, MA 02161
Phone: 781/449-NITS
Website: www.headlice.org

—Materials on treating lice infestations.

National Pest Control Association
8100 Oak Street
Dunn Loring, VA 22027
Phone: 703/573-8330
Website: www.pestworld.org

—Provides referrals for pest control
operators who practice integrated
pest management.

**Northwest Coalition for
Alternatives to Pesticides**
P.O. Box 1393
Eugene, OR 97440
Phone: 541/344-5044
Website: www.efn.org/~ncap

—Works to reduce pesticide use in our
communities through public education and advocacy. Offers fact sheets
on the dangers of pesticides and
alternatives for specific pest
problems.

**Pesticide Action Network
North America (PANNA)**
49 Powell Street, Suite 500
San Francisco, CA 94102
Phone: 415/981-1771
Website: www.panna.org/panna

—Provides information on the dangers
of pesticides and on less toxic alternatives.

Rachel Carson Council
8940 Jones Mill Road
Chevy Chase, MD 20815
Phone: 301/652-1877
Website: members.aol.com/rccouncil/
ourpage/rcc_page.htm

—Clearinghouse and library with
information at both scientific and
consumer levels on pesticide-related
issues. Their "Questionnaire for
Interviewing Pest Control
Specialists" is free if you send a
self-addressed business-size
envelope.

Other Publications

Common-Sense Pest Control. William
Olkowski, Sheila Daar, and Helga Olkowski.
Taunton Press, 1991 (available from Bio-
Integral Resource Center, 510/524-2567).
The "bible" on least-toxic pest control.

**"Citizen's Guide to Pest Control and
Pesticide Safety."** Free EPA booklet avail-
able through the National Center for
Environmental Publications and
Information, P.O. Box 42419, Cincinnati
OH 45242-2419. Phone: 513/489-8190.

RADON

National Safety Council Radon Hotline
Phone: 800/767-7236

—Provides information on how to detect and reduce radon in your home. Pamphlets available: *A Citizen's Guide to Radon,* 2nd Edition, U.S. Environmental Protection Agency, May 1992, Air and Radiation (ANR-464), EPA Document 402-K92-001.

Chapter Six
Caring for Yourself During Pregnancy

GENERAL

Bio-Integral Resources Center
(See listing under chapter 5, "Pesticides.")

Environmental Working Group
(See listing under chapter 5, "Pesticides.")

National Institute of Environmental Health Sciences (See listing under chapter 5.)

National Pesticide Telecommunications Network (See listing under chapter 5, "Pesticides.")

Natural Resources Defense Council
(See listing under chapter 2, "Paints.")

Northwest Coalition for Alternatives to Pesticides (See listing under chapter 5, "Pesticides.")

Washington Toxics Coalition (See listing under chapter 5, "Cleaning Products.")

U.S. Environmental Protection Agency Office of Science and Technology
Website: www.epa.gov/ost

—Surf to the "Program" page of this site to see information on fish advisories, beach safety, and water quality.

FOOD SAFETY

National Audubon Society
700 Broadway
New York, NY 10003
Phone: 212/979-3000
Website: www.audubon.org

—Educational programs related to birds and their habitats as well as broader environmental conservation issues, including wetland preservation, conservation of biological diversity, reduction of air pollution, and protection of water quality. Publishes *Audubon Magazine,* nature field guides, and other books and magazines. For the *Audubon Guide to Seafood,* call 212/979-3127.

The Campaign for Food Safety
860 Highway 61
Little Marais, MN 55614
Phone: 218/226-4164
Website: www.purefood.org

—Campaigns include getting bovine growth hormones out of milk, ending irradiation of foods, and labeling genetically engineered foods.

Center for Science in the Public Interest (CSPI)
1875 Connecticut Avenue, NW, Suite 300
Washington, DC 20009
Phone: 202/332-9110
Website: www.cspinet.org

—Provides food safety information; publishes *Nutrition Action Health Letter* and other food-related publications.

The Humane Society of the United States
2100 L Street, NW
Washington, DC 20037
Phone: 203/452-1100
Website: www.hsus.org

—The world's largest animal protection organization links animal welfare issues with environmental and consumer health concerns. Publishes *Humane Consumer and Producer Guide.*

Mothers & Others for a Livable Planet
40 West 20th Street, 9th Floor
New York, NY 10011-4211
Phone: 212/242-0010, 888/ECO-INFO (888/326-4636)
Website: www.mothers.org/mothers

—Green consumers education organization focusing on environmental health and sustainable agriculture. Publishes *The Green Guide,* which offers practical tips on how to make environmental change through consumer buying power.

Public Voice for Food and Health Policy
1012 14th Street, NW, Suite 800
Washington, DC 20005
Phone: 202/347-6200
Website: www.publicvoice.org

—Provides information on issues such as pesticides, meat and poultry inspection, seafood safety, and sustainable agriculture.

Sea Web
Website: www.seaweb.org

—A multimedia public education project designed to raise awareness of the world's oceans and the life within them.

U.S. Centers for Disease Control and Prevention (See Listing under chapter 2, "Paints.")

U.S. Department of Agriculture Meat & Poultry Hotline
Phone: 800/535-4555
Website: www.usda.gov

—Provides information on food-borne pathogens in meat and poultry and how to safely cook these foods.

U.S. Food and Drug Administration Center for Food and Applied Nutrition
(See listing under chapter 4.)

WATER

Center for Environmental Health
965 Mission Street, Suite 218
San Francisco, CA 94103
Phone: 888/804-1866; 415/974-5028

—Provides information on water filters that may contaminate water with lead.

Chemical Scoreboard
Website: www.scorecard.org

—This database maintained by the Environmental Defense Fund allows users to access information about reported toxic releases in their counties, which may affect air and water quality.

Consumers Union
202 Truman Avenue
Yonkers, NY 10703
Phone: 914/378-2000

—Researches products for safety and works to protect consumer rights. Publishes *Consumer Reports* and buying guides for a variety of products. Back issues available.

International Bottled Water Association
1700 Diagonal Road, Suite 650
Alexandria, VA 22314
Phone: 800/WATER-11
(800/928-3711)
Website: www.bottledwater.org

—Answers questions about different types of bottled water.

National Drinking Water Clearinghouse
Phone: 800/624-8301
Website: www.ndwc.wvu.edu

—Answers questions about drinking water safety; provides assistance in locating testing agencies.

National Sanitation Foundation (NSF)
3475 Plymouth Road
Ann Arbor, MI 48105
Phone: 800/673-8010
Website: www.nsf.org

—Certifies water purifiers and bottled waters. Offers a booklet that lists certified bottled waters and plumbing components, as well as water purifiers and the contaminants they eliminate.

National Testing Labs
6555 Wilson Mills Road, Suite 102
Cleveland, OH 44143
Phone: 800/426-8378
Website: www.watercheck.com

—Tests water samples (sent by mail) for 94 different pollutants, including pesticides and bacteria.

National Water Information Clearinghouse
U.S. Geological Survey
Phone: 800/426-9000

—Information on surface and groundwater quantity and quality.

Safe Drinking Water Hotline:
800/426-4791

—Responds to consumer questions about drinking water quality and federal drinking water regulations, including the maximum allowable levels of all regulated substances in drinking water.

Suburban Water Testing Labs
4600 Kutztown Road
Temple, PA 19560
Phone: 800/433-6595
Website: www.h2otest.com

—Tests water samples (sent by mail) for pesticides, heavy metals, and other toxic contaminants. Recommends treatment methods for determined problem.

U.S. Environmental Protection Agency Center for Environmental Information and Statistics
(See listing under chapter 5, "General Information.")

Other Publications

Eating for Two: A Complete Guide to Nutrition During Pregnancy. Mary Hess and Anne Hunt. Macmillan, 1992.

Eating With Conscience: The Bioethics of Food. Dr. Michael W. Fox. New Sage Press, 1997.

Dying from Dioxin. Lois Marie Gibbs. SouthEnd Press, 1995.

"How to Avoid Food-Borne Illness in the Home." Free from the Consumer Information Center, Dept. 79, Pueblo, CO 81009.

Our Stolen Future. Theo Colborn, Dianne Dumanoski, and John Peterson Myers. Viking Penguin, 1996.

The Sierra Club Guide to Safe Drinking Water. Sierra Club Books, 1996.

The Safe Shopper's Bible (See listing under chapter 5, "General Information.")

What's in Your Cosmetics? Aubrey Hampton. Odonian Press, 1995.

Chapter Seven
Caring for Baby

GENERAL INFORMATION

Council on Economic Priorities
30 Irving Place
New York, NY 10003
Phone: 800/729-4237
Website: www.accesspt.com/cep

—Conducts research on the social and environmental impact of corporations. Publishes *Shopping for a Better World.* Also has a database on their website, which provides information on the social and environmental responsibility of numerous companies.

Humane Society of the United States
(See listing under chapter 6, "Food Safety.")

National Labor Committee
275 Seventh Avenue, 15th Floor
New York, NY 10001
Phone: 212/242-3002

—Works to stop labor abuses such as sweatshop conditions.

People for the Ethical Treatment of Animals (PETA)
P.O. Box 52516
Washington, DC 20015
Phone: 301/770-8950, x398
Website: envirolink.org/arrs/peta

—Publishes the "Shopping Guide for Caring Consumers," a guide to companies that conduct animal testing.

AFL-CIO
Union Label and Service Department
815 16th Street, NW, Room 607
Washington, DC 20006
Phone: 800/522-3591

—Will tell you if a product is union-made.

Washington Toxics Coalition (See listing under chapter 5 "Cleaning Products.")

Other Publications

Your Baby and Child. Penelope Leach. Alfred A. Knopf, 1997.

The First Twelve Months of Life. Theresa Caplan and The Princeton Center for Infancy and Early Childhood. Putnam, 1995.

Mothering Magazine
P.O. Box 1690
Santa Fe, NM 87504
Phone: 800/984-8116

DIAPERS

National Association of Diaper Services (NADS)
994 Old Eagle School Road, Suite 1019
Wayne, PA 19087
Phone: 610/971-4850
Website: www.diapernet.com

—Answers questions about diapering.

Publications

Diaper Changes: The Complete Diapering Book and Resource Guide. Theresa Rodriguez Farrisi. Homekeepers Publishing, 1997.

Whitewash: Exposing the Health and Environmental Dangers of Women's Sanitary Products and Disposable Diapers—What You Can Do About It. Liz Armstrong, Adrienne Scott. HarperCollins Publishers, 1992.

Chapter Eight
Feeding Your Baby

GENERAL INFORMATION

Alliance for Bio-Integrity
406 West Depot Street
Fairfield, IA 52556
Phone: 515/472-5554
Website: www.bio-integrity.org

—Nonprofit coalition that has filed a lawsuit to compel the U.S. Food and Drug Administration to label and conduct safety tests of all genetically modified foods.

The Campaign for Food Safety
(See listing under chapter 6, "Food Safety.")

Consumers International
24 Highbury Crescent
London N5 1RX
Great Britain
Phone: 44 171 226 6663
Website: www.consumersinternational.org

—International nonprofit organization working to strengthen the consumer movement. Represents more than 200 consumer organizations on issues such as product standards, trade, health policy, food, and environment.

Environmental Working Group
(See listing under chapter 5, "Cleaning Products.")

Food Allergy Network
10400 Eaton Place, 107
Fairfax, VA 22030-2208
Phone: 800/929-4040
Website: www.foodallergy.org

—Offers pamphlets, books, and videos on food allergies. Also furnishes recipes for people with food allergies. Has a list of foods with hidden allergens.

Mothers for Natural Law
P.O. Box 1177
Fairfield, IA 52556
Phone: 515/472-2809
Website: www.safe-food.org

—Nonprofit organization working for labeling of genetically modified foods through a petitioning campaign. Website lists foods that claim to be free of genetically modified ingredients.

Union of Concerned Scientists
1616 P Street, NW, Suite 310
Washington, DC 20036
Phone: 202/332-0900
Website: www.ucsusa.org

—Organization representing 75,000 scientists who have joined together to protest the misuse of science and technology. Advocates for responsible public policy in energy, transportation, arms, and sustainable agriculture (including genetically modified food crops).

Vegetarian Resource Group
P.O. Box 1463
Baltimore, MD 21203
Phone: 410/366-VEGE (410/366-8343)
Website: www.vrg.org

—Answers questions about vegetarianism; publishes *Vegetarian Journal,* as well as booklets on vegetarian nutrition in children, cookbooks, and general vegetarian information.

Other Publications

Feeding the Whole Family.
Cynthia Lair. Moon Smile Press, 1997.

The Yale Guide to Children's Nutrition.
edited by William V. Tamborlane, M.D.
Yale University Press, 1997.

BREAST-FEEDING

La Leche League International

Phone: 800-LA LECHE (525-3243) or
847/519-7730

Website: www.lalecheleague.org

—Call to find a local La Leche support
group and obtain information about
breast-feeding. Website has many
articles on breast-feeding.

Promotion of Mother's Milk, Inc.

Website: www.promom.org

Publications

*Bestfeeding: Getting Breastfeeding Right for
You.* Mary Renfrew, Chloe Fisher, and
Suzanne Arms. Celestial Arts, 1990.

The Womanly Art of Breastfeeding.
La Leche League International, edited by
Judy Torgus and Gwen Gorsch. Plume
Books, 1997.

FARMERS MARKETS, CO-OPS, AND COMMUNITY SUPPORTED AGRICULTURE

American Farmland Trust

Publications Office
1 Short Street
Northampton, MA 01060
Phone: 800/370-4879
Website: www.farmland.org

—Works to preserve small family
farms in the face of encroaching
urban development. Publishes
"How to Organize and Run a
Successful Farmers' Market," by
Julia Freedgood.

Community Alliance with Family Farmers

P.O. Box 363
Davis, CA 95617
Phone: 530/756-8518
Website: www.caff.org

—Helps farmers start or improve a
CSA program. Assists consumers
locate local CSA programs.
Publishes *The National Organic
Directory,* updated annually.

Community Supported Agriculture Hotline

Bio-Dynamic Farming & Gardening
Association
Phone: 800/516-7797

—Call to obtain a list of community-
supported or biodynamic farms in
your area.

Community Supported Agriculture of North America

Northeast Sustainable Agriculture Working
Group
P.O. Box 608
Belchertown, MA 01007
Phone: 413/323-4531

—For a CSA-related resource list and
to find a CSA near you, send a self-
addressed stamped envelope. Has
publications on starting and managing CSAs.

Co-op Directory Services

919 21st Avenue South
Minneapolis, MN 55404
Phone: 612/332-0417

—To find a food-buying club, co-op
store, or distributor-wholesaler,
send a self-addressed, stamped,
business-size envelope.

Co-op Network

P.O. Box 57
Randolph, VT 05060
Phone: 802/234-9293
Website: users.quest-
net.com/~george.keller/index.html

—Provides information on locating
local co-op distributors; publishes
National Co-op Directory, which
includes distributors and stores.

National Co-operative Business Association (NCBA)
1401 New York Avenue, NW, Suite 1100
Washington, DC 20005
Phone: 800/636-6222

—Educational materials, including "How to Start a Co-op Food Buying Club" video.

Openair-Market Net
Website: www.openair.org

U.S. Department of Agriculture
202/720-8317
Website:
www.ams.usda.gov/tmd/markets/states.htm

—Farmers' Market Directory available online or by calling.

Chapter Nine
Raising an Environmentally Aware Child

American Academy of Dermatology
P.O. Box 4014
Schaumberg, IL 60168-4014
Phone: 847/330-0230
Website: www.aad.org

—Provides information on skin cancer and sunscreens.

American Council for an Energy Efficient Economy (See listing under chapter 4.)

American Oceans Campaign
725 Arizona Avenue, Suite 102
Santa Monica, CA 90401
Phone: 310/576-6162
Website: www.americanoceans.org

—Works to protect and restore marine environments by educating the public and policy makers.

The Amicus Journal
Magazine of the National Resources Defense Council (See listing under chapter 2, "Paint.")

—Send four dollars for special summer 1998 issue on children's environmental books.

Art and Creative Materials Institute
100 Boyleston Street, Suite 1050
Boston, MA 02116
Phone: 617/426-6400
Website:
www.creativeindustries.com/acmi

—Answers questions about the safety of art and craft supplies. Offers free pamphlet, "What You Need to Know about the Safety of Art and Craft Materials."

Bat Conservation International
P.O. Box 162603
Austin, TX 78716-2603
Phone: 512/327-9721

—Supports bat conservation and habitation preservation and has an Adopt a Bat program.

Bio-Integral Resource Center
(See listing under chapter 5, "Pesticides.")

Brooklyn Botanic Gardens (See listing under chapter 5, "Gardens and Lawn Care.")

Brown Bear Resources
222 North Higgins
Missoula, MT 59802
Phone: 406/549-4896

—Dedicated to the preservation of the grizzly bear in North American through bear adoption programs and public education.

Center for Health, Environment and Justice
P.O. Box 6806
Falls Church, VA 22040
Phone: 703/237-2249
Website: www.essential.org/cchw

—Helps families protect their children

and communities from chemical poisons. Networks with local environmental groups.

Community Right to Know Hotline
(See listing under chapter 5.)

International Wildlife Coalition and Whale Adoption Project
70 East Falmouth Highway
East Falmouth, MA 02536
Phone: 508/548-8328
Website: www.iwc.org
—Wildlife conservation and rescue programs, including whale adoption programs. Funds go to marine and land mammal research and rescue.

Mothers & Others for a Livable Planet
(See listing under chapter 6, "Food Safety.")

National Audubon Society
(See listing under chapter 6, "Food Safety.")

National Coalition Against the Misuse of Pesticides (See listing under chapter 5, "Pesticides.")

National Wildlife Federation
1400 16th Street, NW, Suite 501
Washington, DC 20036
Phone: 202/797-6800
Website: www.nwf.org
—Environmental education programs for youth and teens, outdoor activities, and backyard wildlife.

Natural Resources Defense Council
(See listing under chapter 2, "Paint.")

National Coalition for Alternatives to Pesticides (See listing under chapter 5, "Pesticides.")

Oceanic Society
Fort Mason Center, Building E
San Francisco, CA 94123
Phone: 800/326-7491
Website: www.oceanic-society.org
—Works to protect marine mammals and the marine environment through conservation-based research and environmental education.

Sierra Club
85 2nd Street, 2nd Floor
San Francisco, CA 94105
Phone: 415/977-5500
Website: www.sierraclub.org
—Conservation organization that strives to shape public policy. Publishes *Sierra Magazine*.

Sea Turtle Survival League
424 NW 13th Street, North
Suite A1
Gainesville, FL 32609
Phone: 800/678-7853
—Works to protect sea turtles and their habitats. Has an adoption program.

U.S. Consumer Product Safety Commission (See listing under chapter 2, "Paint.")

U.S. Department of Agriculture (See listing under chapter 6, "Pregnancy.")

U.S. Environmental Protection Agency
Air Now Website: www.epa.gov/airnow
—Provides frequently updated ozone maps for East and Midwest.

Office of Science and Technology Website (See listing under chapter 6, "General.")

Products Available *by* Mail

H ere you'll find contact information for companies mentioned throughout the book, as well as a few more. Most of these companies offer products by mail order. We've also listed some manufacturers that will give you the names of retailers near you.

To help you locate specific products, we've included an index, organized alphabetically by product type. Under each product heading is a list of the companies that sell those types of products. The addresses and phone numbers for those companies are listed in alphabetical order in the following section, "Company Information." Say you are looking for baby bottles. Simply look under the product heading entitled, "Bottles, Nipples, and Sanitizing Racks." Then look up each company listed for contact information.

Index

ALLERGY PRODUCTS

Allergy Control Products, Inc.

Allergy Resources

Allerx

Harmony

Healthy Habitats

InteliHealth Healthy Home

Priorities

Real Goods Trading Company

BABY CARRIERS AND SLINGS

Baby Bjorn (Regal Lager)

Baby Bunz & Co.

Earthlings

Earthwise Basics

Eco-Wise Environmental Products

Gerry Baby Products Company

The Natural Baby Company

New Native Baby Carrier

Patagonia

REI

Sara's Ride

Snugglebundle Baby Products

BATH SUPPLIES

Babyworks

Cloud Cotton

Earth Runnings

Earthlings
Earthsake
Ecobaby
Environmental Home Center
Garnet Hill
GladRags
Harmony
Natureswear
New Native Baby Carrier
Rainbow Organic Fiber Mill
Real Goods Trading Company
Snugglebundle Baby Products
Terra Verde
TerrEssentials
Tomorrow's World
Worldware

BEDDING

Allergy Resources
Babyworks
Coyuchi, Inc.
Crosby Company
Crown City Mattress Company/The
    Natural Bedroom
Earth Runnings
Earth Wear
Earthlings
Earthsake
EarthSpun Heritage Natural Fibers
Ecobaby
Ecosport
Eco-Wise Environmental Products
Environmental Home Center
Forty Oaks Organic Textiles
Furnature
Garnet Hill
Grandma's Blankets

Green Mountain Spinnery
Harmony
Healthy Habitats
Heart of Vermont
Indigenous Designs
InteliHealth Healthy Home
Little Koala
The Natural Baby Company
Natureswear
Naturlich Natural Home
New Native Baby Carrier
Nontoxic Environments
Nontoxic Hotline & Nirvana Safe Haven
Organic Cotton Alternatives
Priorities
Rainbow Organic Fiber Mill
Real Goods Trading Company
Rosie Hippo's Wooden Toys and Games
Snugglebundle Baby Products
Terra Verde
Tomorrow's World
Worldware

BOTTLES, NIPPLES, AND SANITIZING RACKS

Avent America
Ecobaby
Evenflo
Medela
Perfectly Safe
Prince Lionheart

BREAST-FEEDING SUPPLIES

Ameda/Egnell (Hollister)
Avent America
Ecobaby
Eco-Wise Environmental Products

Garnet Hill
GladRags
Little Koala
Medela
Motherwear
The Natural Baby Company

CAR SEATS
Century Products

CARBON MONOXIDE ALARMS
Kidde Safety
North American Detectors, Inc.

CARPETING AND PADS
ABC Carpet & Home
Avalon Carpets
Bellbridge, Inc.
Carousel Carpets
CDC Carpets & Interiors
Colin Campbell & Sons, Ltd.
E.C.O. of New York
EarthSpun Heritage Natural Fibers
Earthweave Carpet Mills, Inc.
Einstein Moomjy
Environmental Home Center
Floorworks
Healthy Habitats
IKEA
Karastan Contract Carpets
Kevyn Woven Hempen Home
Leggett & Platt
A Loomful of Hues
Naturlich Natural Home
Nontoxic Environments
Ortex Rugs
Planetary Solutions
Real Goods Trading Company

Sinan Company
Wools of New Zealand

CLEANING PRODUCTS
Bi-O-Kleen
Dr. Bronner's (see Magic Chain)
Earth Power, Inc.
Ecobaby (Bi-O-Kleen brand)
Ecover
Harmony (Seventh Generation brand)
Life on the Planet
LifeTime Solutions
Magic Chain (for Dr. Bronner's)
N.E.E.D.S.
Nontoxic Environments
RCN Products (EarthRite brand)

CLOTHING
Baby Bunz & Company
Babyworks
Biobottoms
Clean Clothes
Cloud Cottons
Earth Friendly Goods
Earth Wear
Earthlings
Earthsake
EarthSpun Heritage Natural Fibers
Ecobaby
Ecosport
Eco-Wise Environmental Products
Forty Oaks Organic Textiles
Garnet Hill
Globalwear
Hanna Andersson
Harmony
Healthy Habitats
Hemp Culture

HinderCovers

Indigenous Designs

Koala Konnections

L.L.Bean

Lill-ing

Little Koala

The Natural Baby Company

Natureswear

New Day Creations

Nontoxic Hotline & Nirvana Safe Haven

Patagonia

Snugglebundle Baby Products

Sol Lite Active Wear

Solar Protective Factory/Solarweave

SunFun Collection

Sun Precautions

Terra Verde

Tomorrow's World

Tushies Baby Products

Worldware

DIAPERS, COVERS, AND WIPES

Baby Bunz & Company

Babyworks

Biobottoms

Earth Wear

Earthlings

Ecobaby

Eco-Wise Environmental
    Products

GladRags

Harmony

HinderCovers

Lill-ing

Little Koala

The Natural Baby Company

New Native Baby Carrier

Snugglebundle Baby Products

Tushies Baby Products

FABRICS AND YARNS

Coyuchi, Inc.

Designtex, Inc.

EarthSpun Heritage Natural Fibers

Green Mountain Spinnery

Hemp Textiles International, Inc.

Hemp Traders

Kevyn Woven Hempen Home

The Natural Alternative

Rainbow Organic Fiber Mill

Tomorrow's World

FILTERS AND AIR PURIFIERS

Absolute Environmental's Allergy
    Products Store

Allergy Control Products, Inc.

Allergy Resources

Allermed

Allerx

American Environmental Health Store

Ecobaby

E.L. Foust Company, Inc.

Environmental Home Center

General Filters, Inc.

Harmony

Healthy Habitats

InteliHealth Healthy Home

N.E.E.D.S.

Nontoxic Environments

Nontoxic Hotline & Nirvana Safe Haven

Priorities

Pure Air Systems, Inc.

Real Goods Trading Company

Research Products Corporation
3M Company

FLOORING

Aged Woods, Inc.
CDC Carpets & Interiors
Classic Tile
Conklin's Authentic Barnwood
Crossroads Recycled Lumber
Dodge-Regupol, Inc.
E.C.O. of New York
EcoTimber International
Eco-Wise Environmental Products
Endura Hardwoods
Environmental Home Center
Forbo Industries, Inc.
Furlong & Lee Stone Sales
Gerbert Limited
Healthy Habitats
Hoboken Wood Floors
Horse Drawn Pine
International Wood Products, Inc.
Jefferson Recycled Woodworks
Junckers Danish Beech Flooring USA
Korqinc
Mountain Lumber Company
Naturlich Natural Home
Pioneer Millworks
Planetary Solutions
Recycled Lumber Works
Superior Floor Company, Inc.

FOOD

Allergy Resources
Country Life Natural Foods
Crusoe Island Natural Foods

Diamond Organics
Earth's Best, Inc.
Eco-Organics USA
Eco-Wise Environmental Products
Gerber
Walnut Acres
The Well-Fed Baby

FURNITURE

Crate & Barrel Catalog
Crost Furniture & Imports
Earthlings
Earthsake
Ecobaby
Eddie Bauer
Furnature
Gerry Baby Products Company
Green Design Furniture Company
Gridcore Systems International
Hand in Hand
Healthy Habitats
Heart of Vermont
Jefferson Recycled Woodworks
The Loft Bed Store
Miya Shoji & Interiors
Mohr & McPherson
The Natural Alternative
The Natural Baby Company
Pacific Rim
Pioneer Millworks
Sensational Beginnings
Shaker Workshops
Summit Furniture, Inc.
Terra Verde
3-D Interiors
Trestlewood Furniture Co.

GARDENING SUPPLIES

Cook's Garden

Earth Friendly Choices

Hand in Hand

The Natural Baby Company

Sensational Beginnings

HEATERS

Solid State Heating

INSECT REPELLENTS

Avon

Lakon Herbals

KITCHEN SUPPLIES

Back to Basics Products

The Bakers Catalog

Eco-Wise Environmental Products

Natural Baby Catalog

Perfectly Safe

Terra Verde

LAUNDRY POWDERS

Bi-O-Kleen

Ecobaby (Bi-O-Kleen brand)

Ecover

Harmony (Seventh Generation brand)

Logona

LEAD TESTS

Lead Check

Michigan Ceramic Supplies Inc.

LIGHTING

Duro-Test Lighting

Energy Federation, Inc.

General Electric Company

Harmony

Healthy Habitats

Lightolier

Lights of America

Lutron

Osram Sylvania

Real Goods Trading Company

Tomorrow's World

MATTRESSES AND FUTONS

Crown City Mattress Company/
The Natural Bedroom

Earthlings

Earthsake

Ecobaby

Eco-Wise Environmental Products

Environmental Home Center

Furnature

Garnet Hill

Harmony

Healthy Habitats

Heart of Vermont

Natura

Nontoxic Environments

Nontoxic Hotline & Nirvana Safe Haven

Organic Cotton Alternatives

Real Goods Trading Company

Sinan Natural Building Materials
Company

Snugglebundle Baby Products

Terra Verde

Tomorrow's World

Wise & Healthy

PAINTS, FINISHES, AND ADHESIVES

AFM

Benjamin Moore & Company

Best Paint Company

Bioshield (See The Natural Choice)

Chem-Safe Products

Eco-Wise Environmental Products

E.C.O. of New York

Environmental Home Center

Glidden/ICI Paints

Healthy Habitats

Kelly Moore Paint

Kurfees (Progress Paint Manufacturing)

Lisa York

Livos Phytochemistry, Inc.

Miller Paint Company

The Natural Choice

Naturlich Natural Home

N.E.E.D.S.

Nontoxic Environments

Nontoxic Hotline & Nirvana Safe Haven

Pace Chem Industries

Planetary Solutions

Progress Paint Manufacturing
   (Kurfees brand)

Roman Adhesives

Sinan Natural Building Materials
   Company

Terra Verde

PERSONAL CARE PRODUCTS

Aubrey Organics

Baby Bunz & Company

Biobottoms

California Baby

Dr. Bronner's

Ecobaby

Eco-Wise Environmental Products

Lakon Herbals

Logona

The Natural Baby Company

Terra Verde

TerrEssentials

Tom's of Maine

Weleda

Worldware

POTTY CHAIRS

Gerry Baby Products Company

The Natural Baby Company

Perfectly Safe

RADON TESTS

Air Chek

First Alert

Key Technology Radon Gas Testing
   Products

Landauer, Inc.

Nontoxic Environments

RTCA

Teledyne Brown Engineering

SAFETY EQUIPMENT

Perfectly Safe

STROLLERS

Century Products

Kidco (MacLaren brand)

TOYS, GAMES, AND STUFFED ANIMALS

Ampersand Press

Animal Town

Baby Bunz & Company

Binary Arts Company

Earth Friendly Choices

Earth Friendly Goods

Earth Runnings

Earthlin's Environmental Products

Earthlings

Earthsake
Earthwise Basics
Ecobaby
Ecosport
Educational Insights
Emily's Toybox
Frank Schaffer Publications
Hand in Hand
Harmony
Healthy Habitat
Hugg-a-Planet
L.L.Bean
Learning Curve International
Little Koala
The Natural Baby Company
New England Toys
Nontoxic Hotline & Nirvana Safe Haven
North Star Toys
Nova Natural Toys & Crafts
Play Design
The Play Store
Rosie Hippo's Wooden Toys and Games
Sensational Beginnings
Strata Quality Gifts & Toys
    from Nature
T.C. Timber/Habermaass Corporation
Terra Verde
This Country's Toys

VACUUM CLEANERS AND SUPPLIES

Absolute Environmental's Allergy
    Products Store
Allergy Control Products, Inc.
Environmental Home Center
Eureka Company
Euroclean

For Your Health Products
Harmony
Healthy Habitats
InteliHealth Healthy Home
Miele Appliances, Inc.
N.E.E.D.S.
Nilfisk Advance America, Inc.
Nontoxic Environments
Nontoxic Hotline & Nirvana
    Safe Haven
Priorities
3M Products

WALLPAPER

Crown Corporation
E.C.O. of New York
Maya Romanoff Corporation
Pattern People, Inc.

WASHING MACHINES

Frigidaire Home Products

WET CLEANER

Ecomat

WINDOW COVERINGS

Conrad Imports

WOOD

Blue Log Lumber
Conklin's Authentic Barnwood
Crossroads Recycled Lumber
EcoTimber International
Endura Hardwoods
Environmental Home Center
Jefferson Recycled Woodworks
Mountain Lumber Company
Pioneer Millworks
Recycled Lumber Works

Company Information

ABC Carpet & Home
888 Broadway
New York, NY 10003
Phone: 212/473-3000
Website: www.abchome.com

—Rugs made without child labor. Mail order, but no catalog.

Absolute Environmental's Allergy Products Store
3504 South University Drive
Davie, FL 33328
Phone: 800/771-2246
Website: www.allergystore.com

—Vacuum cleaners with HEPA filters; particulate-retaining vacuum cleaner bags; air filters.

AFM (American Formulating and Manufacturing)
350 West Ash Street, Suite 700
San Diego, CA 92101
Phone: 619/239-0321

—Low-VOC paints, stains, sealants, carpet cleaner, and flooring adhesives.

Aged Woods, Inc.
2331 East Market Street
York, PA 17402
Phone: 800/233-9307
Website: www.agedwoods.com

—Antique reclaimed wood flooring.

Air Chek
P.O. Box 2000
Naples, NC 28760
Phone: 800/247-2435
Website: www.airchek.com

—Short-term radon tests recommended by *Consumer Reports*.

Allergy Control Products, Inc.
96 Danbury Road
Ridgefield, CT 06877
Phone: 800/422-3878
Website: www.allergycontrol.com

—Cotton/polyester barrier cloth fabric for make-your-own mattress encasements; air filters; particulate-retaining vacuum cleaner bags.

Allergy Resources
557 Burbank Street, Suite K
Broomfield, CO 80020
Phone: 800/USE-FLAX (800/873-3529)

—Organic cotton mattresses; cotton pillows; unbleached, undyed cotton sheets; organic cotton or polypropylene encasements for crib and standard mattresses; HEPA filters; Organic Baby brand baby food.

Allermed Corporation
31 Steel Road
Wylie, TX 75098
Phone: 214/442-4898

—HEPA air conditioner filters.

Allerx
P.O. Box 1119
Royse City, TX 75189
Phone: 800/447-1100

—High efficiency air conditioner filters; Allersearch X-Mite sprays and powders; cotton/polyester or vinyl/nylon tricot barrier cloth encasements for standard mattresses.

Ameda/Egnell (Hollister)
2000 Hollister Drive
Libertyville, IL 60048
Phone: 800/323-4060
Website: www.hollister.com

—Breast pumps.

267

American Environmental Health Store
8345 Walnut Hill Lane, Suite 225
Dallas, TX 75231
Phone: 800/428-2343, 214/361-9515
—HEPA air filters; air purifiers.

Ampersand Press
750 Lake Street
Port Townsend, WA 98368
Phone: 800/624-4263, 360/379-5187
Website: www.ampersandpress.com
—Children's nature games.

Animal Town
P.O. Box 757
Greenland, NH 03840
Phone: 800/445-8642
Website: www.animaltown.com
—Children's environmental games.

Aubrey Organics
4419 N. Manhattan Avenue
Tampa, FL 33614
Phone: 800/282-7394, 813/877-4186
Website: www.aubrey-organics.com
—Herbal soaps, shampoos, lotions, and sunblocks for children.

Avalon Carpets
P.O. Box 2025
Calhoun, GA 30701
Phone: 800/274-4990
—Wool carpeting, glued onto latex backing, dyed, mothproofed. Will refer you to the nearest retailer.

Avent America
501 Lively Boulevard
Elk Grove Village, IL 60007
Phone: 800/542-8368
Website: www.aventamerica.com
—Baby bottles; breast pumps.

Avon
Phone: 800/FOR-AVON (800/367-2866)
Website: www.avon.com
—Skin So Soft Bug Guard and Skin So Soft Moisturizing Suncare Plus insect-repellent citronella lotions.

Baby Bjorn
Regal Lager
1990 Delk Industrial Boulevard, Suite 105
Marietta, GA 30067
Phone: 800/593-5522
Website: www.babybjorn.com
—Soft baby carriers. Will refer you to nearest retailer or catalog company.

Baby Bunz & Company
P.O. Box 113
Lynden, WA 98264
Phone: 800/676-4559
—Cotton baby slings; organic cotton diapers and wool covers; organic cotton children's clothing; Weleda personal care products; natural fiber dolls and toys.

Babyworks
11725 NW West Road
Portland, OR 97229
Phone: 800/422-2910, 503/645-4349
Website: www.babyworks.com
—Waterproof wool "puddle pads"; unbleached cotton hooded bath towels; cotton or wool diapers and covers; Bumkins all-in-one diapers; wipes; untreated cotton or wool blankets; natural fiber dolls.

Back to Basics Products
11660 South State Street
Draper, UT 84020
Phone: 800/688-1989
Website: www.backtobasicsproducts.com
—Grain grinders; electric flour mills.

The Bakers Catalog
P.O. Box 876
Norwich, VT 05055-0876
Phone: 800/827-6836
Website: www.kingarthurflour.com
—Electric flour mills.

Bellbridge, Inc.
1940 Olivera Road, Suite C
Concord, CA 94520
Phone: 800/227-3408, 925/798-7242
—Dyed New Zealand wool carpets glued onto a jute backing. Will refer you to nearest distributor.

Benjamin Moore & Company
Phone: 800/826-2623, 888/236-6667
Website: www.benjaminmoore.com
—No-VOC "Pristine" paint. Some "Crayola" paints (the lighter shades made with 1-base or 2-base) are low-VOC.

Best Paint Company
5205 Ballard Avenue, NW
Seattle, WA 98107
Phone: 206/783-9938
—Low-VOC paints

Binary Arts Company
1321 Cameron Street
Alexandria, VA 22314
Phone: 703/549-4999
Website: www.puzzles.com,
www.binaryarts.com,
www.webgames.com
—Games and puzzles.

Biobottoms
Phone: 800/766-1254
Website: www.biobottoms.com
—Cotton diapers and clothing.

Bi-O-Kleen Industries, Inc.
P.O. Box 82066
Portland, OR 97282
Phone: 503/557-0216
—Laundry powder; cleaning products. Will refer you to nearest retailer or to a catalog company.

Blue Log Lumber
P.O. Box 804
Mendocino, CA 95460
Phone: 707/937-0918
—Reclaimed and recycled lumber.

California Baby
Phone: 310/277-6430
—Baby shampoos, body washes, and bubble baths.

Carousel Carpets
1 Carousel Lane
Ukiah, CA 95482
Phone: 707/485-0333
—Wool, linen, jute, and cotton carpets with natural latex backings; hand-woven wool, jute, or cotton rugs. Wool is mothproofed. Will refer you to nearest retailer.

CDC Carpets and Interiors
3425 Bee Cave Road
Austin, TX 78746
Phone: 512/327-8326
Website: www.citysearch.com/aus/cdc
—Cork tile flooring; coir (coconut husk), sisal (Agave cactus stalk), or seagrass carpeting with natural latex backing.

Century Products
9600 Valley View Road
Macedonia, OH 44056
Phone: 888/5-CARSEAT, 800/837-4044
Website: www.centuryproducts.com

Century Products (continued)

—Century 1000 STE Classic children's car seats and Century Four in One Pro Sport Plus strollers that convert to car seats, both recommended in *Consumer Reports' Guide to Baby Products*. Will refer you to nearest retailer.

Chem-Safe Products
P.O. Box 33023
San Antonio, TX 78265
Phone: 210/657-5321

—"Enviro-Safe," a no-VOC paint in both light and dark colors.

Classic Tile
325 Pine Street
Elizabeth, NJ 07206
Phone: 800/352-2527

—Cork tile flooring. Will refer you to nearest retailer.

Clean Clothes
1955 Pauline Boulevard, Suite 200
Ann Arbor, MI 48103
Phone: 800/609-8593
Website: www.organicclothes.com

—Organic cotton baby clothing.

Cloud Cottons
1460 East 20th Avenue
Eugene, OR 97403
Phone: 541/345-7479

—Organic cotton infant clothing and towels.

Colin Campbell and Sons, Ltd.
1428 West 7th Avenue
Vancouver, British Columbia,
Canada V6H 1C1
Phone: 800/667-5001
Website: www.colcam.com

—Nature's Carpet brand undyed, untreated wool carpets on a natural latex and jute backing. Will refer you to nearest retailer.

Conklin's Authentic Barnwood
R R 1, Box 70
Susquehanna, PA 18847-9751
Phone: 717/465-3832
Website: www.conklinsbarnwood.com

—Flooring and lumber from reclaimed antique wood.

Conrad Imports
Website: www.conradshades.com

—Window shades of natural grasses, reeds, and fibers handwoven in Asia. Available through interior designers and window covering specialty stores.

Cook's Garden
To order a catalog:
P.O. Box 535
Londonderry, VT 05148
To order products:
P.O. Box 5010
Hodges, SC 29653
Phone: 800/457-9703
Website: www.cooksgarden.com

—Children's flower or vegetable seed collections, gardening gloves, and gardening books.

Country Life Natural Foods
P.O. Box 489
Pullman, MI 49450
Phone: 616/236-5011

—Ships organic foods at wholesale prices.

Coyuchi, Inc.
P.O. Box 845
Pt. Reyes Station, CA 94956
Phone: 415/663-8077

—FoxFibre organic cotton upholstery and curtain fabrics; organic cotton sheets and baby bedding. Sells only fabric by mail order. Will refer you to nearest retailer or to a catalog company for sheets and bedding.

Crate & Barrel Catalog
P.O. Box 9059
Wheeling, IL 60090-9059
Phone: 800/451-8217, 800/323-5461

—Wicker stacking baskets; solid wood children's furniture.

Crosby Company
1080 Calkins Road
Rochester, NY 14623
Phone: 800/955-SNUG
Website: www.staysnug.com

—StaySnug brand blankets with leg pouches.

Crossroads Recycled Lumber
P.O. Box 184
O'Neals, CA 93645
Phone: 209/868-3646

—Recycled and reclaimed lumber and flooring.

Crost Furniture & Imports
1799 Willow Road
Northfield, IL 60093
Phone: 888/98-CROST, 847/501-2550
Website: www.crost.com

—Furniture made from antique and reclaimed lumber.

Crown City Mattress Company/The Natural Bedroom
250 S. San Gabriel Boulevard
San Gabriel, CA 91776
Phone: 626/796-9101, 800/365-6563

—Organic cotton and Pure Grow wool crib and standard mattresses and futons; organic, unbleached, untreated cotton or Pure Grow wool pillows, bumper pads, and comforters.

Crown Corporation
3012 Huron Street, Suite 101
Denver, CO 80202
Phone: 800/422-2099, 303/292-1313

—Wall coverings from recycled cotton and sustainably harvested wood.

Crusoe Island Natural Foods
267 Route 89 South
Savannah, NY 13146
Phone: 800/724-2233
Website: www.crusoeisland.com

—Ships organic foods at wholesale prices.

Designtex, Inc.
200 Varick Street, 8th Floor
New York, NY 10014
Phone: 212/886-8200

—Organic cotton upholstery fabrics. Will refer you to architects or interior designers that sell their products.

Diamond Organics
P.O. Box 2159
Freedom, CA 95019
Phone: 888/ORGANIC (888/674-2642)
Website: www.diamondorganics.com

—Organic foods by mail order; baby-food grinder; organic cotton baby socks.

Dodge-Regupol, Inc.
715 Fountain Avenue
Lancaster, PA 17601
Phone: 717/295-3400
Website: www.regupol.com

—Cork tile flooring.

Duro-Test Lighting
9 Law Drive
Fairfield, NJ 07004
Phone: 973/808-1800
Website: www.durotest.com

—Compact fluorescent lamp bulbs recommended by *Consumer Reports*.

E.C.O. of New York (Environmental Construction Outfitters)
190 Willow Avenue
Bronx, NY 10454
Phone: 800/238-5008
Website: www.environproducts.com

—Nonbiocide, no-VOC, or natural paints; natural finishes and stains; low-VOC flooring adhesives and tile grouts; natural linoleum, cork, and reclaimed wood or sustainably harvested wood flooring; untreated, dyed wool carpeting with jute backing; sisal, jute, coir, and sea-grass carpeting with jute backings; less toxic nylon carpeting; jute carpet padding; low-pollutant wall-papers.

Earth Friendly Choices
157 North Evergreen
Arlington Heights, IL 60004
Phone: 847/394-2050

—Science kits; nature and wooden toys; unbleached organic cotton stuffed animals; children's indoor gardening kits.

Earth Friendly Goods
3701 Stony Creek Road
Fort Worth, TX 76116
Phone: 800/257-2848

—Organic cotton teddy bears and bunnies; organic cotton baby clothing.

Earth Power, Inc.
P.O. Box 205
Glen Rock, NJ 07452
Phone: 201/445-7068
Website: www.ayslcorp.com

—Power Herbal Disinfectant.

Earth Runnings
P.O. Box 3027
Taos, NM 87571
Phone: 505/758-5703
Website: www.ecomall.com/biz/earth.htm

—Hemp bedding, shower curtains, stuffed whales, and children's tipis.

Earth Wear
1007 Swallow Lane
Chattanooga, TN 37421
Phone: 423/894-3674

—Organic cotton children's clothing, diapers, and baby blankets.

Earth's Best, Inc.
Consumer Affairs Division
P.O. Box 28
Pittsburgh, PA 15230-9421
Phone: 800/442-4221
Website: www.earthsbest.com

—Organic baby food. Will refer you to nearest retailer.

Earthlin's Environmental Products
P.O. Box 729
Pomona, CA 91769-0729
Phone: 909/237-1960

—Children's environmental learning games made of recycled paper and water-based paints, with wooden game pieces.

Earthlings
P.O. Box 659
Ojai, CA 93024
Phone: 888/GOBABYO (888/462-2296)
Website: www.earthlings.net

—Organic cotton crib sheets, baby blankets, and crib and standard mattresses; organic cotton baby and children's clothing, diapers, towels, washcloths, and stuffed animals; naturally finished hardwood cribs; Kelty K.I.D.S. Carriers cotton slings; toys.

Earthsake
1817 Second Street
Berkeley, CA 94710
Phone: 510/559-8440
Website: www.earthsake.com

—Sustainably harvested solid maple cribs; organic cotton/wool crib and standard mattresses and futons; organic cotton baby blankets and baby clothing; green cotton bath towels, washcloths, and shower curtains; cotton bath mats with natural latex backing; wooden toys.

EarthSpun Heritage Natural Fibers
c/o CISA
Tillson House
University of Massachusetts
Amherst, MA 01003
Phone: 413/549-6271

—Vegetable-dyed wool yarns, fabrics, rugs, clothing, blankets, and scarves.

Earthweave Carpet Mills, Inc.
P.O. Box 6120
Dalton, GA 30722
Phone: 706/259-0022
Website: www.earthweave.com

—Hemp and wool blended carpets, backed with jute and bonded with less-toxic glue and natural latex.

Earthwise Basics
214 Elliot Street, #2
Brattleboro, VT 05301
Phone: 800/791-3957, 802/254-2235
Website: www.ediapers.com,
www.naturaltoys.com

—Wooden toys; baby slings.

Ecobaby
1475 North Cuyamaca
El Cajon, CA 92020
Phone: 888/ECOBABY, 800/596-7450,
619/562-9606
Website: www.ecobaby.com

—Hardwood cribs, step stools, and high chairs; untreated wool puddle pads; organic cotton or wool crib-size futons; organic cotton crib mattresses, sheets, blankets, comforters, pillows, and bumper pads; organic cotton washcloths, washmits, and bath towels; Critter Cape hooded bath towels; organic cotton baby clothing and diapers; Tushies disposable diapers; wool diaper covers; silicone nipples; nursing pads and bras; Aubrey Organics children's personal care products; organic cotton stuffed and wooden toys; air purifiers; Bi-O-Kleen cleaning products and laundry powders.

Ecomat
147 Palmer Avenue
Mamaroneck, NY 10543
Phone: 800/299-2309

—A nontoxic multiprocess wetcleaning clothing service. Franchises are growing rapidly. Ecomat also offers a mail-in service.

Eco-Organics USA

300 B Communipaw Avenue
Jersey City, NJ 07304
Phone: 888/ECO-ORGANIC
(888/326-3784)
Website: www.eco-organics.com

—Organic food home delivery club. Will send out weekly packages of fresh produce and juice.

Ecosport

92 Kansas Street
Hackensack, NJ 07601
Phone: 800/486-4326,
201/489-0389
Website: www.ecosport.net

—Organic cotton children's clothing, terry cloth teddy bears, crib sheets, and baby blankets. Will refer you to nearest retailer or to a catalog company.

EcoTimber International

1020 Heinz Avenue
Berkeley, CA 94710
Phone: 510/549-3000
Website: www.ecotimber.com

—Sustainably harvested domestic and tropical hardwoods; flooring and lumber from reclaimed, recycled wood.

Ecover

Website: www.ecover.com
Available by mail order through:
Good Eats
5 Louise Drive
Warminster, PA 18974
Phone: 800/490-0044
Website: www.goodeats.com

—Cleaning products and laundry powders. Available at most natural foods stores. Website lists retailers around the country.

Eco-Wise Environmental Products

110 West Elizabeth Street
Austin, TX 78704
Phone: 512/326-4474
Website: www.ecowise.com

—Organic and green cotton diapers, covers, and pads; Bumkins diapers; Tushies disposable diapers; unbleached, untreated cotton nursing pads; organic cotton baby clothing, hats, socks, and bibs; organic cotton crib sheets, blankets, pillows, and crib mattresses; organic cotton baby slings; baby personal care products; organic baby food; baby-food grinders; recycled lumber, cork, and natural linoleum flooring; no-VOC, no-biocide paints.

Eddie Bauer

3834 148th Avenue NE
Redmond, WA 98052
Phone: 800/426-6253
Website: www.eddiebauer.com

—Childcraft solid maple cribs.

Educational Insights

16941 Keegan Avenue
Carson, CA 90746
Phone: 800/933-3277
Website: www.edin.com

—Educational toys.

Einstein Moomjy

150 East 58th Street
New York, NY 10155
Phone: 212/758-0900, 800/864-3633

—Vegetable-dyed wool rugs from Turkey.

E.L. Foust Company, Inc.

P.O. Box 105
Elmhurst, IL 60126
Phone: 800/225-9549

—Activated alumina air filters.

Emily's Toybox
P.O. Box 48
Altamont, NY 12009
Phone: 518/861-6719

—Wooden toys, including timber trains
and blocks. Catalogs, $1.

Endura Hardwoods
1331 NW Kearney Street
Portland, OR 97209
Phone: 503/827-6408

—Certified sustainably harvested or
recycled lumber and flooring.

Energy Federation, Inc.
P.O. Box 4712
Natick, MA 01760
Phone: 800/876-0660, 508/653-4299
Website: www.efi.org/biz/efi/

—Compact fluorescent lamp bulbs;
energy-efficient lighting.

Environmental Home Center
1724 4th Avenue South
Seattle, WA 98134
Phone: 800/281-9785, 206/682-7332
Website: www.enviresource.com

—Pesticide-free wool carpet with natural latex and jute backing; sisal, coir,
seagrass, or jute carpeting; natural
linoleum and cork flooring; organic
cotton mattresses, futons, pillows;
wool mattress pads and pillows;
untreated cotton flannel sheets;
untreated, unbleached cotton bath
towels; cotton shower curtains; air
purifiers; HEPA filters; Miele vacuum cleaners; plant-based paints and
finishes; certified sustainably harvested and recycled lumber.

Eureka Company
1201 East Bell Street
Bloomington, IL 61701
Phone: 800/282-2886

—Vacuum cleaners with HEPA filters.
Will refer you to nearest distributor.

Euroclean
1151 Bryn Mawr Avenue
Itasca, IL 60143
Phone: 800/545-4372
Website: www.eurocleanusa.com

—Vacuum cleaners with HEPA filters.
Will refer you to nearest retailer.

Evenflo
Attn: Feeding Department
1801 Commerce Drive
Piqua, OH 45356
Phone: 800/356-BABY (2229)
Website: www.evenflo.com

—Glass and plastic baby bottles.

First Alert
3901 Liberty Street Road
Aurora, IL 60504
Phone: 800/392-1395
Website: www.firstalert.com

—RD1 short-term radon tests recommended by *Consumer Reports*.

Floorworks
365 Dupont Street
Toronto, Ontario, Canada M5R 1W2
Phone: 416/961-6891

—Wool carpets sewn onto jute or cotton backings, mothproofed. Will
direct you to nearest retailer.

For Your Health Products
P.O. Box 15096
Chevy Chase, MD 20825
Phone: 301/654-1127

—Vacuum cleaners with HEPA filters.

Forbo Industries, Inc.
P.O. Box 667
Hazleton, PA 18201
Phone: 800/342-0604
Website: www.forbo-industries.com

—Natural linoleum. Will refer you to
nearest retailer.

Forty Oaks Organic Textiles
2 Queens Lane
Petaluma, CA 94952
Phone: 707/769-1097

—Organic cotton flannel crib blankets with matching baby caps.

Francis Family Toys
316 Ojodela Vaca
Santa Fe, NM 87505
Phone: 505/473-4501

—Paper-making and other craft kits; wooden toys. Will refer you to nearest retailer.

Frank Schaffer Publications
23740 Hawthorne Blvd.
Torrance, CA 90505
Phone: 800/421-5533
Website: www.frankschaffer.com

—Wooden puzzles, clocks that teach how to tell time.

Frigidaire Home Products
P.O. Box 212378
Augusta, GA 30917
Phone: 800/451-7007,
706/860-4110
Website: www.frigidaire.com

—Front-loading clothes washers that save energy and water. Will refer you to nearest retailer.

Furlong & Lee Stone Sales
51 East 42nd Street
New York, NY 10017
Phone: 212/986-3828

—Natural domestic marble. Will refer you to nearest retailer.

Furnature
319 Washington Street
Brighton, MA 02135-3395
Phone: 617/783-4343
Website: www.furnature.com

—Organic cotton sofas, loveseats, chairs, crib and standard mattresses, and pillows.

Garnet Hill
231 Main Street
Franconia, NH 03580
Phone: 800/622-6216

—Green cotton towels, bath rugs, sheets, baby clothes and maternity clothes; cotton nursing pads and bras; wool mattress pads.

General Electric Company
Phone: 800/435-4448
Website: www.ge.com/lighting/home

—Compact fluorescent lamp bulbs recommended by *Consumer Reports.* Will refer you to nearest retailer.

General Filters, Inc.
P.O. Box 8025
Novi, MI 48376-8025
Phone: 248/476-5100

—Medium-efficiency particulate air filters for central air conditioning or heating systems. Will refer you to local contractors who will install their filters.

Gerber
445 State Street
Fremont, MI 49413
Phone: 800/4-GERBER (800/443-7237)
Website: www.gerber.com

—Gerber Tender Harvest organic baby food. Will refer you to nearest retailer.

Gerbert Limited
715 Fountaina Avenue
Lancaster, PA 17601
Phone: 717/299-5035

—Natural linoleum flooring. Will refer you to nearest representative.

**Gerry Baby Products Company
(Evenflo)**
1801 Commerce Drive
Piqua, OH 45356
Phone: 800/233-5921

—Gerry's Explorer Backpack for child
carriage; wooden potty chairs.

GladRags
P.O. Box 12751
Portland, OR 97212
Phone: 503/282-0436

—Organic cotton nursing pads,
hooded baby towels and diapers.

Glidden
ICI Paints
16651 Sprague Road
Strongsville, OH 44136
Phone: 800/221-4100, 800/984-5444
Website: www.icipaintstores.com

—No-VOC Glidden "Spread 2000" and
ICI "Lifemaster 2000" paints (with
biocide). Will refer you to nearest
retailer.

Globalwear
3432 SE Grant Street
Portland, OR 97214
Phone: 503/236-9699
Website: www/europa.com/~globalwear/

—Organic cotton, hemp, silk, and
recycled fiber clothing for children
ages 2–8.

Grandma's Blankets
5210 Lewis Road, Suite 14
Agoura Hills, CA 91301
Phone: 818/991-3367

—Organic cotton flannel receiving and
baby blankets.

Green Design Furniture Company
267 Commercial Street
Portland, ME 04011
Phone: 800/853-4234
Website: www.greendesigns.com

—Solid wood furniture of interlocking
joinery pieces.

Green Mountain Spinnery
P.O. Box 568
Putney, VT 05346
Phone: 800/321-9665, 802/387-4528
Website: www.spinnery.com

—Undyed, untreated Greenspun
Vermont wool yarns and blankets.

Gridcore Systems International
1400 Canal Avenue
Long Beach, CA 90813
Phone: 562/901-1492
Website: www.gridcore.com

—Shelving and paneling made with
recycled cardboard boxes and
bonded with formaldehyde-free
resin. Will refer you to nearest
retailer.

Hand in Hand
P.O. Box 1605
Secaucus, NJ 07096-1605
Phone: 800/872-9745

—Wooden and cloth toys; wooden
children's furniture; children's gardening tools.

Hanna Andersson
1010 NW Flanders
Portland, OR 97209
Phone: 800/222-0544
Website: www.hannaandersson.com

—Children's clothing.

Harmony

360 Interlocken Boulevard
Broomfield, CO 80021
Phone: 800/456-1177

—Seventh Generation cleaning and recycled paper products; organic and green cotton clothing; untreated cotton sheets and wool blankets; organic cotton baby blankets and mattresses; polyester knit plastic encasements for standard mattresses; cotton-polyester crib and standard barrier cloth mattress encasements; Allersearch X-Mite brand sprays and powders; organic cotton towels and bath rugs; green cotton or hemp shower curtains; organic cotton stuffed bunnies; alcohol-free disposable baby wipes; HEPA air filters; filtered fans; EuroClean HEPA vacuum cleaners; compact fluorescent lamp bulbs.

Healthy Habitats

P.O. Box 1968
Port Townsend, WA 98368
Phone: 888/742-2482, 360/379-3379

—Organic or green cotton baby clothing; organic cotton and wool mattresses, pillows, mattress pads, comforters, blankets and sheets; hand woven bassinets; organic cotton stuffed animals; barrier cloth mattress encasements; vacuum cleaners with HEPA filters; no-VOC and low-VOC paints, stains, and sealants; natural linoleum and cork flooring; wool, sisal, and coir carpets; compact fluorescent lamps; air filters.

Heart of Vermont

P.O. Box 612
Barre, VT 05641
Phone: 800/639-4123, 802/476-3098
Website: www.heartofvermont.com

—Organic cotton or untreated wool crib sheets, blankets, comforters, pillows, and bumper pads; organic cotton / wool crib and standard mattresses and futons; unfinished furniture kits and futon frames.

Hemp Culture

3580 North Main Street
Soquel, CA 95073
Phone: 408/479-8121
Website: www.members.cruzio.com/~scd

—Hemp children's dresses. Catalogs, $1.

Hemp Textiles International, Inc.

3200 30th Street
Bellingham, WA 98225
Phone: 360/650-1684
Website: www.cantiva.com

—Hemp fabrics. Will refer you to nearest retailer or a catalog company.

Hemp Traders

2132 Colby Avenue, #5
Los Angeles, CA 90025
Phone: 310/914-9557
Website: www.hemptraders.com

—Hemp fabrics.

Hoboken Wood Floors

979 Third Avenue
New York, NY 10022
Phone: 212/759-5917

—Unfinished or water-based polyurethane finished wood flooring from recycled and reclaimed lumber.

HinderCovers

5300 Ka Haku Road, Unit 2
Kilavea, HI 96754
Phone: 888/446-3377; 808/826-6719

—Organic cotton diapers and clothing.

Horse Drawn Pine
273 Pendleton Hill Road
North Stonington, CT 06359
Phone: 860/599-4393

—Reclaimed antique timber flooring.

Hugg-a-Planet
247 Rockingstone Avenue
Larchmont, NY 10538
Phone: 800/332-7840, 914/833-0200
Website: www.hugg-a-planet.com

—Foundlings unbleached, organic cotton stuffed animals; educational cotton pillow globes.

IKEA
Phone: 800/434-IKEA (800/434-4532)
Website: www.ikea.com

—Rugs made without child labor.

Indigenous Designs
219 Buckeye Street, Unit B
Redwood City, CA 94063
Phone: 650/568-7360
Website: www.indigenousdesigns.com

—Pesticide-free, undyed wool blankets; natural fiber children's clothing. Will refer you to a catalog company.

InteliHealth Healthy Home
97 Commerce Way, P.O. Box 7007
Dover, DE 19903
Phone: 800/394-3775
Website: www.intelihealth.com

—Crib and standard barrier cloth mattress encasements; AllerSearch X-Mite powder and spray; HEPA air purifiers; EuroClean HEPA vacuum cleaners; unbleached, untreated cotton sheets.

International Wood Products, Inc.
P.O. Box 128
Queen Anne, MD 21657
Phone: 410/364-5031
Website: www.internationalwood.com

—Flooring from reclaimed wood. Will refer you to nearest retailer.

Jefferson Recycled Woodworks
P.O. Box 696
McCloud, CA 96057
Phone: 530/964-2740
Website: www.ecowood.com

—Children's and other furniture, flooring, and lumber from recycled and reclaimed wood.

Junckers Danish Beech Flooring USA
4920 E. Landon Drive
Anaheim, CA 92807
Phone: 800/878-9663,
714/777-6430
Website: www.junckershardwood.com

—Sustainably grown beech flooring. Will refer you to nearest retailer.

Karastan Contract Carpets
Phone: 800/234-1120
Website: www.karastan.com

—Wool carpeting with latex backing, mothproofed, dyed. Will refer you to nearest retailer.

Kelly Moore Paint
1015 Commercial Street
San Carlos, CA 94670
Phone: 415/592-8337

—Envirocoat, no-VOC paint. Will refer you to nearest retailer.

Kevyn Woven Hempen Home
P.O. Box 306
Wolf Creek, OR 97497
Phone: 541/866-2452
Website: www.sirius.com/~flipper/kevyn/

—Handwoven hemp and organic cotton fabrics and yarns; handwoven hemp rugs; Hungarian machine-woven rugs. Specializes in custom orders.

Key Technology Radon Gas Testing Products
Phone: 800/523-4964

—Key-Rad-Kit short-term radon tests and Key-Trac-Kit long-term radon tests recommended by *Consumer Reports*.

Kidco, Inc.
300 Terrace Drive
Mundelein, IL 60060-3836
Phone: 800/553-5529
Website: www.kidcoinc.com

—MacLaren folding umbrella strollers with reclining backs. Will refer you to nearest retailer.

Kidde Safety
1394 South 3rd Street
Mebane, NC 27302
Phone: 800/880-6788
Website: www.kidde.com

—Nighthawk 2000 carbon monoxide alarms. Will refer you to nearest retailer.

Koala Konnections
735 Palomar Drive
Sunnyvale, CA 94086
Phone: 888/GO-KOALA
Website: www.koalakon.com

—Children's sun-protective clothing.

Korqinc
155 East 56th Street
New York, NY 10022
Phone: 212/758-2593

—Cork flooring.

L.L.Bean, Inc.
Freeport, ME 04033-0001
Phone: 800/221-4221
Website: www.llbean.com

—Clothing and outdoor gear.

Lakon Herbals
RR1, Box 4710 Templeton Road
Montpelier, VT 05602
Phone: 800/TO-LAKON (865-2566), 802/223-5563
Website: www.enterit.com/LakonHerbals5563.htm

—Organic herbal baby oil and salves; Bygone Bugz herbal insect.

Landauer, Inc.
2 Science Road
Glenwood, IL 60425-1586
Phone: 800/528-8327
Website: www.landauerinc.com

—RadTrack Alpha-Track Radon Gas Detector, a long-term radon test recommended by *Consumer Reports*.

Lead Check
P.O. Box 1210
Framingham, MA 01701
Phone: 800/262-LEAD
Website: www.leadcheck.com

—Lead check swabs.

Learning Curve International
314 West Superior Avenue, 6th Floor
Chicago, IL 60610
Phone: 800/704-8697
Website: www.learningcurve.com

—Wooden and fabric toys. Will refer you to nearest retailer or to a catalog company.

Leggett & Platt
Hartex Carpet Cushion
Permaloom Carpet Cushion (by Southwest Fibers)
P.O. Box 758
Villa Rica, GA 30180
Phone: 800/237-9640, 714/973-7777

—Less toxic carpet padding. Will refer you to nearest retailer.

Life on the Planet
23852 Pacific Coast Highway, #200
Malibu, CA 90265
Phone: 818/880-5144
Website: www.cleanhouse.com
—Cleaning kit with recipes for non-
toxic cleaners on the label of bottles.

LifeTime Solutions
Jack Mayers
53 Winthrop Road
Manchester, CT 06040
Phone: 860/649-3900
—Cleaning products.

Lightolier
631 Airport Road
Fall River, MA 02720
Phone: 508/679-8131
—Lamp fixtures for compact fluorescent bulbs. Will refer you to nearest
retailer.

Lights of America
Consumer Affairs Department
611 Reyes Drive
Walnut, CA 91789
Phone: 800/321-8100
Website: www.lightsofamerica.com
—Compact fluorescent lamp bulbs rec-
ommended by *Consumer Reports;*
lamp fixtures. Will refer you to near-
est retailer.

Lill-ing
P.O. Box 3571
Vero Beach, FL 32964
Phone: 800/747-WOOL
—Untreated wool baby clothing and
diaper covers.

Lisa York
18 Laurel Avenue
Petaluma, CA 94952
Phone: 707/769-1787
—Natural, petroleum-free paints and
finishes.

Little Koala
614 Bellefonte Street
Shadyside, PA 15232
Phone: 412/687-1239
Website: www.littlekoala.com
—Breast pumps; nursing bras and
organic cotton nursing pads;
unbleached cotton diapers; organic
cotton baby wipes, baby clothing,
and receiving blankets; untreated
wool baby sweaters and blankets;
wooden toys.

Livos Phytochemistry, Inc.
P.O. Box 1740
Mashpee, MA 02649-1740
Phone: 508/477-7955
Website: www.livos.com
—No-VOC and low-VOC natural paints.

The Loft Bed Store
14980 Farm Creek Drive
Woodbridge, VA 22191
Attn. Larry Spinks
Phone: 800/842-6119,
703/643-1044
Website: www.loftbed.com
—Eco Furniture bed frames, dressers,
nightstands, and bookcases from
certified sustainably harvested oak;
toddler furniture of sustainably
harvested wood by request; custom
orders.

Logona Kosmetik
554-E Riverside Drive
Asheville, NC 28801
Phone: 888/456-4662
—Children's shampoos, soaps, baby
oils, sunscreens, nonfluoride tooth-
pastes, and diaper rash creams;
Sodasan laundry soap powder.

A Loomful of Hues
5 East 17th Street, 6th Floor
New York, NY 10003
Phone: 212/691-2821
–Handmade natural fiber area rugs.

Lutron

Website: www.lutron.com

—Light- and motion- sensitive dimmers and controls. Information on where to find products is available only on their website. Available at Home Depot and other chain stores.

Magic Chain (for Dr. Bronner)

2598 Fortune Way, Suite K
Vista, CA 92083
Phone: 800/622-6648

—Castile soaps and cleaning products.

MarketPlace/Handwork of India

1455 Ashland Avenue
Evanston, IL 60201
Phone: 800/726-8905

—Products made with fair trade practices.

Maya Romanoff Corporation

1730 W. Greenleaf
Chicago, IL 60626
Phone: 773/465-6909

—Low-pollutant, natural fiber wall coverings. Will refer you to nearest retailer.

Medela, Inc.

4610 Prime Parkway
McHenry, IL 60050-7005
Phone: 800/TELL-YOU
Website: www.medela.com

—Baby bottles; breast pumps; nursing bras and pads; USP purified lanolin. Will refer you to local retailers and breast-feeding specialists.

Michigan Ceramic Supplies Inc.

4048 Seventh Street
Wyandotte, MI 48192
Phone: 800/860-2332, 734/281-2300

—Lead Inspector Kit

Miele Appliances, Inc.

22 D Worlds Fair Drive
Somerset, NJ 08873
Phone: 800/289-MIELE
Website: www.miele.com

—Vacuum cleaners with HEPA filters. Will refer you to nearest retailer.

Miller Paint Company

317 SE Grand Avenue
Portland, OR 97214
Phone: 503/233-4491

—Low-VOC, biocide-free paints.

Miya Shoji & Interiors

109 West 17th Street
New York, NY 10011
Phone: 212/243-6774

—Screens and room dividers of paper and natural wood; solid wood furniture and beds, unfinished by request. Custom orders only.

Mohr & McPherson

290 Concord Avenue
Cambridge, MA 02138
Phone: 617/354-6662

—Furniture made from reclaimed teak and mahogany. Custom orders only.

Motherwear

320 Riverside Drive
Northampton, MA 01062
Phone: 800/950-2500
Website: www.motherwear.com

—Breast pumps; USP purified lanolin; nursing bras, pads, and clothing; maternity clothing.

Mountain Lumber Company

P.O. Box 289
Ruckersville, VA 22968
Phone: 800/445-2671,
804/985-3646
Website: www.mountainlumber.com

—Reclaimed antique wood flooring and lumber.

Natura

680 Bishop Street North
Cambridge, Ontario, Canada N3H 4V6
Phone: 800/215-3002

—Organic cotton and wool mattresses. Will refer you to nearest retailer.

The Natural Alternative
11577 124th Street N
Hugo, MN 55038
Phone: 612/351-7165
Website: www.dgsoft.com/tna
—Organic cotton sofas, loveseats, and chairs with removable washable upholstery; organic cotton fabrics and filling.

The Natural Baby Company
7835 Freedom Avenue, NW
North Canton, OH 44720-6907
Phone: 800/388-BABY
(800/388-2229)
—Pine toddler beds and furniture with water-based finishes; wooden high chairs, potty chairs, and foot stools; organic and unbleached cotton blankets; pesticide-free wool blankets; wool crib mattress pads; Sara's Ride hip carriers; organic cotton baby clothing and diapers; wipes; diaper covers; cotton diaper-changing pads; nursing pads and bras; baby-food grinders; personal care products; wooden toys; Wachsfarben beeswax block crayons.

The Natural Choice
1365 Rufina Circle
Santa Fe, NM 87505
Phone: 800/621-2591,
505/438-3448
Website: www.irisinc.com
—Bioshield organic paint and pigments to mix your own wall paints; Bioshield milk (casein) paint; Auro and Livos plant- and mineral-based, low-VOC paints and stains; no-VOC paints; cork flooring; organic cotton towels and baby blankets; cleaners.

Natureswear
650 5th Street, Suite 204
San Francisco, CA 94107
Phone: 800-252-COTN (2686),
415/543-2785
—Organic cotton baby clothing, sun hats, bibs; organic and green cotton baby blankets and washcloths; green cotton crib sheets.

Naturlich Natural Home
P.O. Box 1677
Sebastopol, CA 95473
Phone: 707/824-0914
—Pesticide-free, untreated wool carpet with jute and natural latex backing; jute, sisal, seagrass, or camel hair carpets sewn onto jute backing; wool carpet pads; Enviro-tech low-VOC carpet glue; untreated hardwood, natural linoleum, and cork flooring; low-VOC paints, finishes, and flooring adhesives; untreated wool, organic cotton, untreated cotton, or hemp bedding.

N.E.E.D.S.
527 Charles Avenue, 12-A
Syracuse, NY 13209
Phone: 800/634-1380, 315/488-6312
Website: www.needs.com
—AFM nonbiocide, low-VOC, water-based paints, stains, and sealants; AFM flooring adhesives; Nilfisk vacuum cleaners with ULPA filters; air filters; AFM SafeChoice carpet shampoo; cleaners; personal care products.

New Day Creations
1283 12th Avenue
San Francisco, CA 94122
Phone: 415/665-9604
—Hemp overalls for infants and toddlers.

New England Toys
44 Kent Road
Warren, CT 06754
Phone: 888/588-8697, 860/868-2557

—Natural fiber stuffed animals; environmental children's books; wooden toys; swings made of recycled tires; nature games.

New Native Baby Carrier
P.O. Box 247
Davenport, CA 95017
Phone: 800/646-1682, 408/458-3398
Website: www.cruzio.com/~newnativ

—Organic cotton sling-style carriers, baby blankets, bibs, washcloths, and diapers.

Nilfisk Advance America, Inc.
300 Technology Drive
Malvern, PA 19355
Phone: 800-NILFISK (800/645-3475)
Website: www.pa.nilfisk-advance.com

—Vacuum cleaners with ULPA filters. Will refer you to nearest retailer.

Nontoxic Environments
P.O. Box 384
Newmarket, NH 03857
Phone: 800/789-4348
Website: www.nontoxicenvironments.com

—Nonbiocide, no-VOC paints; radon tests; AFM SafeChoice carpet shampoo; Crystal Air water-based polyurethane sealant; untreated wool crib comforters; organic cotton and wool crib and standard futons and mattresses; vacuum supplies; vacuum cleaners with HEPA filters; air filters.

Nontoxic Hotline & Nirvana Safe Haven
3441 Golden Rain Road, #3
Walnut Creek, CA 94595
Phone: 800/968-9355, 925/472-8868
Website: www.nontoxic.com

—Organic cotton and wool crib and standard mattresses; air filters; vacuum cleaners with Alta filters; EcoSport organic cotton children's clothing, teddy bears, bibs, baby blankets, and crib sheets; low-VOC paints and sealants.

North American Detectors, Inc.
100 Tempo Avenue
Toronto, Ontario, Canada M2H 3S5
Phone: 800/387-4219, 416/496-5900
Website: www.nadi.com

—CO920 carbon monoxide alarm recommended by *Consumer Reports*.

North Star Toys
HC81, Box 617
Questa, NM 87556
Phone: 505/586-0112

—Wooden toys and puzzles.

Nova Natural Toys & Crafts
817 Chestnut Ridge Road
Chestnut Ridge, NY 10977
Phone: 914/426-3757
Website: www.novanatural.com

—Wooden toys; cotton and wool stuffed animals.

Organic Cotton Alternatives
3120 Central Avenue, SE
Albuquerque, NM 87106
Phone: 888/645-4452, 505/268-9738
Website: www.organiccottonalts.com

—Organic cotton crib futons.

Ortex Rugs
Schermerhorn Brothers Company, distributor
225 Executive Drive
Moorestown, NJ 08057
Phone: 800/231-1043

—Hungarian hemp rugs with hemp backing.

Osram Sylvania
100 Endicott Street
Danvers, MA 01923-3623
Phone: 800/544-4828
Website: www.sylvania.com

—Compact fluorescent lamp bulbs
recommended by *Consumer Reports*.
Will refer you to nearest retailer.

Pace Chem Industries
3050 Westwood Drive, B10
Las Vegas, NV 89109
Phone: 800/350-2912

—Crystal Shield low-VOC paint and
floor sealant; Crystal Air cabinet and
furniture sealant.

Pacific Rim
P.O. Box 2844
Eugene, OR 97402
Phone: 541/342-4508

—Sustainably harvested hardwood
cribs, unfinished or finished with
plant-based stain, which convert to
twin-size toddler beds. Will refer you
to nearest retailer.

Patagonia Mail Order
8550 White Fir Street
Reno, NV 89533
Phone: 800/638-6464
Website: www.patagonia.com

—Organic cotton children's clothing;
Baby Bunting sacks; sun-protective
hats.

Pattern People, Inc.
10 Floyd Road
Derry, NH 03038
Phone: 603/432-7180

—Low-pollutant wallpapers.

Perfectly Safe
7835 Freedom Avenue NW, Suite 3
North Canton, OH 44720-6907
Phone: 800/837-KIDS (800/837-5437)

—Oven latches; stove guards; cabinet
and drawer handle restraints;
Gerry wooden potty chairs; safety
gates; electrical outlet plates;
sanitizing dishwasher baskets for
bottles and nipples; baby-food
grinders.

Pioneer Millworks
1755 Pioneer Road
Shortsville, NY 14548
Phone: 716/289-3090
Website: www.pioneermillworks.com

—Flooring, lumber, custom furniture,
and other products from reclaimed
wood.

Planetary Solutions
P.O. Box 1049
Boulder, CO 80306
Phone: 303/442-6228

—Glidden low-VOC paints; wool or
recycled natural fiber carpet pads;
cork and natural linoleum flooring;
Nature's Carpet undyed, unmoth-
proofed wool carpet with jute backing; naturally dyed wool rugs;
low-VOC finishes, sealants; flooring
adhesives; AFM SafeCoat carpet
cleaners.

Play Design
21 Guernsey Avenue
Montpelier, VT 06502
Phone: 802/454-7318

—Handmade wooden puzzles with
nature motifs.

The Play Store
508 University Avenue
Palo Alto, CA 94301
Phone: 650/326-9070,
Toll-free: 877/876-1111

—Natural wooden, wool and cotton
stuffed toys.

Prince Lionheart

2421 S. Westgate Road
Santa Maria, CA 93455
Phone: 800/544-1132
Website: www.princelionheart.com

—Sanitizing dishwasher baskets for bottles and nipples.

Priorities

1451 Concord Street, Suite 2
Framingham, MA 01701
Phone: 800/553-5398
Website: www.priorities.com

—Allersearch X-Mite brand sprays and powders; mattress encasements; 3M Filtrete air conditioner filters and air filters; particulate-retaining vacuum cleaner bags; Nilfisk Alta filter and Windsor HEPA filter vacuum cleaners.

Progress Paint Manufacturing (for Kurfees)

201 E. Market Street
Louisville, KY 40202
Phone: 800/626-6407, 502/584-0151

—Low-VOC, biocide-free Kurfees Fresh Air paints.

Pure Air Systems, Inc.

P.O. Box 418
Plainfield, IN 46168
Phone: 800/869-8025
Website: www.pureairsystems.com

—HEPA air filtration systems. Will refer you to nearest retailer.

RCN Products

P.O. Box 2006
Greenwich, CT 06831-2006
Phone: 800/284-2023

—EarthRite brand cleaning products. Will refer you to nearest retailer or to a catalog company.

REI (Recreational Equipment, Inc.)

1700 45th Street East
Sumner, WA 98390
Phone: 800/426-4840
Website: www.rei.com

—Hiking gear for children; Kelty K.I.D.S. Kangaroo Child Carriers and Explorer Child Carriers for hiking trips.

Rainbow Organic Fiber Mill

P.O. Box 760
North Bennington, VT 05257
Phone: 802/442-0871
Website: www.rofm.com

—Organic cotton bath mats, washcloths, hooded baby and bath towels, bibs; terry fabrics and sheets.

Real Goods Trading Company

555 Leslie Street
Ukiah, CA 95482-5576
Phone: 800/762-7325, 707/468-9214
Website: www.realgoods.com

—Barrier cloth mattress encasements; compact fluorescent lamp bulbs; Allersearch X-Mite powders and sprays; organic cotton or hemp mattresses; organic cotton or wool pillows; unbleached, untreated cotton bath towels and shower curtains; Dharmic hemp rugs with cotton backing and vegetable dyes; HEPA air purifiers.

Recycled Lumber Works

596 Park Boulevard
Ukiah, CA 95482
Phone: 707/462-2567

—Reclaimed vintage timber and flooring.

Research Products Corporation
P.O. Box 1467
Madison, WI 53701-1467
Phone: 800/545-2219
Website: www.resprod.com

—Medium-efficiency particulate air
   filters. Will refer you to nearest
   retailer.

Roman Adhesives
824 State Street
Calumet City, IL 60409
Phone: 800/488-6117,
708/891-0188

—Natural, low-VOC wallpaper glues.
   Will refer you to nearest retailer.

Rosie Hippo's Wooden Toys and Games
P.O. Box 2068
Port Townsend, WA 98368
Phone: 800/385-2620, 360/385-2620
Website: www.rosiehippo.com

—Wooden toys, puzzles, and games;
   gardening and insect games;
   organic cotton stuffed animals;
   silk receiving blankets.

RTCA
2 Hays Street
Elmsford, NY 10523
Phone: 800-457-2366

—Short-term radon tests recommended
   by *Consumer Reports.*

Sara's Ride
2737 Larimer Street
Denver, CO 80205
Phone: 800/394-6519, 303/292-2224

—Hip carriers.

Sensational Beginnings
P.O. Box 2009
Monroe, MI 48161
Phone: 800/444-2147
Website: www.sb-kids.com

—Wooden puzzles, children's furniture,
   and stepping stools; wildlife drawing
   sets; gardening tools for children.

Shaker Workshops
P.O. Box 8001
Ashburnham, MA 01430
Phone: 800/840-9121,
781/646-8985
Website: www.shakerworkshops.com

—Unfinished wood furniture kits,
   including a toddler high chair.

Sinan Company
P.O. Box 857
Davis, CA 95617-0857
Phone: 530/753-3104
Website: www.dcn.davis.ca.us/go/sinan

—Natural, low-VOC wallpaper glues;
   pesticide-free wool carpet; natural
   fiber rugs; low-VOC floor waxes; cotton and wool futons; Auro
   natural paints.

Snugglebundle Baby Products
444A N. Main Street, #165
East Longmeadow, MA 01028
Phone: 888/449-7482, 413/525-1972
Website: www.snugglebundle.com

—Organic cotton crib futons; green and
   organic cotton layettes, crib quilts,
   bumper pads, sheets, and baby clothing; untreated wool puddle pads;
   hemp baby blankets; organic cotton
   diapers, bath towels, washcloths, and
   baby slings; wool diaper covers;
   organic cotton.

Solar Protective Factory/Solarweave
3469 Quail Haven Lane
Carmichael, CA 95608
Phone: 916/944-2387
Website: www.solarweave.com

—Children's sun-protective cloth. Will
   refer you to clothing brand names
   and retailers.

Solid State Heating
P.O. Box 769
Old Saybrook, CT 06475
Phone: 800/544-5182
Website: www.sshcinc.com
—Radiant heaters.

Strata Quality Gifts & Toys from Nature
58 Central Street
Wellesley, MA 02482
Phone: 888/237-2992
Website: www.2strata.com
—Environmental education and wooden toys; children's nature books.

Summit Furniture, Inc.
5 Harris Court, Bldg. W
Monterey, CA 93940
Phone: 408/375-7811
—Garden furniture made with SmartWood certified lumber.

SunFun Collection
751 Laurel Street, #707
San Carlos, CA 94070
Phone: 800-4-SUN-FUN
(800/478-6386)
—Sun-protective children's clothing.

Sun Precautions, Inc.
2815 Wetmore Avenue
Everett, WA 98201
Phone: 800/882-7860
Website: www.sunprecautions.com
—Sun-protective children's clothing.

Superior Floor Company, Inc.
901 E. Thomas Street
Wausau, WI 54403
Phone: 800/247-4705, 715/842-5358
Website: www.superiorfloor.com
—Untreated hardwood flooring.

T.C. Timber/Habermaass Corporation
P.O. Box 42
4407 Jordan Road
Skaneateles, NY 13152
Phone: 800/245-7622
—Wooden toys.

Teledyne Brown Engineering
50 Van Buren Avenue
Westwood, NJ 07675
Phone: 800/666-0222
—Short-term radon test recommended by *Consumer Reports*.

Terra Verde
120 Wooster Street
New York, NY 10012
Phone: 212/925-4533
—Hardwood, nontoxic-finish furniture; Pacific Rim hardwood cribs; organic cotton crib mattresses; organic, untreated cotton or wool bedding; untreated or organic cotton baby clothing, towels, and bath rugs; untreated, undyed cotton stuffed animals; lead-free pottery; organic pigments to mix your own paints; personal care products; plant-based watercolors for children.

TerrEssentials
2650 Old National Pike
Middletown, MD 21769-8817
Phone: 301/371-7333
—Organic cotton washcloths; herbal baby soaps and hair cleansers; talc-free baby powder; Lakon Herbals salves and baby oils.

This Country's Toys
P.O. Box 41479
Providence, RI 02940-1479
Phone: 800/359-1233
—Wooden building blocks and train sets by t.c. timber.

3-D Interiors
1312 Haight Street
San Francisco, CA 94117
Phone: 415/863-0373

—Solid wood furniture with interlocking joinery pieces.

3M Company
3M Do It Yourself Division
Box 33053
St. Paul, MN 55133-3053
Phone: 800/388-3458
Website: www.mmm.com

—3M Filtrete filters; particulate-retaining vacuum cleaner bags. Mail order or will refer you to nearest retailer.

Tom's of Maine
P.O. Box 710
Kennebunk, ME 04043
Phone: 800/985-3874, 800/775-2388
Website: www.tomsofmaine.com

—Children's soaps, toothpastes, and shampoos.

Tomorrow's World
194 West Oceanview Avenue
Norfolk, VA 23503
Phone: 800/229-7571
Website: www.tomorrowsworld.com

—Hemp and organic cotton fabrics; organic cotton crib and standard sheets, receiving blankets, towels, washcloths, and baby clothing; organic cotton and wool crib comforters; organic cotton/wool crib and standard mattresses and futons; compact fluorescent lamp bulbs; hemp and untreated, undyed cotton shower curtains.

Trestlewood Furniture Co.
1035 South 800 West
Salt Lake City, UT 84104

Phone: 801/972-9970
Website: www.trestlewood.com

—Recycled redwood outdoor furniture.

Tushies Baby Products
P.O. Box 102
Delta, CO 81416
Phone: 800/344-6379
Website: www.ecomall.com

—Recycled fiber, nonchlorine-bleached, chemical-free disposable diapers and liner pads; alcohol-free baby wipes; organic cotton baby T-shirts.

Walnut Acres
Penns Creek, PA 17862
Phone: 800/433-3998
Website: www.walnutacres.com

—Organic food.

Weleda, Inc.
175 North Route 9W
Congers, NY 10920
Phone: 800/241-1030
Website: www.weleda.com

—Soaps, creams, and shampoos for children; baby oils and lotions; diaper rash ointments; talc-free baby powders; Dr. Hauschka children's sunblocks.

The Well-Fed Baby
11835 Carmel Mountain Road, #350
San Diego, CA 92128
Phone: 888/WELL-FED, 619/486-4412

—Organic vegetarian baby food.

Wise & Healthy
Phone: 800/583-8882
Website: www.wiseandhealthy.com

—Natura brand organic cotton and wool mattresses.

Wools of New Zealand
700 Galleria Parkway, Suite 300
Atlanta, GA 30339
Phone: 800/452-8864
Website: www.fernmark.com

—Wool carpeting, mothproofed, some undyed. Atelier, Avalon, Bellbridge, Bloomsburg, Karastan, Woolshire, and Wools of New Zealand brands, each with different backings, all for less than $40 per square yard. Will refer you to nearest retailer.

Worldware
336 Hayes Street
San Francisco, CA 94102
Phone: 415/487-9030
Website: www.worldwaresf.com

—Organic cotton crib sheets, baby blankets, quilts, baby clothing, towels; hemp baby clothing; green cotton hooded baby towels, talc-free baby powder.

Select
Bibliography

Chapter One

Colborn, Theo, Dianne Dumanoski, and John P. Myers. *Our Stolen Future: Are We Threatening Our Fertility, Intelligence, and Survival? A Scientific Detective Story.* New York: Viking Penguin, 1996.

Di Gangi, Joseph. *Lead and Cadmium in Vinyl Children's Products.* Washington, D.C.: Greenpeace USA, 1997.

Fano, Alix. "Environmental Factors in the Rise of Children's Cancer." *The Green Guide,* Vol. 54/55 (1998), pp. 1–3.

Gibbs, Lois Marie. *Dying from Dioxin: A Citizen's Guide to Reclaiming Our Health and Rebuilding Democracy.* Boston: South End Press, 1995.

Gurunathan, Somia, et al. "Accumulation of Chlorpyrifos on Residential Surfaces and Toys Accessible to Children." *Environmental Health Perspectives,* Vol. 106, No. 1 (1999), pp. 9–16.

Healing the Harm: Eliminating the Pollution from Health Care Practices. Washington, D.C.: Health Care Without Harm/Environmental Working Group, 1997.

Indoor Air Pollution Fact Sheet: Formaldehyde. New York: American Lung Association, 1995.

Inside Story: Guide to Indoor Air Quality. U.S. Environmental Protection Agency, Office of Air and Radiation, and U.S. Consumer Product Safety Commission (EPA/402/K93/007). Washington, D.C.: 1993.

Introduction to Indoor Air Quality: A Reference Manual. U.S. Environmental Protection Agency, Office of Air and Radiation (EPA/400/3-91/003). Washington, D.C.: 1993.

Kessel, Irene, and John T. O'Connor. *Getting the Lead Out: The Complete Resource on How to Prevent and Cope with Lead Poisoning.* New York: Plenum, 1997.

Landrigan, Philip, and Herbert Needleman. *Raising Children Toxic Free.* New York: Avon Books, 1995.

Lowengart, Ruth A., et al. "Childhood Leukemia and Parents' Occupational and Home Exposures." *Journal of the National Cancer Institute,* Vol. 79, No.1 (1987), pp. 39–46.

Øie, Leif, Lars-Georg Hersoug, and J.Ø. Madsen. "Residential Exposure to Plasticizers and Its Possible Role in the Pathogenesis of Asthma." *Environmental Health Perspectives,* Vol. 105, No. 9 (1997), pp. 972–78.

Ott, Wayne R., and John W. Roberts. "Everyday Exposure to Toxic Pollutants." *Scientific American,* Vol. 278, No. 2 (1998), pp. 86–91.

Overexposed: Organophosphate Insecticides in Children's Food. Washington, D.C.: Environmental Working Group, 1998.

Pesticides in the Diets of Infants and Children. Washington, D.C.: National Academy Press, 1993.

Rauch, Molly E. "Screening Out Neurotoxins." *The Green Guide,* Vol. 56/7 (1998), pp. 1–3.

Respiratory Health Effects of Passive Smoking: Lung Cancer and Other Disorders. U.S. Environmental Protection Agency, Office of Research and Development, Office of Air and Radiation (EPA/600/6-90/006F). Washington, D.C.: 1992.

Schmidt, Charles W. "Childhood Cancer: A Growing Problem." *Environmental Health Perspectives,* Vol. 106, No. 1 (1998), pp. 18–23.

Screening Young Children for Lead Poisoning: Guidance for State and Local Public Health Officials. U.S. Centers for Disease Control and Prevention. Atlanta, Georgia: 1997.

Starrels, Jennifer. "Hand-Me-Down Poisons: An Update on Hormone Disruption." *The Green Guide,* Vol. 42 (1997), pp. 1–3.

Stringer, Ruth, et al. *Determination of the Composition and Quantity of Phthalate Ester Additives in PVC Children's Toys.* Exeter, U.K.: Greenpeace Research Laboratories, University of Exeter, 1997.

Targeting Indoor Air Pollution: EPA's Approach and Progress. U.S. Environmental Protection Agency (EPA/400/R-92/012). Washington, D.C.: 1992.

Toxicity Testing: Strategies to Determine Needs and Priorities. Washington, D.C.: National Academy Press, 1984.

Update on Formaldehyde, An. U.S. Consumer Product Safety Commission (Doc. #725). Washington, D.C.: 1997.

U.S. Centers for Disease Control and Prevention. "Mortality and Hospitalization Among Children and Adults, 1980–1993." *Morbidity and Mortality Weekly Report,* Vol. 45, No. 17 (1996), pp. 350–53.

Chapter Two

General

Bower, John. *The Healthy House,* 3rd Ed. Bloomington, Ind.: The Healthy House Institute, 1997.

Gibbs, Lois Marie. *Dying from Dioxin: A Citizen's Guide to Reclaiming Our Health and Rebuilding Democracy.* Boston: South End Press, 1995.

Leach, Penelope. *Your Baby and Child: From Birth to Age Five.* New York: Alfred A. Knopf, 1997.

Marinelli, Janet, and Paul Bierman-Lytle. *Your Natural Home.* New York: Little, Brown, 1995.

Mott, Lawrie. *Our Children at Risk: The Five Worst Environmental Threats to Their Health.* New York: Natural Resources Defense Council, 1997.

Øie, Leif, Lars-Georg Hersoug, and J.Ø. Madsen. "Residential Exposure to Plasticizers and Its Possible Role in the Pathogenesis of Asthma." *Environmental Health Perspectives,* Vol. 105, No. 9 (1997), pp. 972–78.

Pearson, David. *The Natural House Book: Creating a Healthy, Harmonious, and Ecologically Sound Home Environment.* New York: Simon & Schuster, 1989.

Potkotter, Louis. *The Natural Nursery: The Parent's Guide to Ecologically Sound, Nontoxic, Safe, and Healthy Baby Care.* Chicago: Contemporary Books, 1994.

Van der Meer, Antonia. *Great Beginnings: An Illustrated Guide to You and Your Baby's First Year.* New York: Dell Publishing, 1994.

LEAD

CPSC Finds Lead Poisoning Hazard for Young Children in Imported Vinyl Miniblinds. U.S. Consumer Product Safety Commission (Release #96-150). Washington, D.C.: 1996.

Kessel, Irene, and John T. O'Connor. *Getting the Lead Out: The Complete Resource on How to Prevent and Cope with Lead Poisoning.* New York: Plenum, 1997.

Marino, Phyllis E., et al. "A Case Report of Lead Paint Poisoning During Renovation of a Victorian Farmhouse." *American Journal of Public Health,* Vol. 80, No. 10 (1990), pp. 1183–85.

Rauch, Molly E. "Screening Out Neurotoxins." *The Green Guide,* Vol. 56/7 (1998), pp. 1–3.

Report on the National Survey of Lead-Based Paint in Housing: Base Report. U.S. Environmental Protection Agency, Office of Pollution Prevention and Toxics (EPA/747/R95/003). Washington, D.C.: 1995.

Screening Young Children for Lead Poisoning: Guidance for State and Local Public Health Officials. U.S. Centers for Disease Control and Prevention. Atlanta, Georgia: 1997.

PAINTS

Choose Green: Interior Latex Paints. Washington, D.C.: Green Seal, 1996.

Introduction to Indoor Air Quality: A Reference Manual. U.S. Environmental Protection Agency, Office of Air and Radiation (EPA/400/3-91/003). Washington, D.C.: 1993.

CARPETS

Abrams, Robert, et al. *Carpets and Indoor Air: What You Should Know.* Attorney General's Environmental Protection and Consumer Protection Bureau and the Office of Public Information (0029-NYDL-93-032). New York: 1993.

Anderson, Julius H. "Reactions to Carpet Emissions: A Case Series." *Journal of Nutritional & Environmental Medicine,* Vol. 7 (1997), pp. 177–85.

Carpet and Indoor Air Quality in Schools. Maryland State Department of Education, Division of Business Services, School Facilities Branch. Baltimore: 1993.

Choose Green: Carpets. Washington, D.C.: Green Seal, 1996.

Duehring, Cindy. "Carpet: Laying It Safe." *The Green Guide,* Vol. 19 (1996), pp. 1–3.

Iovine, Julie V. "Must-Have Label: Rug Makers and Sellers are Seeking Ways to Trumpet Compliance with a New Child-Labor Law." *The New York Times,* October 16, 1997.

CRIBS AND BEDDING

Baby Product Safety Tips: Safety Alert. U.S. Consumer Product Safety Commission (Doc. #5082). Washington, D.C.: 1993.

CPSC Warns of Strangulation with Crib Toys: Safety Alert. U.S. Consumer Product Safety Commission (Doc. #5024). Washington, D.C.: 1992.

Indoor Air Pollution Fact Sheet: Formaldehyde. New York: American Lung Association, 1995.

Lyman, Francesca. "The Natural Bedroom." *The Green Guide,* Vol. 45 (1997), pp. 1–3.

Marquardt, Sandra. "Pick Your Cotton." *The Green Guide,* Vol. 22 (1996), pp. 1–3.

Marquardt, Sandra, and Aisha Ikramuddin. "Natural Fibers of the Future." *The Green Guide,* Vol. 45 (1997), p. 5.

Pennybacker, Mindy. "Breathing Space: What You Can Do to Stop the Rise of Asthma." *The Green Guide,* Vol. 21 (1996), pp. 1–4.

———. "The Ghettoization of Asthma." *The Green Guide,* Vol. 56/57 (1998), pp. 1, 4–6.

Protect Your Child. U.S. Consumer Product Safety Commission (Doc. #4241). Washington, D.C.:

Some Crib Cornerposts May Be Dangerous: Safety Alert. U.S. Consumer Product Safety Commission (Doc. #5027). Washington, D.C.: 1991.

Update on Formaldehyde, An. U.S. Consumer Product Safety Commission (Doc. #725). Washington, D.C.: 1997.

Your Used Crib Could Be Deadly: Safety Alert. U.S. Consumer Product Safety Commission (Doc. #5020). Washington, D.C.: 1995.

SUDDEN INFANT DEATH SYNDROME

Choukas-Bradley, Melanie. "Advances in the War on SIDS." The Washington Post, December 20, 1996.

McKenna, James J. "Sudden Infant Death Syndrome: Making Sense of Current Research." *Mothering,* Vol. 81 (1996), pp. 74–80.

Schwartz, Peter J., et al. "Prolongation of the QT Interval and the Sudden Infant Death Syndrome." *New England Journal of Medicine,* Vol. 338, No. 24 (1998), pp. 1709–14.

Soft Bedding Products and Sleep Position Contribute to Infant Suffocation Deaths: Safety Alert. U.S. Consumer Product Safety Commission (Doc. #5049). Washington, D.C.: 1993.

What Every Parent Should Know: Facts About Sudden Infant Death Syndrome and Reducing the Risks for SIDS. Ledyard, Conn.: SIDS Network, 1996.

What is SIDS? National Sudden Infant Death Syndrome Resource Center, National Center for Education in Maternal and Child Health, U.S. Department of Health and Human Services, 1993.

LIGHTING

Caldwell, Chris. "Zap Energy Waste and Save Dollars in Your Home." *The Green Guide,* Vol. 34 (1997), pp. 1–3.

Heede, Richard. *Homemade Money: How to Save Energy and Dollars in Your Home.* Snowmass, Colorado: Rocky Mountain Institute, 1995.

"Light Bulbs: The Best and the Brightest." *Consumer Reports,* Vol. 61, No. 7 (1996), p. 7.

Rembert, Tracey. "The Eternal Flame: Compact Fluorescents Are Cheap, Earth-Friendly and May Last Forever." *E Magazine,* Vol. 7, No. 4 (1996), pp. 44–45.

Wilson, Alex, and John Morrill. *Consumer Guide to Home Energy Savings,* 6th Ed. Washington, D.C.: American Council for an Energy-Efficient Economy, 1998.

Chapter Three

Brody, Jane E. "Baby Walkers May Slow Infants' Development." *The New York Times,* October 14, 1997.

CPSC Offers Safety Tips for Infant Carrier Seats: Safety Alert. U.S. Consumer Product Safety Commission (Doc. # 5048), 1992.

Jones, Sandy, Werner Freitag, and the editors of *Consumer Reports. Guide to Baby Products,* 5th Ed. Yonkers, New York: Consumer Reports Books, 1996.

Safety and Accident Prevention: Baby Product Safety. American Medical Association, Kids Health at the AMA Website (http://www.ama-assn.org), 1998.

Testing the Waters. New York: Natural Resources Defense Council, 1998.

Tips for Your Baby's Safety. U.S. Consumer Product Safety Commission (Doc. #4200). Washington, D.C.

"Child's Death Underscores Urgency of Returning Recalled Cribs." Washington, D.C.: Associated Press.

Chapter Four

GREEN BUILDING

Bower, John. *The Healthy House,* 3rd Ed. Bloomington, Indiana: The Healthy House Institute, 1997.

Indoor Air Pollution Fact Sheet: Formaldehyde. New York: American Lung Association, 1995.

Inside Story: Guide to Indoor Air Quality. U.S. Environmental Protection Agency, Office of Air and Radiation, and U.S. Consumer Product Safety Commission (EPA/402/K93/007). Washington, D.C.: 1993.

Introduction to Indoor Air Quality: A Reference Manual. U.S. Environmental Protection Agency, Office of Air and Radiation (EPA/400/3-91/003). Washington, D.C.: 1993.

Marinelli, Janet, and Paul Bierman-Lytle. *Your Natural Home.* New York: Little, Brown, 1995.

Pearson, David. *The Natural House Book: Creating a Healthy, Harmonious, and Ecologically Sound & Home Environment.* New York: Simon & Schuster, 1989.

Update on Formaldehyde, An. U.S. Consumer Product and Safety Commission (Doc. #725). Washington, D.C.: 1997.

LEAD-FREE DISHES

Mott, Lawrie. *Our Children at Risk: The Five Worst Environmental Threats to Their Health.* New York: Natural Resources Defense Council, 1997.

What You Should Know About Lead in China Dishes. New York: Environmental Defense Fund, 1994.

CHILD SAFETY

Jones, Sandy, Werner Freitag, and the editors of *Consumer Reports. Guide to Baby Products,* 5th Ed. Yonkers, New York: Consumer Reports Books, 1996.

Safety and Accident Prevention: Preventing Common Household Accidents. American Medical Association, Kids Health at the AMA Website (http://www.ama-assn.org), 1998.

Stringer, Ruth, et al. *Determination of the Composition and Quantity of Phthalate Ester Additives in PVC Children's Toys.* Exeter, U.K.: Greenpeace Research Laboratories, University of Exeter, 1997.

Tips for Your Baby's Safety. U.S. Consumer Product Safety Commission (Doc. #4200). Washington, D.C.

ENERGY-EFFICIENCY

Caldwell, Chris. "Zap Energy Waste and Save Dollars in Your Home." *The Green Guide,* Vol. 34 (1997), pp. 1–3.

Heede, Richard. *Homemade Money: How to Save Energy and Dollars in Your Home.* Snowmass, Colorado: Rocky Mountain Institute, 1995.

Wilson, Alex, and John Morrill. *Consumer's Guide to Home Energy Savings.* Washington, D.C.: American Council for an Energy-Efficient Economy, 1997.

Chapter Five

GENERAL

Bower, John. *The Healthy House,* 3rd Ed. Bloomington, Indiana: The Healthy House Institute, 1997.

Inside Story: Guide to Indoor Air Quality. U.S. Environmental Protection Agency, Office of Air and Radiation, and U.S. Consumer Product Safety Commission (EPA/402/K93/007). Washington, D.C.: 1993.

Ott, Wayne R., and John W. Roberts. "Everyday Exposure to Toxic Pollutants." *Scientific American,* Vol. 278, No. 2 (1998), pp. 86–91.

COMBUSTION POLLUTANTS

Burning Charcoal in Homes, Vehicles and Tents Causes 25 Deaths from Carbon Monoxide Each Year. U.S. Consumer Product Safety Commission (Doc. #5012). Washington, D.C.: 1992.

Combustion Pollutants in Your Home. California Environmental Protection Agency, Air Resources Board, Research Division. Sacramento: 1994.

Combustion Appliances and Indoor Air Pollution. U.S. Environmental Protection Agency, U.S. Consumer Product Safety Commission, and American Lung Association. Washington, D.C.: 1994.

CPSC and NKHA Stress Kerosene Safety. U.S. Consumer Product Safety Commission (Doc. #5052). Washington, D.C.: 1992.

Health Effects of Wood Smoke. Washington State Department of Ecology, Air Quality Program (Brochure No. 92–46). Olympia, Wash.: 1997.

"Redesigned CO Detectors Earn High Marks." *Consumer Reports,* Vol. 62, No. 5 (1997), p. 9.

"Sleeping Safely (Carbon Monoxide Detectors Can Spot This Poisonous Gas Before It's Too Late)." *Consumer Reports,* Vol. 61, No. 11 (1996), pp. 58–59.

The "Senseless" Killer: Can You Tell What It Is? U.S. Consumer Product Safety Commission (Doc. #4464). Washington, D.C.: 1993.

What You Should Know About Space Heaters. U.S. Consumer Product Safety Commission. Washington, D.C.: 1988.

CLEANERS

Berthold-Bond, Annie. *Clean and Green.* Woodstock, N.Y.: Ceres Press, 1994.

Colborn, Theo, Dianne Dumanoski, and John Peterson Myers. *Our Stolen Future: Are We Threatening Our Fertility, Intelligence, and Survival? A Scientific Detective Story.* New York: Viking Penguin, 1996.

Dickey, Philip. *Buy Smart, Buy Safe: A Consumer's Guide to Less-Toxic Products.* Seattle: Washington Toxics Coalition, 1994.

———. *Hormones in Your Haircolor?* Seattle: Washington Toxics Coalition, 1997.

———. *Safer Cleaning Products.* Seattle: Washington Toxics Coalition, 1998.

———. *Troubling Bubbles: The Case for Replacing Alkylphenol Ethoxylate Surfactants.* Seattle: Washington Toxics Coalition, 1997.

Epstein, Samuel, and David Steinman. *The Safe Shopper's Bible: A Consumer's Guide to Nontoxic Household Products, Cosmetics and Food.* New York: Macmillan, 1995.

"Fish Sex Hormones." *Rachel's Environment & Health Weekly,* Vol. 545 (1997).

Ikramuddin, Aisha. "The Cleaning Blues." *The Green Guide,* Vol. 53 (1998), p. 5.

Litovitz, T.L., et al. "1996 Annual Report of the American Association of Poison Control Centers Toxic Exposure Surveillance System." *Journal of Emergency Medicine,* Vol. 15 (1997), pp. 447–500.

Logan, Karen. *Clean House, Clean Planet.* New York: Pocket Books, 1997.

DRY CLEANING/WET CLEANING

"Dry-Cleaning Test: Cutting Clothing Care Costs: Must You Obey That Label?" *Consumer Reports,* Vol. 62, No. 2 (1997), pp. 52–53.

Ebbert, Kristin. "Greenwashing: Safer Alternatives to Dry Cleaning." *The Green Guide,* Vol. 46 (1997), pp. 1–3.

"Household Risks: Dry-Cleaning and Health." *Consumer Reports,* Vol. 61, No. 3 (1996), p. 6.

Ruder, Avima M., et al. "Cancer Mortality in Female and Male Dry-Cleaning Workers." *Journal of Mortality,* Vol. 36, No. 8 (1994), pp. 867–74.

Wallace, Deborah, and Edward Groth. *Perchloroethylene Exposure from Dry Cleaned Clothes.* Yonkers, New York: Consumers Union, 1996.

Wallace, Deborah, et al. *Upstairs, Downstairs: Perchloroethylene in the Air in Apartments Above New York City Dry Cleaners.* Yonkers, New York: Consumers Union, 1995.

PESTICIDES

Bormann, Herbert, Diana Balmori, and Gordon T. Geballe. *Redesigning the American Lawn: A Search for Environmental Harmony.* New Haven, Conn.: Yale University Press, 1993.

Leiss, J.K., and D.A. Savitz. "Home Pesticide Use and Childhood Cancer: A Case-Control Study." *American Journal of Public Health,* Vol. 85, No. 2 (1995), pp. 249–52.

Lowengart, R.A., et al. "Childhood Leukemia and Parents' Occupational and Home Exposures." *Journal of the National Cancer Institute,* Vol. 79, No. 1 (1987), pp. 39–46.

Marquardt, Sandra. "Golf's Green Handicap." *The Green Guide,* Vol. 37 (1997), pp. 1–3.

Nishioka, Marcia, et al. "Measuring Transport of Lawn-Applied Herbicide Acids from Turf to Home: Correlation of Dislodgeable 2,4-D Turf Residues with Carpet Dust and Carpet Surface Residues." *Environmental Science and Technology,* Vol. 30, No. 11 (1996), pp. 3313–20.

Olkowski, William, Sheila Daar, and Helga Olkowski. *Common-Sense Pest Control: Least-Toxic Solutions for Your Home, Garden, Pets and Community.* Newtown, Conn.: Taunton Press, 1991.

Pogoda, Janice M., and Susan Preston-Martin. "Household Pesticides and Risk of Pediatric Brain Tumors." *Environmental Health Perspectives,* Vol. 105, No. 11 (1997), pp. 1214–20.

Schultz, Warren. *The Chemical-Free Lawn: The Newest Varieties and Techniques to Grow Lush, Hardy Grass.* Emmaus, Pa.: Rodale Press, 1996.

Wiles, Richard, et al. *Tap Water Blues: Herbicides in Drinking Water.* Washington, D.C.: Environmental Working Group, 1994.

RADON

Brookins, Douglas G. *The Indoor Radon Problem.* New York: Columbia University Press, 1990.

Leary, Warren E. "Research Ties Radon to as Many as 21,800 Deaths Each Year." *The New York Times,* February 20, 1998.

"Radon—Lung Cancer Risk High for Smokers." *Science News,* Vol. 153 (1998), p. 159.

"Radon: Worth Learning About." *Consumer Reports,* Vol. 60, No. 7 (1995), pp. 464–65.

Reducing Radon Risks. U.S. Environmental Protection Agency, Air and Radiation (EPA 520/1-89-027). Washington, D.C.: 1992.

ASBESTOS

Asbestos in the Home. U.S. Consumer Product Safety Commission (Doc. #453). Washington, D.C.

Cancer Hazard! CPSC Warns about Asbestos in Consumer Products: Safety Alert. U.S. Consumer Product Safety Commission (Doc. #5080). Washington, D.C.: 1986.

Toxics Information Series: Asbestos. U.S. Environmental Protection Agency, Office of Pesticides and Toxic Substances (TS-793). Washington, D.C.: 1980.

MOLD

Biological Pollutants in Your Home. U.S. Environmental Protection Agency (EPA/402/F90/102). Washington, D.C.: 1990.

Holloway, Lynette. "Poisonous Mold Shuts a Renovated Library in Staten Island." *The New York Times,* October 4, 1997.

"Indoor Mold Growth and Infant Pulmonary Hemorrhage." *Journal of Environmental Health,* Vol. 59, No. 8 (1997), p. 25.

Meredith, Robyn. "Infants' Lung Bleeding Traced to Toxic Mold." *The New York Times,* January 24, 1997.

Verhoeff, A.P., and H.A Burge. "Health Risk Assessment of Fungi in Home Environments." *Annals of Allergy, Asthma and Immunology,* Vol. 78, No. 6 (1997), pp. 544–54.

HUMIDIFIERS

CPSC Issues Alert About Care of Room Humidifiers: Safety Alert. U.S. Consumer Product Safety Commission (Doc. #5046). Washington, D.C.: 1988.

IMPROVING AIR QUALITY WITH AIR CONDITIONERS, VACUUM CLEANERS, AND FILTERS

Heede, Richard. *Homemade Money: How to Save Energy and Dollars in Your Home.* Snowmass, Colorado: Rocky Mountain Institute, 1995.

"Household Air Cleaners: Our Tests Show That These Machines Can Reduce Dust and Smoke, But They Can't Get Rid of Odors." *Consumer Reports,* Vol. 57, No. 10 (1992), pp. 657–59, 662.

Residential Air-Cleaning Devices: A Summary of Available Information. U.S. Environmental Protection Agency, Air and Radiation (EPA 400/1-90-002). Washington, D.C.: 1990.

Roberts, John W., et al. "Exposure of Children to Pollutants in House Dust and Indoor Air." *Reviews of Environmental Contamination and Toxicology,* Vol. 143 (1995), pp. 59–76.

Wilson, Alex, and John Morrill. *Consumer's Guide to Home Energy Savings.* Washington, D.C.: American Council for an Energy-Efficient Economy, 1997.

ELECTROMAGNETIC FIELDS

Questions and Answers About Electric and Magnetic Fields Associated with the Use of Electric Power. National Institute of Environmental Health Sciences, and U.S. Department of Energy (DOE/EE-0040). Washington, D.C.: 1995.

"EMFs May Cause Some Cancers, Blue Ribbon Panel Concludes." *Environment News Service (ENS),* June 26, 1998.

Chapter Six

GENERAL

Colborn, Theo, Dianne Dumanoski, and John Peterson Myers. *Our Stolen Future: Are We Threatening Our Fertility, Intelligence, and Survival? A Scientific Detective Story.* New York: Viking Penguin, 1996.

Fano, Alix. "Environmental Factors in the Rise of Children's Cancer." *The Green Guide,* Vol. 54/55 (1998), pp. 1–3.

Haynes, R.C. "A Tradition of Focusing on Children's Health." *Environmental Health Perspectives,* Vol. 106, No. 1 (1998), pp. A14–16.

Landrigan, Philip, and Herbert Needleman. *Raising Children Toxic Free.* New York: Farrar Straus & Giroux, 1994.

Myers, S.R., et al. "Characterization of 4-aminobiphenyl-hemoglobin adducts in maternal and fetal blood samples." *Journal of Toxicology and Environmental Health,* Vol. 47, No. 6, pp. 553–66.

PESTICIDES

Buckley, J.D., et al. "Occupational Exposures of Parents of Children with Acute Nonlymphocytic Leukemia: A Report from the Children's Cancer Study Group." *Cancer Research,* Vol. 49, No. 14 (1989), pp. 4030–37.

Daniels, Julie L., et al. "Pesticides and Childhood Cancers." *Environmental Health Perspectives,* Vol. 105, No. 10 (1997), pp. 1068–77.

RADIATION

Kodama, K., et al. "A Long-Term Cohort Study of the Atomic-Bomb Survivors." *Journal of Epidemiology,* Vol. 6, No. 3 Suppl. (1996), pp. S95–S105.

Shea, K.M., and R.E. Little. "Is There an Association Between Preconception Paternal X-Ray Exposure and Birth Outcome?" *American Journal of Industrial Medicine,* Vol. 145, No. 6 (1997), pp. 546–51.

Wiley, Lynn M., et al. "Impaired Cell Proliferation in Mice that Persists Across at Least Two Generations after Paternal Irradiation." *Radiation Research,* Vol. 148, No. 2 (1997), pp. 145–51.

Yoshimoto, Y., et al. "Malignant Tumors During the First Two Decades of Life in the Offspring of Atomic Bomb Survivors." *American Journal of Human Genetics,* Vol. 46, No. 6 (1990), pp. 1041–52.

PCBs, DIOXINS, AND OTHER HORMONE DISRUPTORS

Chao, W., C. Hsu, and Y.L. Guo. "Middle-Ear Disease in Children Exposed Prenatally to Polychlorinated Biphenyls and Polychlorinated Dibenzofurans." *Archives of Environmental Health,* Vol. 52, No. 4 (1997), p. 257.

Davis, Devra Lee, Michelle B. Gottleib, and Julie R. Stampnitzky. "Reduced Ratio of Male to Female Births in Several Industrial Countries: A Sentinel Health Indicator?" *Journal of the American Medical Association,* Vol. 279 (1998), pp. 1018–23.

Ebbert, Kristin, and Becky Gillette. "Hormonal Imbalance: How Pollution Skews Sexual Development." *The Green Guide,* Vol. 54/55 (1998), pp. 1, 4–6.

Gibbs, Lois Marie. *Dying from Dioxin: A Citizen's Guide to Reclaiming Our Health and Rebuilding Democracy.* Boston: South End Press, 1995.

Pennybacker, Mindy, and Kristin Ebbert. "Our Barbies, Ourselves." *The Green Guide,* Vol. 23 (1996), pp. 1–3.

Rogan, Walter, et al. "Congenital Poisoning by Polychlorinated Biphenyls and Their Contaminants in Taiwan." *Science,* Vol. 241 (1988), pp. 334–36.

HEAVY METALS: LEAD AND MERCURY

Andrews, K.W., D.A. Savitz, and I. Hertz-Picciotto. "Prenatal Lead Exposure in Relation to Gestational Age and Birth Weight: A Review of Epidemiological Studies." *American Journal of Industrial Medicine,* Vol. 26, No. 1 (1994), pp. 13–32.

Gonzalez-Cossio, Teresa, et al. "Decrease in Birthweight in Relation to Maternal Bone-Lead Burden." *Pediatrics,* Vol. 100, No. 5 (1997), p. 856.

Goyer, R.A. "Transplacental Transport of Lead."*Environmental Health Perspectives,* Vol. 89 (1990), pp. 101–105.

Grandjean, P., et al. "Cognitive Deficit in 7-Year-Old Children with Prenatal Exposure to Methylmercury." *Neurotoxicology and Teratology,* Vol. 19, No. 6 (1997), pp. 417–28.

Min, Y.I., et al. "Parental Occupational Lead Exposure and Low Birth Weight." *Amercian Journal of Industrial Medicine,* Vol. 30, No. 5 (1996), pp. 569–78.

Myers, G.J., et al. "Effects of Prenatal Methylmercury Exposure from a High Fish Diet on Developmental Milestones in the Seychelles Child Development Study." *Neurotoxicology,* Vol. 18, No. 3 (1997), pp. 819–29.

Myers, G.J., and P.W. Davidson. "Prenatal Methylmercury Exposure and Children: Neurologic, Developmental, and Behavioral Research." *Environmental Health Perspectives,* Vol. 106, Suppl. 3 (1998), pp. 841–47.

Rauch, Molly E. "Screening Out Neurotoxins." *The Green Guide,* Vol. 56/57 (1998), pp. 1–3.

Silbergeld, E.K. "Lead in Bone: Implications for Toxicology During Pregnancy and Lactation." *Environmental Health Perspectives,* Vol. 91 (1991), pp. 63–70.

ALCOHOL

Connor, P.D., and A.P. Streissguth. "Effects of Prenatal Exposure to Alcohol Across the Life Span." *Alcohol Health and Research World,* Vol. 20, No. 3 (1996), pp. 170–74.

FOOD SAFETY

Catching the Limit: Mercury Contamination of America's Food. Washington, D.C.: Environmental Working Group, 1997.

Earle, Sylvia. *Sea Change.* New York: G.P. Putnam's Sons, 1995.

Ebbert, Kristin. "Blue Acres: Fish Farming." *The Green Guide,* Vol. 44 (1997), p. 5.

Fox, Nicols. S*poiled: The Dangerous Truth About a Food Chain Gone Haywire.* New York: Basic Books/HarperCollins, 1997.

Hess, Mary Abbott, and Anne Elise Hunt. *Eating for Two: The Complete Guide to Nutrition During Pregnancy.* New York: Macmillan, 1994.

Hook Line and Sinking: The Crisis in Marine Fisheries. New York: Natural Resources Defense Council, 1997.

Ikramuddin, Aisha, and Leila Mead. "Slaughterhouse 5: Factory Farming of Meat and Poultry." *The Green Guide,* Vol. 51 (1998), pp. 1–3.

Ikramuddin, Aisha. "Strawberries: In a Jam." *The Green Guide,* Vol. 40 (1997), p. 5.

Overexposed: Organophosphate Insecticides in Children's Food. Washington, D.C.: Environmental Working Group, 1998.

Pennybacker, Mindy. "The Last Wild Fish in the Sea." *The Green Guide,* Vol. 35 (1997), pp. 1–3.

Pesticides in Children's Food. Washington, D.C.: Environmental Working Group, 1993.

Shopper's Guide to Pesticides in Produce, A. Washington, D.C.: Environmental Working Group, 1995.

State of the World: 1995. New York: W.W. Norton, 1995.

WATER

Evans, Nancy, and Marguerite Young. "Turning on the Tap May Be Risky." *The San Francisco Chronicle,* April 14, 1998.

Gordon, Wendy. "Toxins on Tap." *The Green Guide,* Vol. 27 (1996), pp. 1–3.

Mansur, Michael. "Water Woes Stir Concerns of Wider Contamination." *The Kansas City Star,* February 14, 1998.

Olson, Eric D. *Trouble on Tap.* New York: Natural Resources Defense Council, 1995.

The Sierra Club Guide to Safe Drinking Water. San Francisco: Sierra Club Books, 1996.

"Should You Use a Water Filter?" *Consumer Reports,* Vol. 62, No. 7 (1997), pp. 27–29.

The Sierra Club Guide to Safe Drinking Water. San Francisco: Sierra Club Books, 1996.

Wiles, Richard, et al. *Tap Water Blues: Herbicides in Drinking Water.* Washington, D.C.: Environmental Working Group, 1994.

PERSONAL CARE PRODUCTS

Dickey, Philip. *Hormones in Your Haircolor?* Seattle: Washington Toxics Coalition, 1997.

Ebbert, Kristin. "The Cosmetic Mask." *The Green Guide,* Vol. 31 (1996), pp. 1–3.

Hampton, Aubrey. *What's in Your Cosmetics?* Tucson, Ariz.: Odonian Press, 1995.

Chapter Seven

Brazelton, T. Berry. *Touchpoints: The Essential Reference.* MA: Perseus Books, 1995.

Caplan, Theresa, and the Princeton Center for Infancy and Early Childhood. *The First Twelve Months of Life.* New York: Putnam, 1995.

Di Gangi, Joseph. *Lead and Cadmium in Vinyl Children's Products.* Washington, D.C.: Greenpeace USA, 1997.

"Diaper Wars: As Brands Battle for Your Business, Know What to Look For—And What's Just Hype." *Consumer Reports,* Vol. 63, No. 8 (1998), pp. 53–55.

Ebbert, Kristin. "The Cosmetic Mask." *The Green Guide,* Vol. 31 (1996), pp. 1–3.

Epstein, Samuel, and David Steinman. *The Safe Shopper's Bible: A Consumer's Guide to Nontoxic Household Products, Cosmetics and Food.* New York: Macmillan, 1995.

Farrisi, Theresa R. *Diaper Changes: The Complete Diapering Book and Resource Guide.* Richland, Pa.: Homekeeping Publishing, 1997.

Hampton, Aubrey. *What's in Your Cosmetics?* Tucson, Ariz.: Odonian Press, 1995.

Jusczyk, Peter W., and Elizabeth A. Hohne. "Infants' Memory for Spoken Words." *Science,* Vol. 277 (1997), pp. 1984–86.

Leach, Penelope. *Your Baby and Child: From Birth toAge Five.* New York: Alfred A. Knopf, 1997.

Potential Health Hazards of Cosmetic Products, (Serial 99–68). Hearings before the Subcommittee on Regulation and Business Opportunities, U.S. House of Representatives. Washington, D.C.: 1998.

Potkotter, Louis. *The Natural Nursery: The Parent's Guide to Ecologically Sound, Nontoxic, Safe, and Healthy Baby Care.* Chicago: Contemporary Books, 1994.

Stringer, Ruth, et al. *Determination of the Composition and Quantity of Phthalate Ester Additives in PVC Children's Toys.* Exeter, U.K.: Greenpeace Research Laboratories, University of Exeter, 1997.

Van der Meer, Antonia. *Great Beginnings: An Illustrated Guide to You and Your Baby's First Year.* New York: Dell Publishing, 1994.

Winter, Ruth. *A Consumer's Dictionary of Cosmetic Ingredients.* New York: Crown Publishers, 1974.

Chapter Eight

BREAST-FEEDING

American Academy of Pediatrics. "Breastfeeding and the Use of Human Milk." *Pediatrics,* Vol. 100, No. 6 (1997), pp. 1035–39.

Christoffel, Katherine K., and A. Ariza. "The Epidemiology of Overweight in Children: Relevance for Clinical Care." *Pediatrics,* Vol. 101, No. 1 (1998), pp. 103–105.

Dietz, William H. "Health Consequences of Obesity in Youth: Childhood Predictors of Adult Disease." *Pediatrics,* Vol. 101, No. 3 (1998), pp. 518–25.

Horwood, L.J., and D.M. Fergusson. "Breastfeeding and Later Cognitive and Academic Outcomes." *Pediatrics,* Vol. 101, No. 1 (1998), p. E9.

Leach, Penelope. *Your Baby and Child: From Birth to Age Five.* New York: Alfred A. Knopf, 1997.

Potkotter, Louis. *The Natural Nursery: The Parent's Guide to Ecologically Sound, Nontoxic, Safe, and Healthy Baby Care.* Chicago: Contemporary Books, 1994.

Troiano, R.P., and K.M. Flegel. "Overweight Children: Description, Epidemiology, and Demographics." *Pediatrics,* Vol. 101, No. 3 (1998), pp. 497–504.

CONTAMINANTS IN BREAST MILK

Colborn, Theo, Dianne Dumanoski, and John P. Myers. *Our Stolen Future: Are We Threatening Our Fertility, Intelligence, and Survival? A Scientific Detective Story.* New York: Viking Penguin, 1996.

Freudenheim, J., et al. "Exposure to Breast Milk in Infancy and the Risk of Breast Cancer." *Epidemiology,* Vol. 5 (1994), pp. 324–31.

Gibbs, Lois Marie. *Dying from Dioxin: A Citizen's Guide to Reclaiming Our Health and Rebuilding Democracy.* Boston: South End Press, 1995.

Gulson, B.L., et al. "Relationships of Lead in Breast Milk to Lead in Blood, Urine, and Diet of the Infant and Mother." *Environmental Health Perspectives,* Vol. 106, No. 10 (1998), pp. 667–74.

Huotari, Carol. "Alcohol and Motherhood." *Leaven,* Vol. 33, No. 2 (1997), pp. 30–31.

Hylander, M.A., et al. "Human Milk Feedings and Infection Among Very Low Birth Weight Infants." *Pediatrics,* Vol. 102, No. 3 (1998), pp. E38.

Little, R.E., et al. "Maternal Alcohol Use During Breast-Feeding and Infant Mental and Motor Development at One Year." *New England Journal of Medicine,* Vol. 321, No. 7 (1989), pp. 425–30.

Plant, M.L. "Alcohol and Breast Cancer: A Review." *International Journal of Addiction,* Vol. 27, No. 2 (1992), pp. 107–28.

Schulte, P. "Minimizing Alcohol Exposure of the Breastfeeding Infant." *The Journal of Human Lactation,* Vol. 11, No. 4 (1995), 317–19.

Smith-Warner, Stephanie A., et al. "Alcohol and Breast Cancer in Women: A Pooled Analysis of Cohort Studies." *Journal of the American Medical Association,* Vol. 279, No. 7 (1998), pp. 535–40.

STORING BREAST MILK

Arnold, Lois D.W. "Currents in Human Milk Banking: Storage Containers for Human Milk: An Issue Revisited." *Journal of Human Lactation,* Vol. 11, No. 4 (1995), pp. 325–28.

Garza, C., et al. "Effects of Methods of Collection and Storage on Nutrients in Human Milk." *Early Human Development,* Vol. 6 (1982), pp. 295–303.

Goldblum, R.M., et al. "Human Milk Banking I: Effects of Container Upon Immunologic Factors in Mature Milk." *Nutrition Research,* Vol. 1 (1981), pp. 449–59.

Pittard, W.B., and K. Bill. "Human Milk Banking: Effect of Refrigeration on Cellular Components." *Clinical Pediatrics,* Vol. 20 (1981), pp. 31–33.

BOTTLE-FEEDING

Mountfort, K.A., et al. "Investigations into the Potential Degradation of Polycarbonate Baby Bottles During Sterilization with Consequent Release of Bisphenol A." *Food Additive Contaminants,* Vol. 14, Nos. 6–7 (1997), pp. 737–40.

Raloff, Janet. "Lacing Food with an Estrogen Mimic." *Science News,* Vol. 152, No. 16 (1997), p. 255.

———. "A Pollutant That Can Alter Growth." *Science News,* Vol. 152, No. 16 (1997), p. 255.

Scariati, P.C., L.M. Grummer-Strawn, and S.B. Fein. "Water Supplementation of Infants in the First Month of Life." *Archives of Pediatric Adolescent Medicine,* Vol. 151, No. 8, pp. 830–32.

INFANT FORMULA

Goozner, Merrill. "Formula is New, But Improved?" *Chicago Tribune,* May 21, 1997.

Hill, Alma E., "Formula Improves, But Can't Replace Mom: Similac Blend Still No Substitute for Breast-Feeding." *The Atlanta Constitution,* June 2, 1997.

FOOD SAFETY

Fox, Nicols. *Spoiled: The Dangerous Truth About a Food Chain Gone Haywire.* New York: Basic Books/HarperCollins, 1997.

Hess, Mary Abbott, and Anne Elise Hunt. *Eating for Two: The Complete Guide to Nutrition During Pregnancy.* New York: Macmillan, 1994.

Ikramuddin, Aisha. "Strawberries: In a Jam." *The Green Guide,* Vol. 40 (1997), p. 5.

Overexposed: Organophosphate Insecticides in Children's Food. Washington, D. C.: Environmental Working Group, 1998.

Pesticides in Children's Food. Washington, D. C.: Environmental Working Group, 1993.

Shopper's Guide to Pesticides in Produce, A. Washington, D.C.: Environmental Working Group, 1995.

"USDA Releases Pesticide Data Program Report for 1996 Residues on Fruits and Vegetables." *Pesticide & Toxic Chemical News,* April 9, 1998.

Wiles, Richard, and Kert Davies. *Pesticides in Baby Food.* Washington, D.C.: Environmental Working Group, 1995.

Zeiger, Robert S. "Can Food Allergies Be Prevented?" *Food Allergy News,* Vol. 3, No. 4 (1994), pp. 6–7.

Chapter Nine

INDOOR AND OUTDOOR ACTIVITIES

Testing the Waters. New York: Natural Resources Defense Council, 1998.

PROTECTING YOUR CHILD OUTSIDE

Autier, P., J.F. Dore, and H. Luther. "The Case for Sunscreens Revisited." *Archives of Dermatology,* Vol. 134, No. 4 (1998), pp. 509–11.

Brody, Jane E. "Protecting Children From Bugs That Bite." *The New York Times,* July 7, 1998.

Camas, Joanne. "Sand Trap?" *The Green Guide,* Vol. 34 (1997), p. 6.

Cournoyer, Michelle. "Backyard Habitats Aid Ecosystems." *Honolulu Star-Bulletin,* June 29, 1998.

CPSC Finds Lead Poisoning Hazard for Young Children on Public Playground Equipment. U.S. Consumer Product Safety Commission (Release #97-001). Washington, D.C.: 1996.

DeCicco, John, and Martin Thomas. *Green Guide to Cars & Trucks, Model Year 1998.* Washington, D.C.: American Council for an Energy-Efficient Economy, 1998.

Law Requires Review and Labeling of Art Materials Including Children's Art and Drawing Products. U.S. Consumer Product Safety Commission (Doc. #5016). Washington, D.C.: 1988.

Lytle, Lisa. "Sunscreen Still Worthwhile." *The Honolulu Advertiser,* June 30, 1998.

Marquardt, Sandra. "Golf's Green Handicap." *The Green Guide,* Vol. 37 (1997), pp. 1–3.

Olkowski, William, Sheila Daaar, and Helga Olkowski. *Common-Sense Pest Control: Least-Toxic Solutions for Your Home, Garden, Pets, and Community.* Newtown, Conn.: Taunton Press, 1991.

Pennybacker, Mindy. "Breathing Space: What You Can Do to Stop the Rise of Asthma." *The Green Guide,* Vol. 21 (1996), pp. 1–4.

———. "The Ghettoization of Asthma." *The Green Guide,* Vol. 56/57 (1998), pp. 1, 4–6.

Rauch, Molly E. "De-Buzzing Mosquitoes the Natural Way." *The Green Guide,* Vol. 41 (1997), p. 5.

"Rebuffing Summer's Bugs." *The Green Guide,* Vol. 28 (1996), p. 6.

acetone, 36
acid rain, 79
aerosol sprays, 93
aflatoxin, 133
AIDS, 130, 137, 194
air conditioners, 79, 104, 105, 108–9, 111
air filtration. *See* air purifiers; filters
air fresheners, 95
air pollution, 229–30
    indoor, 12–13, 28, 81–83, 86–91, 143
    perchloroethylene and, 96
    sulfur dioxide and, 79
    See also industry, wastes; smoke
air purifiers, 68–69, 81, 109, 110–11
air quality watch, 229–30
alachlor, 138
alcohol
    breast-feeding and, 191, 193–94
    pregnancy avoidance, 122, 134
alkylphenol ethoxylates, 92, 142, 156
allergies
    to baby-care products, 155, 156
    breast-fed babies and, 191–92
    to cleaning products, 91
    fan usage and, 111
    mold symptoms, 105
    preventive measures, 9, 80–83
    See also asthma; food allergies
alpha particles, 101
ammonia, 28, 91, 92, 94, 96, 173
amphetamines, 117
amyl acetate, 142
animals
    children's activities with, 220, 226, 227
    dander, 14, 42, 69, 71
    flea sprays, 15, 98, 99

animals, toy. *See* stuffed animals
antibiotics, 124
antihistamines, 193
antiques, 37, 38, 71
APEs. *See* alkylphenol ethoxylates
appliances
    asbestos in, 102
    combustion pollutants, 88–89
    electromagnetic fields, 112
    energy-efficient, 79, 80
    filters for, 109–10
    mold prevention, 105
    professional maintenance of, 90–91
    venting of, 88–89
    water-saving, 76, 79
    See also specific types
arsenic, 137
art supplies, 228
asbestiform tremolite, 237
asbestos, 102–3, 137
asbestosis, 237
asthma, 9
    combustion pollutants and, 87, 88
    down/feathers and, 49
    dust mites and, 14, 42, 50
    fan usage, 111
    formaldehyde and, 18
    nitrogen dioxide and, 87
    phthalate and, 16, 36, 176
    rise of, 14–15, 229
    smoke and, 87
    sulfur dioxide and, 88
    trigger prevention, 80–82, 111, 229–30
atomic bomb, radiation from, 117
atrazine, 15, 135, 138
attic fans, 104

automobiles
baby safety seats, 58–59
emissions, 28, 87, 89, 90
environmental impact, 229
water-saving washing tips, 76
wax ingredients, 94, 95

baby clothing, 166–74
baby equipment, 36–50, 57–63 (*see also specific items*)
baby food, 203–9
baby monitors, 112
babyproofing, 76–78, 96
backdrafts, 88–89, 108
backing, carpet, 33
backpack baby carriers, 59
backyard wildlife habitats, 225–26
bacterial contaminants
air conditioner/humidifier, 104
drinking water, 135, 136
food, 123–25, 212
swimming pools, 235
bags, plastic and shopping, 73
baked goods, 132
baking soda, 28, 92, 159, 163, 167
basements, mold in, 104, 105
bathing, baby, 148–57
bath products, 153–59
safety, 148, 152, 153
water temperature, 78, 152, 153
bathrooms
cleaning products, 92, 93, 94, 95
mold and mildew, 103–7, 154
safety, 74–75
water conservation, 76
beans, 132–33, 210, 211
bedding
crib, 12, 42–50
electric blankets, 103, 113
laundering, 50, 82
parents', 67–68
beeswax, 40
behavioral problems, 17, 118, 121
benzene, 18, 28, 31, 89, 121, 135, 138
benzo-a-pyrene, 88
bicycle helmets, 229
biocides, 29
birth defects, 17, 116, 118, 122, 134, 139
bisphenol-A, 185, 200
black flies, 233

bladder cancer, 19, 88, 138
blankets. *See* bedding
bleach, chlorine, 92, 173
bleeding lung syndrome, 104
blinds, window, 50–51
Blue Baby Syndrome, 137
boating safety, 236
books, 178, 221–24
borax, 93, 106, 163, 173
boric acid, 100
bottled water, 141–42, 215
bottle-feeding, 183, 198–203
dental care and, 202–3
equipment, 71–72, 184–85, 200–201
equipment sterilization, 198, 201–2
formula, 183, 189, 195, 198–200
glass vs. plastic bottles, 72, 184–85, 196, 200–201
weaning, 215
botulism, 212
brain cancer, 120
brain development, 16, 17, 118, 121, 134
brain tumors, 15, 99
breast cancer, 15, 92, 187, 194
breast-feeding, 183–98
advantages, 183–87
how-to tips, 187–89
maternal diet, 183, 191–92, 205–6
in parents' bed, 66
problems, 189–91
SIDS risk decreased by, 47, 186
weaning, 215
breast milk
alcohol and, 193–94
freezing, 196, 197
health benefits, 185–86
pumping and storing, 194–97, 198
toxins in, 18, 117, 137, 192–93
bronchitis, 87, 88, 121
bubble bath, baby, 155
bumper pads, crib, 49
burns, 76, 78, 92, 95, 167
butane, 93
butyl cellosolve, 94

cabinets, kitchen, 74, 78
cadmium, 51, 130, 135, 137, 176
caffeine, 122, 191
calcium, 119, 121, 130, 191
Campylobacter jejuni, 123

cancer
  asbestos and, 102
  breast-feeding and, 187, 194
  carcinogenic home-product ingredients,
    9, 15, 94, 95
  childhood rate rise, 15
  combustion pollutants and, 87, 88
  dioxins, 17–18, 117–18
  electromagnetic fields and, 112
  formaldehyde and, 12, 18–19
  fungi and, 104
  hormone disruptors and, 15
  mycotoxins and, 104
  nitrosamines and, 21, 95, 133, 142, 201
  PCBs and, 117–18
  perchloroethylene and, 96, 97
  pesticides and, 9, 15, 99, 116, 120, 138
  phthalates and, 16, 176
  prevention diet, 127
  radiation and, 120
  SOCs and, 138
  See also specific types
carbamate pesticides, 121
carbaryl, 121
carbon monoxide
  alarms, 76, 81, 89, 144
  exposure symptoms, 87
carcinogens. *See* cancer
cardiopulmonary resuscitation, 181
carpets, 12, 18, 31–35, 68–69
  cleaning, 34
  dust mites in, 11, 31, 69
  dust mite spray, 81
  installation precautions, 11, 143
  mold and, 104, 105
  natural fibers vs. synthetics, 31, 32, 33
  recommended manufacturers, 34–35
  vacuuming, 34, 68–69, 108
carriages, baby, 60
carriers, infant, 59–60
cars. *See* automobiles
car seats, 58–59
central nervous system
  alcohol and, 134
  cleaning products and, 94, 95
  cocaine and, 121
  mercury and, 119
  neurotoxins and, 16, 138
  pesticides and, 121
  solvents and, 19

ceramic glazes, 72–73
cereals. *See* grains
cervical cancer, 15
CFCs. *See* chlorofluorocarbons
chairs, 70–71
  baby feeding, 62
changing table, 37, 165
charcoal filters, 109
charcoal grill, indoor use hazard, 90
chemical fertilizers, 113–14
Chernobyl nuclear accident, 138
chicken. *See* poultry
child labor, product cautions, 35, 172–73
chilling, signs of baby's, 166
chimneys, 88–89, 90, 91
chlorine, 94, 137, 138, 139
chlorine bleach, 92, 96, 173
chlorine gas, 92
chlorofluorocarbons, 79, 93
chloroform, 138
chlorpyrifos, 18, 19, 113, 121, 210
choking hazards, 77, 171, 177, 180, 201, 208
cigarette smoke. *See* smoke
citronella, 232, 233
Clean Air Act, 229
cleaning products, 91–96
  babyproofing, 74, 91
  baby's sensitivity to, 91
  for carpets, 34
  hazardous ingredients, 18, 91–95, 138
  mixture warning, 92
  pregnancy avoidance, 143
  safer alternatives, 93, 96
  for upholstery, 71
cloth diapers. *See* diapers
clothes dryers, 80, 88, 89, 103
clothes washers, 79, 80
clothing
  for baby, 166–74
  flame-retardant, 45, 167
  natural fabric, 171
  protective, 231, 233, 234
  safety tips, 171–72
  sleep, 43, 167
  See also laundering
cocaine, 121, 193
colostrum, 185, 186
combustion pollutants, 87–91
comforters (bedding), 49, 67
community supported agriculture, 213

computers, infant/toddler precautions, 113
cool-spray humidifiers, 106
cork flooring, 36, 70
cornstarch, 156, 157, 160
cotton
    baby clothes, 167, 168, 171
    bathroom accessories, 75, 154
    bedding, 48, 68
    conventional, green, and organic, 43–44
    fire retardant for, 45
    mattresses, 67
couches, 70–71
CPR (cardiopulmonary resuscitation),
        181
craft supplies, 228
cribs, 37–40
    mattresses and bedding, 42–50
    placement in nursery, 38–39, 112
    safety standards, 38–39, 61
    toy precautions, 39, 176, 177
Cryptosporidium parvum, 124, 137
crystal, leaded, 73
cupboards, kitchen, 74
cups, weaning to, 215
curtains and drapes, 12, 50, 82, 108
cyanazine, 138
cyanide, 137

dairy products, 129, 130
dander, animal, 14, 42, 69, 71
DDE, 120, 192
DDT, 15, 16, 98, 120–21, 130, 192
DEA. *See* diethanolamine
deer ticks, 148, 230–31
DEET, 231, 232, 233
dehumidifiers, 105
dental care, 202–3
    fluoride, 139, 202
    mercury amalgam fillings, 119, 143, 203
    sealants, 203
    teeth cleaning, 202
    X-ray avoidance, 120
deodorizers
    diaper pail cakes, 163
    room, 69, 95
DES (diethylstilbestrol), 15, 117, 121
detergent, laundry, 92, 93, 94
    safer alternatives, 96, 173
developmental problems, 118
diaper rash, 159, 173

diapers, 159–66
    cloth equipment, 164–65
    cloth vs. disposable, 160–62, 166
    diapering procedure, 162–63
    laundering, 163, 173–74
    newborn's layette, 169
    pins and fasteners, 164
    swim, 236
    wipes, 163
diatomaceous earth, 100
diazinon, 121
diet. *See* food and diet
diethanolamine, 142, 156
diethylstilbestrol. *See* DES
diet pills, 193
Dilantin, 117
dioxin, 15, 16, 17–18, 138
    in breast milk, 18, 192
    fetal exposure hazards, 18, 117–18
    in vinyl production, 17–18, 30
    in water, 130, 135
dishes, lead-free, 72–73, 144
dishwashers, 75, 76
disinfectants, 93, 94, 137, 138–39
disposable diapers, 160–62
    more ecologically correct, 166
disposable nursers, 196, 201
distillers, water, 140
doormats, 86
drapes. *See* curtains and drapes
drawers, kitchen, 74, 78
drinking water. *See* water
drowning, 74, 148, 235
drugs
    breast-feeding and, 193
    fetal exposure to, 121–22
dry-cleaning solvents, 19, 95, 96–97, 143
dryers. *See* clothes dryers; hair dryers
Dursban, 113
dust, 71, 88
    lead, 17, 24, 25, 26, 51, 86
dust mites, 80–81
    asthma and, 14, 42, 50
    bedding, 11, 42, 49, 68
    carpeting, 11, 31, 69, 81
    curtains and drapes, 50
    removal of, 69, 81, 82, 108
    upholstery, 71
dyes
    baby clothing, 168

carpet fibers, 33
fabric, 43
hair, 92, 142, 143, 193
wall coverings, 30

E. coli, 93, 124, 134, 135, 212
ecological practices
    home, 238–39
    preschool, 237–38
eggs, 124, 125, 129, 130
electric blankets, 103, 113
electromagnetic fields, 55, 111–13, 120
emergency information, 78
endocrine disruptors. *See* hormone
    disruptors
endometriosis, 15
energy-efficient products, 78–80
engorgement, breast, 190, 191, 194
essential fatty acids (Omega-3), 130
ethanol, 28
ethoxylated alcohols, 94
evaporative humidifier, caution against, 106
exercise, for babies, 180–82
exhaust fans, 89, 102, 105, 107

fabric
    dyes in, 43
    formaldehyde in, 12, 45, 167
    mold in, 104
    natural, 50, 75, 96, 154, 171
    removing finishes of, 46, 167
    synthetic, 45–46
    See also specific types
fabric softeners, 96, 173
fans, 102, 104, 105, 107, 108, 111
    backdrafts, 89
farmers' markets, 213
farm-raised fish, 131
faucet guards, 75
fecal coliform, 135, 136, 137
fertilizers, 113–14, 137
fetal risks, 115–22
    cigarette smoke, 11, 89, 121
    heavy metals, 15, 118–20, 137
    hormone disruptors crossing placenta,
        9, 15
    maternal alcohol consumption, 134
    toxins crossing placenta, 9, 11, 18, 24,
        115, 117–22
    See also birth defects

filters, 109–10
    air, 82, 108–9
    air conditioner, 108, 111
    vaccuum, 34, 69, 71, 81, 82, 106, 108,
        109, 110
    water, 139–41
fingernails, cutting baby's, 151
fingers, hazards to baby's, 42, 60
fire extinguisher, 76
fireplaces, 87, 88, 89, 90
fire safety, 47–48, 76
    smoke alarms, 45, 48, 76, 81, 144
    See also flame-retardant finishes
first-aid kits, 78
fish, 130–31
    contaminants, 17, 118, 119–20, 130, 131
    extinction threats, 226
    food poisoning precautions, 125
flame retardant finishes, 45, 47–48, 67,
    167
flea sprays, 15, 98, 99
floor coverings, 35–36, 70, 103 (*see also*
    carpets)
flour, 133
flues, chimney, 88, 90
fluorescent lighting, 54
fluoride, 139, 202
fly repellents, 223
folic acid, 127
food allergies, 81, 205–6, 208, 214
    breast-feeding and, 191–92
food and diet, 122–34
    for babies, 203–9, 210, 211–12
    bacterial contaminants, 123–25, 212
    breast-feeding mothers and, 184, 191–92,
        205–6
    genetically modified, 214–15
    healthier, green food choices, 125–26
    organic, IPM, or local, 127–29, 209–10
    packaged, 126, 133–34
    pregnancy, 122–23, 130, 143, 144
    shopping tips, 127–34, 212–14
    See also bottle-feeding, breast-feeding
food cooperatives, 213
food poisoning, 93, 123–25, 130, 134, 212
Food Quality Protection Act of 1996, 99
formaldehyde
    in carpeting, 18, 31
    charcoal filters and, 109
    in cigarette smoke, 12, 89

formaldehyde *(continued)*
 in cleaning products, 94
 in fabric, 12, 45, 167
 health effects, 12
 in paint, 12, 28
 in personal care products, 142, 156
formula. *See* bottle-feeding
fragrances, 69, 142, 154–55, 156
fruits and vegetables, 127–29
 diet tips, 126
 food poisoning cautions, 124, 125
 locally grown, 126, 128–29
 organic, 127–29, 204, 210
 pesticide contamination, 209, 210
 wax coatings, 124, 128
 See also juices
fumes, 91, 96–97
 volatile organic compounds, 11–12, 18
 See also smoke
fungi. *See* mold and mildew
fungicides, 15, 28, 29, 51, 128
furans, 15
furnaces, 79, 88, 90, 108, 109
furniture
 bedroom, 67–68
 living room, 70–71
 nursery, 36–42
 particleboard, 12, 18, 70, 143
 upholstered, 71, 108
 used, 71
 See also cribs
furniture polish, 94
futons, 67, 68, 71
 crib-sized, 48

galactosemia, 186
games, board, 227–28
gardens and lawns, 113–14, 230
 children's activities, 225–26
 nitrogen fertilizers, 137
 pesticide use, 113, 121
gas appliances, 14, 87, 88, 89, 90–91
gases, 87, 88, 92, 100–104
gasoline, 12, 17, 18, 25, 86
gates, child safety, 62, 77, 78
genetically modified foods, 214–15
Giardia lamblia, 124, 137
giardiasis, 136
glues, 12, 18, 31, 94, 138
glycols, 28

golf courses, pesticides and, 86, 113, 121, 230
grains, 126, 131–32
 baby cereals, 205
 grinding own, 211, 212
 organic alternatives, 209
 packaged cereals, 133–34
 toasting, 212
grass. *See* gardens and lawns
green cotton, 44
grilling food, 89, 90
gyms, crib, 39, 176, 177

hair dryers, 102
hair dye, 92, 142, 143, 193
halogen lamps, 54–55, 80
hardwoods, 35, 41
head lice, 98
heaters
 combustion pollutants, 88, 90, 91
 hot water, 78, 80, 91, 153
 as mold preventive, 106
heating, home, 80, 90, 106
heavy metals, 15, 137
 in fabric dyes, 168
 fetal exposure to, 117
 in vinyl, 51
 See also lead; *other specific metals*
hemolytic uremic syndrome, 124
HEPA filters, 34, 69, 71, 81, 82, 106, 108, 111
 advantages of, 110
hepatitis, 136
herbal supplements, pregnancy cautions, 122
herbicides, 15, 18, 113, 138, 214
herpes simplex virus, 93
high chairs, 62
high efficiency particulate arresting filters. *See* HEPA filters
hiking, 228–29
Hiroshima, 117
HIV. *See* AIDS
homemade baby food, 203, 211–12
homemade cleaners, 93, 96
hooded towels, 153–54
hormone disruptors
 in cleaners, 92–93, 95
 examples and effects, 15–16
 in hair dye, 142
 in plastic baby bottles, 185, 196, 200

pregnancy risks, 9, 15
  See also APEs; bisphenol-A; PCBs; pesti-
    cides; phthalates
hot water heaters
  and combustion pollutants, 88, 91
  temperature setting, 78, 80, 153
houseplants, mold and, 104, 105
humidifiers, 104, 105, 106–7
humidistat, 107
hydrochloric acid, 94
hydrofluoric acid, 94
hydrogen peroxide, 106
hygrometer, 107
hypoallergenic products, 155–56
hypospadias, 15

illness
  breast-feeding and maternal, 194
  breast-milk benefits for babies, 185
  water-borne, 136
  See also specific conditions
immune system, 104, 136–37, 186
industry
  child labor products, 35, 172–73
  power plant pollution, 79
  wastes, 15–16, 135, 137, 138, 139–40,
    229–30
infertility, 15
insect bites, 230–33
insect growth regulators, 100
insecticides. *See* pesticides
Integrated Pest Management, 99–100, 114,
    127, 204, 209, 210, 230
ipecac, 77

Japanese shoji screens, 53–54
juices
  for baby, 203, 208, 215
  organic, 134
  pasteurization protection, 124, 212

kerosene, 28, 87, 94
kerosene heaters, 88, 90
kidney problems, 28, 94, 95, 124, 176
kitchens, 71–74
  babyproofing, 74, 78
  cleaning products, 74, 92–96
  combustion pollutants, 88, 89
  exhaust fans, 89, 107
  mold prevention, 105

supplies, 72
water conservation, 75–76

lambskin, 47
lamps. *See* lighting
landfills, 93, 100, 160
latches, 37, 78
latex paint, 28, 29
laundering
  baby clothes, 168, 173–74
  bedding, 50, 82
  detergent, 92, 93, 94, 96, 173
  diapers, 163, 173–74
  handwashing dry-clean-only garments,
    97, 98
lawnmowers, power, 89, 90
lawns. *See* gardens and lawns
layette, 165, 169–71
lead, 86
  in breast milk, 192
  in crystal and china, 72–73, 144
  detection of, 25–26
  fetal exposure hazards, 17, 24, 117, 119
  in paint, 16–17, 24–27, 38
  in plastic and shopping bags, 73
  in playground equipment, 237
  in shellfish, 130
  in soil, 17, 26, 86
  toxic effects of, 16–17, 24, 25, 27, 237
  in vinyl home products, 18, 51
  in vinyl toys, 176
  in water, 25, 135, 136, 137, 140
learning problems, 17, 118, 121, 134
Legionnaire's disease, 136
lentils, 132–33
leukemia, 15, 18, 99, 116, 120
life vests, child, 236
light bulbs
  energy-efficient, 80
  halogen, 54
lighting, 54–55
linoleum, 36, 70
Listeria, 123, 129, 130
listeriosis, 123
liver problems, 19, 28, 95, 176
living room/playroom, 69–71
low-birth-weight babies, 11, 47, 117, 118
lung cancer, 18, 87, 88, 100, 101, 102, 237
lung problems. *See* respiratory problems
lye, 91–92, 94

Lyme disease, 148, 230
lymphoma, 18

MADs. *See* Mosquito Abatement Districts
malathion, 121
marijuana, 193
massage, 157, 159
mastitis, 190–91
mattresses, crib, 38, 42, 47–50
mattresses, parent's, 67
meat, 124, 125, 126, 129–30
meconium, 185
medication. *See* drugs
melanoma. *See* skin cancer
mercury, 17, 117, 119–20
  in breast milk, 117, 192
  in dental fillings, 119, 143, 203
  in fish, 17, 119–20, 130
  in paint, 28
  in water, 135, 137
metal polishes, 94, 95
methylene chloride, 156
methylmercury, 17, 119
microwave ovens, 125, 197
mildew. *See* mold and mildew
milk
  organic, 130, 209
  rBGH-free, 130, 209
  See also bottle-feeding; breast milk
milk paints, 29, 30
minerals, 127, 130
  pregnancy supplement, 122
miscarriage, 118, 136, 137, 139
mobiles, crib, 176, 177
mold and mildew, 103–7
  asthma and, 14
  in bedding, 42
  low-biocide paint and, 29
  prevention, 104–5, 154
  removal, 105–6, 109
  in upholstery, 71
Mosquito Abatement Districts, 230
mosquitoes, 121, 230, 232
mothballs, 95, 167
multiple chemical sensitivities, 23
mushrooms, poisonous, 237
mycotoxins, 104

Nagasaki, 117
naphthalene, 95

natural fibers, 32, 33, 50, 75, 96, 154, 171
natural food stores, 212–13
"natural" product labels, 129, 142, 156
nature activities, 219–20, 225–29
negative-ion generators, 110–11
neurological problems
  fetal risks, 118, 119, 134, 137
  folic acid prevention, 127
  solvents and, 138
neurotoxins, 16–17, 19, 138
  See also carbamates; lead; mercury;
    organophosphates
nipples, baby bottle, 71–72, 201
nipples, maternal, 189–90
nitrates, 135, 137
nitrites, 95, 135, 137
nitrogen dioxide, 87
nitrogen fertilizers, 137
nitrosamines, 21, 95, 137, 142, 156, 201
nonasbestiform tremolite, 237
nonmetallic inorganics, 137–38
nuclear accidents, 117, 138
nucleotides, 198
nursery, 19–22, 112
  furniture, 36–42
  painting, 24–30
  safety, 38–39
nursing. *See* breast-feeding
nutrition. *See* food and diet
nuts and seeds, 126, 133
nylon, 45

offgassing, 12
  carpets, 31–32
  paint, 28
  phthalates, 16
  vinyl, 30
oil-based paint, 28
Omega-3 acids, 130
organic cotton, 44, 75, 154
organic diapers, 164
organic fertilizers, 114
organic food, 126, 127–28, 130, 209–10
  baby food, 203–4
organic gardening, 114
organic paint, 29, 30
organochlorine pesticides, 18, 120
organophosphate pesticides, 15, 17, 121,
  210, 230
osteoporosis, 187

outdoor activities, 224–27
outdoor pollutants, 86, 89, 113–14, 143
    (*see also* air pollution; pesticides)
ovarian cancer, 187
oven cleaning, 89, 92
overheating, signs of baby's, 47, 166, 172
ozone, 28, 79, 93, 110–11, 139, 229, 233
ozone machines, 110

pacifiers, 71, 201
packaged foods, 126, 133–34
PAHs (polycyclic aromatic hydrocarbons),
    88, 121
paint
    formaldehyde in, 12, 18
    lead in, 16–17, 24–27, 38
    mercury in, 28
    nursery precautions, 24–30
    pesticides in, 28, 98
    pregnancy avoidance, 11, 24, 143, 193
    solvents in, 138
    types, 28, 29, 30
    volatile organic compounds in, 19, 28
paper, chlorine bleaching of, 17
parabens, 156–57
paradichlorobenzenes, 95
parasites, 124, 136, 137
particleboard, 12, 18, 39, 70, 143
particulates, 14, 88, 229
pathogens
    drinking water, 136–37
    food, 123–125, 212
PCBs (polychlorinated biphenyls), 15–16
    in breast milk, 192
    fetal exposure to, 117–18
    in fish, 118, 130
    in water, 15–16, 135
p-dichlorobenzene, 138
peanut allergies, 81
perchloroethylene, 19, 95, 96–97
perfume. *See* fragrances
permethrin, 232
personal care products
    adult, 92, 142–43, 193
    alternative, 157
    baby, 154–59
pesticides, 51, 97–100
    alternatives, 99–100, 114, 127, 231–33
    in breast milk, 192
    conventionally grown cotton, 43–44

in food, 203–4, 210
    health hazards, 9, 15, 17, 99, 116, 120
    hormone disruptors and, 15, 92
    indoor pollution by, 18, 19, 113
    outdoor pollution by, 230
    in paint, 28, 98
    pregnancy avoidance, 120–21, 143
    in sponges, 98
    in water, 98, 135, 138
petrochemicals, 45
petroleum distillates, 93, 95
pets. *See* animals
phenols, 138
phenylketonuria, 186
phosphates, 93
phosphoric acid, 94, 95
phthalates, 138
    asthma and, 16, 36, 176
    in home products, 18
    in pacifiers, 201
    in PVC plastic, 16, 30, 72, 185
    in toys, 175–76
pillows, 49–50, 66, 67
pine resin, 29, 36
PKU (phenylketonuria), 186
placenta. *See* fetal risks
plants, 76, 104, 105, 237
plastic, 12
    baby bottles, 72, 184–85, 196, 200–201
    bags, 73
    safe toys, 179
    See also vinyl
play activities
    for babies, 174–82
    for children, 224–29
    water sports, 235–36
playground hazards, 237
playpens, 60–61
plumbing, mold and, 104
plywood furniture, 70, 143
pneumonia, 87, 121
poisoning
    babyproofing against, 77
    carbon monoxide, 87
    cleaning chemicals, 91
    diaper pail deodorizer cakes, 163
    lead, 16–17, 24, 25, 27, 237
    mercury, 119
    plant, 237
    See also food poisoning; pesticides

pollen, 42, 109, 111
pollutants, indoor, 12–13, 81–83, 85–114
    protection against outdoor sources, 86, 89,
        113–14
    See also air pollution; *specific pollutants and
        pollutant types*
polychlorinated biphenyls. *See* PCBs
polycyclic aromatic hydrocarbons, 88, 121
polyester, 45
polyethylene, 196, 200
polypropylene, 196, 200
polyurethane finishes, 35, 40
polyurethane foam, 47, 48, 70
polyvinyl chloride (PVC). *See* vinyl
portable air purifiers. *See* air purifiers
portable cribs, 61
portable radiant heater, 106
postpartum hemorrhaging, 187
poultry safety, 123, 124, 129–30
pregnancy precautions, 9–13, 143, 193 (*see
    also* fetal risks)
premature babies
    bottle equipment sterilization, 201–2
    breast milk benefits, 185, 186
    fetal lead exposure and, 118
    listeriosis and, 123
    SIDS and, 47
preschool environmental education, 237–38
preservatives, 29
processed foods, 126, 129, 210
produce. *See* fruits and vegetables
propane, 93
pulmonary hemorrhage, 104
purifiers. *See* air purifiers
PVC. *See* vinyl
pyrethrin, 15

radiant heaters, 106
radiation/radioactivity, 101, 117, 120, 138, 143
radium, 138
radon, 100–102, 117, 120, 138, 144
rashes, 159, 173
raw foods, 130, 143
rectal cancer, 138
recycling, 227, 238–39, 239
refrigerators, 79, 80
reproductive problems, 9, 121, 137, 138, 139
respiratory problems
    asbestos and, 102, 237
    cleaning products and, 92

nitrogen dioxide and, 87
phthalates and, 176
smog and, 79
smoke and, 87, 88, 89, 121
toxic mold and, 104
volatile organic compounds and, 28
See also asthma; lung cancer
rice, 132, 209
roach control, 99
Rocky Mountain spotted fever, 231
room dividers, 52–54
rooting reflex, 188
rugs. *See* carpets
running strollers, 60

safety. *See* babyproofing; *specific products
    and subjects*
Salmonella, 93, 124, 212
sand, playground, 237
sanding, 24
scalds, 75, 78, 152, 153
seafood. *See* fish
sealants, dental, 203
sealants, polyurethane, 35, 40
seashore activities, 226–27
secondhand smoke, 87, 89, 121
shades, window, 51
shampoo, carpet, 34
shampoo, hair, 92, 142, 156
    babies and, 149, 152, 155, 157
sheepskin, 45, 47
sheets, crib, 48–49
shoes, 86, 171
shopping bags, 73
shower cleaners, 94, 95
shower curtains, 16, 75, 154
SIDS. *See* Sudden Infant Death Syndrome
silica aerogel, 100
silicone, baby-bottle nipples, 71–72, 201
simazine, 138
skin cancer, 88, 233, 234, 235
sleep
    baby bottles and, 202
    clothing for, 43, 167
    positioning baby, 46–47, 66
smog, 14, 28, 79, 86, 229
smoke, 12, 18
    asthma and, 14
    as carcinogen, 89, 121
    fetal effects, 11, 87, 89, 121

as irritant, 82
    pregnancy avoidance, 11, 143
    respiratory problems and, 87, 88, 89, 121
    SIDS and, 47, 89
smoke alarms, 45, 48, 76, 81, 144
soap, 92, 149, 152, 154–55, 157
sodium bisulfate, 95
soil, lead in, 17, 26, 86
solvents, 9, 18, 19
    in drinking water, 15, 138
    dry-cleaning, 19, 95, 96–97, 143
    in paints, 28
soybean oil, 231–32
sperm count, 15, 16, 116, 120
spina bifida, 127
sponge baths, 149–51
sponges, pesticides in, 98
spot removers, 93, 95
Stachybotrys atra, 104
Staphylococcus aureus, 93
steam humidifiers, 106
sterilization, baby-bottle equipment, 198,
        201–2
stillbirth, 118, 123
stomach cancer, 88
stoves
    babyproofing, 74
    cleaning products, 92, 94
    combustion pollutants, 87, 88, 89, 90,
        103
strangulation cautions, 39, 171–72
strawberries, tainted, 124, 209
strollers, 60
strontium, 138
stuffed animals, 82, 178
    crib safety, 39
    mold growth in, 104
styrene, 19, 28, 31, 135, 138
sucking reflex, 188
Sudden Infant Death Syndrome, 46–47
    bedding and, 45, 47, 49, 67
    breast-feeding reducing risk of, 47, 186
    maternal smoking and, 89, 121
    sleep position and, 46–47, 66
suffocation hazards, 66, 67
sugars, 133
sulfur dioxide, 79, 88
sun protection, 171, 233–35
supplements, nutritional, 122
surfactants, 92

swaddling, 66
swimming, 227, 235–36
swings, indoor, 63
synthetic fabrics, 45–46
synthetic organic compound, 138

talc, 156, 157
tannic acid, 69, 71, 81
TEA *See* triethanolamine
teeth. *See* dental care
teethers, 16, 176
teething, 208
Teflon, 72
temperature
    room, 80, 149, 166
    water, 75, 78, 80, 152, 153
tetrachloroethylene, 95, 135
thalidomide, 117
thermometer, mercury, 119
thermostat settings, 80, 153
THMs (trihalomethanes), 138–39
thyroid, 9, 118, 138
ticks, 148, 230–31
toilet bowls, 74, 76, 92, 94, 95
toiletries. *See* personal care products
toilet training, 75
toluene, 19, 28, 31, 36, 47, 95
toothpaste, 202
towels, 75, 153–54
toy chests, 37
toys, 175–82
    age appropriate, 176–78
    crib safety, 39
    nontoxic, 174–80
    pesticides absorption, 19
    stuffed animals, 82, 104, 178
trichloroethylene, 28, 95, 138
triethanolamine, 21, 95, 142, 156
trihalomethanes (TMSs), 138–39
trisodium nitrilotriacetate, 95
tuberculosis, 194
tung oil, 29, 35, 40
turpentine, 29

ULPA filters, 34, 108, 110
umbrella strollers, 60
upholstery, 70–71, 108
uranium, 100, 138
used furniture, 71
    crib precautions, 37–38

vacuuming
  carpets, 34, 68–69, 108
  filters, 34, 69, 71, 81, 82, 106, 108, 109, 110
  as pollutant removal, 108
  upholstered furniture, 71
vegetables. *See* fruits and vegetables
ventilation, 107–8
  importance of, 12, 81, 87, 88, 89
  for mold/mildew prevention, 103, 105
  as radon remediation, 101
vinegar, 106, 163, 173
vinyl
  baby bottles, 72, 200
  breast-milk storage cautions, 196
  dioxins in production and incineration, 17–18, 30
  flooring, 36, 103
  miniblinds, 51
  pacifiers, 201
  phthalates in, 16, 30, 72, 185
  shower curtain alternative, 75
  toys, 175–76
  wallpaper, 30
vinyl chloride, 36, 138
viruses, 136, 137
vitamin A, 122, 127, 130
vitamin C, 127, 191
vitamin D, 130
vitamin supplements, 122
volatile organic compounds (VOCs), 12, 18–19, 82
  in aerosol sprays, 93
  baby clothes and, 167
  in carpet, 31–33
  in floor coverings, 35
  in furniture, 70
  in paint, 28
  pregnancy avoidance, 143
  See also offgassing

walkers, baby, 62–63
wall coverings, 30–31, 98
wall-to-wall carpeting. *See* carpets
warmth, baby's need for, 149, 153, 166
washcloths, 153
washing machines, 79, 80
wastes
  hazardous sites, 93
  incineration, 17–18

industrial, 15–16, 135, 137, 138, 139–40, 229–30
landfills, 93, 100, 160
pesticide disposal, 100
recycling, 227, 237–38, 239
water, 134–42
  baby's drinking, 215
  bottled, 141–42, 215
  conservation, 75–76
  contaminants, 15–16, 25, 93, 98, 104, 119, 124, 130, 135–39, 140, 235
  filters, 139–41
  heaters. *See* hot water heaters
  temperature, 75, 78, 80, 152, 153
  testing, 135, 139
water-borne illnesses, 136
waterproof diaper covers, 165
water sports, 124, 227, 235–36
waterways pollution, 227, 235
waxes, car, 94, 95
waxes, produce coating, 124, 128
weaning, 215
weatherstripping, 80, 90
windows
  cleaning product hazards, 94
  coverings, 12, 50–51, 82, 108
wipes, baby, 163
wood, 39–42
  certified, 41
  crib, 39–40
  finishes and stains, 18, 28
  flooring, 35
  formaldehyde in pressed, 12
  furniture, 70
  potty chair, 75
  toys, 178, 179–80
wood smoke, 87
wood stoves, 87, 88, 89, 90, 103
wool, 44–45
  bedding, 67–68
  carpeting, 33
  clothing, 167–68, 171
  crib mattress, 48
  diaper covers, 165
  upholstery, 70–71

X rays, 117, 120, 143
xylene, 28, 31, 36

zinc, 135
zoos, 220

"As a scientist, I can vouch for the ecological principles underlying this best-of-all-possible guides for toxic-free baby care, which balances the issues in a direct, nonpartisan way. As an expectant, first-time mother, I plan to keep a copy right next to the changing table. Bravo to Mothers & Others for this uniquely valuable and very honest resource."

—Sandra Steingraber, Ph.D.,
author of *Living Downstream*

"An invaluable and necessary guide for parents in our polluted world."

—Natasha Richardson
and Liam Neeson

"This is a wonderfully comprehensive guide to a safe home environment for children—from pregnancy through childhood. It provides intelligent and practical advice to parents on what they can do to protect their children from toxic exposures during their most vulnerable years."

—Frederica Pereira, Dr. P. H., professor,
Center for Children's Environmental Health,
Columbia School of Public Health

"As babies and children are much more vulnerable to the hazardous exposures of our modern world, it is essential that there is a book that addresses their own special needs. Mothers & Others does an outstanding job of offering a natural and healthy way to raise your child."

—Debra Lynn Dadd,
author of *Home Safe Home*

Join Us in Protecting the Future of Our Children
—Become a Member of Mothers & Others

Mothers & Others for a Livable Planet is a national, nonprofit organization seeking to effect lasting protection of children's health and the environment through consumer education and action.

Member Benefits

For your tax-deductible donation of $25 a year, you'll receive:

- Our award-winning newsletter.

- A year's subscription to our monthly newsletter, *The Green Guide,* an up-to-date resource on the latest environmental news and what it means for your family's well-being.

- Researched responses to your individual questions, such as where you can have your water tested, the safest ways to store food, how to eliminate ants without toxic chemicals, and much more.

- Two free back issues of *The Green Guide,* two free fact sheets, and discounts on our other books and products.

- Quarterly reports on Mothers & Others' Shoppers Campaign and other programs.

How to Join

It's easy! Just give us your name, address, phone number, and dues of $25 by check or credit card. You can call our toll free number:

1-888-ECO-INFO (in New York City, please call (212) 242-0010).

Or write us at:

Mothers & Others for a Livable Planet
40 West 20th Street, 9th Floor
New York, NY 10011

To find out more about us, please visit our Website at **www.mothers.org**

For a **free** issue of *The Green Guide,* see the back of this page.

Special Offer for Readers of
Mothers & Others Guide to Natural Baby Care

Call us and receive a *free* issue of *The Green Guide,* the nation's only green consumer action newsletter and the winner of the 1998 *Utne Reader* Alternative Press Award for 'General Excellence in Newsletters.' Get the latest environmental health news in six easy-to-read pages. You'll find practical steps you can take in your daily life to protect your family and the environment.

Some recent issues have covered:

- Children's Environmental Health
- Women's Health and the Environment
- Men's Health
- Bioengineered Food and the Consumer's Right to Know
- Sane, Safe Building and Decorating Supplies
- The Green Home
- The Natural Bedroom
- Factory Farming and Food Safety
- How to Get Organic Food
- Least Toxic Ways to Deal with Mosquitoes, Termites, and Other Pests
- Green Cleaning

Call our toll-free hotline: 888-ECO-INFO

Please ask for the free *The Green Guide* offer from the *Natural Baby Care* book.